BELLIGERENT REPRISALS FROM ENFORCEMENT TO RECIPROCITY

This book challenges the traditional understanding of belligerent reprisals as a mechanism aimed at enforcing the laws of armed conflict. By re-instating reciprocity at the core of belligerent reprisals, it construes them as tools designed to re-calibrate the legal relationship between parties to armed conflict and pursue the belligerents' equality of rights and obligations in both a formal and a substantive sense. It combines an inquiry into the conceptual issues surrounding the notion of belligerent reprisals, with an analysis of State and international practice on their purpose and function. Encompassing international and non-international armed conflicts, it provides a first comprehensive account of the role of reprisals in governing legal interaction during wartime, and offers new grounds to address questions on their applicability, lawfulness, regulation and desirability. This title is part of the Flip it Open Programme and may also be available Open Access. Check our website Cambridge Core for details.

FRANCESCO ROMANI is a Research Fellow at the Geneva Academy of International Humanitarian Law and Human Rights, where he co-ordinates the IHL Expert Pool. He is also Visiting Professor on international responsibility and litigation at the Law Faculty of Lille Catholic University and holds a PhD in International Law from the Graduate Institute of International and Development Studies (Geneva). His research interests include international humanitarian law, human rights and cultural heritage law.

BELLIGERENT REPRISALS FROM ENFORCEMENT TO RECIPROCITY

A New Theory of Retaliation in Conflict

FRANCESCO ROMANI
Geneva Academy of International Humanitarian Law and Human Rights

CAMBRIDGE
UNIVERSITY PRESS

CAMBRIDGE
UNIVERSITY PRESS

Shaftesbury Road, Cambridge CB2 8EA, United Kingdom

One Liberty Plaza, 20th Floor, New York, NY 10006, USA

477 Williamstown Road, Port Melbourne, VIC 3207, Australia

314–321, 3rd Floor, Plot 3, Splendor Forum, Jasola District Centre, New Delhi – 110025, India

103 Penang Road, #05–06/07, Visioncrest Commercial, Singapore 238467

Cambridge University Press is part of Cambridge University Press & Assessment, a department of the University of Cambridge.

We share the University's mission to contribute to society through the pursuit of education, learning and research at the highest international levels of excellence.

www.cambridge.org
Information on this title: www.cambridge.org/9781108831840

DOI: 10.1017/9781108912327

First published 2025

A catalogue record for this publication is available from the British Library

A Cataloging-in-Publication data record for this book is available from the Library of Congress

ISBN 978-1-108-83184-0 Hardback
ISBN 978-1-108-92742-0 Paperback

To Marilena,
Alessandra,
Gianpaolo,
Tru and Shali

CONTENTS

ACKNOWLEDGEMENTS

As a reader, I have always thought of books as vessels that take me to faraway spaces and introduce me to characters through the power of imagination. As I happen to write one, I have found that the real people and places that I have encountered in its drafting were by no means less extraordinary. To all of them I owe a huge debt of gratitude. I feel extremely privileged for all the moments of intellectual enquiry and exchange that I have had the opportunity to share with them. And as I beg their forgiveness for all the mistakes that they will inevitably find, I also hope that this book will reflect the depth of their insights and contributions.

The Graduate Institute of International and Development Studies in Geneva is the place where the seeds of this book were first sown and carefully grown. Paola Gaeta and Andrew Clapham have been two exceptional mentors that have accompanied and directed the coming into being of this book for nearly ten years – first as PhD supervisors, then as patient advisors. Their mastery of the discipline and their unrelenting incitement have been a precious light in navigating the troubled waters of this topic. I cannot thank Andrea Bianchi enough for his stimulating lectures and encouragement to challenge the theoretical assumptions of the discipline – and of my own thinking. With all his experience and kindness, Jakob Kellenberger has been an inspiration from both a professional and a human point of view. With his feedback, Robert Heinsch has been a challenging reader, helping me push the horizon of my research one step further. I have spent wonderful hours with Alessandra La Vaccara and Antonio Coco, nurturing together our research and friendship in different corners of the world.

My research stay at the University of Michigan was a decisive turning point in my approach to the topic. Monica Hakimi, Steven R. Ratner and James D. Morrow have provided me with a new conceptual framework that has accompanied my reflection ever since. Besides being wonderful hosts in the Law Quadrangle, they have given me the tools to ask the correct questions, even before finding the right answers. At Harvard Law School,

Gabriella Blum, Naz K. Modirzadeh and Dustin A. Lewis have opened for me the doors of the Program on International Law and Armed Conflict; in so doing, they have allowed me to benefit from a most innovative research environment, capturing me with their contagious enthusiasm and cutting-edge projects. I am also thankful to Sasha Radin and the US Naval War College for giving me the opportunity to present my research at the Stockton Center for the Study of International Law and receive key feedback from the experienced lawyers, officers and researchers gathered there.

At Cambridge University, the Lauterpacht Centre for International Law was a unique environment to exchange on my research ideas. On several occasions, Sarah Nouwen, Federica Paddeu, Eyal Benvenisti, Christopher Greenwood and Giovanni Mantilla enriched my reflections with key insights. My work at the Customary IHL project with the ICRC and the British Red Cross has allowed me to delve into fundamental questions of IHL methodology and substance, and I am indebted to Claudia Maritano and Michael M. Meyer for their support and kind guidance. I also wish to thank Finola O'Sullivan, Marianne Nield, Gemma Smith, Tobias Ginsberg, Aiswarya Narayanan, Nomita Dasgupta and the anonymous reviewers from Cambridge University Press – their patience, advice and help in structuring, editing and producing this book have been exceptional throughout these years. Last but not least, a heartfelt thank you goes to Rob Gibson for his outstanding support with the indexing process.

As I embarked on this long journey, I was afraid that writing a book could turn out to be a very lonely activity. If that has not been the case, most of the credit goes to my family. For all these years, they have always encouraged, supported (and been patient with) me. They have provided me with materials and suggestions, and constantly offered an attentive ear, a kind word and a supportive shoulder. They have always advised me in the wisest terms, and helped me bear the brunt and pressure. Thank you to my mother, Marilena, for being a safe harbor when the weather is stormy and a vast, deep sea when it is nice, whose example and countless talents always prompt us to aim for what is good and beautiful; to my sister, Alessandra, for being so bright in her personality and intellect, for always believing in me and for being ready to share her swirling passion and brilliant ideas; to my father, Gianpaolo, for attaching so much importance and pride to my little accomplishments and for offering to help accordingly; and to our foxies, Tru and Shali, for always pumping in some energy and fun when worries and fatigue are about to prevail. This book on reciprocity is dedicated to them – the shiniest examples of unconditional love I could ever hope for.

TABLE OF TREATIES

Declaration Renouncing the Use, in Time of War, of Explosive Projectiles under 400 Grammes Weight, Saint Petersburg, 11 December 1868, in force 11 December 1868, Schindler & Toman (1988) 102

Hague Convention II with respect to the Laws and Customs of War on Land (with Annexed Regulations), The Hague, 29 July 1899, in force 4 September 1900, 32 Stat. 1803; T.S. No. 403; 91 BFSP 988

Declaration IV (2) concerning Asphyxiating Gases, The Hague, 29 July 1899, in force 4 September 1900, Schindler & Toman (1988) 105

Hague Convention IV on the Laws and Customs of Warfare on Land (with Annexed Regulations), The Hague, 18 October 1907, in force 26 January 1910, 205 CTS 277; USTS 539; 100 BFSP 338; 2 US Treaties 2269; UKTS 9 (1910), Cd 5030

Hague Convention V concerning Rights and Duties of Neutral Powers and Persons in Case of War on Land, The Hague, 18 October 1907, in force 26 January 1910, 100 BFSP 359; 2 US Treaties 2290; 205 CTS 299; USTS 545

Hague Convention IX respecting Bombardment by Naval Forces in Time of War, The Hague, 18 October 1907, in force 26 January 1910, 100 BFSP 401; 2 US Treaties 2314; UKTS 13 (1910); 205 CTS 345

Hague Convention XIII concerning Rights and Duties of Neutral Powers in Maritime Warfare, The Hague, 18 October 1907, in force 26 January 1910, 100 BFSP 448; 2 US Treaties 2352; 205 CTS 395; USTS N545

Declaration XIV Prohibiting the Discharge of Projectiles and Explosives from Balloons, The Hague, 18 October 1907, in force 27 November 1909, UKTS 15 (1910)

Protocol for the Prohibition of the Use in War of Asphyxiating, Poisonous or Other Gases, and of Bacteriological Methods of Warfare, Geneva, 17 June 1925, in force 8 February 1928, 94 LNTS 65; UKTS 24 (1930), Cmd 3604; 126 BFSP 324; 26 UST 571; TIAS 8061

Convention for the Amelioration of the Condition of Wounded and Sick of Armies in the Field, Geneva, 27 July 1929, in force 19 June 1931; no longer in operation following the universal acceptance of the Geneva Conventions of 1949, 47 Stat. 2074; T.S. No. 847; 118 L.N.T.S. 303

Convention Relative to the Treatment of Prisoners of War, Geneva, 27 July 1929, in force 19 June 1931, no longer in operation following the universal acceptance of the

Geneva Conventions of 1949, 47 Stat. 2021; T.S. No. 846; 118 L.N.T.S. 343; 130 BFSP 239

Charter of the United Nations, San Francisco, 26 June 1945, in force 24 October 1945, 1 UNTS XVI

Agreement for the Prosecution and Punishment of the Major War Criminals of the European Axis, with Charter of the International Military Tribunal, London, 8 August 1945, in force 9 August 1945, 82 UNTC 280

Geneva Conventions Relative to the Protection of the Victims of International Armed Conflicts, Geneva, 12 August 1949, in force 21 October 1950, 75 UNTS 31; UKTS 39 (1958), Cmd 550; 157 BFSP 229; 6 UST 3114; TIAS 3362; ATS 21 (1958)

Geneva Convention for the Amelioration of the Condition of the Wounded and Sick in Armed Forces in the Field (Geneva Convention I), Geneva, 12 August 1949, in force 21 October 1950, 75 UNTS 31; 157 BFSP 234; UKTS 39 (1958); TIAS 3362; 6 UST 3114

Geneva Convention for the Amelioration of the Condition of Wounded, Sick and Shipwrecked Members of the Armed Forces at Sea (Geneva Convention II), Geneva, 12 August 1949, in force 21 October 1950, 75 UNTS 85; 157 BFSP 262; UKTS 39 (1958); TIAS 3363; 6 UST 3217

Geneva Convention Relative to the Treatment of Prisoners of War (Geneva Convention III), Geneva, 12 August 1949, in force 21 October 1950, 75 UNTS 135; 157 BFSP 284; UKTS 39 (1958); TIAS 3364; 6 UST 3316

Geneva Convention Relative to the Protection of Civilian Persons in Time of War (Geneva Convention IV), Geneva, 12 August 1949, in force 21 October 1950, 75 UNTS 287; 157 BFSP 355; UKTS 39 (1958), Cmd 550; TIAS 3365; 6 UST 3516

Hague Convention for the Protection of Cultural Property in the Event of Armed Conflict, The Hague, 14 May 1954, in force 7 August 1956, 249 UNTS 215

African Convention on the Conservation of Nature and Natural Resources, Algiers, 15 September 1968, in force 16 June 1969, 1001 UNTS 1

Vienna Convention on the Law of Treaties, Vienna, 23 May 1969, in force 27 January 1980, 1155 UNTS 331

Convention on the Prohibition of the Development, Production and Stockpiling of Bacteriological (Biological) and Toxin Weapons and on Their Destruction, Washington, DC/Moscow/London, 10 April 1972, in force 26 March 1975, 1015 UNTS 163

Protocol Additional to the Geneva Conventions of 12 August 1949, and relating to the Protection of Victims of International Armed Conflicts (Protocol I), Geneva, 8 June 1977, in force 7 December 1978, 1125 UNTS 3

Protocol Additional to the Geneva Conventions of 12 August 1949, and relating to the Protection of Victims of Non-international Armed Conflicts (Protocol II), Geneva, 8 June 1977, in force 7 December 1978, 1125 UNTS 609

Convention on Prohibitions or Restrictions on the Use of Certain Conventional Weapons which may be deemed to be Excessively Injurious or to have

Indiscriminate Effects (with Protocols I, II and III), Geneva, 10 October 1980, in force 2 December 1983, 1342 UNTS 137

Protocol on Prohibitions or Restrictions on the Use of Mines, Booby-Traps and Other Devices (Protocol II) annexed to the Convention on Prohibitions or Restrictions on the Use of Certain Conventional Weapons which may be deemed to be Excessively Injurious or to have Indiscriminate Effects, Geneva, 10 October 1980, in force 2 December 1983, 1342 UNTS 137

Protocol on Prohibitions or Restrictions on the Use of Incendiary Weapons (Protocol III) annexed to the Convention on Prohibitions or Restrictions on the Use of Certain Conventional Weapons which may be deemed to be Excessively Injurious or to have Indiscriminate Effects, Geneva, 10 October 1980, in force 2 December 1983, 1342 UNTS 137

Convention on the Prohibition of the Development, Production, Stockpiling and Use of Chemical Weapons and on their Destruction, Geneva, 3 September 1992, in force 29 April 1997, 1975 UNTS 45

Additional Protocol to the Convention on Prohibitions or Restrictions on the Use of Certain Conventional Weapons which may be deemed to be Excessively Injurious or to have Indiscriminate Effects (Protocol IV, entitled Protocol on Blinding Laser Weapons), Vienna, 13 October 1995, in force 30 July 1998, 1380 UNTS 370

Protocol on Prohibitions or Restrictions on the Use of Mines, Booby-Traps and Other Devices as amended on 3 May 1996 (Protocol II, as amended on 3 May 1996) annexed to the Convention on Prohibitions or Restrictions on the Use of Certain Conventional Weapons which may be deemed to be Excessively Injurious or to have Indiscriminate Effects, Geneva, 3 May 1996, in force 3 December 1998, 2048 UNTS 93

Convention on the Prohibition of the Use, Stockpiling, Production and Transfer of Anti-Personnel Mines and on their Destruction, Oslo, 18 September 1997, in force 1 March 1999, 2056 UNTS 211

Rome Statute of the International Criminal Court, Rome, 17 July 1998, in force 1 July 2002, 2187 UNTS 3

Second Protocol to The Hague Convention of 1954 for the Protection of Cultural Property in the Event of Armed Conflict, The Hague, 26 March 1999, in force 9 March 2004, 2253 UNTS 172

Amendment to Article 1 of the Convention on Prohibitions or Restrictions on the Use of Certain Conventional Weapons which may be deemed to be Excessively Injurious or to have Indiscriminate Effects, Geneva, 21 December 2001, in force 18 May 2004, 2260 UNTS 82

Revised African Convention on the Conservation of Nature and Natural Resources, Maputo, 11 July 2003, in force 23 July 2016

Convention on Cluster Munitions, Dublin, 30 May 2008, 1 August 2010, 2688 UNTS 39

Treaty on the Prohibition of Nuclear Weapons, New York, 7 July 2017, in force 22 January 2021, 3379 UNTS

TABLE OF CASES

International

International Court of Justice

Armed Activities on the Territory of the Congo (New Application: 2002) (Democratic Republic of the Congo *v.* Uganda), Jurisdiction and Admissibility, Judgment, I.C.J. Reports 2006, p. 6

Gabčíkovo-Nagymaros Project (Hungary/Slovakia), Judgment, I.C.J. Reports 1997, p. 7

Legal Consequences for States of the Continued Presence of South Africa in Namibia (South West Africa) notwithstanding Security Council Resolution 276 (1970), Advisory Opinion, I.C.J. Reports 1971, p. 16

Legal Consequences of the Construction of a Wall in the Occupied Palestinian Territory, Advisory Opinion, I.C.J. Reports 2004, p. 136

Legality of the Threat or Use of Nuclear Weapons, Advisory Opinion, I.C.J. Reports 1996, p. 226

Military and Paramilitary Activities in and against Nicaragua (Nicaragua *v.* United States of America), Merits, Judgment, I.C.J. Reports 1986, p. 14

Permanent Court of International Justice

Factory at Chorzów (Germany *v.* Poland), Merits, Judgment No. 13, 1928, P.C.I.J., Series A, No. 17

International Military Tribunal

France and Others *v.* Göring (Hermann) and Others, Judgment and Sentence, 1 October 1946

International Criminal Tribunal for the Former Yugoslavia

The Prosecutor *v.* Kupreškić et al. (IT-95-16-T), Trial Chamber II, Judgment, 14 January 2000

The Prosecutor *v.* Kupreškić et al. (IT-95-16-A), Appeals Chamber, Appeal Judgment, 23 October 2001

The Prosecutor *v.* Martić (IT-95-11-R61), Trial Chamber I, Decision (Rule 61), 8 March 1996

The Prosecutor *v.* Martić (IT-95-11-TC), Trial Chamber I, Judgment, 12 June 2007

The Prosecutor *v.* Martić (IT-95-11-A), Appeals Chamber, Appeal Judgment, 8 October 2008

The Prosecutor *v.* Tadić (IT-94-1-AR72), Appeals Chamber, Decision on the Defence Motion for Interlocutory Appeal on Jurisdiction, 2 October 1995

The Prosecutor *v.* Tadić (IT-94-1-T), Trial Chamber, Judgment, 7 May 1997

Eritrea-Ethiopia Claims Commission

Partial Award: Prisoners of War – Eritrea's Claim 17, 1 July 2003, in (2009) 26 *Reports of International Arbitral Awards*, p. 23

Arbitral Tribunals

Arbitration between Portugal and Germany (*Naulilaa* case), Award, 31 July 1928, in (1929) 2 *Reports of International Arbitral Awards*, p. 1011

Case concerning the Difference between New Zealand and France concerning the Interpretation or Application of Two Agreements, concluded on 9 July 1986 between the Two States and which Related to the Problems Arising from the Rainbow Warrior Affair, Arbitral award, 30 April 1990, in (1990) 20 *Reports of International Arbitral Awards*, p. 215

International Centre for the Settlement of International Disputes

Corn Products International, Inc. *v.* The United Mexican States, ICSID Case No. ARB (AF)/04/01, Arbitral award, 15 January 2008

National

Belgium

In re Von Falkenhausen, Military Tribunal of Brussels (2nd Chamber), Judgment, 9 March 1951

Bosnia and Herzegovina

In re Lučić, Court of Bosnia and Herzegovina, Judgment, 19 September 2007

Colombia

Constitutional Case no. C-291/07, Constitutional Court of Colombia (Plenary Chamber), Judgment, 25 April 2007

Germany

Italian Partisans case, Federal Court of Justice, Judgment, 25 October 2010

Italy

In re Albers et al., Military Tribunal of La Spezia, Judgment No. 1, 13 January 2007 (available at www.eccidiomarzabotto.com/processi.php)

In re Albers et al., Military Court of Appeals of Rome, Judgment No. 25/08, 7 May 2008, Case No. 1/2008 R.G. (available at www.eccidiomarzabotto.com/docs/sentenza7maggio2008.pdf)

In re Engel, Military Tribunal of Turin, Judgment, 15 November 1999, Case Nos. 2046/96 R.N.R. and 0111/99 R.G.U.D. (available at https://portalegiustiziamilitare.difesa.it/default.aspx?Id=1126)

In re Hass and Priebke, Military Tribunal of Rome, Judgment, 22 July 1997 (available at www.difesa.it/Giustizia_Militare/rassegna/Processi/Priebke/Pagine/6Sentenza220797.aspx)

In re Hass and Priebke, Military Court of Appeals of Rome, Judgment, 7 March 1998 (available at www.difesa.it/Giustizia_Militare/rassegna/Processi/Priebke/Pagine/11Sentenza070398.aspx)

In re Hass and Priebke, Supreme Court of Cassation, Judgment, 16 November 1998 (available at www.difesa.it/Giustizia_Militare/rassegna/Processi/Priebke/Pagine/12Sentenza161198.aspx)

In re Kappler, Military Tribunal of Rome, Judgment, 20 July 1948, Case No. 631 (available at www.difesa.it/Giustizia_Militare/rassegna/Processi/Kappler/Pagine/02sentenza631.aspx)

In re Kappler, Supreme Military Tribunal, Judgment, 25 October 1952, Case No. 1714 (available at www.difesa.it/Giustizia_Militare/rassegna/Processi/Kappler/Pagine/07sentenza1714.aspx)

In re Kappler, Supreme Court of Cassation, Judgment, 19 December 1953, Case No. 26 (available at www.difesa.it/Giustizia_Militare/rassegna/Processi/Kappler/Pagine/08sentenza26.aspx)

In re Milde et al., Military Tribunal of La Spezia, Judgment No. 49, 10 October 2006, Case No. 64/05 (available at http://archiviodellamemoriacivitellavaldichiana.it/archivio_documenti/Sentenza%20Tribunale%20Militare%20della%20Spezia%20n.%2049%2010-10-2006.pdf)

In re Milde, Military Court of Appeals of Rome, Judgment No. 72/07, 18 December 2007, Case No. 52/2007 R.G. (available at www.archiviodellamemoriacivitellavaldichiana.it/prodotto/n-72-del-18-12-2007-sentenza-di-2-grado-con-cui-la-corte-militare-di-appello-rigetta-le-impugnaz-sentenza-di-appello/)

In re Milde, Supreme Court of Cassation, Judgment, 13 January 2009, Case No. 1072/2009, 92 Riv Dir Int 618, ILDC 1224 (IT 2009) (available at https://opil.ouplaw.com/display/10.1093/law:ildc/1224it09.case.1/law-ildc-1224it09)

In re Saevecke, Military Tribunal of Turin, Judgment, 9 June 1999, Cases No. 1619/96 R.N.R. and 0409/97 R.G.U.D. (available at www.difesa.it/Giustizia_Militare/rassegna/Processi/Pagine/SaeveckeTheodorEmil.aspx)

In re Sommer et al., Military Tribunal of La Spezia, Judgment, 22 June 2005, Case No. 45/2005 (available at www.difesa.it/Giustizia_Militare/rassegna/Processi/Sommer_Schoneberg_Bruss/Pagine/default.aspx)

In re Sommer et al., Military Court of Appeals of Rome, Judgment No. 65, 21 November 2006 (available at www.difesa.it/Giustizia_Militare/rassegna/Processi/Sommer_Schoneberg_Bruss/Pagine/SentenzaCorteMilitareAppelloRoma.aspx)

In re Sommer et al., Supreme Court of Cassation, Judgment No. 1362/07, 8 November 2007 (available at www.difesa.it/Giustizia_Militare/rassegna/Processi/Sommer_Schoneberg_Bruss/Pagine/SentenzaCorteSupremaCassazione.aspx)

In re Winkler et al., Military Tribunal of Verona, Judgment No. 43/2011, 6 July 2011, Case Nos. 172/08 and 80/09 (available at https://archiviodpc.dirittopenaleuomo.org/d/940-ergastolo-per-gli-eccidi-nazisti-commessi-nel-1944-lungo-l-appennino-tosco-emiliano-esclusi-stato-d)

In re Winkler et al., Supreme Court of Cassation, Judgment No. 23288, 19 March 2014

The Netherlands

In re Rauter, Special Criminal Court in The Hague, Judgment, 4 May 1948, Case No. 193, in (1949) 16 *Annual Digest and Reports of Public International Law Cases*, p. 509

In re Rauter, Special Court of Cassation, Judgment, 12 January 1949, Case No. 193, in (1949) 16 *Annual Digest and Reports of Public International Law Cases*, p. 509

United Kingdom

Trial of Field Marshal Kesselring, British Military Court in Rome, 17 February–6 May 1947, Case No. 44, VIII *Law Reports of Trials of War Criminals*, p. 9

Trial of Generals Von Mackensen and Maelzer, British Military Court in Rome, 18–30 November 1945, Case No. 43, VIII *Law Reports of Trials of War Criminals*, p. 1

United States of America

In re Dostler, Military Commission in Rome, Judgment, 12 October 1945, Case No. 2, I *Law Reports of Trials of War Criminals*, p. 22

The United States of America *v.* Otto Ohlendorf and Others (The Einsatzgruppen case), Nürnberg Military Tribunal II-A, 8–9 April 1948, in *Trials of War Criminals before the Nuernberg Military Tribunals* (Washington, DC: US Government Printing Office, 1950), vol. IV, p. 1

The United States of America *v.* Wilhelm List and Others (The Hostage Case), Nürnberg Military Tribunal V, 19 February 1948, in *Trials of War Criminals before the Nuernberg Military Tribunals* (Washington, DC: US Government Printing Office, 1950), vol. XI, p. 757

The United States of America *v.* Wilhelm von Leeb and Others (The High Command case), Nürnberg Military Tribunal V-A, 27 October 1948, in *Trials of War Criminals before the Nuernberg Military Tribunals* (Washington, DC: US Government Printing Office, 1950), vols. X–XI

Fact-Finding

International Humanitarian Fact-Finding Commission[1]

Executive Summary of the Report of the Independent Forensic Investigation in relation to the Incident affecting an OSCE Special Monitoring Mission to Ukraine (SMM) Patrol on 23 April 2017, 7 September 2017

Commission on Human Rights in South Sudan

UN Doc. A/HRC/34/63, *Report*, 6 March 2017

UN Doc. A/HRC/37/CRP.2, *Report*, 23 February 2018

UN Doc. A/HRC/37/71, *Report*, 13 March 2018

UN Doc. A/HRC/40/CRP.1, *Report*, 20 February 2019

UN Doc. A/HRC/45/CRP.3, *'There is nothing left for us': starvation as a method of warfare in South Sudan – Conference room paper*, 5 October 2020

UN Doc. A/HRC/45/CRP.4, *Transitional justice and accountability: a roadmap for sustainable peace in South Sudan – Conference room paper*, 5 October 2020

UN Doc. A/HRC/49/78, *Report*, 15 February 2022

UN Doc. A/HRC/49/CRP.4, *Conflict-related sexual violence against women and girls in South Sudan – Conference room paper*, 21 March 2022

[1] All news releases available at the News Archive website: www.ihffc.org/index.asp?Language=EN&page=news&mode=newsarchive.

Group of Eminent International and Regional Experts on Yemen

UN Doc. A/HRC/39/43, *Report*, 17 August 2018
UN Doc. A/HRC/42/17, *Report*, 9 August 2019
UN Doc. A/HRC/42/CRP.1, *Detailed Findings*, 3 September 2019
UN Doc. A/HRC/45/6, *Report*, 28 September 2020
UN Doc. A/HRC/45/CRP.7, *Detailed Findings*, 29 September 2020
UN Doc. A/HRC/48/20, *Report*, 13 September 2021
UN Doc. A/HRC/48/CRP.4, *Accountability Update*, 14 September 2021

Independent Fact-Finding Mission on Libya

UN Doc. A/HRC/48/83, *Report*, 29 November 2021

Independent International Commission of Inquiry on the Syrian Arab Republic

UN Doc. A/HRC/19/69, *Report*, 22 February 2012
UN Doc. A/HRC/21/50, *Report*, 16 August 2012
UN Doc. A/HRC/23/58, *Report*, 18 July 2013
UN Doc. A/HRC/24/46, *Report*, 16 August 2013
UN Doc. A/HRC/25/65, *Report*, 12 February 2014
UN Doc. A/HRC/27/60, *Report*, 13 August 2014
UN Doc. A/HRC/28/69, *Report*, 5 February 2015
UN Doc. A/HRC/31/68, *Report*, 11 February 2016
UN Doc. A/HRC/33/55, *Report*, 11 August 2016
UN Doc. A/HRC/37/72, *Report*, 1 February 2018
UN Doc. A/HRC/37/CRP.3, *'I lost my dignity': Sexual and gender-based violence in the Syrian Arab Republic – Conference room paper*, 8 March 2018
UN Doc. A/HRC/38/CRP.3, *The siege and recapture of eastern Ghouta*, 20 June 2018
UN Doc. A/HRC/39/65, *Report*, 9 August 2018
UN Doc. A/HRC/46/55, *Report*, 11 March 2021
UN Doc. A/HRC/49/77, *Report*, 8 February 2022

Independent International Fact-Finding Mission on Myanmar

UN Doc. A/HRC/39/CRP.2, *Report*, 17 September 2018
UN Doc. A/HRC/42/CRP.5, *Detailed Findings*, 16 September 2019
UN Doc. A/HRC/51/4, *Report*, 12 July 2022

International Commission of Human Rights Experts on Ethiopia

UN Doc. A/HRC/51/46, *Report*, 19 September 2022

Investigation by the Office of the UN High Commissioner for Human Rights on Libya

UN Doc. A/HRC/31/CRP.3, *Detailed Findings*, 23 February 2016

Panel of Experts on Yemen

UN Doc. S/2015/125, *Final Report*, 20 February 2015
UN Doc. S/2018/192, *Final Report*, 26 January 2016
UN Doc. S/2018/594, *Final Report*, 26 January 2018
UN Doc. S/2019/83, *Final Report*, 25 January 2019
UN Doc. S/2020/326, *Final Report*, 28 April 2020
UN Doc. S/2021/79, *Final Report*, 25 January 2021
UN Doc. S/2022/50, *Final Report*, 26 January 2022

TABLE OF KEY DOCUMENTS

International Organizations

United Nations[1]

Security Council

Resolution 540 (1983), UN Doc. S/RES/540 (1983), 31 October 1983

UN Doc. S/PV.2663, *Provisional Verbatim Record of the Two Thousand Six Hundred and Sixty-Third Meeting*, 18 February 1986

Resolution 598 (1987), UN Doc. S/RES/598 (1987), 20 July 1987

Statute of the International Tribunal for the Prosecution of Persons Responsible for Serious Violations of International Humanitarian Law Committed in the Territory of the Former Yugoslavia since 1991, UN Doc. S/25704, 3 May 1993, Annex, p. 36; UN Doc. S/25704/Add.1, 19 May 1993; UN Doc. S/RES/827 (1993), 25 May 1993

Resolution 2140 (2014), UN Doc. S/RES/2140 (2014), 26 February 2014

Resolution 2216 (2015), UN Doc. S/RES/2216 (2015), 14 April 2015

General Assembly

Resolution 2444 (XXIII), UN Doc. A/RES/2444 (XXIII), 19 December 1968, *Respect for Human Rights in Armed Conflict*

Resolution 2597 (XXIV), UN Doc. A/RES/2597 (XXIV), 16 December 1969, *Respect for Human Rights in Armed Conflict*

Resolution 2603 (XXIV), UN Doc. A/RES/2603 (XXIV) A, 16 December 1969, *Question of Chemical and Bacteriological (Biological) Weapons*

Resolution 2625 (XXV), UN Doc. A/RES/2625 (XXV), 24 October 1970, *Declaration on Principles of International Law concerning Friendly Relations and Co-operation among States in accordance with the Charter of the United Nations*

Resolution 2674 (XXV), UN Doc. A/RES/2674 (XXV), 9 December 1970, *Respect for Human Rights in Armed Conflict*

Resolution 2675 (XXV), UN Doc. A/RES/2675 (XXV), 9 December 1970, *Basic Principles for the Protection of Civilian Populations in Armed Conflict*

[1] For States' and UN communications related to the Iran–Iraq War, see Appendix.

Resolution 32/77, UN Doc. A/RES/32/77, 12 December 1977, *Chemical and Bacteriological (Biological) Weapons*

Resolution 56/82, UN Doc. A/RES/56/82, 28 January 2002, *Report of the International Law Commission on the Work of Its Fifty-Third Session*

Resolution 70/57, UN Doc. A/RES/70/57, 7 December 2015, Annex *Universal Declaration on the Achievement of a Nuclear-Weapon Free World*

Resolution 70/62, UN Doc. A/RES/70/62, 11 December 2015

Secretary-General

UN Doc. S/16962, 22 February 1985, *Prisoners of War in Iran and Iraq. The Report of a Mission Dispatched by the Secretary-General – January 1985*

Grundberg, Hans, 'Briefing to the United Nations by the Special Envoy of the Secretary-General for Yemen', 16 January 2023 (available at https://osesgy.unmissions.org/sites/default/files/en_jan_unsc_briefing_final.pdf)

UN Doc. A/HRC/54/61, 21 August 2023, *Report of the UN Secretary-General on Cooperation with the United Nations, Its Representatives and Mechanisms in the Field of Human Rights*

Human Rights Council

Resolution 12/2, UN Doc. A/HRC/RES/12/2, 12 October 2009

Resolution 24/24, UN Doc. A/HRC/RES/24/24, 9 October 2013

Resolution 36/31, UN Doc. A/HRC/RES/36/31, 3 October 2017

Resolution 36/21, UN Doc. A/HRC/RES/36/21, 6 October 2017

Resolution 42/28, UN Doc. A/HRC/RES/42/28, 1 October 2019

United Nations Educational, Scientific and Cultural Organization (UNESCO)

World Heritage Centre, *Operational Guidelines for the Implementation of the World Heritage Convention*, WHC.21/01, 31 July 2021

International Law Commission

State Responsibility

ILC, 'Text of Articles 28 to 32, with Commentaries thereto, Adopted by the Commission at Its Thirty-First Session', UN Doc. A/34/10 and Corr. 1, in (1979) II(1) ILC Ybk

Ago, Roberto, 'Addendum to the Eighth Report on State Responsibility', UN Doc. A/CN.4/318/Add. 5–7, in (1980) II(1) ILC Ybk

Arangio-Ruiz, Gaetano, 'Third Report on State Responsibility', UN Doc. A/CN.4/440 and Add. 1, in (1991) II(1) ILC Ybk

Arangio-Ruiz, Gaetano, 'Fourth Report on State Responsibility', UN Doc. A/CN.4/444 and Add. 1-3, in (1992) II(1) ILC Ybk

ILC, 'Report of the Commission to the General Assembly on the work of Its Forty-seventh session', UN Doc. A/CN.4/SER.A/1995/Add.1 (Part 2), in (1995) II(2) ILC Ybk

ILC, 'Text of Draft Articles 42 (Para. 3), 47, 48 and 51 to 53 with Commentaries thereto Provisionally Adopted by the Commission at Its Forty-Eight Session', in (1996) II(2) ILC Ybk

ILC, 'Draft Articles on the Responsibility of States for Internationally Wrongful Acts, as Provisionally Adopted by the International Law Commission on First Reading', UN Doc. A/CN.4/SER.A/1996/Add.1 (Part II), in (1996) II(2) ILC Ybk

ILC, 'State Responsibility: Comments and Observations Received from Governments', UN Doc. A/CN.4/488, in (1998) II(1) ILC Ybk

ILC, 'State Responsibility: Comments and Observations Received from Governments', Doc. A/CN.4/488/Add. 3, in (1998) II(1) ILC Ybk

Crawford, James, 'Second Report on State Responsibility, Addendum 2', UN Doc. A/CN.4/498/Add. 4, in (1999) II(1) ILC Ybk

Crawford, James, 'Third Report on State Responsibility, Addendum 3', UN Doc. A/CN.4/507/Add. 3, in (2000) II(1) ILC Ybk

Crawford, James, 'Third Report on State Responsibility, Addendum 4', UN Doc. A/CN.4/507/Add. 4, in (2000) II(1) ILC Ybk

ILC, 'Articles on Responsibility of States for Internationally Wrongful Acts, with Commentaries', UN Doc. A/56/10, in (2001) II(2) ILC Ybk

ILC, 'Responsibility of States for Internationally Wrongful Acts', UN Doc. A/RES/56/83, 28 January 2002 (corrected by document A/56/49(Vol. I)/Corr.4)

Reservations to Treaties

ILC, 'Guide to Practice on Reservations to Treaties', in (2011) II(2) ILC Ybk

Identification of Customary International Law

ILC, 'Draft Conclusions on Identification of Customary International Law, with Commentaries', in (2018) II(2) ILC Ybk

Protection of the Environment in Relation to Armed Conflicts

Jacobsson, Marie G., 'Second report on the protection of the environment in relation to armed conflicts', UN Doc. A/CN.4/685, 28 May 2015

ILC, 'Report of the ILC on the work of its sixty-seventh session, 4 May–5 June and 6 July–7 August 2015', UN Doc. A/70/10

ILC, 'Topical summary of the discussion held in the Sixth Committee of the General Assembly during its seventieth session', UN Doc. A/CN.4/689, 28 January 2016

Jacobsson, Marie G., 'Third report on the protection of the environment in relation to armed conflicts', UN Doc. A/CN.4/700, 3 June 2016

ILC, 'Report of the ILC on the work of its sixty-eighth session, 2 May–10 June and 4 July–12 August 2016', UN Doc. A/71/10

Switzerland, 'Observations concernant la pratique et les instruments de la Suisse visant à protéger l'environnement en relation avec un conflit armé ainsi que des observations additionnelles sur le projet de principes', Comment during the 68th session of the ILC, 2016 (available at https://legal.un.org/ilc/sessions/68/pdfs/french/poe_switzerland.pdf)

ILC, 'Topical summary of the discussion held in the Sixth Committee of the General Assembly during its seventy-first session', UN Doc. A/CN.4/703, 22 February 2017

Lehto, Marja, 'Second report on protection of the environment in relation to armed conflicts', UN Doc. A/CN.4/728, 27 March 2019

ILC, 'Report of the ILC on the work of its seventy-first session, 29 April–7 June and 8 July–9 August 2019', UN Doc. A/74/10

ILC, 'Topical summary of the discussion held in the Sixth Committee of the General Assembly during its seventy-fourth session', UN Doc. A/CN.4/734, 12 February 2020

Kingdom of the Netherlands, 'Comment' during the 73rd session of the ILC, 2022 (available at https://legal.un.org/ilc/sessions/73/pdfs/english/poe_netherlands.pdf)

ILC, 'Protection of the environment in relation to armed conflicts – Comments and observations received from Governments, international organizations and others', UN Doc. A/CN.4/749, 17 January 2022

Lehto, Marja, 'Third report on protection of the environment in relation to armed conflicts, UN Doc. A/CN.4/750, 16 March 2022

ILC, 'Draft principles on protection of the environment in relation to Armed Conflicts', UN Doc. A/77/10, in (2022) II(2) ILC Ybk

Meeting of States Parties to the Treaty on the Prohibition of Nuclear Weapons

UN Doc. TPNW/MSP/2022/6, *Report of the first Meeting of States Parties to the Treaty on the Prohibition of Nuclear Weapons*, 21 July 2022

Other UN Documents

(1990) 40 *Yearbook of the United Nations 1986* (Dordrech/Boston/London: Martinus Nijhoff, 1990)

UN Doc. S/20012, 13 July 1988, *Letter Dated 11 July 1988 from the Acting Permanent Representative of the Islamic Republic of Iran to the United Nations Addressed to the Secretary-General*

UN Doc. S/20754, 2 August 1989, *Letter Dated 27 July 1989 from the Chargé d'affaires a.i. of the Permanent Mission of Iraq to the United Nations Addressed to the Secretary-General*

UN Doc. S/21104, 24 January 1990, *Letter Dated 24 January 1990 from the Permanent Representative of the Permanent Mission of the Islamic Republic of Iran to the United Nations addressed to the Secretary-General*

League of Nations

Assembly, *Resolution on Protection of Civilian Populations against Bombing from the Air in Case of War*, 30 September 1938, Schindler & Toman (2004) 329

League of Arab States

Council, *Resolution 2676*, 15 September 1970

Organizations and Associations

International Committee of the Red Cross

Resolution XIV, 16th International Red Cross Conference, London, 1938

Draft Rules for the Limitation of the Dangers Incurred by the Civilian Population in Time of War, 15 October 1956 (Geneva: ICRC, 1956)

Report on the Reaffirmation and Development of the Laws and Customs Applicable in Armed Conflicts – Report Submitted by the ICRC at the XXI International Conference of the Red Cross (Istanbul, September 1969), Geneva, 1969

ICRC Appeal, October 1973 (1973) 152 IRRC, p. 583

Memorandum from the International Committee of the Red Cross to the States Parties to the Geneva Conventions of August 12, 1949 concerning the conflict between Islamic Republic of Iran and Republic of Iraq, Geneva, 7 May 1983

Annual Report 1983 (Geneva: ICRC, 1984)

Second Memorandum from the International Committee of the Red Cross to the States Parties to the Geneva Conventions of August 12, 1949 concerning the conflict between Islamic Republic of Iran and Republic of Iraq, Geneva, 10 February 1984

Bombing of Iraqi and Iranian Cities, Press Release No. 1489, 7 June 1984

Annual Report 1984 (Geneva: ICRC, 1985)

ICRC Appeal, 28 May 1985

Annual Report 1985 (Geneva: ICRC, 1986)

Annual Report 1986 (Geneva: ICRC, 1987)

Annual Report 1987 (Geneva: ICRC, 1988)

Press Release No. 1567, 23 March 1988

Annual Report 1988 (Geneva: ICRC, 1989)

International Humanitarian Law and the challenges of contemporary armed conflicts – Report prepared by the International Committee of the Red Cross for the 28th International Conference of the Red Cross and Red Crescent, 03/IC/09, Geneva, 2003

International Humanitarian Law and the challenges of contemporary armed conflicts – Report prepared by the International Committee of the Red Cross for the 31st International Conference of the Red Cross and Red Crescent (Geneva, 28 November–1 December 2011), 31IC/11/5.1.2, Geneva, 2011

Draft '0' Resolution on 'Strengthening Compliance with International Humanitarian Law' (with the Swiss Federal Department of Foreign Affairs), Geneva, September 2015

Strengthening Compliance with International Humanitarian Law – Draft Resolution and Concluding Report (with the Swiss Federal Department of Foreign Affairs), Doc. 32IC/15/19.2, Geneva, October 2015

International Humanitarian Law and the challenges of contemporary armed conflicts – Report prepared by the International Committee of the Red Cross for the 32nd International Conference of the Red Cross and Red Crescent (Geneva, 8–10 December 2015), 32IC/15/11, Geneva, 2015

Guidelines on the Protection of the Natural Environment in Armed Conflict, 25 September 2020

'The ICRC's legal and policy position on nuclear weapons' (2022) 104 IRRC, pp. 1477–99

International Red Cross and Red Crescent Movement

20th International Conference of the Red Cross (1965), *Resolution XXVIII on the Protection of Civilian Populations against the Dangers of Indiscriminate Warfare* (1965) 56 IRRC, pp. 589 f.

24th International Conference of the Red Cross (1981), *Resolution XIII on Disarmament, Weapons of Mass Destruction and Respect for Non-combatants* (1981) 225 IRRC, p. 330

Statutes of the International Red Cross and Red Crescent Movement (adopted by the 25th International Conference of the Red Cross at Geneva in 1986, and amended in 1995 and 2006)

32nd International Conference of the Red Cross and Red Crescent (2015), *Strengthening Compliance with International Humanitarian Law*, Resolution 32IC/15/R2, Geneva, 8–10 December 2015

International Humanitarian Fact-Finding Commission[2]

'Update to the IHFFC Statement of 8 October 2015', News Release, 14 October 2015

'Organization of American States adopts resolution referring to IHFFC', News Release, 5 June 2018

'IHFFC has proposed its services', News Release, 29 January 2019

'Launch of the Group of Friends of the IHFFC at the United Nations', News Release, 13 November 2019

[2] All news releases available at the News Archive website: www.ihffc.org/index.asp?Language=EN&page=news&mode=newsarchive.

'Support for the IHFFC at the 33rd International Conference', News Release, 12 December 2019

'IHFFC has proposed its services', News Release, 23 October 2020

'Ethiopia: IHFFC has proposed its services', News Release, 21 January 2021

'IHFFC has proposed its services', News Release, 10 March 2022

Commission on the Responsibility of the Authors of the War and on Enforcement of Penalties

Report Presented to the Preliminary Peace Conference, 29 March 1919, in (1920) 14 AJIL

Hague Commission of Jurists

Draft Rules of Aerial Warfare, The Hague, 19 February 1923, 17 AJIL Supp. 245, 32 AJIL Supp. 1

Harvard Program on Humanitarian Policy and Conflict Research

Manual on International Law Applicable to Air and Missile Warfare (Cambridge: Cambridge University Press, 2013)

Harvard Research in International Law

Draft Convention on the Law of Treaties (1935) 29 AJIL, Supplement: Research in International Law, pp. 653 ff.

Institut de Droit International

'Conclusion IX', in (1877) 1 *Annuaire de l'Institut de Droit International*

'The Manual on the Laws of War on Land', Oxford, 9 September 1880, in (1881–1882) 5 *Annuaire de l'Institut de Droit International*; Hans Wehberg (ed.), *Institut de Droit International. Tableau Général des Résolutions (1873–1956)* (Basel: Éditions juridiques et sociologiques, 1957), pp. 180–98

Politis, Nikolaos, 'Rapport et projets de résolution de règlement', in (1934) *Annuaire de l'Institut de Droit International*

'Résolution I. – Régime des représailles en temps de paix', in (1934) *Annuaire de l'Institut de Droit International*

'Resolution on the Distinction between Military Objectives and Non-military Objects in General and Particularly the Problems Associated with Weapons of Mass Destruction', 9 September 1969, in (1969) 53 *Annuaire de l'Institut de Droit International*

International Conference on Human Rights

Resolution XXIII, 12 May 1968, *Human Rights in Armed Conflict*

International Group of Experts at the Invitation of the NATO Cooperative Cyber Defence Centre of Excellence

Schmitt, Michael N. (ed.), *Tallinn Manual on the International Law Applicable to Cyber Warfare* (Cambridge: Cambridge University Press, 2013)
Schmitt, Michael N. (ed.), *Tallinn Manual 2.0 on the International Law Applicable to Cyber Warfare* (Cambridge: Cambridge University Press, 2017, 2nd ed.)

International Institute of Humanitarian Law

The Manual on the Law of Non-international Armed Conflict, with Commentary, San Remo, 2006

International Law Association

Draft Convention for the Protection of Civilian Populations against New Engines of War, Amsterdam, 2 September 1938, Schindler & Toman (1988) 223

International Conferences

Conference of Brussels (1874)

'Project of an International Declaration concerning the Laws and Customs of War', 27 August 1874, Schindler, Dietrich and Toman, Jiri (eds.), *The Laws of Armed Conflicts* (Dordrecht: Martinus Nijhoff, 1988), pp. 22–34

United Nations Conference on the Law of Treaties (1968–1969)

UN Doc. A/CONF.39/11, *Official Records of the United Nations Conference on the Law of Treaties, First Session (Summary records of the plenary meetings and of the meetings of the Committee of the Whole)* (New York: UN, 1969)
UN Doc. A/CONF.39/11/Add.1, *Official Records of the United Nations Conference on the Law of Treaties, Second Session (Summary records of the plenary meetings and of the meetings of the Committee of the Whole)* (New York: UN, 1970)
UN Doc. A/CONF.39/11/Add.2, *Official Records of the United Nations Conference on the Law of Treaties, Documents of the Conference* (New York: UN, 1971)

Diplomatic Conference on the Reaffirmation and Development of International Humanitarian Law Applicable in Armed Conflicts (Geneva, 1974–1977)

Swiss Federal Political Department, *Official Records of the Diplomatic Conference on the Reaffirmation and Development of International Humanitarian Law Applicable in Armed Conflicts – Geneva (1974–1977)* (Bern: 1978), 17 vols.

Swiss Federal Political Department, *Actes de la Conférence Diplomatique sur la réaffirmation et le développement du Droit international humanitaire applicable dans les conflits armés – Genève (1974–1977)* (Berne: 1978), 17 vols.

State Documents[3]

China

'Joint Statement of the Leaders of the Five Nuclear-Weapon States On Preventing Nuclear War and Avoiding Arms Races', 3 January 2022

Egypt

Declaration upon ratification of the 1977 Additional Protocols to the 1949 Geneva Conventions, 9 October 1992

France

Reservation upon accession to Additional Protocol I to the 1949 Geneva Conventions, 11 April 2001

'Joint Statement of the Leaders of the Five Nuclear-Weapon States On Preventing Nuclear War and Avoiding Arms Races', 3 January 2022

'Ministerial Statement of the French Republic, the United Kingdom of Great Britain and Northern Ireland, and the United States of America', 1 August 2022

Ministry of the Armies, Direction des affaires juridiques – État-major des armées, *Manuel de droit des opérations militaires* (2022 ed.)

Germany

Control Council for Germany, Law No. 10, 'Punishment of Persons Guilty of War Crimes, Crimes against Peace and against Humanity', 20 December 1945, in 3 *Official Gazette of the Control Council for Germany*, p. 12

[3] For States' and UN communications related to the Iran–Iraq War, see Appendix.

Declarations made at the time of ratification of the 1977 Additional Protocols to the 1949 Geneva Conventions, 14 February 1991

Federal Ministry of Defence, *Law of Armed Conflict Manual*, Joint Service Regulation (ZDv) 15/2, 1 May 2013

Italy

Legge di Guerra, promulgated with Regio Decreto No. 1415, 8 July 1938-XVI, 'Approvazione dei testi della legge di guerra e della legge di neutralità', in (1938) 211 *Supplemento ordinario alla Gazzetta Ufficiale*, Allegato A, p. 3

Declaration made at the time of ratification of Additional Protocol I to the 1949 Geneva Conventions, 27 February 1986

Chiefs of Defence Staff, *Manuale di Diritto umanitario*, SMD-G-014, 1991

Russian Federation

'Joint Statement of the Leaders of the Five Nuclear-Weapon States On Preventing Nuclear War and Avoiding Arms Races', 3 January 2022

Saudi Arabia

UN Doc. S/2018/266, *Letter Dated 26 March 2018 from the Permanent Representative of Saudi Arabia to the United Nations addressed to the President of the Security Council*, 27 March 2018

Saudi Press Agency, 'Joint Incidents Assessment Team Refutes Allegations against Coalition Forces', 25 November 2020 (available at www.spa.gov.sa/2161522)

United Kingdom

War Office, *The Law of War on Land being Part III of the Manual of Military Law*, HMSO, 1958

Declarations and reservations made upon ratification of Additional Protocol I to the 1949 Geneva Conventions, 28 January 1998

Ministry of Defence, *The Joint Service Manual of the Law of Armed Conflict*, JSP 383, 2004 edition with amendments

'Joint Statement of the Leaders of the Five Nuclear-Weapon States On Preventing Nuclear War and Avoiding Arms Races', 3 January 2022

'Ministerial Statement of the French Republic, the United Kingdom of Great Britain and Northern Ireland, and the United States of America', 1 August 2022

United Arab Emirates

Emirates News Agency, 'Coalition to Restore Legitimacy in Yemen announces reopening of ports Hudaydah, Sanaa tomorrow', 22 November 2017 (available at https://wam.ae/en/details/1395302648875)

Emirates News Agency, 'Royal Saudi Air Defence intercepts, destroys Houthi UAV: Arab Coalition', 8 April 2019 (available at www.wam.ae/en/details/1395302753854)

Emirates News Agency, '"We will take urgent and timely measures against Houthi militia": Coalition to Restore Legitimacy in Yemen', 24 June 2019 (available at www.wam.ae/en/details/1395302769701)

Emirates News Agency, 'Coalition downs Saudi-bound Houthi drone', 10 September 2019 (available at https://wam.ae/en/details/1395302785466) and 11 September 2019 (available at https://wam.ae/en/details/1395302785730)

Emirates News Agency, 'Coalition forces target ballistic missile capabilities in Sana'a', 23 February 2020 (available at www.wam.ae/en/details/1395302826195)

United States of America

Lieber, Francis, *Instructions for the Government of Armies of the United States in the Field*, promulgated by US President Abraham Lincoln as General Orders No. 100 of the US War Department, 24 April 1865

Department of the Army, *Field Manual 27-10, The Law of Land Warfare*, 18 July 1956, as modified by Change No. 1, 15 July 1976

Department of the Air Force, *Air Force Pamphlet 110-31, International Law – The Conduct of Armed Conflict and Air Operations*, 1976

Central Intelligence Agency, *Iran–Iraq: Ballistic Missile Warfare and Its Regional Implications. An Intelligence Assessment*, March 1986

Department of State, *Report Annexed to Message from the President of the United States*, 100th Congress, 1st Session, Treaty Doc. 100-2 (Washington, DC: US Government Printing Office, 1987)

Naval War College, Oceans Law and Policy Department, Centre for Naval Warfare Studies, *Annotated Supplement to the Commander's Handbook on the Law of Naval Operations*, November 1997

'Joint Statement of the Leaders of the Five Nuclear-Weapon States On Preventing Nuclear War and Avoiding Arms Races', 3 January 2022

'Ministerial Statement of the French Republic, the United Kingdom of Great Britain and Northern Ireland, and the United States of America', 1 August 2022

Department of Defense, Office of General Counsel, *Law of War Manual*, June 2015 (Updated July 2023)

Yemen

Yemen News Agency, 'Leader of Yemen's Revolution announces new phase of military escalation', 20 December 2017 (available at www.saba.ye/en/news482164.htm)

Yemen News Agency, 'Yemeni ballistic missiles hopes to Level Playing Field in Saudi War: Report', 5 March 2019 (available at www.saba.ye/en/news528335.htm)

Yemen News Agency, 'Riyadh screams of Yemeni missiles', 27 May 2019 (available at www.saba.ye/en/news537414.htm)

Yemen News Agency, 'Al-Houthi to al-Jazeera: the war is open with Saudi Arabia if it does not stop its aggression against Yemen', 18 August 2020 (available at www.saba.ye/en/news3106042.htm)

Yemen News Agency, 'Seventh year will be year of victory, decisiveness: Army's spokesman', 22 March 2021 (available at www.saba.ye/en/news3133512.htm)

Yemen News Agency, 'President announces suspension of missile strikes, drones, military operations for 3 days', 27 March 2022 (available at www.saba.ye/en/news3181022.htm)

ABBREVIATIONS

AC	Appeals Chamber
AJIL	*American Journal of International Law*
AP(s)	Additional Protocol(s) to the 1949 Geneva Conventions
BYIL	*British Yearbook of International Law*
CCW	1980 Convention on Prohibitions or Restrictions on the Use of Certain Conventional Weapons which may be deemed to be Excessively Injurious or to have Indiscriminate Effects
CDDH	Diplomatic Conference on the Reaffirmation and Development of International Humanitarian Law Applicable in Armed Conflicts, Geneva 1974–77
CHR-SoSu	Commission on Human Rights in South Sudan
CoI-S	Independent International Commission of Inquiry on the Syrian Arab Republic
CWC	1992 Chemical Weapons Convention
EJIL	*European Journal of International Law*
GC(s)	1949 Geneva Convention(s)
GEE-Y	Group of Eminent International and Regional Experts on Yemen
HRC	Human Rights Council
IAC	international armed conflict
ICJ	International Court of Justice
ICLQ	*International and Comparative Law Quarterly*
ICoHRE-E	International Commission of Human Rights Experts on Ethiopia
ICRC	International Committee of the Red Cross
IDI	Institut de Droit International
IHFFC	International Humanitarian Fact-Finding Commission
IHL	international humanitarian law
IIFFM-M	Independent International Fact-Finding Mission on Myanmar
ILA	International Law Association
ILC	International Law Commission
ILC Ybk	*Yearbook of the International Law Commission*
ISIL	Islamic State of Iraq and the Levant
JIAT	Joint Incidents Assessment Team

NAFTA	North American Free Trade Agreement
NIAC	non-international armed conflict
NSAG	non-State armed group
NYIL	*Netherlands Yearbook of International Law*
OHCHR	Office of the UN High Commissioner for Human Rights
PCIJ	Permanent Court of International Justice
PoE-Y	Panel of Experts on Yemen
RGDIP	*Revue Générale de Droit International Public*
TC	Trial Chamber
TPNW	2017 Treaty on the Prohibition of Nuclear Weapons
UN	United Nations
US DoD	US Department of Defense
VCLT	1969 Vienna Convention on the Law of Treaties

Introduction

I.1 Belligerent Reprisals: The Eternal Recurrence of the Same?

In the spring of 330 BC, Alexander the Great set fire to the royal palaces of Persepolis, the ceremonial capital of the Achaemenid Empire. Several centuries later, ancient historians were puzzled and upset by the ominous fate of 'the capital of the entire Orient, from which so many nations previously sought jurisdiction, the birthplace of so many kings'.[1] Their accounts diverge as to what exactly prompted the destruction of the city:[2] whether it was a premeditated act which Alexander pursued against the advice of his senior generals,[3] or the spontaneous initiative of a drunken mob to which the king acceded out of impulse.[4] Despite this uncertainty, all versions agree on the core motivation behind this act – that is, the desire to retaliate against the burning of Athens and its Acropolis, carried out by the Achaemenid king Xerxes I during the Second Persian War (482–479 BC). For its symbolic value, selected target and modes of execution, the fire of Persepolis mirrored the profanation of the sacred hill of Athens;[5] its avowed objective was to 'avenge Greece'[6] and retaliate

[1] Quintus Curtius Rufus, *History of Alexander* (tr. John C. Rolfe), 2 vols. (Cambridge, MA: Harvard University Press, 1946), vol. I, p. 389, at V.vii.8 [footnotes omitted].

[2] Plutarch, *Plutarch's Lives* (tr. Bernadotte Perrin), 11 vols. (Cambridge, MA: Harvard University Press, 1958), vol. VII, *Life of Alexander*, p. 339, at 38.

[3] Arrian, *The Anabasis of Alexander* (tr. Edward J. Chinnock) (London: Hodder and Stoughton, 1884), p. 178, at III.xviii.

[4] Diodorus Siculus, *Library of History* (tr. Charles Bradford Welles), 12 vols. (Cambridge, MA: Harvard University Press, 1963), vol. VIII, p. 325, at XVII.72; Plutarch, *Plutarch's Lives*, vol. VII, pp. 337, 339, at 38; Curtius Rufus, *History of Alexander*, vol. I, pp. 387, 389, at V.vii.2–7.

[5] Plutarch, *Plutarch's Lives*, vol. VII, p. 337, at 38 (who draws a link between the burning of Xerxes's palace and the latter's setting ablaze of Athens); Diodorus Siculus, *Library of History*, vol. VIII, p. 327, at XVII.72 (highlighting the identical treatment incurred by the two monuments).

[6] Curtius Rufus, *History of Alexander*, vol. I, p. 387, at V.vii.4.

for the crimes committed against the Hellenic temples and sanctuaries.[7] In an extremely insightful glimpse into human psychology, the Roman historian Quintus Curtius Rufus sketches the reaction of the Macedonian troops: oscillating between the shame for the obliteration of such a famous city and their desire to justify it, they 'forced themselves to believe that it was right that it should be wiped out in exactly that manner'.[8]

Undoubtedly, international law has undergone enormous developments since the time of Alexander's campaign – including by establishing a very sophisticated framework to govern warfare, conduct hostilities and protect victims of war.[9] However, references to retaliation and vengeance are anything but rare in today's discourse on armed conflict. Three recent examples, drawn from different contexts, are particularly telling. The first one dates from 2020, and nearly drew a stunning parallelism with the events that took place during the invasion of Persia more than two millennia ago. Fearing retaliation for the drone strike that had killed Iranian major general Qassem Suleimani, the then-President of the United States threatened to target fifty-two Iranian sites, including some 'at a very high level & important to Iran & the Iranian culture' [sic], should Americans or US assets be hit.[10] The second instance brings us to Eastern Europe. On several occasions in 2022 and 2023, the Russian

[7] Diodorus Siculus, *Library of History*, vol. VIII, p. 325, at XVII.72; Arrian, *Anabasis of Alexander*, pp. 178–79, at III.xviii (who, however, considered the destruction of Persepolis unwise and, in any case, did not believe in the rationale of punishing the Persians: ibid.).

[8] Curtius Rufus, *History of Alexander*, vol. I, p. 389, at V.vii.10 [footnote omitted].

[9] Throughout this work, we will use the terms "the laws of armed conflict", "international humanitarian law", "*ius in bello*" and "the laws of war" interchangeably, unless otherwise specified.

[10] M. Chulov, J. Borger, G. Abdul-Ahad, and agencies, 'Trump vows to hit 52 sites "very hard" if Iran retaliates over Suleimani killing', *The Guardian*, 5 January 2020 (available at www.theguardian.com/world/2020/jan/05/donald-trump-vows-to-hit-52-sites-very-hard-if-iran-retaliates-for-suleimani-killing). After re-affirming the threat on a handful of occasions, the President stepped back after receiving considerable criticism not only from Iranian officials, but also from key allies, international organizations and senior officials in the US administration (including the Secretary of State and the Defense Secretary): see A. Woodcock, R. Merrick and A. Cowburn, 'Iran crisis: Boris Johnson warns Trump not to break international law by bombing cultural sites', *The Independent*, 6 January 2020 (available at www.independent.co.uk/news/uk/politics/iran-war-trump-boris-johnson-cultural-sites-soleimani-iraq-a9272076.html); BBC News, 'Trump under fire for threat to Iranian cultural sites', 6 January 2020 (available at www.bbc.com/news/world-middle-east-51014237); D. Smith and agencies, 'Trump defends "war crime" threat to target cultural sites in Iran', *The Guardian*, 7 January 2020 (available at www.theguardian.com/world/2020/jan/06/suleimani-killing-donald-trump-defends-threat-to-hit-cultural-sites-in-iran); D. Superville, 'Trump retreats from threat to attack Iranian

leadership portrayed its strikes on population centres and power infrastructures in Ukraine as 'tit-for-tat measures' made necessary, and allegedly justified, by enemy attacks on, for example, the Kerch Strait bridge, the power lines of the Kursk nuclear power station, and the residential areas of Moscow.[11] This, in turn, has prompted threats of revenge and punishment from the counterpart.[12] The third illustration relates to the latest round of hostilities in the Gaza Strip since October 2023. In that context, reciprocity has characterized several statements accompanying the 'Operation Al-Aqsa Flood' just as much as 'Operation Iron Sword'. On the one hand, Hamas and the Palestinian Islamic Jihad have repeatedly lamented Israeli 'violation of all international norms, laws and human rights conventions' in the context of the belligerent occupation of Palestine;[13] on the other, recourse by Israel to specific methods of warfare (such as completely cutting off the supply of electricity, food, water and fuel to the Gaza Strip) was framed by senior Israeli political officials not only as a punishment for previous enemy

cultural sites', Associated Press, 8 January 2020 (available at https://apnews.com/article/e456bc97066894a04b23b384fec6cded).

[11] See the statements by the President and the Foreign Ministry of Russia quoted in: M. Hunder and J. Landay, 'Russia launches biggest air strikes since start of Ukraine war', Reuters, 11 October 2020 (available at www.reuters.com/world/europe/russias-ria-state-agency-reports-fuel-tank-fire-kerch-bridge-crimea-2022-10-08/); F. Ebel, 'Putin admits attacks on civilian infrastructure, asking: "Who started it?"', *The Washington Post*, 8 December 2022 (available at www.washingtonpost.com/world/2022/12/08/russia-attacks-ukraine-infrastructure-putin/); M. Seddon and C. Miller, 'Vladimir Putin vows retaliation for drone attack on Moscow', *Financial Times*, 30 May 2023 (available at www.ft.com/content/cdde0e44-0e90-41c0-a3be-e5f6849b706b); G. Jones and A. Heavens, 'Russia vows retaliation for Ukraine's "terrorist attack" on Crimean Bridge', Reuters, 12 August 2023 (available at www.reuters.com/world/europe/russia-vows-retaliation-ukraines-terrorist-attack-crimean-bridge-2023-08-12/). For a legal analysis of the October 2022 attack on the Kerch Strait Bridge, see Marko Milanovic and Michael N. Schmitt, 'Ukraine Symposium – The Kerch Strait Bridge Attack, Retaliation, and International Law', *Articles of War*, 12 October 2022 (available at https://lieber.westpoint.edu/kerch-strait-bridge-attack-retaliation-international-law/).

[12] See the statement by Ukraine's Defence Ministry reproduced in P. Beaumont, C. Higgins and A. Mazhulin, 'Putin warns of further retaliation as Ukraine hit by massive wave of strikes', *The Guardian*, 10 October 2022 (available at www.theguardian.com/world/2022/oct/10/explosions-kyiv-ukraine-war-russia-crimea-putin-bridge).

[13] Middle East Monitor, 'Statement by Hamas's Al-Qassam Brigades top military commander', 7 October 2023 (available at www.middleeastmonitor.com/20231007-statement-by-hamass-al-qassam-brigades-top-military-commander/); see also Euronews, 'Hamas claims responsibility for deadly Jerusalem shooting', 30 November 2023 (available at www.euronews.com/2023/11/30/hamas-claims-responsibility-for-deadly-jerusalem-shooting).

misconduct,[14] but also as a way of coercing the enemy into ceasing current violations of international humanitarian law (IHL) (i.e., the taking of hostages).[15]

The result of these statements has been the cautious, half-whispered re-appearance in academic and policy discussions of the topic of belligerent reprisals.[16] In its most essential definition, this notion indicates an act that would violate the laws of armed conflict, were it not for its being taken in response to a previous unlawful breach of that body of rules by the counterpart.[17] To be clear, this topic has never ceased to interrogate

[14] See the statements by Israel's Defence Minister quoted in E. Fabian, 'Defense minister announces "complete siege" of Gaza: No power, food or fuel', *The Times of Israel*, 9 October 2023 (available at www.timesofisrael.com/liveblog_entry/defense-minister-announces-complete-siege-of-gaza-no-power-food-or-fuel/); by the President of Israel reproduced in R. Omaar, 'Israeli president Isaac Herzog says Gazans could have risen up to fight "evil" Hamas', ITV, 13 October 2023 (available at www.itv.com/news/2023-10-13/israeli-president-says-gazans-could-have-risen-up-to-fight-hamas); and by the Prime Minister of Israel quoted in L. Berman, 'Netanyahu: Goal of war is "to defeat the murderous enemy, ensure our existence in our land"', *The Times of Israel*, 28 October 2023 (available at www.timesofisrael.com/liveblog_entry/netanyahu-goal-of-war-is-to-defeat-the-murderous-enemy-ensure-our-existence-in-our-land/).

[15] See the statement by Israel's Energy Minister reproduced in N. Slawson, 'First Thing: no power, water or fuel for Gaza until hostages are freed, Israel says', *The Guardian*, 12 October 2023 (available at www.theguardian.com/us-news/2023/oct/12/first-thing-no-power-water-fuel-gaza-until-hostages-freed-israel-says).

[16] See, for instance, Adil A. Haque, 'Renouncing Reprisals: An Opportunity for the Biden Administration', *Just Security*, 1 April 2021 (available at www.justsecurity.org/75553/renouncing-reprisals-an-opportunity-for-the-biden-administration/), as well as Michael N. Schmitt, 'Ukraine Symposium – Reprisals in International Humanitarian Law', *Articles of War*, 6 March 2023 (available at https://lieber.westpoint.edu/reprisals-international-humanitarian-law/). See also, in relation to the hostilities between Armenia and Azerbaijan over Nagorno-Karabakh in September 2020, the reference to reprisals in Human Rights Watch, 'Armenia/Azerbaijan: Don't Attack Civilians. Respect Absolute Ban on Targeting Civilians, Civilian Objects', 30 September 2020 (available at www.hrw.org/news/2020/09/30/armenia/azerbaijan-dont-attack-civilians).

[17] Similar (albeit not identical) definitions can be found in different scholarly works on the topic. Kalshoven stated that '[r]eprisals . . . consist of the intentional violation of a rule of international law in reaction to an act equally violative of such a norm' (Frits Kalshoven, *Belligerent Reprisals* (Leiden: Sijthoff, 1971; re-published Leiden/Boston: Martinus Nijhoff, 2005), p. 29). Bierzanek defined the measure as 'retaliation upon the state having committed unlawful acts by means of other unlawful acts' (Remigiusz Bierzanek, 'Reprisals in Armed Conflict' (1987–88) 14 *Syracuse Journal of International and Comparative Law*, p. 829). Watts, on his part, submitted that '[d]efined simply, reprisals are violations of international law undertaken in response to unauthorized violations by another subject of international law' (Sean Watts, 'Reciprocity and the Law of War' (2009) 50 *Harvard International Law Journal*, p. 382). Finally, Greenwood has written that '[a] belligerent reprisal consists of action which would normally be contrary to the

legal scholars: whether on the sly or head-on, the issue peeps out on a recurrent basis, in connection with the adoption of a treaty, the rendering of a judgment, the identification of a custom or the monitoring of a conflict. And yet, notwithstanding the knowledge that has accrued over the past decades, belligerent reprisals continue to prove an elusive concept. This is the result of three, cumulative sets of problems.

I.2 Conceptual, Normative and Policy Difficulties

The first issue is one of *semantics*. Over time, the term "reprisal" has taken up a variety of meanings, making it more and more difficult to grasp its significance and regulate its role in armed conflict. For instance, in UN parlance, the word is often associated with acts of intimidation and harm against those cooperating with the organization in the field of human rights.[18] At a deeper level, the theory and language of international law are not always aligned with the practice of belligerent reprisals. Sometimes, the position of parties to armed conflicts undermines clear-cut theoretical distinctions. By way of example, belligerent reprisals have been traditionally contrasted to so-called armed reprisals: whereas the former notion represents a *ius in bello* mechanism, the latter falls in the province of *ius ad bellum*, and indicates measures involving recourse to armed force and characterized by a punitive character.[19] This has not prevented belligerents from conflating the two regimes, for instance by invoking belligerent reprisals as a way to justify IHL violations even when the underlying intent was to chastise the initiation of an armed conflict or bring about its end.[20]

laws governing the conduct of armed conflict (the *ius in bello*) but which is justified because it is taken by one party to an armed conflict against another party in response to the latter's violation of the *ius in bello*' (Christopher Greenwood, 'The Twilight of the Law of Belligerent Reprisals' (1989) 20 *Netherlands Yearbook of International Law*, p. 38).

18 See, for instance, UN Doc. A/HRC/54/61, *Report of the UN Secretary-General on Cooperation with the United Nations, Its Representatives and Mechanisms in the Field of Human Rights*, 21 August 2023, *passim*.

19 See Evelyn Speyer Colbert, *Retaliation in International Law* (New York: King's Crown Press, 1948), *passim*; Richard A. Falk, 'The Beirut Raid and the International Law of Retaliation' (1969) 63 AJIL, pp. 428–31; Derek Bowett, 'Reprisals Involving Recourse to Armed Force' (1972) 66 AJIL, pp. 1–3. See also UN Doc. A/RES/2625(XXV), *Declaration on Principles of International Law concerning Friendly Relations and Co-operation among States in accordance with the Charter of the United Nations*, 24 October 1970, para. 1: 'States have a duty to refrain from acts of reprisal involving the use of force'.

20 For a paradigmatic example taken from the Iran–Iraq War, see UN Doc. S/18704, 18 February 1987, p. 2, whereby Iraq would consider itself released from its commitment not to bombard Iranian towns for two weeks not only 'if the forces of the Iranian régime

On other occasions, it is legal theory that fails to recognize or formalize the presence of belligerent reprisals, setting up novel notions with little prescriptive standing (such as that of "other countermeasures" in relation to non-international armed conflict).[21]

The second problem concerns the *regulation* of belligerent reprisals. As we shall see in greater detail below, there exists a significant degree of uncertainty regarding both the procedural and the substantive requirements that must accompany the adoption of belligerent reprisals.[22] In addition to that, defining the precise scope for lawful recourse to belligerent reprisals has proved highly controversial – not only under customary IHL, but also to some extent under treaty law.[23] Historically, the phenomenon of belligerent reprisals has been approached by means of incremental prohibitions that excluded recourse to such measures when taken against certain targets or when using certain weapons. This way of proceeding (coherent with the State-driven nature of IHL law-making) seems to presuppose a belief in the residual nature of the entitlement to resort to belligerent reprisals when they have not been outlawed (yet).[24] At the same time, this conclusion could be challenged on two grounds: from the outside, by looking at the interplay of IHL with other legal frameworks, most notably international human rights law (IHRL);[25] but also from the inside, by taking into account current research on the permissive or prohibitive nature of IHL itself.[26]

shell Iraqi towns and residential areas', but also '*if the Iranian régime launches a new assault against Iraqi territory and Iraq's international borders*', and in any case if Iran did not 'espouse a *new position consistent with international law [with regard to peace]*' [emphasis added].

[21] Jean-Marie Henckaerts and Louise Doswald-Beck, *Customary International Humanitarian Law*, 2 vols. (Cambridge: Cambridge University Press, 2005), vol. I, p. 526, Rule 148.

[22] See Section 1.2.1.3.

[23] See Section 1.2.1.2.

[24] On *a contrario* reasoning in case of specific prohibitions, see Stanislaw E. Nahlik, 'Belligerent Reprisals As Seen in the Light of the Diplomatic Conference on Humanitarian Law, Geneva, 1974–1977' (1978) 42 *Law and Contemporary Problems*, pp. 64–66.

[25] For a comprehensive analysis of the topic, see Robert Kolb, Gloria Gaggioli and Pavle Kilibarda (eds.), *Research Handbook on Human Rights and Humanitarian Law. Further Reflections and Perspectives*, 2nd ed. (Cheltenham: Edward Elgar, 2022); in relation to belligerent reprisals, see Shane Darcy, *Collective Responsibility and Accountability under International Law* (Leiden: Transnational Publishers, 2007), pp. 175–82.

[26] For the reference book on the topic, see Anne Quintin, *The Nature of International Humanitarian Law: A Permissive or Restrictive Regime?* (Cheltenham: Edward Elgar, 2020).

The third question is one of *policy*. Recent contributions from the social sciences testify to the widespread recourse to conducts defended as belligerent reprisals. Morrow has demonstrated that in international armed conflicts, retaliation for violations of the laws of war is near ubiquitous, swift, and leading to better compliance.[27] Building on this evidence, Osiel has remarked a paradoxical situation – that is, recourse to belligerent reprisals appears to be more frequent precisely in those situations where it is prohibited by the 1949 Geneva Conventions and their 1977 Additional Protocols.[28] When it comes to civil wars, Jo has shown that, due to the rebel groups' quest for legitimacy, reciprocal behaviours are less ubiquitous for certain types of violations (especially in the field of child soldiering and detention access), but still at work for others (e.g., the killing of civilians).[29] Thus, current practice seems to resist the long-standing attempt by international law to progressively curb (or, in the case of non-international armed conflicts, completely rule out) the ability to adopt belligerent reprisals. As a result, not only does the prospective of adding *new* prohibitions on belligerent reprisals look more and more remote – the risk is actually that even *existing* prohibitions are called into question by means of contrary practice, and that an increased role for reciprocity is 'reinject[ed] . . . back into humanitarian law by way of custom, even as treaties have increasingly sought to reject it'.[30]

In sum, international law is losing its grip over belligerent reprisals: it fails to define it conceptually, govern it normatively, and constrain it factually. The notion has always sat, as Bílková has written, at the

[27] James D. Morrow, *Order within Anarchy: The Laws of War as an International Institution* (Cambridge: Cambridge University Press, 2014), p. 144.

[28] Mark Osiel, *The End of Reciprocity: Terror, Torture and the Law of War* (Cambridge: Cambridge University Press, 2009), p. 278. Geneva Conventions Relative to the Protection of the Victims of International Armed Conflicts, Geneva, 12 August 1949, in force 21 October 1950, 75 UNTS 31; UKTS 39 (1958), Cmd 550; 157 BFSP 229; 6 UST 3114; TIAS 3362; ATS 21 (1958). Protocol Additional to the Geneva Conventions of 12 August 1949, and relating to the Protection of Victims of International Armed Conflicts (Protocol I), Geneva, 8 June 1977, in force 7 December 1978, 1125 UNTS 3; Protocol Additional to the Geneva Conventions of 12 August 1949, and relating to the Protection of Victims of Non-International Armed Conflicts (Protocol II), Geneva, 8 June 1977, in force 7 December 1978, 1125 UNTS 609.

[29] Hyeran Jo, *Compliant Rebels: Rebel Groups and International Law in World Politics* (New York: Cambridge University Press, 2015), pp. 74, 132–33, 165, 199.

[30] Osiel, *End of Reciprocity*, p. 279.

vanishing point of IHL,[31] stretching to its very limits the normative reach of international regulation. How can we prevent it from slipping behind that edge, and escaping all attempts at legal governance?

I.3 The *causa* of Belligerent Reprisals: Purpose and Function of the Mechanism

At first sight, these three sets of problems touch on very different aspects – with law being only one of them. Yet, they can also be seen as different declinations of a unitary, deeper legal issue – that of the *causa* of belligerent reprisals. Having its roots in Roman law, this notion identifies, as Salmon put it, 'the legal basis and rationale of a juridical institution'.[32] As such, it could be seen as encompassing two complementary aspects. A first, static trait would relate to the *purpose* of a given legal tool, and would investigate the abstract objectives attributed to it by the legal order. A second, more dynamic facet would focus on the *function* of the mechanism, considering its inner dynamics and its relationship with other notions under international law. The identification of the *causa* is therefore vested with a paramount role in the process of legal qualification. When considered together, these elements provide an exact depiction of a legal mechanism, both in itself and *vis-à-vis* other institutions; when they are lacking, what stands jeopardized is not only the autonomous standing and specific conceptualization of any legal notion, but also the very possibility of deriving its specific regulation and subjecting it to effective governance.

In my view, the conceptual, normative and policy difficulties looming over belligerent reprisals are but symptoms of a wider conundrum – that is, the failure on the part of international law to correctly analyse and formalize their *causa*. If the notion of belligerent reprisals is blurred, prone to abuse and difficult to distinguish from other legal concepts; if the margin of application and regulation of the mechanism is unclear; if recourse to it persists (and actually expands) notwithstanding all the attempts at reducing and ultimately removing it – then it is reasonable to infer that international legal doctrine has a problem in construing the

[31] Veronika Bílková, 'Belligerent Reprisals in Non-International Armed Conflicts' (2014) 63 ICLQ, p. 31.

[32] Jean Salmon, *Dictionnaire de droit international public* (Bruxelles: Bruylant, 2001), p. 154 (translation by the author; in the original: '[l]e fondement, la raison d'une institution juridique').

purpose and function of belligerent reprisals. This is so in at least two senses.

The first issue has to do with the approach that international law has taken to formalize the purpose and function of belligerent reprisals (the question of "how"). Writing on the provisions of the 1977 Additional Protocols, Almond has remarked that '[belligerent] reprisals ... are completely ignored except in the sense of providing prohibitions'.[33] Whereas the drafters of those treaties failed to ask the question on the *causa* of belligerent reprisals altogether, following scholars and practitioners have approached the issue – but in flawed terms. True, virtually all recent contributions on belligerent reprisals contain notations on the purpose of the mechanism; however, they have downgraded the *causa*, from being *the* criterion to *legally qualify* a given behaviour as a belligerent reprisal, into being *one out of* many conditions to verify *whether the measure is lawful*.[34] In other words, the element that is necessary to legally recognize a conduct as belligerent reprisal has been transformed into one of the parameters to evaluate it. If one looks carefully, this turns the order of the analysis upside down. A stakeholder (be it the addressee of the measure, a third State, or any legal observer) cannot assess the lawfulness of a conduct, without first being able to subsume it under a legal construct that determines the applicable norms. As the tragedy of Oedipus teaches us, the ability to recognize and identify something not only precedes any evaluation that we can make of it – it is what makes that very judgment possible.[35]

Despite the fallacy of this methodological approach, we could always argue that at least international law has embarked on a reflection on this fundamental issue. We might be looking at the topic from the wrong angle – so the argument would go – but we do have a rather solid consensus that belligerent reprisals are characterized by a specific purpose, which consists in the enforcement of the laws of armed conflict.[36]

[33] Harry H. Almond, 'Reprisals: The Global Community Is Not Yet Ready to Abandon Them' (1980) 74 *Proceedings of the American Society of International Law*, p. 197.

[34] Henckaerts and Doswald-Beck, *Customary IHL Study*, vol. I, p. 515; Greenwood, 'Twilight of Reprisals', p. 40; Shane Darcy, 'The Evolution of the Law of Belligerent Reprisals' (2003) 175 *Military Law Review*, p. 187.

[35] Sophocles, *King Oedipus* (tr. William B. Yeats) (London: Macmillan, 1928), pp. 14 ('though you have your sight, you cannot see'), 42 ('All truth! Now O Light, may I look my last upon you').

[36] On the enforcement purpose of belligerent reprisals, see for example Henckaerts and Doswald-Beck, *Customary IHL Study*, vol. I, pp. 515–16; Greenwood, 'Twilight of

But that is precisely where the second, more important issue enters the picture – and it has to do with the solution that international law has given to the question of the *causa* of belligerent reprisals (the question of "what"). By attributing to this mechanism the objective of coercing a return to compliance with IHL, international law has operated a skilful operation of embellishment (some would say whitewash) of belligerent reprisals. This strategy has played out along two, mutually reinforcing axes – which will be duly analysed in the book. On the one hand, concerned with the functioning of the measure, belligerent reprisals have been construed on the basis of the blueprint provided by the law of countermeasures. On the other hand, related to the purpose of the notion, belligerent reprisals have been interpreted as a forward-looking tool, interested in the positive value of enforcing breached norms and strengthening the legal order.

With all likelihood, the main aspiration behind this move was to rein in by way of interpretation a mechanism that was notably impervious to legal constraints. However laudable the attempt, there are serious weaknesses in the legal underpinnings of this construction. From a purely conceptual viewpoint, the analogy between countermeasures and belligerent reprisals could well stand; however, it is a rather long shot to assume that the motivations, stakes and incentives for retaliatory breaches are the same as we deal with IHL during wartime, on the one hand, and for other international obligations mostly during peacetime, on the other. The same artificiality characterizes the acknowledgement (often expressed in the legal scholarship) that other motives can legitimately characterize recourse to belligerent reprisals, provided that the enforcement purpose be present.[37] If it is admitted that enforcement of the law might not always be the primary objective, singling it out as *the* decisive criterion to identify and assess belligerent reprisals is just a form of cherry-picking – the move could well be coherent with the overall objective of shoring up and sustaining the legal order, but it remains an arbitrary choice of attributing legal relevance to one element at the exclusion of all the others.

Additionally, we must wonder if the attribution of an enforcement purpose to belligerent reprisals and their assimilation with countermeasures has fulfilled its aspirations, or if instead it has done more harm than

Reprisals', pp. 45–46; Darcy, 'Evolution of Reprisals', p. 191; Bílková, 'Reprisals in NIACs', p. 33. For a general overview of the scholarship on the issue, see Section 2.4.3.2.

[37] Kalshoven, *Belligerent Reprisals*, p. 24; Greenwood, 'Twilight of Reprisals', p. 46.

good. It is probably excessive to argue that this interpretation of the *causa* of belligerent reprisals is the sole responsible for the legimitization and perpetuation of the mechanism. But it is undeniable that it has prejudiced our analytical tools, by altering our understanding of the purpose and function of belligerent reprisals and ultimately by preventing an unbiased appreciation of their place in the regulation of contemporary warfare.

I.4 Main Claim, Structure and Objectives of the Book

It is both timely and appropriate to re-consider the purpose and function that international law attributes to belligerent reprisals. This book challenges the mainstream understanding of belligerent reprisals as a tool interested in enforcing compliance with the laws of armed conflict; by re-instating reciprocity at the core of the mechanism, it argues that belligerent reprisals aim at re-calibrating the legal relationship between parties to an armed conflict and at ensuring parity of arms both in a formal and in a substantive sense.

In line with this claim, the book will be divided in six chapters. Chapter 1 will introduce the notion of belligerent reprisals, and present the two competing paradigms that have served as reference models for its formalization – that is, enforcement (embodied by non-forcible countermeasures) and reciprocity (represented by the unilateral suspension and termination of international obligations). Chapter 2 will follow the trajectory by which belligerent reprisals have been subsumed progressively under the enforcement paradigm, at the expense of their features inspired by reciprocity. Chapter 3 will analyse several instances of State practice (both verbal and physical ones) that testify to the resilience and persisting influence of reciprocity in structuring the purpose and function of belligerent reprisals. Building on this analysis, Chapter 4 will focus on two aspects of the Iran–Iraq War of 1980–88 as case-studies to test how belligerents have articulated the *causa* of belligerent reprisals in international armed conflict; retaliatory instances of chemical warfare and the "war of the cities" during that conflict will demonstrate that enforcement and reciprocity converge (instead of mutually exclude each other) in defining the functioning of belligerent reprisals, and that these measures can take on a variety of purposes far exceeding that of bringing about compliance with the laws of war. Chapter 5 will draw the conceptual framework to analyse belligerent reprisals in non-international armed conflicts (NIACs), placing the mechanism between the competing pulls of inequality of status and equality of rights and obligations and witnessing the role that reciprocity plays also in this context. Chapter 6 will then distinguish between lawful and unlawful belligerent reprisals in non-international armed conflict, before analysing how their purpose and function have been construed by several bodies monitoring IHL compliance. Finally, the Conclusion will discuss some key implications of these findings: it will disentangle belligerent reprisals from theories of law-making, discuss their specificity *vis-à-vis* compliance mechanisms, and highlight the importance of a new formalization of the mechanism for future regulation and reform.

By placing the question of the *causa* at the centre of the legal reflection on belligerent reprisals, I aim at two objectives. On the short term, by re-considering their purpose and function, I wish to draw a new legal perimeter, within which still pending questions over the regulation of the mechanism could be finally solved. Answering the primary question as to how and for what purposes belligerent reprisals work will make it possible for future contributions to approach the secondary questions concerning, for instance, the degree of proportionality, the authority and the quality of the authorizing entity, the beginning and the cessation, and the residual scope for lawful recourse to such measures. On the longer run, the book provides legal scholars, military officials and political decision-makers with a novel viewpoint on the practice and the law of belligerent reprisals. In so doing, it offers a firmer ground to discuss what place (if any) belligerent reprisals should occupy in any future IHL regime. This should ensure that, whatever the decision on belligerent reprisals (whether they are maintained as an indispensable feature in the legal governance of armed conflict, or whether they are dismissed once and for all from the books and the practice of warfare), at least we would have looked into the abyss with unobstructed gaze.

1

Reciprocity and Countermeasures

Competing Paradigms to Understand Belligerent Reprisals

1.1 *Dramatis personae*

As the International Committee of the Red Cross (ICRC) has noted, the 1949 Geneva Conventions and their 1977 Additional Protocols do not 'provide a definition of "[belligerent] reprisal"', nor do they set forth 'the requirements for legitimate reprisals in case where they are not explicitly prohibited'.[1] With IHL treaties focusing exclusively on the prohibition of certain belligerent reprisals, the challenge of clarifying the conceptual and normative tenets of the notion has been taken up by legal scholars, State officials and judicial authorities. However, most interpreters have derived the fundamental traits of belligerent reprisals by means of logical deduction or a priori distinctions *vis-à-vis* other notions of international law.[2] Searching for legal underpinnings to belligerent reprisals in the rich fabric of international law, they considered two paradigms as particularly apt to formalize the purpose and function of the mechanism: one inspired by reciprocity, the other by enforcement. After sketching the international regulation of belligerent reprisals, this chapter will present

1 Henckaerts and Doswald-Beck, *Customary IHL Study*, vol. II, p. 3302, para. 60; Geneva Conventions Relative to the Protection of the Victims of International Armed Conflicts, Geneva, 12 August 1949, in force 21 October 1950, 75 UNTS 31; UKTS 39 (1958), Cmd 550; 157 BFSP 229; 6 UST 3114; TIAS 3362; ATS 21 (1958); Protocol Additional to the Geneva Conventions of 12 August 1949, and relating to the Protection of Victims of International Armed Conflicts (Protocol I), Geneva, 8 June 1977, in force 7 December 1978, 1125 UNTS 3; Protocol Additional to the Geneva Conventions of 12 August 1949, and relating to the Protection of Victims of Non-International Armed Conflicts (Protocol II), Geneva, 8 June 1977, in force 7 December 1978, 1125 UNTS 609.

2 For a few, paradigmatic examples of this tendency, see Françoise J. Hampson, 'Belligerent Reprisals and the 1977 Protocols to the Geneva Conventions of 1949' (1998) 37 ICLQ, pp. 819–21; Edward Kwakwa, 'Belligerent Reprisals in the Law of Armed Conflict' (1990–91) 27 *Stanford Journal of International Law*, p. 51.

the constitutive elements of these two archetypes, as well as the trajectory by which they were progressively detached and, ultimately, considered as mutually exclusive. Belligerent reprisals came thus to be confronted with the fundamental dilemma still hollowing them to this day – that is, that of choosing between reciprocity and enforcement as the paradigm structuring and inspiring their purpose and function.

1.2 Belligerent Reprisals under International Law

1.2.1 The International Regulation of Belligerent Reprisals

Even if retaliation has been a component of warfare since antiquity, it was not until the late nineteenth century that international lawyers tackled the phenomenon of belligerent reprisals. Early attempts at codifying the laws of war (be they conducted by governmental conferences or by non-governmental institutions) provided the first venue where the topic could be raised, discussed and often dropped.[3] Thus, while the 1880 Oxford Manual compiled by the Institut de Droit International (IDI) contained two provisions on belligerent reprisals,[4] the Peace Conferences that took place in 1874 in Brussels, and in 1899 and 1907 in The Hague, failed to openly address the topic.[5] As the field of the laws of war grew increasingly sophisticated in the twentieth century,

[3] Kalshoven, *Belligerent Reprisals*, pp. 45, 68.

[4] Institut de Droit International, 'The Manual on the Laws of War on Land', Oxford, 9 September 1880 (1881–82) 5 *Annuaire de l'Institut de Droit International*; Hans Wehberg (ed.), *Institut de Droit International. Tableau Général des Résolutions (1873–1956)* (Basel: Éditions juridiques et sociologiques, 1957), pp. 180–98. Article 85 provided that '[r]eprisals are formally prohibited in case the injury complained of has been repaired' (Wehberg, *ibid.*, p. 197). Article 86, on its part, provided that '[i]n grave cases in which reprisals appear to be absolutely necessary, their nature and scope shall never exceed the measure of the infraction of the laws of war committed by the enemy. They can only be resorted to with the authorization of the commander in chief. They must conform in all cases to the laws of humanity and morality' (*ibid.*, p. 198).

[5] Kalshoven, *Belligerent Reprisals*, p. 66. On the possibility to construe Article 50 of the Regulations annexed to the 1899 and 1907 Hague Conventions as a 'clear, albeit feeble, attempt to grapple with the problem of belligerent reprisals', see Kwakwa, 'Belligerent Reprisals', p. 54, footnote 23 and, partially, Darcy, 'Evolution of Reprisals', p. 197. Hague Convention No II with respect to the Laws and Customs of War on Land (with Annexed Regulations), The Hague, 29 July 1899, in force 4 September 1900, 32 Stat. 1803; T.S. No. 403; 91 BFSP 988; Hague Convention No IV on the Laws and Customs of Warfare on Land (with Annexed Regulations), The Hague, 18 October 1907, in force 26 January 1910, 205 CTS 277; USTS 539; 100 BFSP 338; 2 US Treaties 2269; UKTS 9 (1910), Cd 5030.

the rules applicable to belligerent reprisals also developed along two, converging axes.

1.2.1.1 Treaty Provisions Prohibiting Recourse to Belligerent Reprisals

The first leg of this process (largely promoted by means of treaty law) has resulted in a wide range of prohibitions that curtail the parties' right to adopt belligerent reprisals.[6] The 1929 Convention Relative to the Treatment of Prisoners of War ushered in this movement by prohibiting belligerent reprisals against prisoners of war.[7] Whereas the Third Geneva Convention of 1949 (GC III) reaffirmed that provision,[8] the other three Geneva Conventions of 1949 significantly broadened the category of persons and objects protected from belligerent reprisals. These instruments forbade taking belligerent reprisals 'against the wounded, sick, personnel, buildings or equipment protected' by the First Geneva Convention (GC I);[9] 'against the wounded, sick and shipwrecked persons, the personnel, the vessels or the equipment protected' by the Second Geneva Convention (GC II);[10] and against those civilian persons (and their property) 'who, at a given moment and in any manner whatsoever, find themselves, in case of a conflict or occupation, in the hands of a Party to the conflict or Occupying Power of which they are not nationals', as per the wording of the Fourth Geneva Convention

[6] For the national and international criminal judgments that preceded, consolidated and expanded these treaty provisions, see Sections 2.2.3.1, 2.2.3.3 and 2.4.3.1, as well as Section 3.4.2.

[7] Article 2(3), Convention Relative to the Treatment of Prisoners of War, Geneva, 27 July 1929, in force 19 June 1931, no longer in operation following the universal acceptance of the Geneva Conventions of 1949, 47 Stat. 2021; T.S. No. 846; 118 L.N.T.S. 343; 130 BFSP 239: '[m]easures of reprisal against them [*scil.*, prisoners of war] are forbidden'.

[8] Article 13(3), Geneva Convention Relative to the Treatment of Prisoners of War (Geneva Convention III), Geneva, 12 August 1949, in force 21 October 1950, 75 UNTS 135; 157 BFSP 284; UKTS 39 (1958); TIAS 3364; 6 UST 3316: '[m]easures of reprisal against prisoners of war are prohibited'.

[9] Article 46, Geneva Convention for the Amelioration of the Condition of the Wounded and Sick in Armed Forces in the Field (Geneva Convention I), Geneva, 12 August 1949, in force 21 October 1950, 75 UNTS 31; 157 BFSP 234; UKTS 39 (1958); TIAS 3362; 6 UST 3114.

[10] Article 47, Geneva Convention for the Amelioration of the Condition of Wounded, Sick and Shipwrecked Members of the Armed Forces at Sea (Geneva Convention II), Geneva, 12 August 1949, in force 21 October 1950, 75 UNTS 85; 157 BFSP 262; UKTS 39 (1958); TIAS 3363; 6 UST 3217.

(GC IV).[11] Just a few years later, the 1954 Hague Convention for the Protection of Cultural Property in the Event of Armed Conflict prohibited the adoption of 'any act directed by way of reprisals against cultural property'.[12]

Against this background, the 1977 Protocol I additional to the 1949 Geneva Conventions (AP I) further narrowed the scope of belligerent reprisals in international armed conflicts (IACs), in a qualitative as well as a quantitative sense. On the one hand, building on the safeguards offered by GCs I and II, it 'extend[ed] the sphere of protected persons by widening the definitions of wounded, sick, and shipwrecked persons in Article 8 [of AP I], and by including several new objects and persons for protection'.[13] On the other, it included a set of new and crucial provisions that safeguarded civilian persons and objects from reprisal action well beyond the scope of GC IV. Belligerent reprisals on the civilian population or civilians were prohibited[14] in absolute and peremptory terms;[15] these categories would benefit from this safeguard even if they do not find themselves 'in the hands of a Party to the conflict or Occupying Power of which they are not nationals' (as was the case under GC IV),[16] and even in situations of 'actual military hostilities of an international armed conflict'.[17] At the same time (and in addition to the general protection from attack or reprisal now afforded civilian objects),[18]

[11] See Article 4 in conjunction with Article 33(3), Geneva Convention Relative to the Protection of Civilian Persons in Time of War (Geneva Convention IV), Geneva, 12 August 1949, in force 21 October 1950, 75 UNTS 287; 157 BFSP 355; UKTS 39 (1958), Cmd 550; TIAS 3365; 6 UST 3516.

[12] Article 4(4), Hague Convention for the Protection of Cultural Property in the Event of Armed Conflict, The Hague, 14 May 1954, in force 7 August 1956, 249 UNTS 215. On the similarity between Article 11(1) of that Convention (concerning the withdrawal of immunity from cultural property under special protection) and the functioning of belligerent reprisals, see René Provost, *International Human Rights and Humanitarian Law* (Cambridge: Cambridge University Press, 2002), p. 176. On the applicability of this prohibition to non-international armed conflicts, see Section 5.1.1.

[13] Darcy, 'Evolution of Reprisals', p. 203. The latter category listed includes 'medical personnel, religious personnel, medical units, medical transports and transportations, medical vehicles, ships, crafts, and aircraft': see *ibid.*

[14] Article 51(6) AP I reads as follows: '[a]ttacks against the civilian population or civilians by way of reprisals are prohibited'.

[15] Yves Sandoz, Christophe Swinarski and Bruno Zimmermann (eds.), *Commentary on the Additional Protocols of 8 June 1977 to the Geneva Conventions of 12 August 1949* (Geneva: ICRC/Martinus Nijhoff, 1987), p. 626, para. 1984.

[16] See Article 33(3) GC IV in conjunction with Article 4 GC IV.

[17] Darcy, 'Evolution of Reprisals', p. 205.

[18] Article 52(1) AP I: '[c]ivilian objects shall not be the object of attack or of reprisals'.

a number of targets were specifically shielded from retaliatory action, including cultural objects and places of worship,[19] objects indispensable to the survival of the civilian population,[20] the natural environment[21] as well as works and installations containing dangerous forces.[22]

Further prohibitions on belligerent reprisals could be found, either in explicit terms or by way of interpretation, in the field of weapons law. A first case in point is the II Protocol on Prohibitions or Restrictions on the Use of Mines, Booby-Traps and Other Devices, annexed to the 1980 Convention on Prohibitions or Restrictions on the Use of Certain Conventional Weapons which may be deemed to be Excessively Injurious or to have Indiscriminate Effects (CCW).[23] Both in the original version of 1980[24] and in its amended version of 1996,[25] the II Protocol to the CCW endorses the enhanced protection from reprisals granted to the civilian population and civilian objects by AP I to the GCs. In its most

[19] Article 53 AP I:

> [w]ithout prejudice to the provisions of the Hague Convention for the Protection of Cultural Property in the Event of Armed Conflict of 14 May 1954, and of other relevant international instruments, it is prohibited ... (c) to make such objects [*scil.*, historic monuments, works of art or places of worship which constitute the cultural or spiritual heritage of peoples] the object of reprisals.

[20] Article 54(4) AP I.

[21] Article 55(2) AP I.

[22] Article 56(4) AP I: '[i]t is prohibited to make any of the works, installations or military objectives mentioned in paragraph 1 [*scil.*, works or installations containing dangerous forces, namely dams, dykes and nuclear electrical generating stations] the object of reprisals'.

[23] Convention on Prohibitions or Restrictions on the Use of Certain Conventional Weapons which may be deemed to be Excessively Injurious or to have Indiscriminate Effects (with Protocols I, II and III), Geneva, 10 October 1980, in force 2 December 1983, 1342 UNTS 137.

[24] Article 3(2), Protocol on Prohibitions or Restrictions on the Use of Mines, Booby-Traps and Other Devices (Protocol II) annexed to the Convention on Prohibitions or Restrictions on the Use of Certain Conventional Weapons which may be deemed to be Excessively Injurious or to have Indiscriminate Effects, Geneva, 10 October 1980, in force 2 December 1983, 1342 UNTS 137: 'It is prohibited in all circumstances to direct weapons to which this Article applies, either in offence, defence or by way of reprisals, against the civilian population as such or against individual civilians'.

[25] Protocol on Prohibitions or Restrictions on the Use of Mines, Booby-Traps and Other Devices as amended on 3 May 1996 (Protocol II, as amended on 3 May 1996) annexed to the Convention on Prohibitions or Restrictions on the Use of Certain Conventional Weapons which may be deemed to be Excessively Injurious or to have Indiscriminate Effects, Geneva, 3 May 1996, in force 3 December 1998, 2048 UNTS 93.

recent wording, the II Protocol to the CCW prohibits to direct mines, booby-traps and a range of other devices specified in its Article 3 'by way of reprisals, against the civilian population as such or against individual civilians or civilian objects'.[26] Likewise, the provisions contained in the 1972 Biological Weapons Convention and in the 1992 Chemical Weapons Convention (CWC) might also be construed as restricting the ability to use the weapons covered in those treaties by way of reprisal. The obligation set forth in Article I of the former instrument (to 'never in any circumstances' develop, produce, acquire or retain biological or bacteriological weapons)[27] has been interpreted by both the ICRC and part of the scholarship as including, *a fortiori*, a prohibition against their retaliatory use.[28] Moving to the CWC, the fact that under Article I thereof States Parties undertake explicitly 'never under any circumstances . . . [t]o use chemical weapons',[29] coupled with the predisposition of extensive compliance arrangements,[30] has led to a similar conclusion.[31] In this regard, it is important to mention that, according to these views, the use of such biological agents and toxic chemicals as a form of belligerent reprisals would not be included in the provisions that provide for exceptions to the obligations set forth in Article I of the respective conventions.[32]

[26] *Ibid.*, Article 3(7). On the applicability of this prohibition to non-international armed conflicts, see Section 5.1.1.

[27] Article I, Convention on the Prohibition of the Development, Production and Stockpiling of Bacteriological (Biological) and Toxin Weapons and on Their Destruction, Washington/Moscow/London, 10 April 1972, in force 26 March 1975, 1015 UNTS 163.

[28] See Jozef Goldblat, 'The Biological Weapons Convention: An Overview' (1997) 37 IRRC, p. 257 ('use presupposes possession'); Henckaerts and Doswald-Beck, *Customary IHL Study*, vol. I, p. 257; William Boothby, *Weapons and the Law of Armed Conflict* (Oxford: Oxford University Press, 2016), p. 129.

[29] Article I(1)(b), Convention on the Prohibition of the Development, Production, Stockpiling and Use of Chemical Weapons and on Their Destruction, Geneva, 3 September 1992, in force 29 April 1997, 1975 UNTS 45.

[30] See particularly *ibid.*, Article VII, as well as the Annex on Implementation and Verification.

[31] See Boothby, *Weapons and the Law*, p. 137; Henckaerts and Doswald-Beck, *Customary IHL Study*, vol. I, p. 260.

[32] Belligerent reprisals would not amount to one of the 'protective' purposes that allow retention of a certain type and amount of biological agents under Article I(1) of the Biological Weapons Convention: see Goldblat, 'Biological Weapons Convention', p. 254. Nor would belligerent reprisals represent a case of law enforcement that justifies the retention of toxic chemicals under Article II(9)(d) CWC: see Boothby, *Weapons and the Law*, p. 132.

1.2.1.2 The Remaining Scope for Lawful Recourse to Belligerent Reprisals

As a result of these developments and prohibitions, the most recent contributions have acknowledged the limited but persistent availability of belligerent reprisals – at least in IACs.[33] There exists a general understanding that, as a matter of treaty law, belligerent reprisals could only be taken against 'military objectives'[34] and 'members of enemy's armed forces still actively engaged in hostilities and other persons who are participating directly in hostilities'.[35] As these categories are 'in principle legitimate [targets] anyway',[36] recourse to belligerent reprisals would 'involve either the unlawful use of a lawful weapon or the use of an unlawful weapon'[37] – unless, however, applicable treaty prohibitions excluded the use of such weapons even by way of reprisal.[38]

This leaves open the important question whether it is *always* possible to draw a prohibition of belligerent reprisals from those clauses prohibiting recourse to certain weapons 'in all circumstances' or obliging States 'never under any circumstances' to use them, or if that inference is only permissible when other conditions and safeguards are present.[39] Although the former interpretation is at times advanced in military manuals,[40] it does not appear to be applied coherently throughout the

[33] For their availability in non-international armed conflicts, see specifically Chapters 5 and 6.

[34] Jérôme De Hemptinne, 'Prohibition of Reprisals', in Andrew Clapham, Paola Gaeta and Marco Sassòli (eds.), *The 1949 Geneva Conventions: A Commentary* (Oxford: Oxford University Press, 2015), p. 581; Hampson, 'Reprisals and the 1977 Protocols', pp. 828–29.

[35] Greenwood, 'Twilight of Reprisals', p. 53; see also De Hemptinne, 'Prohibition of Reprisals', p. 581.

[36] De Hemptinne, 'Prohibition of Reprisals', p. 582.

[37] Hampson, 'Reprisals and the 1977 Protocols', p. 829.

[38] See, in this sense, De Hemptinne, 'Prohibition of Reprisals', p. 582; Darcy, 'Evolution of Reprisals', p. 211.

[39] Besides the examples cited in Section 1.2.1.1 and in this section, this language appears in provisions such as: Article 2(1)–(2) of the Protocol on Prohibitions or Restrictions on the Use of Incendiary Weapons (Protocol III) annexed to the CCW, Geneva, 10 October 1980, in force 2 December 1983, 1342 UNTS 137; Article 1(1) of the Convention on the Prohibition of the Use, Stockpiling, Production and Transfer of Anti-Personnel Mines and on Their Destruction, Oslo, 18 September 1997, in force 1 March 1999, 2056 UNTS 211; Article 1(1) of the Convention on Cluster Munitions, Dublin, 30 May 2008, 1 August 2010, 2688 UNTS 39.

[40] UK Ministry of Defence, *The Joint Service Manual of the Law of Armed Conflict*, JSP 383 (2004 edition with amendments), p. 111, footnote 41, whereby the prohibition of launching incendiary attacks on the civilian population, civilians, and civilian objects

spectrum of similar provisions,[41] nor is it always reflected in the lists of prohibited reprisals that those instruments set forth.[42]

Beside military objectives, members of enemy armed forces and persons directly participating in hostilities, there have been various suggestions arguing that specific categories of individuals and objects could still be targeted by way of reprisals. Greenwood, for instance, has relied on Article 49(3) AP I to claim that 'the main reprisal provisions [contained therein] do not apply to ship-to-ship, ship-to-air or air-to-air combat unless that has an incidental effect on civilians or civilian objects on land'.[43] On his part, Nahlik has argued that the decision by the Geneva Diplomatic Conference of 1974–77 to include only specific prohibitions against belligerent reprisals, at the exclusion of any general provision, left unprotected against the adoption of such measures certain groups of individuals and objects.[44]

With regard to customary law applicable to IACs, it has been noted that this body of rules protects much fewer categories of persons and

'in all circumstances' (as set forth in Article 2(1) of the 1980 Protocol III to the CCW) would 'preclude the use of incendiary weapons for the purpose of reprisals'.

41 For example, the UK MoD *Joint Service Manual* does not mention reprisals in relation to the obligations flowing from other weapons law treaties to which it is party and that display a similarly sweeping language, such as the 1997 Anti-Personnel Mine Ban Convention (*ibid.*, para. 6.13, as amended by Amendment no. 4 of July 2011) and the 2008 Convention on Cluster Munitions (*ibid.*, paras. 6.17 *ter* and 6.22, introduced respectively by Amendment no. 3 of September 2010 and Amendment no. 4 of July 2011).

42 *Ibid.*, paras. 16.18–16.19.1. See also US Department of Defense, Office of General Counsel, *Law of War Manual*, June 2015 (Updated July 2023), para. 18.18.3; German Federal Ministry of Defence, *Law of Armed Conflict Manual*, Joint Service Regulation (ZDv) 15/2, 1 May 2013, para. 490. See also French Ministry of the Armies, Direction des affaires juridiques – Etat-major des armées, *Manuel de droit des opérations militaires* (2022 ed.), *passim*.

43 Greenwood, 'Twilight of Reprisals', pp. 53–54. For a similar view, see Darcy, 'Evolution of Reprisals', pp. 210–11. Against this view, see Andrew D. Mitchell, 'Does One Illegality Merit Another?' (2001) 170 *Military Law Review*, p. 170.

44 Nahlik, 'Reprisals in Light of Diplomatic Conference', p. 56 (quoting a statement by the delegate of Poland). These groups would include 'remains of the deceased, enemies *hors de combat*, occupants of aircraft, members of the armed forces and military units assigned to civil defense organization, women and children vulnerable to rape, forced prostitution, or indecent assault, and, finally, undefended localities and demilitarized zones' (*ibid.*). For a qualified acceptance of Nahlik's analysis, see Hampson, 'Reprisals and the 1977 Protocols', p. 829, footnote 54. Darcy, on his part, argues that 'an instrument whose ultimate goal is one of "protecting the victims of armed conflict" could hardly sanction taking such reprisals, particularly those [against women and children]': see Darcy, 'Evolution of Reprisals', pp. 209–10.

objects than treaty law.[45] Most contentious is the question whether the categories shielded from belligerent reprisals in Part IV of AP I would also be protected as a matter of general international law. The failure by many military powers to ratify AP I (sometimes specifically in light of those provisions),[46] the reservations and declarations appended by numerous other States,[47] and especially State practice[48] suggest that belligerent reprisals would still be permissible during the conduct of hostilities against most of the civilians, civilian population and civilian objects mentioned in Articles 51 to 56 AP I.[49] While hesitating to 'assert that a right to resort to such reprisals continues to exist',[50] the ICRC concedes in its *Customary IHL Study* that 'it is difficult to conclude that there has yet crystallized a customary rule specifically prohibiting reprisals against civilians during the conduct of hostilities'.[51]

All these difficulties are magnified in relation to nuclear weapons. Several elements in the 2017 Treaty on the Prohibition of Nuclear Weapons (TPNW) could be interpreted as adding a further prohibition on the use of such weapons by way of belligerent reprisal.[52] Similarly to the CWC, States Parties to the TPNW undertake 'never under any circumstances to ... [u]se or threaten to use nuclear weapons or other nuclear explosive devices'.[53] Other provisions in the treaty prohibit to

45 Darcy, 'Evolution of Reprisals', p. 244.

46 Especially the United States: see Section 3.4.1.

47 See Section 3.3.

48 See Section 3.4.2 and Chapter 4.

49 See Greenwood, 'Twilight of Reprisals', p. 64; Darcy, 'Evolution of Reprisals', pp. 243–44. A possible exception would be Article 53(c) AP I, which 'adds little to those prohibitions already established under the 1954 Hague Cultural Property Convention' (Darcy, *ibid.*, p. 205); Greenwood notes, however, that 'the Hague Convention was by no means universally accepted' (Greenwood, 'Twilight of Reprisals', p. 64).

50 Henckaerts and Doswald-Beck, *Customary IHL Study*, vol. I, p. 523.

51 *Ibid.*

52 Treaty on the Prohibition of Nuclear Weapons, New York, 7 July 2017, in force 22 January 2021, 3379 UNTS.

53 Article 1(1)(d) TPNW. Criticizing the opportunity of waiving reciprocal sanctions in the domain of nuclear warfare from the CWC framework, Rühle has written that 'if some regimes ultimately chose to refrain from using chemical weapons, as did Saddam Hussein in the first Gulf War (after having employed them against Iran in the 1980–1988 Iran-Iraq War), it was not because they feared the moral outrage of the international community, but serious military reprisals': Michael Rühle, 'The Nuclear Weapons Ban Treaty: Reasons for Scepticism', *NATO Review*, 19 May 2017 (available at www.nato.int/docu/review/articles/2017/05/19/the-nuclear-weapons-ban-treaty-reasons-for-scepticism/index.html).

'acquire, possess or stockpile' such weapons;[54] set forth procedures aimed at their 'total elimination';[55] and rule out the possibility of appending reservations.[56] Taken together, and read in light of those paragraphs in the Preamble reaffirming that 'any use of nuclear weapons would be contrary to the laws of armed conflict' and 'abhorrent to the principles of humanity and the dictates of public conscience',[57] these provisions could be construed as implying an *a fortiori* prohibition of belligerent reprisals involving nuclear weapons.[58] At the same time, the TPNW does not contain an explicit prohibition on the use of nuclear weapons 'by way of reprisal' (such as the one appearing in the II Protocol to the CCW on Prohibitions or Restrictions on the Use of Mines, Booby-Traps and Other Devices mentioned above),[59] and its Preamble acknowledges 'the continued reliance on nuclear weapons in military and security concepts, doctrines and policies'.[60]

Even if the elements of the TPNW supporting a prohibition of belligerent reprisals were to prevail, the treaty's most challenging aspect lies in the fact that no State possessing nuclear weapons has acceded to it (yet).[61] This leaves the question as to the legality of any reprisal involving nuclear weapons to be governed by customary law – which is however particularly unsettled on the matter, especially after the International Court of Justice (ICJ) failed to provide meaningful guidance on the topic.[62] The ICRC considers it 'doubtful' that any use of nuclear weapons

[54] Article 1(1)(a) TPNW. For an overview of these obligations, see Gail Lythgoe, 'Nuclear Weapons and International Law: The Impact of the Treaty on the Prohibition of Nuclear Weapons', *EJIL:Talk!*, 2 December 2020 (available at www.ejiltalk.org/nuclear-weapons-and-international-law-the-impact-of-the-treaty-on-the-prohibition-of-nuclear-weapons/).

[55] Article 4 TPNW.

[56] Article 16 TPNW.

[57] Preamble of the TPNW, paras. 10–11.

[58] See UN Doc. A/RES/70/57, 7 December 2015, Annex *Universal Declaration on the Achievement of a Nuclear-Weapon Free World*, para. 4; UN Doc. A/RES/70/62, 11 December 2015, para. 1.

[59] See Section 1.2.1.1.

[60] Preamble of the TPNW, para. 14. See also *ibid.*, Article 17(2), admitting the possibility for a State Party to withdraw from the treaty 'if it decides that extraordinary events related to [its] subject matter have jeopardized the supreme interests of its country'. See also Section 1.4.1.3(2)(b).

[61] As of 2023, these are Russia, USA, China, France, United Kingdom, Pakistan, India, Israel, North Korea: see ICAN, 'Which countries have nuclear weapons?' (available at www.icanw.org/nuclear_arsenals).

[62] ICJ, *Legality of the Threat or Use of Nuclear Weapons, Advisory Opinion*, I.C.J. Reports 1996, p. 226, paras. 31 and especially 46 (whereby it did not 'have to pronounce on the question of belligerent reprisals save to observe that in any case any right of recourse to

by way of reprisal (even against enemy first use of such weapons against the civilian population) could ever meet the conditions of legality (including those related to the purpose and subsidiarity of the measure);[63] and even if that were possible, it maintains that such retaliatory use would still be 'contrary to the principles of humanity and the dictates of public conscience'.[64] Although the First Meeting of States Parties to the TPNW has reaffirmed that 'any use or threat of use of nuclear weapons is a violation of international law',[65] nuclear powers have continued to uphold the value of nuclear weapons for 'defensive purposes' even after the entry into force of the TPNW.[66] Between these competing pulls, the scholarship refrains from clear-cut conclusions on the legality or illegality of resorting to belligerent reprisals involving the use of nuclear weapons, preferring instead to stress the difficulty of envisaging situations where such conduct would actually meet the necessary criteria for the measure to be lawful.[67]

Finally, the scarcity and inconclusive nature of treaty provisions addressing belligerent reprisals in NIACs have left international lawyers

such reprisals would, like self-defence, be governed *inter alia* by the principle of proportionality').

63 ICRC, 'The ICRC's Legal and Policy Position on Nuclear Weapons' (2022) 104 IRRC, p. 1492.

64 *Ibid.*, p. 1497.

65 UN Doc. TPNW/MSP/2022/6, *Report of the First Meeting of States Parties to the Treaty on the Prohibition of Nuclear Weapons*, 21 July 2022, para. 4.

66 China, Russia, France, United Kingdom, United States, 'Joint Statement of the Leaders of the Five Nuclear-Weapon States on Preventing Nuclear War and Avoiding Arms Races', 3 January 2022 (available at www.whitehouse.gov/briefing-room/statements-releases/2022/01/03/p5-statement-on-preventing-nuclear-war-and-avoiding-arms-races/); France, United Kingdom, United States, 'Ministerial Statement of the French Republic, the United Kingdom of Great Britain and Northern Ireland, and the United States of America', 1 August 2022 (available at www.state.gov/ministerial-statement-of-the-french-republic-the-united-kingdom-of-great-britain-and-northern-ireland-and-the-united-states-of-america/).

67 Stuart Casey-Maslen, 'The Use of Nuclear Weapons as a Reprisal under International Humanitarian Law', in Stuart Casey-Maslen, Gro Nystuen and Annie Golden Bersagel (eds.), *Nuclear Weapons under International Law* (Cambridge: Cambridge University Press, 2014), p. 190; Louis Maresca and Eleanor Mitchell, 'The Human Costs and Legal Consequences of Nuclear Weapons under International Humanitarian Law' (2015) 97 IRRC, p. 643; Darcy, 'Evolution of Reprisals', p. 215. For the view whereby the use of nuclear weapons would be permissible not only 'as a reprisal for its actual prior use by the enemy or his allies', but also if the enemy 'violates the rules of the law of war on a scale so vast as to put himself altogether outside the orbit of considerations of humanity and compassion', see Hersch Lauterpacht, *Oppenheim's International Law*, 7th ed. (London: Longmans, 1952), pp. 350 f.

wondering about the very applicability of the notion in that context.[68] Scholarly works on the topic diverge considerably, both in the answer given and in the reasoning adopted. Certain authors have excluded reprisals from the purview of NIACs on the basis of such varied elements as the peremptory character of IHL norms and the application of international human rights law,[69] or extralegal considerations coupled with the general theoretical framework of IHL.[70] While claiming that the concept of lawful reprisals has not materialized outside of inter-State relations,[71] the ICRC has focused on the practical scope of protection, arguing that even in NIACs it is prohibited to direct 'reprisals' against persons who do not or who have ceased to take a direct part in hostilities,[72] especially when the measure would be incompatible with the requirement of humane treatment and entail any of the acts prohibited 'at any time and in any place whatsoever' under Article 3 GCs.[73] Yet, other authors have maintained that although recourse to reprisals is not to be encouraged, the notion is 'in fact applicable' in NIACs.[74] Furthermore, even scholars reluctant to acknowledge this applicability have noticed a gradual shift since the end of the Cold War, with international and State practice moving towards an approach where belligerent reprisals do form part of the legal regime governing NIAC, subject to certain legal constraints.[75]

1.2.1.3 Requirements for the Adoption of Belligerent Reprisals under Customary Law

The second axis in the process of sophistication of the law applicable to belligerent reprisals bears a customary character, and has resulted from the interaction of international case-law, national legislation, military manuals and the scholarship. While the international conventions mentioned above limited themselves to outlawing certain retaliatory

[68] See in this chapter, footnotes 12 and 26, and more broadly, Chapters 5 and 6.
[69] Darcy, *Collective Responsibility and Accountability*, pp. 179–81.
[70] Bílková, 'Reprisals in NIACs', pp. 63–64.
[71] Henckaerts and Doswald-Beck, *Customary IHL Study*, vol. I, pp. 527–28; ICRC, *Commentary on the Third Geneva Convention*, 2nd ed. (Cambridge: Cambridge University Press, 2021), para. 944.
[72] Henckaerts and Doswald-Beck, *Customary IHL Study*, vol. I, p. 526, Rule 148.
[73] ICRC, *Commentary on GC III*, 2nd ed., para. 946.
[74] Sandesh Sivakumaran, *The Law of Non-International Armed Conflict* (Oxford: Oxford University Press, 2012), p. 473; see also *ibid.*, pp. 452–53 and 457. For a discussion of permissible targets of belligerent reprisals in NIAC, see Section 6.2.
[75] See Bílková, 'Reprisals in NIACs', pp. 64–65 and, more in detail, Chapters 5 and 6.

conducts, the main thrust of this second leg has consisted in crafting a regulation for those belligerent reprisals that have not been prohibited (yet). Since the regulation of belligerent reprisals has been a decisive aspect of their assimilation to countermeasures, it will be treated in detail in Chapter 2; however, it is worthwhile to sketch its defining moments already at this juncture, to highlight their interaction with the process of prohibitions and restrictions outlined above.

The seeds for setting out a regulation of belligerent reprisals had already been sown in the early codification efforts over the nineteenth and the early twentieth century,[76] but the most powerful impulse in this direction came in the aftermath of the two World Wars. In an unprecedented judicial dialogue between courts, post-war tribunals worked out the first, coherent systematization of the substantive and procedural rules applicable to belligerent reprisals.[77] If the "fog of war" had blurred the contours of the notion, these few but significant pronouncements gave belligerent reprisals a clear and specific physiognomy – at least with regard to the conditions of substance and procedure that had to be met for a lawful resort to the mechanism.

With greater awareness came increased willingness to discuss the measure in international fora – at least up to a certain point. Delegations negotiating the 1977 Additional Protocols to the 1949 GCs debated at length the opportunity of introducing a specific regulation for the case of legitimate belligerent reprisals in both IACs and NIACs.[78] Those attempts at agreeing on a black-letter law at the international level eventually failed, and the various inputs given during the Diplomatic Conference only featured in sporadic reservations to the 1977 Additional Protocols.[79] At the domestic level, however, the *travaux préparatoires* sparked an intense reflection in military as well as political circles. Provisions on belligerent reprisals were given careful consideration in military manuals and national legislation worldwide, and contributed to

[76] IDI, 'Oxford Manual', Article 86.

[77] See specifically the 1948 judgment in the *Hostage Case (The United States of America v. Wilhelm List and Others)* by the Nürnberg Military Tribunal V, and those *in re Rauter* by the Special Criminal Court in The Hague and the Special Court of Cassation of the Netherlands, respectively in 1948 and 1949 – discussed in Section 2.2.3.1. See also the judgments *in re Kappler* by the Military Tribunal in Rome, the Supreme Military Tribunal, and the Supreme Court of Cassation of Italy (in 1948, 1952 and 1953 respectively) – analysed in Section 3.4.2.1.

[78] See Sections 3.2 and 5.2.

[79] See Section 3.3.

refining the understanding of the notion under customary international law.[80]

At the turn of the twenty-first century, domestic as well as international case-law had an additional chance to re-examine the notion of belligerent reprisals in a few cases dealing with World War II[81] and the armed conflict(s) in the former Yugoslavia.[82] Capitalizing on this unfaltering attention for the topic, the ICRC devoted four rules of its *Customary IHL Study* to belligerent reprisals, setting out, among other things, the 'conditions [to] be met in order for belligerent reprisals against permitted categories of persons and objects not to be unlawful'.[83] According to the Commentary to Rule 145, these conditions demand that belligerent reprisals be a proportionate measure of last resort, that they be authorized at the highest level of government, and that they cease as soon as their purpose has been achieved.[84]

However important, these developments have not solved all the questions associated with the regulation of belligerent reprisals. It has proved impossible, for instance, to determine conclusively whether the proportionality of the belligerent reprisal should be measured against the original unlawful act,[85] the damage suffered,[86] the purpose of the reaction,[87] or some combination of all these factors.[88] Nor is it clear whether the authority to order recourse to belligerent reprisals only rests with the highest level of government,[89] or if the highest military echelons are also vested with such power.[90] Even with regard to the subsidiarity

[80] See Henckaerts and Doswald-Beck, *Customary IHL Study*, vol. II, pp. 3302–60.

[81] See particularly the Italian case-law discussed in Section 3.4.2.

[82] See the judgments by the International Criminal Tribunal for the former Yugoslavia *in re Martič* and *in re Kupreškić*, analysed in Sections 2.2.3.3(1)–(2).

[83] Henckaerts and Doswald-Beck, *Customary IHL Study*, vol. I, p. 515.

[84] *Ibid.*, pp. 515–18.

[85] Kalshoven, *Belligerent Reprisals*, p. 342.

[86] Mentioned by Henckaerts and Doswald-Beck, *Customary IHL Study*, vol. I, p. 518.

[87] Myres S. McDougal and Florentino P. Feliciano, *Law and Minimum World Public Order: The Legal Regulation of International Coercion* (New Haven: Yale University Press, 1961), p. 682.

[88] Greenwood, 'Twilight of Reprisals', p. 44.

[89] See Henckaerts and Doswald-Beck, *Customary IHL Study*, vol. I, p. 518; Dieter Fleck (ed.), *The Handbook of International Humanitarian Law*, 3rd ed. (Oxford: Oxford University Press, 2013), p. 205; Gerald I. A. D. Draper, 'The Enforcement and Implementation of the Geneva Conventions of 1949 and of the Two Additional Protocols of 1978', in (1979) 164 *Recueil des cours de l'Académie de droit international de La Haye, 1979-III*, p. 34.

[90] IDI, 'Oxford Manual', Article 86. Darcy maintains that a customary norm has not crystallized on this element yet (Darcy, 'Evolution of Reprisals', p. 193).

requirement (a principle whose application to belligerent reprisals is hardly in dispute), it might be a matter of highly subjective appreciation to determine if and when all other lawful measures have been exhausted; even more so, that subjectivity would be exacerbated for those situations 'where the fruitlessness of any other remedy but reprisals is apparent from the outset'.[91]

1.3 Appreciating the Relevance of the *causa* of Belligerent Reprisals

1.3.1 Outstanding Questions in the Law of Belligerent Reprisals

For nearly a century and a half, the two trajectories just outlined (the one focused on prohibiting belligerent reprisals, the other interested in regulating them) have crossed paths, determining the different approaches by which international law would deal with the mechanism. Throughout this time, they have also crossed swords, as they were taken to embody two competing stances *vis-à-vis* retaliation in warfare: on one hand, it was feared that agreeing on a regulation of the measure would imply a legitimization of its use; on the other, it was submitted that prohibition alone would fail to answer the legitimate requests for guidance that a wronged belligerent might seek before embarking on retaliation.[92] Beyond this superficial opposition, however, both strategies responded to a chiefly humanitarian concern: that is, that of subjecting previously unrestricted measures to a double set of constraints, comprising of absolute prohibitions as well as relative conditions of exercise. In line with this wider policy goal, the law of belligerent reprisals has steadily evolved in a univocal direction, restricting the choice of legitimate targets and means for retaliatory measures while augmenting and enhancing the substantive and procedural conditions to lawfully adopt them.

At the same time, we have seen that the coherence of international law in progressively curbing the scope of belligerent reprisals does not necessarily mean that all the questions raised by the notion have been exhausted. Some of the outstanding difficulties relate to the set of absolute prohibitions that derive from the first axis, and revolve around the

[91] Kalshoven, *Belligerent Reprisals*, p. 340.

[92] See, for instance, the different attitudes recalled by Kalshoven (*ibid.*, p. 48) with regard to the Brussels Conference of 1874: while the Russian delegate proposed a text on belligerent reprisals with the intent 'to limit reprisals, not to legitimise them', the Belgian one proposed 'to sacrifice the article as it is on the altar of humanity' [translations by the author].

precise contours of the proscriptions or their crystallization into custom. Others are linked to the relative conditions enshrined in the second axis, and affect the parameters of legality that must accompany the adoption of reprisals that have not been outlawed. Besides, the question as to the very applicability and limits of the notion of belligerent reprisals in NIACs gives traditional challenges a further twist, considering the particular features of these conflicts and of the actors involved therein.

It might be contended that these outstanding doubts are unavoidable, given the customary nature of many of the rules governing the adoption of belligerent reprisals and the need to keep the measure flexible enough to adapt to different scenarios. While overlooking the extent of agreement that States have been able to achieve on the issue of belligerent reprisals, this argument underestimates both the operational difficulties that these open questions engender, and the theoretical issues that they conceal. In reality, beneath the impossibility to clarify the law of belligerent reprisals lies a deeper problem – that is, the failure to correctly identify the *causa* of the mechanism. In other words, by renouncing or mistaking to understand the purpose of belligerent reprisals and the legal dynamics underpinning their adoption, international legal theory has precluded to itself the ability to inquire meaningfully into the applicability, the margin of recourse, and the substantive and procedural requirements of the measure.

If legal theory proves unable to assign a determined objective and functioning to the abstract notion of belligerent reprisal, this necessarily has a trickle-down effect on the whole governing legal framework. First, without a clear outline of the *causa*, it is impossible to situate belligerent reprisals *vis-à-vis* the theoretical underpinnings of IHL in NIACs, and approach the issue of the applicability of the notion in that context. Second, understanding the purpose and function would shed light on the factors that hamper any further prohibition of the measures in IACs (whether under treaty or customary law), and craft paths for reform accordingly. Moving on to the regulation aspects, if the aims of the measure are not properly articulated, one of the most significant parameters in testing compliance with the principle of proportionality would be missing. Similarly, failing to understand what belligerent reprisals aim at prevents a proper understanding of the policy goals and stakes involved in the adoption of the measure, thus making it difficult to apportion authority for the decision-making process between civilian and military leaders. Finally, unless we identify the legal mechanism underlying belligerent reprisals (and with it, the exact effect of those measures on the set of obligations between the parties to the armed conflict), it will not be possible to fully understand the implications on the principle of subsidiarity.

Therefore, the *causa* of belligerent reprisals represents the missing keystone in the complex edifice erected by international law around this troublesome mechanism. Interestingly, scholars writing at the dawn of IHL devoted particular attention to the purpose and function of the mechanism – by turning to them we will retrace the roots of the problem and identify the fundamental alternatives offered to any legal theory of belligerent reprisals.

1.3.2 Early Formalizations of the Purpose and Function of Belligerent Reprisals

On closer inspection, the terms that would structure the debate on the purpose and function of belligerent reprisals throughout the twentieth century were already present in the earliest codifications and scholarly systematizations of the topic. These logical tensions are aptly showcased in the pioneering work of three lawyers, all writing before the time when belligerent reprisals were the object of the twofold process of prohibition and codification outlined above. A brief analysis of their contributions will highlight how, within a unitary framework, a certain view of the purpose of belligerent reprisals could be matched with a conflicting interpretation as to the mechanisms governing the operation of the measure.

1.3.2.1 Francis Lieber

Francis Lieber is credited with the compilation of a document that, 'although formally no more than part of the internal legislation of the United States [, . . . has] come to be regarded as "the first codification of International Articles of War"'.[93] The *Instructions for the Government of Armies of the United States in the Field* were promulgated by US President Abraham Lincoln as General Orders No. 100 of the War Department on 24 April 1865,[94] in order to govern the conduct of Union forces during the American War of Secession. Section I of the

[93] *Ibid.*, p. 45.

[94] Francis Lieber, *Instructions for the Government of Armies of the United States in the Field*, promulgated by US President Abraham Lincoln as General Orders No. 100 of the US War Department, 24 April 1865.

document contains two provisions (*scil.*, Articles 27 and 28) devoted to what Lieber constantly refers to as 'retaliation'.[95] Even if the wording 'belligerent reprisal' was never used in the text of the *Instructions* or in following works by Lieber, the two rules contained in the Lieber Code have been constantly recognized as the first reflection on the topic, and would rank prominently in the minds of those who would soon endeavour to formalize the modern laws of war on the other side of the Atlantic.[96] Therefore, Articles 27 and 28 provide a faithful depiction of (and an essential matrix for) how belligerent reprisals were thought of in the late nineteenth century.

With regard to the purpose attached to the measure under scrutiny, the provisions in the *Instructions* indicate cessation of the unlawful conduct as the ultimate objective of retaliation, and indirectly construe retaliatory measures as a tool of enforcing compliance with existing legal rules. That aim is not only adamant in the affirmation that retaliation seeks to avoid 'repetition of barbarous outrage';[97] it also inspires the characteristics that retaliation is required to meet in order to be legitimate. The scope and features of the measure taken in reaction to a previous breach must be such as to uphold 'the mitigating rules of a regular war'; at the same time, supporting future abidance by the laws of war is seen as the only way of avoiding 'the internecine wars of savages'.[98] But if we focus on the way retaliation is operationalized, the picture is considerably different. Retaliation seems to be chiefly concerned, not with safeguarding the legal order, but with maintaining the symmetry of obligations

[95] The two provisions read as follows:

> Article 27. The law of war can no more wholly dispense with retaliation than can the law of nations, of which it is a branch. Yet civilized nations acknowledge retaliation as the sternest feature of war. A reckless enemy often leaves to his opponent no other means of securing himself against the repetition of barbarous outrage.
>
> Article 28. Retaliation will, therefore, never be resorted to as a measure of mere revenge, but only as a means of protective retribution, and, moreover, cautiously and unavoidably; that is to say, retaliation shall only be resorted to after careful inquiry into the real occurrence, and the character of the misdeeds that may demand retribution.
>
> Unjust or inconsiderate retaliation removes the belligerents farther and farther from the mitigating rules of a regular war, and by rapid steps leads them nearer to the internecine wars of savages.

[96] See Kalshoven, *Belligerent Reprisals*, pp. 45–46.

[97] Lieber, *Instructions*, Article 27.

[98] *Ibid.*, Article 28.

between the parties. The self-interested concern for formal equality between belligerents is evident in the belief that retaliation acts as 'a means of protective retribution',[99] resorted to by a wronged belligerent to 'secur[e] himself' against future misconduct.[100]

The same divergence can be spotted in a telling letter that Lieber sent to General Henry Halleck soon after the *Instructions* had been issued.[101] A general had recently threatened to 'hang ten Confederate officers for every Union officer hung by the Confederates',[102] and the drafter of the document governing the conduct of Union troops decided to analyse the conformity of such measures with the requirement of proportionality set forth in Articles 27 and 28 of the Code. Once more, Lieber unmistakably put at the core of retaliation the preoccupation with cessation of the wrongful conduct and the restoration of breached norms, when it mentioned the need 'promptly to stop' barbarous outrage committed by the enemy.[103] At the same time, however, he made the case for a form of 'quick retaliation' based on 'the elementary principle which prevails all the world over – *tit for tat*, or eye for eye',[104] that is, on a mechanism that is scarcely concerned with restoring compliance, but that looks first and foremost at the restoration of the formal equality between adversaries. Overall, the first scholar who ever tried to formalize the notion of belligerent reprisals found himself pulled between two diverging understandings of the measure: one that stressed the element of norm enforcement, another which gave pride of place to levelling the playing field between belligerents.

1.3.2.2 The French Doctrine in the Interwar Period

Lieber's was not the only theory of belligerent reprisals characterized by the co-existence of these two poles. More than fifty years after the end of the American War of Secession, those conflicting accounts of the purpose and function of the measure featured in the work of two eminent French scholars who thoroughly analysed retaliation: Louis Le Fur and Yves de La Brière. Both jurists posited, as a basic tenet of their contributions, that belligerent reprisals aimed at compelling the enemy to cease an unlawful

[99] *Ibid.*

[100] *Ibid.*, Article 27.

[101] Quoted in George B. Davis, 'Doctor Francis Lieber's Instructions' (1907) 1 AJIL, p. 21, and re-produced by Kalshoven, *Belligerent Reprisals*, p. 46, footnote 5.

[102] *Ibid.*

[103] *Ibid.*

[104] *Ibid.*

conduct and ensuring observance with the laws of war. Cessation of ongoing breaches and future respect for *ius in bello* represented the two sides of a unique paradigm, which was centred on the notion of enforcement and presupposed the continued validity of the breached norms. The definitions that these authors provided for belligerent reprisals insist on the strong connection between the elements of cessation of the breach, compliance with the norm, and re-affirmation of the legal order.[105] However, as soon as they inquired into what legal mechanisms govern the operation of belligerent reprisals, the two authors embraced Lieber's emphasis on the element of formal equality and parity of arms between parties to an armed conflict.

Le Fur submitted that, by supplying the tool of belligerent reprisals, 'international law itself endeavours, in the name of the principles of *reciprocity* and self-defence, to re-establish in part *the equality of opportunities between the belligerents* [*l'égalité des chances entre les belligérants*], without renouncing the rules of justice and humanity that are at its basis'.[106] In the sphere of treaty law, belligerent reprisals represent 'the pure and simple application of a general principle of law, i.e., the *termination* of agreements because of non-compliance by one party'.[107] According to this theory, the principle of reciprocity is considered to be at the basis of all conventions,[108] and a *conditio inadimpleti contractus* underpins every treaty undertaking;[109] as a consequence, any breach of a treaty norm would entitle the victim to refuse performance of its own obligations[110] and consider itself released from its treaty commitments.[111] In this sense, Le Fur can affirm that 'reprisals are simply the name given in international law to the application of a general principle that rests both on equity and on common sense'.[112] Relying on the ideas of tacit consent, self-help and self-defence, the author then claims that the notion of belligerent reprisals can safely apply also in the field of customary obligations.[113] The breach of a customary rule of the

105 Louis Le Fur, *Des Représailles en temps de guerre* (Paris: Recueil Sirey, 1919), p. 19; Yves de La Brière, 'Évolution de la doctrine et de la pratique en matière de représailles', in (1929) 22 *Recueil des cours de l'Académie de droit international de La Haye, 1928-II*, p. 259.

106 Le Fur, *Des Représailles*, p. 133 [translation by the author, emphasis added].

107 *Ibid.*, p. 24 [translation by the author, emphasis added].

108 *Ibid.*

109 *Ibid.*

110 *Ibid.*, pp. 24 f.

111 *Ibid.*, p. 25.

112 *Ibid.* [translation by the author].

113 *Ibid.*, pp. 26 ff. For the different grounds, see *ibid.*, pp. 27 f. (tacit consent), pp. 28–31 (self-help) and pp. 31–32 (self-defence).

laws of war is said to disrupt the general principle of juridical equality and, as a consequence, bestows upon the victim special rights.[114] In this sense, the right to adopt belligerent reprisals is seen not only as flowing directly from the disturbance in the bundle of legal relationships, but also and foremost as an attempt at remedying that upset.[115]

Similar considerations are developed by La Brière, who highlighted the 'actual, immediate and tangible advantage' acquired by the original wrongdoer by violating the laws of war.[116] The author distinguished between unlawful and lawful belligerent reprisals – the former, being prohibited by some higher and universal principles of morality, humanity and civilization, independently from positive rules;[117] the latter, only derogating from the international customs and conventions that make up the legal regime applicable to the war between civilized nations.[118] These international conventions and customs were construed as 'a solemn or tacit agreement with *a synallagmatic character*, engaging one party *vis-à-vis* the others, on the basis of *reciprocity*'.[119] As a consequence, a violation by one party automatically releases the wronged belligerent from the corresponding obligations:[120] recourse to a belligerent reprisal, when exercised in accordance with all substantive and procedural requirements, is not deemed to contravene any rule of the laws of war, insofar as the breach by the original violator has already broken the (solemn or tacit) agreement.[121] Once more, the functioning of belligerent reprisals was grounded in the principle of reciprocity of contractual obligations.[122]

1.3.3 *The Horns of the Dilemma: Belligerent Reprisals between Enforcement and Reciprocity*

In conclusion, those few doctrinal contributions that had taken up the topic of belligerent reprisals before the great codification effort in the

114 *Ibid.*, p. 32.
115 On the concern that belligerents fight by the same rules and the relevance of a 'state of real inferiority' in relation to belligerent reprisals and clauses of denunciation, see *ibid.*, pp. 61–62 [translation by the author].
116 La Brière, 'Évolution de la doctrine', p. 260 [translation by the author].
117 *Ibid.*, p. 267.
118 *Ibid.*, pp. 267 f.
119 *Ibid.*, p. 268 [translation by the author, emphasis added].
120 *Ibid.*
121 *Ibid.*
122 *Ibid.*

mid-twentieth-century feature similar dilemmas. While the purpose of belligerent reprisals was constantly framed as one of enforcement of the legal order, the functioning of the measure was governed by considerations based in reciprocity. The two aspects that made up the *causa* of the notion were thus interpreted as following different logics. Whereas the international legal theory developed between the nineteenth and the twentieth century, still in its nascent form, could still hope to harmonize these two paradigms within a single framework, the growing sophistication that the codification of the laws of war would undergo since the interwar period would soon dictate a choice. Lacking authoritative indications as to what the *causa* of belligerent reprisals was, two competing frameworks provided available blue-prints for the formalization of the notion. The first, which stressed the element of equality before the law, sought guidance in the various mechanisms associated with reciprocity; the second, inspired by a spirit of law enforcement, looked at the new (only in its name) notion of non-forcible countermeasures adopted in peace-time.

1.4 Reciprocity

1.4.1 The Tripartite Systematization of Reciprocity

The existence of a balance of rights and obligations between parties to a legal relationship is a fundamental interest in a legal system such as the international one, which has historically revolved around the foundational principle of sovereign equality of States and structured itself as a horizontal juridical order. This central concern is protected and enforced throughout the different phases that make up the interaction between subjects of international law. For one thing, the emphasis placed by the predominant discourse on the consensual nature of the norm-setting process has allowed States to assess *ex ante* the merits and advantages of entering a certain legal relationship. At the same time, in the absence of a central authority for the enforcement of international law, tools of varying force have allowed victims to restore *ex post* the equilibrium in a legal relationship unduly altered by the wrongdoings of the counterpart. In sum, some of these safeguards establish equilibrium by allowing the creation of the *vinculum iuris*, whereas others enforce it by re-balancing the scope of rights and obligations. All of them, however, operate according to a single mechanism and can be seen as specific manifestations of a unique principle, that is, the principle of reciprocity.

If it is 'almost a truism to state that reciprocity plays an important rôle in international law',[123] its place in the application of the laws of war is particularly contested. The adoption of the GCs has undoubtedly spearheaded a movement stressing the non-reciprocal nature of IHL.[124] At the same time, even the most recent scholarship characterizes the role of reciprocity in creating and developing treaty and customary IHL norms as 'omnipresent'.[125] Pervasive as the principle of reciprocity might be, the dynamics that it follows in governing social action are not necessarily uniform.[126] This notwithstanding, a tripartite systematization of reciprocity can be retrieved and built upon by combining and adjusting seminal contributions from the worlds of academia (such as the work of Watts)[127] and practice (such as the *Law of War Manual* published by the US Department of Defense).[128] This model is applicable in treaty (and, at least according to some accounts, also customary) *ius in bello*.[129]

During an armed conflict, the fundamental interest in balancing the rights and obligations between belligerents *might* be embodied in 'the idea that whether a law of war rule applies to a party to a conflict depends on whether its opponent has accepted and complies with that same rule

[123] Bruno Simma, 'Reflections on Article 60 of the Vienna Convention on the Law of Treaties and Its Background in General International Law' (1970) 20 *Österreichische Zeitschrift für öffentliches Recht*, p. 7.

[124] Henckaerts and Doswald-Beck, *Customary IHL Study*, vol. I, p. 498, Rule 140; ICRC, *Commentary on GC III*, 2nd ed., para. 221; Theodor Meron, 'The Humanization of Humanitarian Law' (2000) 94 AJIL, pp. 247–49.

[125] Jann K. Kleffner, 'The Unilateralization of International Humanitarian Law' (2022) 104 IRRC, p. 2160; see also Watts, 'Reciprocity and Law of War', p. 366. For an earlier articulation of the position, see Hersch Lauterpacht, 'The Limits of the Operation of the Law of War' (1953) 30 BYIL, p. 212; for an empirical analysis, see Bryan Peeler, *The Persistence of Reciprocity in International Humanitarian Law* (Cambridge: Cambridge University Press, 2019), *passim*.

[126] See for instance Robert O. Keohane, 'Reciprocity in International Relations' (1986) 25 *International Organization*, p. 4 (distinguishing between specific and diffuse reciprocity).

[127] Watts, 'Reciprocity and Law of War', *passim* (see in more detail in Sections 1.4.1.1–1.4.1.3).

[128] US Department of Defense, Office of General Counsel, *Law of War Manual*, June 2015 (Updated July 2023).

[129] See Section 1.3.2.2 (reciprocity permeating both treaty and customary law, according to Le Fur). For a critical view, see Simma, 'Reflections on Article 60', p. 23. For a nuanced approach, see Mark E. Villiger, *Customary International Law and Treaties: A Manual on the Theory and Practice of the Interrelation of Sources* (The Hague/London/Boston: Kluwer, 1997), p. 273, paras. 433 f. On reciprocity in relation to custom, see also Watts, 'Reciprocity and Law of War', p. 381 (on persistent objector) and p. 382 (on observational reciprocity), as well as the discussion below.

or a corresponding rule'.[130] In other words, for a belligerent the existence, extent and continued validity of a given obligation (or right) is strictly linked to the counterpart's being subject to a corresponding duty (or enjoying a corresponding entitlement). Within this framework, the idea of reciprocity could have a bearing on the parties' legal positions in three ways: first, by determining whether a rule applies; second, by controlling how a rule operates; and third, by conditioning the continued application of the rule on the counterpart's behaviour.[131]

1.4.1.1 Obligational Reciprocity

The first manifestation of the principle has been labelled by Watts 'obligational reciprocity',[132] and relates to those legal tools that, in one way or another, ensure that a certain set of rights and obligations shape in identical ways the legal position of subjects. The treaty law of war is filled with instruments addressing this concern.[133] In its most basic form, obligational reciprocity is mirrored in the fact that 'states are generally bound by treaties only in their relations with states that have consented to be bound by the same treaty'.[134] Over time, more and more refined clauses have been devised to address the concern with balance of rights and obligations for those cases of armed conflict where not all belligerents were also parties to a potentially applicable instrument. Thus, so-called *si omnes* clauses (also named general participation clauses) provided that a certain treaty 'only applie[d] to an armed conflict if all the parties to the armed conflict [we]re also Parties to the treaty'.[135] Other provisions envisage, for cases where both Parties and non-Parties

[130] US DoD, *Law of War Manual*, para. 3.6.

[131] *Ibid.*

[132] Watts, 'Reciprocity and Law of War', p. 371.

[133] See, on this element, US DoD, *Law of War Manual*, para. 3.6.1.

[134] Watts, 'Reciprocity and Law of War', p. 371. See also US DoD, *Law of War Manual*, para. 3.6.1.

[135] US DoD, *Law of War Manual*, para. 3.6.1. The *Law of War Manual* (para. 3.6.1, footnote 107) provides as examples, *inter alia*: Article 2 of the 1907 Hague Convention IV; Article 20 of the 1907 Hague Convention V concerning Rights and Duties of Neutral Powers and Persons in Case of War on Land, The Hague, 18 October 1907, in force 26 January 1910 (100 BFSP 359; 2 US Treaties 2290; 205 CTS 299; USTS 545); Article 8 of the Hague Convention IX respecting Bombardment by Naval Forces in Time of War, The Hague, 18 October 1907, in force 26 January 1910 (100 BFSP 401; 2 US Treaties 2314; UKTS 13 (1910); 205 CTS 345); and Article 28 of the Hague Convention XIII concerning Rights and Duties of Neutral Powers in Maritime Warfare, The Hague, 18 October 1907, in force 26 January 1910 (100 BFSP 448; 2 US Treaties 2352; 205 CTS 395; USTS N545).

to a treaty find themselves in a situation of armed conflict, that the treaty will only apply in the mutual relations between those States that are Parties to it (but not in the relations between Parties and non-Parties, nor, *a fortiori*, between non-Parties).[136]

Watts has correctly observed that the current practice of treaty reservations, as set forth in the 1969 Vienna Convention on the Law of Treaties (VCLT),[137] provides another form of obligational reciprocity.[138] While the traditional law had 'required the acceptance of *all* States for the reservation to take effect',[139] States are now at liberty to append reservations, provided the latter are compatible with the object and purpose of the treaty and the other contracting States have a right to object thereto.[140] In this way, the principle of reciprocity ensures better satisfaction of individual preferences by operating at a decentralized stage. By upholding the liberty to reserve and by focusing on the acceptance or rejection by the single States, the modern law allows contracting Parties to modify multilateral conventions according to their bilateral preferences.[141]

Obligational reciprocity might be seen as operating in the field of customary international law as well. It is true that customary norms dispense with the notion of reciprocity, to the extent that they 'bind States regardless of formal or express indicia of consent';[142] Watts has however observed that, as long as the notion of persistent objector is maintained, it is at least 'foreseeable that states bound by a customary norm would decline to apply that norm to persistent objectors on the

[136] Even if the *Law of War Manual* lists them in the first category just recalled above (see *ibid.*, para. 3.6.1, footnote 107), this is actually the category to which belong Article 82 of the 1929 Prisoner of War Convention, and Article 25 of the 1929 Convention for the Amelioration of the Condition of Wounded and Sick of Armies in the Field, Geneva, 27 July 1929, in force 19 June 1931 (no longer in operation following the universal acceptance of the Geneva Conventions of 1949, 47 Stat. 2074; T.S. No. 847; 118 L.N.T.S. 303). Correctly, the *Law of War Manual* also includes in this category the first sentence of Article 2 Common to the 1949 GCs, as well Article 7(1) of the CCW (see *ibid.*, para. 3.6.1, footnote 109).

[137] Vienna Convention on the Law of Treaties, Vienna, 23 May 1969, in force 27 January 1980, 1155 UNTS 331. See also International Law Commission, *Guide to Practice on Reservations to Treaties*, in (2011) II(2) ILC Ybk.

[138] See Watts, 'Reciprocity and Law of War', p. 374.

[139] Mark E. Villiger, *Commentary on the 1969 Vienna Convention on the Law of Treaties* (Leiden/Boston: Martinus Nijhoff, 2009), pp. 262 ff., para. 1.

[140] See Articles 19–23 VCLT.

[141] See, in this regard, Watts, 'Reciprocity and Law of War', p. 374.

[142] *Ibid.*, p. 380.

basis of lack of reciprocal obligation'.[143] Obligational reciprocity would thus exert its effect by levelling "to the bottom" the set of legal obligations applicable between parties.

A final notation imposes itself with regard to so-called positive reciprocity. The notion refers to those situations where, even if a State might have sufficient grounds to refuse compliance with a norm by which it would be normally bound, it nonetheless pledges respect with a view to inducing other actors to also observe the norm on a basis of reciprocity. Although this notion is sometimes interpreted outside of obligational reciprocity,[144] it is submitted here that it falls squarely within that category.[145] Indeed, the main thrust of positive reciprocity is that of determining the applicability of a legal norm *ab initio* and creating a legal bond, rather than determine whether such norm continues to apply. This is made abundantly clear by the GCs and AP I, whenever the operation of a certain instrument for a party to the conflict (and the application of the corresponding obligations) is brought about by the initiative of another party.[146]

1.4.1.2 Incorporation of Reciprocity in the Operation of Given Norms

In its second form, the principle of reciprocity manifests itself in those instances where a given rule of the laws of war applies, but the exact contours of its application depend on how the opponent behaves.[147] Reciprocity here no longer represents a condition for a particular norm to exert effects, but is nonetheless 'incorporated into [its] operation'.[148] In this case as well, reciprocity takes different forms and operates along various axes. For one thing, the principle of reciprocity is the legal

[143] *Ibid.*, p. 381.

[144] For instance, the US DoD, *Law of War Manual*, para. 3.6.2 sees it as a strain of observational reciprocity (discussed in Section 1.4.1.3). See, however, *ibid.*, para. 3.6.1, footnote 110, providing that parties to an armed conflict that are Parties to a treaty will be bound by it in relation to a non-Party, if the latter accepts and applies the treaty's provisions, and listing as examples Article 7(2) of the CCW, as well as the second sentence of Article 2 Common to 1949 GCs.

[145] Of an identical opinion is Watts, 'Reciprocity and Law of War', p. 377.

[146] Frits Kalshoven and Liesbeth Zegveld, *Constraints on the Waging of War: An Introduction to International Humanitarian Law*, 4th ed. (Cambridge: Cambridge University Press, 2020), pp. 74 and 155–56 (quoting respectively common Article 2(3) GCs and Articles 1(4) and 96(3) AP I).

[147] US DoD, *Law of War Manual*, para. 3.6.3.

[148] *Ibid.*

formulation of the 'golden rule'[149] identified by Jean Pictet at the basis of humanitarian law and prescribing to 'do others what you would have done to yourself'.[150] It would therefore lie at the basis, for instance, of those expectations that, in releasing prisoners of war, 'each party's conduct with respect to the[ir] repatriation ... will be reasonable and broadly commensurate with the conduct of the other'.[151] The principle of reciprocity has also been detected in those provisions of the laws of war requiring that a party takes on certain burdens in order to enjoy certain benefits.[152] As an example of norms falling into this category, one could mention the rules that grant a particular protection to a class of objects on condition that they not be used for military purposes,[153] or to a class of persons on condition that they satisfy specific criteria.[154] Finally, reciprocity is also incorporated in those rules of the laws of war where 'the ability of a party to comply with a particular duty may be affected by whether its opponent has complied with a corresponding duty'.[155]

1.4.1.3 Negative Reciprocity

The third way in which the principle of reciprocity manifests itself is referred to as negative reciprocity (or, in Watt's terms, 'observational reciprocity'):[156] this notion encompasses all those situations where the

149 *Ibid.*, para. 3.6.3.1.

150 Jean Pictet, 'The Principles of International Humanitarian Law' (1966) 6 IRRC, p. 462 (also cited by US DoD, *Law of War Manual*, para. 3.6.3.1).

151 Eritrea-Ethiopia Claims Commission, *Partial Award: Prisoners of War – Eritrea's Claim 17*, 1 July 2003, in (2009) 26 *Reports of International Arbitral Awards*, pp. 23–72, at para. 149 (also mentioned in US DoD, *Law of War Manual*, para. 9.37.1, footnote 883).

152 US DoD, *Law of War Manual*, para. 3.6.3.2.

153 The *Law of War Manual*, para. 3.6.3.2, mentions in this regard the rules that protect from capture as well as attack hospital ships and rescue craft, provided they not be used for military purposes, as well as those that condition the granting of special protection under the 1954 Hague Convention to refuges and centres on their not being used for military purposes.

154 The classical *locus* for this category is once more found in the sphere of protection for prisoners of war (PoWs), and more precisely in those provisions of GC III that detail the criteria to be satisfied for members of militias, volunteer corps and resistance movements to qualify as PoWs: see Watts, 'Reciprocity and Law of War', pp. 414–15; US DoD, *Law of War Manual*, para. 3.6.3.2. On Articles 43–44 AP I, see Watts, 'Reciprocity and Law of War', pp. 428–29.

155 US DoD, *Law of War Manual*, para. 3.6.3.3, noting that 'the ability of a party to discriminate in conducting attacks may be affected by whether its adversary has properly distinguished its military objectives from the civilian population and other protected persons and objects'.

156 Watts, 'Reciprocity and Law of War', pp. 375–78.

continued cogency of an already applicable rule is conditioned on the counterpart's behaviour. Crudely expressed, negative reciprocity implies that, '[o]nce the parties bind themselves, the continued force of a treaty is contingent on reciprocal observation by states parties'.[157] Based on the maxims *inadimplenti non est adimplendum* and *frangenti fidem non est fides servanda*,[158] legal theory has formalized the principle in the strictly related measures of termination of an agreement, and suspension of its application, as a consequence of breach.

(1) The 1969 Vienna Convention on the Law of Treaties Codifying but also progressively developing a centuries-long practice, the VCLT sets forth the conditions and procedures for a victim party to seek permanent or temporary release from a violated agreement (or parts thereof): the relevant norms are contained in Articles 60, 65–68, 70 and 72 VCLT, as well as in the Annex thereto. Upon adoption, the reach of these provisions was partially curbed by significant factors: the norms incorporating the right to terminate a treaty or suspend its operation as a consequence of its breach only constituted *leges generales* open to party derogation;[159] they were only applicable *qua* treaty law to treaties which were concluded by States after the entry into force of the Convention with regard to such States;[160] and departed in few but significant respects from previous practice.[161] On the other hand, these provisions have been greeted as the 'successful result of scrutinies which exceed by far the entire scholarly work formerly accomplished in the matter in accuracy and appropriate differentiation',[162] and most of the norms contained therein 'have [since] influenced the general international law regime of responses against treaty violations'.[163]

[157] *Ibid.*, p. 375.
[158] Simma, 'Reflections on Article 60', p. 35.
[159] Article 60(4) VCLT.
[160] Article 4 VCLT.
[161] Simma, 'Reflections on Article 60', *passim* (of special importance is the fact that a 'material breach' is only defined by the essential character of the provision breached, but not also by the considerable extent of the breach: see *ibid.*, pp. 61 f.).
[162] *Ibid.*, p. 83.
[163] Bruno Simma and Christian J. Tams, 'Commentary to Article 60', in Olivier Corten and Pierre Klein (eds.), *The Vienna Conventions on the Law of Treaties: A Commentary* (Oxford: Oxford University Press, 2011), vol. II, p. 1356, para. 10; doubts are said to remain with regard to 'the differentiated regime governing responses to multilateral treaties, or the procedural rules governing the invocation of Article 60': *ibid.*, vol. II, p. 1357, para. 10).

(a) Termination and Suspension as a Consequence of Material Breach Article 60 VCLT is the provision that codifies the right for parties to terminate or suspend the operation of a treaty, as a consequence of its being materially breached by a defaulting party and subject to certain conditions.[164] It thus tempers the principle *pacta sunt servanda* with considerations based in negative reciprocity,[165] and strikes a balance between 'the stability of treaty relations' and the 'interest of States to free themselves, temporarily or permanently, from treaty obligations that have lost their benefit due to a prior breach by a defaulting State'.[166] The norm operates differently, depending on the character and category of the treaty, and on the number and identity of reacting parties.

First of all, the party to a bilateral treaty that has been injured by a material breach committed by the counterpart may invoke that breach as a ground for terminating it or suspending its operation in whole or in part.[167] In case the material breach by one of its parties affects a multilateral treaty, Article 60 distinguishes among several scenarios.[168] The reaction could be of a collective type: the other parties might, by unanimous agreement, suspend the operation of the treaty in whole or in part, or terminate it either in the relations between themselves and the defaulting party, or as between all the parties.[169] Alternatively, injured parties may prefer to react individually – in which case, the scope of the reaction would be restricted to suspension of the operation of the treaty.[170] A party specially affected by the material breach may thus choose to 'invoke it as a ground for suspending the operation of the treaty in whole or in part' in its relations with the defaulting State.[171] If, moreover, the material breach affects the provision of a treaty 'the objective of which can only be achieved through the interdependent performance of

[164] See Article 60(3) VCLT for the definition of 'material breach'.

[165] See in this regard, Simma and Tams, 'Commentary to Article 60', vol. II, p. 1353, para. 3.

[166] *Ibid.* See also Villiger, *Commentary on VCLT*, p. 738, para. 5.

[167] Article 60(1) VCLT: '[a] material breach of a bilateral treaty by one of the parties entitles the other to invoke the breach as a ground for terminating the treaty or suspending its operation in whole or in part'.

[168] Article 60(2) VCLT.

[169] Article 60(2)(a)(i)–(ii) VCLT.

[170] Simma and Tams note that this limitation is due to 'the drafter's intention to maintain the stability of treaty relations and . . . their conviction that, as a general rule, multilateral treaties did not necessarily give rise to reciprocal rights and duties': see 'Commentary to Article 60', vol. II, p. 1363, para. 31.

[171] Article 60(2)(c) VCLT.

obligations by all parties',[172] any party other than the defaulting one is entitled to invoke it as a ground for total or partial suspension of its operation with respect to itself.[173] As can be inferred from the ICJ's Advisory Opinion on *Legal Consequences for States of the Continued Presence of South Africa in Namibia (South West Africa) notwithstanding Security Council 276 (1970)*, reactions on account of a breach cannot be subject to the wrongdoer giving its consent:[174] the final choice between termination or suspension of the treaty, on one side, and continued validity and effectiveness thereof, on the other, only rests on the innocent parties.[175]

The VCLT, however, devised other channels to restrict the faculties of the injured State. For scholars writing both before and after its drafting, the breach of the contractual synallagma entitled the injured State to extinguish those treaties or treaty provisions that 'form[ed] *the counterpart or consideration* of the broken treaty or treaty provision'.[176] In light of the principle *quid pro quo*, breach of a treaty would allow termination or suspension also of those interdependent treaties that are 'so closely interrelated that the breach of one frustrate[s] the object and purpose of the other'.[177] The wording of Article 60 VCLT, however, excludes this possibility: it restricts the right to terminate or suspend to the *same* treaty breached by the defaulting State[178] – arguably going against the very concept of reciprocity on which it is grounded.[179]

(b) The Exercise and Consequences of the Right to Terminate or Suspend The VCLT also introduced considerable novelties with regard to the exercise of the rights established under Article 60. From the times of Grotius and Vattel up until the interwar period, the traditional approach to the matter had entitled a party injured from any

172 Simma and Tams, 'Commentary to Article 60', vol. II, p. 1365, para. 38, who also refer to these treaties as 'integral' ones (*ibid.*). On its part, Article 60(3)(c) VCLT uses the following wording: 'if the treaty is of such a character that a material breach of its provisions by one party radically changes the position of every party with respect to the further performance of its obligations under the treaty'.

173 Article 60(3)(c) VCLT.

174 ICJ, *Legal Consequences for States of the Continued Presence of South Africa in Namibia (South West Africa) notwithstanding Security Council Resolution 276 (1970), Advisory Opinion*, I.C.J. Reports 1971, p. 49, para. 101.

175 Villiger, *Commentary on VCLT*, pp. 738 f., para. 6.

176 Simma, 'Reflections on Article 60', p. 21 [emphasis added]; see also Nikolaos Politis, 'Rapport et projets de resolution de règlement', in *Annuaire de l'Institut de Droit International* (1934), p. 10.

177 Simma and Tams, 'Commentary to Article 60', vol. II, p. 1371, para. 54.

178 *Ibid.*

179 *Ibid.*, footnote 118.

violation of a treaty to denounce it unilaterally.[180] In more recent times, scholars had claimed that termination or suspension were conditioned on the failure to reach an agreement with the responsible State,[181] but the attempts at subjecting these remedies to a specific procedure were seen as *de lege ferenda*.[182] The VCLT represents, in this regard, a marked departure and advancement from previous practice. Except for the case of unanimous agreement to terminate or suspend a multilateral agreement, invocation of the material breach by the injured party has no direct effect: indeed, Articles 65–68 VCLT set forth a detailed procedure to be followed in order to obtain, *inter alia*, termination or suspension of the operation of a treaty.[183] While being harshly questioned for their dubious customary basis[184] and their silence on the fundamental question of provisional suspension,[185] these provisions were originally devised by the International Law Commission (ILC) as 'proper safeguards against arbitrary denunciation of a treaty on the ground of an alleged breach'.[186]

If none of the parties to the treaty raises an objection (and also, it must be believed, if all attempts at settling the dispute pursuant to the VCLT have failed),[187] Articles 70–72 VCLT set forth the consequences of

[180] Simma, 'Reflections on Article 60', pp. 26 f.; Bhek Pati Sinha, *Unilateral Denunciation of Treaty because of Prior Violations of Obligations by Other Party* (The Hague: Martinus Nijhoff, 1966), p. 26.

[181] See, for a general overview of the main scholarly contributions, Simma, 'Reflections on Article 60', pp. 31 f.

[182] This is, for instance, the conclusion that Sinha reaches with regard to Article 27 of the Draft Convention on the Law of Treaties, adopted in 1935 by the Harvard Research in International Law (see Sinha, *Unilateral Denunciation*, p. 26; the draft convention is published in (1935) 29 AJIL, Supplement: Research in International Law, pp. 653 ff.).

[183] Articles 65–68 VCLT.

[184] As recently as 2006, the ICJ concluded that 'the rules contained in Article 66 of the Vienna Convention are not of [a customary] character' (see *Armed Activities on the Territory of the Congo (New Application: 2002) (Democratic Republic of the Congo* v. *Uganda), Jurisdiction and Admissibility, Judgment*, I.C.J. Reports 2006, p. 52, para. 125. See also Villiger, *Commentary on the VCLT*, p. 813, para. 27: '[s]ince 1969, States and international courts have given mixed signals as to the customary basis of Articles 65 and 66'.

[185] From Articles 65–68 VCLT, Villiger draws the allegedly logical conclusion that 'Article 60 does not even permit immediate provisional suspension (see *ibid.*, p. 741, para. 12); Simma, on the other hand, recognizes 'the legality of provisional suspension as a complement necessary for the functioning of Article 60 as a remedy to an injured party' (see 'Reflections on Article 60', p. 81).

[186] ILC, 'Report of the International Law Commission on the Work of Its Eighteenth Session, 4 May – 19 July 1966', Doc. A/CN.4/191, in Official Records of the General Assembly, Twenty-First Session, Supplement No. 9 (A/6309/Rev.1), vol. II, p. 254, para. 5 (extract from II ILC Ybk (1966)).

[187] This is the conclusion reached by Simma, 'Reflections on Article 60', p. 82.

carrying out the measures provided by Article 60.[188] According to the former provisions, termination 'releases the parties from any obligation further to perform the treaty';[189] suspension, on its part, only produces such release in the relations between concerned parties 'for the period of the suspension'.[190] In either case, the legal relations established by the treaty or through its execution prior to the adoption of the measure are safeguarded.[191] It is important to properly understand which profiles distinguish these two measures, and which profiles they have in common. Whereas the legal nexus between the parties that had been established by the treaty is *extinguished* as a consequence of termination,[192] in the case of suspension it 'remains intact and ... it is only the operation of its provisions which is suspended'.[193] In both cases, however, the principle *inadimplenti non est adimplendum* that underlies both termination and suspension under Article 60 VCLT aims 'at re-establishing the contractual balance of benefits between the parties'.[194]

(2) Negative Reciprocity and the Laws of War

(a) Article 60(5) VCLT Notably, the operation of negative reciprocity embodied in Article 60 VCLT is significantly curtailed by its paragraph 5.

[188] Both Article 70 and Article 72 VCLT provide the possibility that 'the treaty otherwise provides or the parties otherwise agree' with respect to the consequences of termination or suspension, respectively.

[189] Article 70(1)(a) VCLT.

[190] Article 72(1)(a) VCLT. It is debated what this 'period' amounts to: compare Villiger, *Commentary on VCLT*, p. 887, para. 3 (decision by the parties) with *ibid.*, p. 740, para. 9 (quoting Waldock's answer to the ILC, Doc. A/CN.4/SER.A/1963, in (1963) I ILC Ybk, p. 132, para. 35, and opting for 'until the [defaulting party] carries out its obligations'). The ICJ has interpreted the wording as meaning that 'the Treaty may be ineffective as long as the condition of necessity continues to exist' (ICJ, *Gabčíkovo-Nagymaros Project (Hungary/Slovakia), Judgment*, I.C.J. Reports 1997, p. 62, para. 101). For the conclusion that the question 'will have to be settled on a case-by-case basis', see Philippe Couvreur and Carlos Espaliú Berdud, 'Commentary to Article 72', in Corten and Klein (eds.), *The Vienna Conventions on the Law of Treaties*, vol. II, p. 1632, para. 17.

[191] See Article 70(1)(b) VCLT, as well as Article 72(1)(b) VCLT. In case of suspension of the operation of a treaty, Article 72(2) VCLT obliges the parties to 'refrain from acts tending to obstruct the resumption of the operation of the treaty'.

[192] See, in this respect, Simma, 'Reflections on Article 60', p. 26.

[193] See ILC, 'Report of the International Law Commission on the Work of Its Eighteenth Session, 4 May – 19 July 1966', Doc. A/CN.4/191, p. 267, para. 3. See also Villiger, *Commentary on VCLT*, p. 887, para. 1: '[t]he purpose of suspension is that a treaty becomes inoperative for the parties for a particular time though the treaty regime itself is not affected'.

[194] Simma and Tams, 'Commentary to Article 60', vol. II, p. 1366, para. 40.

This provision has the effect of shielding against the effects of termination and suspension those 'provisions relating to the protection of the human person contained in treaties of a humanitarian character, in particular ... provisions prohibiting any form of reprisals against persons protected by such treaties'.[195] Also in light of the late introduction of the paragraph in the draft of the VCLT and the limited debates that accompanied its adoption,[196] the exact scope of application of this provision is particularly challenging to pinpoint.

The precursor to Article 60(5) VCLT (an oral amendment to draft Article 57) was presented by the Swiss delegation during the first session of the Vienna Conference. In its original wording, the provision read as follows:

> [t]he foregoing rules do not apply to humanitarian conventions concluded with or between States not bound by multilateral conventions for the protection of the human person which prohibit reprisals against individuals. Agreements of this kind must be observed in all circumstances.[197]

According to the Swiss representative, the 1949 GCs (with their prohibitions of reprisals against protected persons) were 'still the subject of some doubts and reservations';[198] pending their universal ratification, it was advisable that 'bilateral or partial agreements or the registration with a neutral intermediary of concordant declarations by States which were not parties to the [Geneva] Conventions ... should not be exposed to termination or suspension that would endanger human life'.[199] He would then expand this reading to also cover 'conventions of equal importance concerning the status of refugees, the prevention of slavery, the prohibition of genocide and the protection of human rights in general'.[200] Although this proposal was not put to the vote because it had not been introduced in writing,[201] a similar amendment was submitted by

[195] Article 60(5) VCLT.

[196] See Simma, 'Reflections on Article 60', pp. 74–75.

[197] UN Doc. A/CONF.39/C.1/SR.61, 61st Meeting of the Committee of the Whole, in UN Doc. A/CONF.39/11, *Official Records of the United Nations Conference on the Law of Treaties, First Session (Summary Records of the Plenary Meetings and of the Meetings of the Committee of the Whole)* (New York: UN, 1969), pp. 354–55, para. 12 (also quoted in Simma, 'Reflections on Article 60', p. 57, footnote 228).

[198] UN Doc. A/CONF.39/C.1/SR.61, p. 354, para. 12.

[199] *Ibid.*

[200] *Ibid.*

[201] *Ibid.*, p. 359, para. 80.

Switzerland during the second session of the Conference.[202] Ultimately leading to the adoption of Article 60(5) VCLT, it was designed to 'put a curb on the harmful effects that [termination and suspension] could have on individuals' and act as 'a saving clause to protect human beings'.[203]

The broad interpretation of Article 60(5) VCLT advocated for by Switzerland has been taken up by the majority of scholars.[204] With regard to the laws of war (and leaving aside the relationship of this provision with the issue of belligerent reprisals, which will be discussed below),[205] the provision has been construed as excluding the role of reciprocity for those norms relating to the protection of the human person that are contained not only in humanitarian treaties,[206] but also in mixed agreements safeguarding both inter-state and humanitarian interests.[207] The provision would thus cover arms control agreements such as the 1972 Biological Weapons Convention, the 1992 CWC, and the 1997 Anti-Personnel Mine Ban Convention.[208] On the other hand, the extent to which Article 60(5) VCLT would apply to capital instruments such as the GCs and the 1977 APs is a matter of debate. For one thing, applying that provision *qua* treaty law would be barred by the general rule of non-retroactive effect contained in Article 4 VCLT:[209] since the GCs and the 1977 APs had been concluded before the entry into force of the VCLT on

202 UN Doc. A/CONF.39/L.31, Switzerland: Amendment to Article 57, in UN Doc. A/CONF.39/11/Add.2, *Official Records of the United Nations Conference on the Law of Treaties, Documents of the Conference* (New York: UN, 1971), p. 269.

203 UN Doc. A/CONF.39/SR.21, Twenty-First Plenary Meeting, in UN Doc. A/CONF.39/11/Add.1, *Official Records of the United Nations Conference on the Law of Treaties, Second Session (Summary Records of the Plenary Meetings and of the Meetings of the Committee of the Whole)* (New York: UN, 1970), p. 112, para. 22.

204 See Giuseppe Barile, 'The Protection of Human Rights in Article 60, Paragraph 5 of the Vienna Convention on the Law of Treaties', in *International Law at the Time of its Codification: Essays in Honour of Roberto Ago* (Milan: Giuffrè, 1987), vol. II, pp. 3–14; Egon Schwelb, 'The Law of Treaties and Human Rights' (1973–75) 16 *Archiv des Völkerrechts*, pp. 23 f.; Simma and Tams, 'Commentary to Article 60', vol. II, p. 1368, paras. 45–47. For a slightly divergent view, see Villiger, *Commentary on VCLT*, p. 747, para. 24.

205 See Section 1.6.2.

206 Simma and Tams, 'Commentary to Article 60', vol. II, p. 1368, para. 45.

207 Mohammed Gomaa, *Suspension or Termination of Treaties for Grounds of Breach* (Leiden: Brill, 1966), pp. 110–11, as well as Simma and Tams, 'Commentary to Article 60', vol. II, p. 1368, para. 47.

208 *Ibid.*, vol. II, p. 1368, para. 47, footnote 103.

209 Article 4 VCLT states that '[w]ithout prejudice to the application of any rules set forth in the present Convention to which treaties would be subject under international law independently of the Convention, the Convention applies only to treaties which are

27 January 1980, their provisions would not be subject to the general framework on the law of treaties enshrined therein. Moreover, the difference of opinions as to the extent to which the principle embodied in Article 60(5) VCLT had a customary basis at the time of its adoption makes it difficult to claim that it applied to the 1949 GCs and the 1977 APs as a matter of general international law even prior to, and independently from, the VCLT.[210] To shield the GCs and AP I from the effects of negative reciprocity, legal theory has therefore relied on specific provisions contained in those treaties, including common Article 1 GCs,[211] Article 1 AP I,[212] as well as the various articles devoted to denunciation.[213]

concluded by States after the entry into force of the present Convention with regard to such States'.

210 In this regard, the position of the majority of authorities is in the sense that Article 60(5) VCLT had no basis in customary international law: see Elizabeth Zoller, *Peacetime Unilateral Remedies: An Analysis of Countermeasures* (New York: Transnational Publishers, 1984), pp. 17 f.; Watts, 'Reciprocity and Law of War', p. 425. For the view that a customary basis can only be found in relation to paragraph 1 of Article 60 VCLT, see Villiger, *Commentary on VCLT*, p. 750, para. 29. In favour of the existing grounding of the provision in general law, see Gomaa, *Suspension or Termination*, p. 113. In its advisory opinion in the *Namibia* case, the ICJ has stated that '[t]he rules laid down by the Vienna Convention on the Law of Treaties concerning termination of a treaty relationship on account of breach may in many respects be considered as a codification of existing customary law on the subject' (see ICJ, *Legal Consequences for States of the Continued Presence of South Africa in Namibia (South West Africa) notwithstanding Security Council Resolution 276 (1970)*, p. 47, para. 94). This statement, however, was chiefly preoccupied with defining the notion of material breach (*ibid.*: '*[i]n the light of these rules*, only a material breach of a treaty justifies termination' [emphasis added]) – a notion that had been thoroughly investigated by legal theory in the general law of treaties even prior to the Vienna Convention (Simma, 'Reflections on Article 60', pp. 28–31); it does not, on the other hand, contain any reference to the other rules that make up the complex edifice of Article 60 VCLT – quite the contrary, the wording 'may in many respects' seems to caution against easy conclusions.

211 Article 1 common to the 1949 GCs reads as follows: '[t]he High Contracting Parties undertake to respect and to ensure respect for the present Convention in all circumstances'. See Jean Pictet (ed.), *Commentary to the I Geneva Convention for the Amelioration of the Condition of the Wounded and Sick in Armed Forces in the Field* (Geneva: ICRC, 1952), p. 25; ICRC, *Commentary on GC III*, 2nd ed., para. 221.

212 Article 1 AP I provides that '[t]he High Contracting Parties undertake to respect and to ensure respect for this Protocol in all circumstances'. See Sandoz, Swinarski and Zimmermann (eds.), *Commentary on the APs*, pp. 37 f., paras. 48–51.

213 The relevant norms are set forth in Articles 63, 62, 142 and 158 of the four 1949 GCs respectively, and Article 99(1) AP I. See in this sense Françoise Bouchet-Saulnier, *The Practical Guide to Humanitarian Law* (Lanham, MD: Rowman & Littlefield, 2014), p. 137; for the view that treaty restrictions of the ability to withdraw from the Geneva

(b) Remaining Scope for Negative Reciprocity in *Ius in Bello* These difficulties in barring observational reciprocity from affecting humanitarian conventions might account for the fact that the principle still informs the reaction to the breach of relatively few, but paramount rules of the laws of armed conflict. An example is provided by the many reservations appended to the 1925 Geneva Protocol for the Prohibition of the Use in War of Asphyxiating, Poisonous or Other Gases, and of Bacteriological Methods of Warfare,[214] to the extent that they have not been superseded by following accession to the 1972 Biological Weapons Convention and the 1992 CWC.[215] Typically, those reservations provided that the instrument would cease to be binding on the victim State 'with respect to any enemy Power the armed forces of which or the armed forces allied with which fail to respect the interdictions which form the subject of [the] protocol'.[216] The evident aim of this and similar manifestations of will was to 'equalize the duties of states under the

Conventions would not entirely dispose of observational reciprocity, see Watts, 'Reciprocity and Law of War', pp. 416–17.

[214] Protocol for the Prohibition of the Use in War of Asphyxiating, Poisonous or Other Gases, and of Bacteriological Methods of Warfare, Geneva, 17 June 1925, in force 8 February 1928, 94 LNTS 65; UKTS 24 (1930), Cmd 3604; 126 BFSP 324; 26 UST 571; TIAS 8061.

[215] As noted by the ICRC, by 2005 there were twenty-one States left who had maintained such reservation to the 1925 Geneva Protocol with regard to chemical weapons, and twenty with reference to biological weapons (Henckaerts and Doswald-Beck, *Customary IHL Study*, vol. I, pp. 256 and 260–61). Out of those States, the majority have subsequently become party to the 1992 CWC and the 1972 Biological Weapons Convention – two instruments whose prohibition to retain such weapons is generally taken to also include a prohibition against retaliatory use (see Section 1.2.1.1). As a result, only two States (Israel, who signed but not ratified the CWC, and North Korea) would still be permitted, as a matter of treaty law, to invoke their reservation and use chemical weapons by way of retaliation (but see their statements whereby they would never use chemical weapons: *ibid.*, pp. 260–61), and only one (Israel) to do so with biological ones. Additional scope for negative reciprocity would remain if the 1925 Geneva Protocol were interpreted only as a no-first use treaty, and a State party to it (whether or not it appended reservations) has not also become a party to one of the following conventions prohibiting biological or chemical weapons.

[216] Thus sounded the reservation formulated by the United Kingdom, as quoted in Richard R. Baxter and Thomas Buergenthal, 'Legal Aspects of the Geneva Protocol of 1925' (1970) 64 AJIL, p. 871. In some cases, such as the Spanish reservation, the principle of reciprocity was explicitly recalled in the text: '[d]eclares this Protocol as compulsory *ipso facto* and without special agreement, in relation to any other Member or State accepting and *executing* the same obligation, that is to say, *on condition of reciprocity*' [emphasis added] (see George Bunn, 'Banning Poison and Germ Warfare: Should the United States Agree?' (1969) 69 *Wisconsin Law Review*, pp. 419 f.).

protocol, thereby producing that mutuality of obligation which states customarily desire'.[217]

The concern for parity of arms has also informed States' policy with regard to nuclear warfare. The operationalization of negative reciprocity enshrined in the reservations to the 1925 Geneva Protocol provided the precedent for threats to reciprocate against the use of nuclear weapons during the Cold War.[218] The concern that an unlawful use of nuclear weapons could give the violator an illegitimate military advantage and irremediably tip the balance in favour of the first user was well present to the minds of international legal scholarship.[219] Even more importantly, the 'policy of deterrence' was one of the prominent factors that the ICJ took into consideration when determining that it could not 'reach a definitive conclusion as to the legality or illegality of the use of nuclear weapons by a State in an extreme circumstance of self-defence, in which its very survival would be at stake'.[220] As Watts has noted, framing the discourse on nuclear exchanges in terms of suspension (if not termination) of the entire norm prohibiting their use 'further undermines the claim that reciprocity has been eliminated as a condition of observance of the law of war'.[221]

To sum up: albeit with notable and growing restrictions, international law (and the laws of war in particular) still formalize measures that enable a wronged belligerent to restore the balance of rights and duties in its legal relationship with the wrongdoer, when that balance has been unduly disturbed by the breach of an applicable norm. It is not surprising that belligerent reprisals have been interpreted as serving this objective and obeying this logic by some of the authors that have inquired into their legal features. The reciprocity model offered a suitable blue-print for belligerent reprisals because of the legal dynamics by which it operates, with the opportunity to seek release from obligations that the enemy does not comply with. The overlap is all the more evident if we consider the

[217] Bunn, 'Banning Poison', p. 393.

[218] For examples on the Cuban missile crisis and the doctrine of 'Mutually Assured Destruction', see respectively *ibid.* and Watts, 'Reciprocity and Law of War', p. 430.

[219] Nagendra Singh and Edward MacWhinney, *Nuclear Weapons and Contemporary International Law* (Dordrecht/Boston: Martinus Nijhoff, 1989), p. 174.

[220] ICJ, *Legality of the Threat or Use of Nuclear Weapons*, p. 263, para. 96. See also *ibid.*, p. 254, para. 66, and Singh and MacWhinney, *Nuclear Weapons*, p. 174: 'short of destruction of the human race and the world, the only permissible use of thermonuclear weapons would appear to be retaliation in kind alone'.

[221] Watts, 'Reciprocity and Law of War', p. 431.

similarity in the affected norms, with the scope of both mechanisms being restricted to the fields of weapons law and the conduct of hostilities. However, a different understanding of belligerent reprisals was equally possible – one that was founded on the framework of enforcement and that drew inspiration from the dynamics of another self-help measure: non-forcible countermeasures.

1.5 Countermeasures

1.5.1 The Consequences of an Internationally Wrongful Act

The notion of countermeasures encompasses those 'pacific unilateral reactions which are intrinsically unlawful, which are adopted by one or more States against another State, when the former consider that the latter has committed an internationally wrongful act which could justify such a reaction'.[222] As 'a legitimate form of peaceful self-help under general international law',[223] these measures represent 'a necessary feature of the framework of "private justice" in a decentralized system'.[224] Similarly to the mechanisms of termination and suspension on account of breach, countermeasures constitute an entitlement grounded in the wrongdoing imputable to the counterpart in a legal relationship. But whereas negative reciprocity 'dispos[es] of an agreement which has turned out to contain only burden without corresponding benefits',[225] countermeasures are motivated by the opposite objective of enforcement: by recurring to them, 'injured States may seek to vindicate their rights and to *restore* the legal relationship with the responsible State which has been ruptured by the internationally wrongful act'.[226] It is on the basis of this interest in upholding international norms, rather than dispose of the corresponding obligations, that international legal theory has formalized both the purposes associated with the adoption of countermeasures, and

[222] Denis Alland, 'The Definition of Countermeasures', in James Crawford, Alain Pellet and Simon Olleson (eds.), *The Law of International Responsibility* (Oxford: Oxford University Press, 2010), p. 1135.

[223] James Crawford, *State Responsibility: The General Part* (Cambridge: Cambridge University Press, 2013), p. 684.

[224] *Ibid.*

[225] Simma, 'Reflections on Article 60', p. 21.

[226] ILC, 'Articles on Responsibility of States for Internationally Wrongful Acts, with Commentaries', UN Doc. A/56/10, in (2001) II(2) ILC Ybk (2001), p. 128, Introductory remarks to Part Three, Chapter II, para. 1 [emphasis added].

the ways in which its functioning affects the legal relationships created by the norm.

The most recent appraisal of the law applicable to countermeasures is found in the Articles on the Responsibility of States for Internationally Wrongful Acts (ARSIWA),[227] adopted by the ILC in 2001 after a decades-long gestation and commended by the UN General Assembly the following year.[228] Even though the rules on countermeasures formulated therein had been a source of constant confrontation throughout the drafting process,[229] they have recently been held to represent customary international law by a North American Free Trade Agreement (NAFTA) Chapter 11 tribunal[230] and, in most of its parts, by the scholarship.[231] While the final version of the ARSIWA does not define countermeasures as such,[232] the notion appears in different sections of the document: first, in Part One, Chapter V, when it is listed as one of the circumstances precluding wrongfulness of an otherwise unlawful conduct;[233] then, in Part Three, Chapter II, as means of implementing the international responsibility of a State.[234] Thus, whereas the latter provisions set forth the substantive and procedural conditions for a countermeasure to be

[227] ILC, 'Responsibility of States for Internationally Wrongful Acts', UN Doc. A/RES/56/83, 28 January 2002 (corrected by document A/56/49(Vol. I)/Corr.4).

[228] UN Doc. A/RES/56/82, 28 January 2002, p. 2, at para. 3.

[229] See, for instance, the variations throughout some of the most recent reports by special rapporteurs to the Commission on the issue of countermeasures: Roberto Ago, 'Addendum to the Eighth Report on State Responsibility', UN Doc. A/CN.4/318/Add. 5-7, in (1980) II(1) ILC Ybk; Gaetano Arangio-Ruiz, 'Third Report on State Responsibility', UN Doc. A/CN.4/440 and Add. 1, in (1991) II(1) ILC Ybk, as well as 'Fourth Report on State Responsibility', UN Doc. A/CN.4/444 and Add. 1–3, in (1992) II (1) ILC Ybk; James Crawford, 'Second Report on State Responsibility, Addendum 2', UN Doc. A/CN.4/498/Add. 4, in (1999) II(1) ILC Ybk, as well as 'Third Report on State Responsibility, Addendum 3', UN Doc. A/CN.4/507/Add. 3, in (2000) II(1) ILC Ybk.

[230] See International Centre for the Settlement of International Disputes, *Corn Products International, Inc.* v. *The United Mexican States*, arbitral award, 15 January 2008, ICSID Case No. ARB(AF)/04/01, pp. 68–70, paras. 145–49.

[231] The most controversial issue being the notion of collective countermeasures addressed in Article 54 ARSIWA: see Crawford, *State Responsibility*, p. 684.

[232] A definition was, however, contained in Draft Article 47, para. 1, adopted on first reading: '[f]or the purposes of the present articles, the taking of countermeasures means that an injured State does not comply with one or more of its obligations towards a State which has committed an internationally wrongful act in order to induce it to comply with its obligations under articles 41 to 46, as long as it has not complied with those obligations and as necessary in light of its response to the demands of the injured State that it do so': see Crawford, *State Responsibility*, p. 685, footnote 60.

[233] Article 22 ARSIWA.

[234] These are Articles 49–54 ARSIWA.

legitimate, the former explains how a lawful countermeasure operates in the framework of State responsibility.

The law applicable to countermeasures can only be understood with reference to the legal consequences of an internationally wrongful act and the international responsibility that that act entails for a State. Building on a tradition that dates back to the pioneering work of Anzilotti,[235] and unless special rules provide otherwise,[236] the ILC considers that the commission by a State of an internationally wrongful act[237] leads to the establishment of a new legal relationship between the responsible and the injured State.[238] It is precisely this new legal relationship that 'constitutes the substance or content of the international responsibility of a State'.[239] The core and general legal consequences that derive from the commission of *any* internationally wrongful act are described in Articles 30 and 31 ARSIWA.[240] For one thing, the responsible State is obliged to cease the internationally wrongful act, if the latter is continuing,[241] and 'to offer appropriate assurances and guarantees of non-repetition, if circumstances so require'.[242] At the same time, the responsible State shall 'make full reparation for the injury caused by the internationally wrongful act'.[243]

[235] According to whom the only consequence that international norms attach to a wrongful act consists in 'the establishment of a new legal relationship between the State to which the relevant act is attributable (which has an obligation to repair) and the State towards whom the obligation that was not complied with was due (which can demand reparation)': see Dionisio Anzilotti, *Teoria Generale della responsabilità dello Stato nel diritto internazionale* (Firenze: Lumachi, 1902), Part I, p. 96 [translation by the author].

[236] Article 55 ARSIWA.

[237] Article 2 ARSIWA indicates the two elements that must be cumulatively present for an act to be internationally wrongful: it must be 'attributable to the State under international law', and it must 'constitute a breach of an international obligation of the State'.

[238] ILC, 'Commentary to ARSIWA', p. 86, Commentary to Part Two, para. 1. The ILC stressed that the legal consequences arising out of an internationally wrongful act are not restricted to those established under the framework of State responsibility, and recalled the rules on termination and suspension on account of a material breach (*ibid.*).

[239] *Ibid.*

[240] For certain *particular* consequences of a *serious* breach of an obligation arising under a peremptory norm of general international law, see Part Two, Chapter III ARSIWA, especially Article 41.

[241] Article 30 ARSIWA, as well as ILC, 'Commentary to ARSIWA', p. 89, para. 5.

[242] Article 30 ARSIWA.

[243] Article 31(1) ARSIWA. Paragraph 2 of the same Article defines the notion of injury as 'includ[ing] any damage, whether material or moral, caused by the internationally wrongful act'. See ILC, 'Commentary to ARSIWA', p. 91, para. 2, quoting Permanent Court of International Justice, *Factory at Chorzów (Germany* v. *Poland), Merits*, Judgment No. 13, 1928, P.C.I.J., Series A, No. 17, p. 47.

1.5.2 The Modern Concept of Countermeasures in ARSIWA

1.5.2.1 Distinction of Countermeasures from Other Institutions

No matter how carefully the legal consequences of the internationally wrongful act are defined, 'the impartial settlement of disputes through due process of law is not yet guaranteed' in the existing international system.[244] International law has therefore acknowledged the existence of countermeasures, that is, of 'essentially temporary measures'[245] 'that would otherwise be contrary to the international obligations of an injured State *vis-à-vis* the responsible State, if they were not taken by the former in response to an internationally wrongful act by the latter'[246] and 'to achieve a specific end'.[247] Through the ARSIWA, the ILC has endeavoured to craft an operational system that takes into account the exceptional character of the institution and prevents abuse through appropriate conditions and limitations.[248] In so doing, it explicitly curbed the scope of its inquiry to those *non-forcible* measures that are *not associated with armed conflict*, thus operating a double exclusion. On the one hand, the ILC ignores the practice associated with 'forcible action, taken by way of self-help in response to a breach'[249] – even more so, it clearly states in Article 50 ARSIWA that countermeasures shall not affect the obligation to refrain from the threat or use of force as embodied in the UN Charter.[250] On the other hand, the ARSIWA do not purport to address the matter of belligerent reprisals in international armed conflict – a domain traditionally reserved for the activity of the ICRC.[251] Confining the ARSIWA to the domain of secondary rules of State responsibility, the ILC left to 'the relevant primary rules' the duty to answer '[q]uestions concerning the use of force in international relations and of the legality of belligerent reprisals'.[252]

After stressing that acts of retorsion also fall short of the notion under scrutiny,[253] the ILC contrasts countermeasures with termination or

244 ILC, 'Commentary to ARSIWA', p. 136, Commentary to Article 52, para. 2.
245 *Ibid.*, p. 129, Introductory remarks to Part Three, Chapter II, para. 4.
246 *Ibid.*, p. 128, Introductory remarks to Part Three, Chapter II, para. 1.
247 *Ibid.*, p. 129, Introductory remarks to Part Three, Chapter II, para. 4.
248 *Ibid.*, p. 128, Introductory remarks to Part Three, Chapter II, para. 2.
249 *Ibid.*, p. 128, Introductory remarks to Part Three, Chapter II, para. 3.
250 See *ibid.*, p. 131, as well as p. 132, para. 5.
251 *Ibid.*, p. 128, Introductory remarks to Part Three, Chapter II, para. 3.
252 *Ibid.*
253 *Ibid.* This exclusion is due to the fact that, by definition, a State taking acts of retorsion does not breach any obligation *vis-à-vis* the target State.

suspension of treaty relations on account of a material breach.[254] The mechanisms inspired by negative reciprocity are seen as encroaching not on isolated obligations, but on the very agreement from which these obligations derive: that agreement will (in whole or in part, for ever or for the time being) cease to be an applicable legal standard for the parties.[255] The functioning of countermeasures, however, is seen as completely different from the one characterizing measures under Article 60 VCLT, both in its effects on the international norm and in its purpose. The adoption of countermeasures does not suspend, much less terminate, the underlying obligation – it only precludes the wrongfulness of the conduct in question if, and for so long as, the conditions are met for a countermeasure to be taken.[256] As Article 49(2) ARSIWA puts it, countermeasures 'are limited to the *non-performance for the time being of international obligations* of the State taking the measures towards the responsible State':[257] instead of setting aside an agreement, they simply 'derogat[e] from a subsisting treaty obligation ... as a necessary and proportionate response to an internationally wrongful act'.[258] The various wordings used by the ILC to describe the functioning of the institution aptly show that the taking of countermeasures is not meant to seek release from an obligation, but only to justify temporary non-compliance with an obligation that continues to exist.[259]

254 *Ibid.*, p. 128, Introductory remarks to Part Three, Chapter II, para. 4.

255 See Crawford, *State Responsibility*, p. 683, and ILC, 'Commentary to ARSIWA', p. 71, Introductory remarks to Part One, Chapter V, paras. 2–4.

256 *Ibid.*, p. 75, Commentary to Article 22, para. 4. Article 22 ARSIWA reads as follows: '[t]he wrongfulness of an act of a State not in conformity with an international obligation towards another State is precluded if and to the extent that the act constitutes a countermeasure taken against the latter State in accordance with Chapter II of Part Three'.

257 Article 49 ARSIWA [emphasis added]. The ILC also remarks that '[i]n taking countermeasures, the injured State effectively *withholds performance* for the time being of one or more international obligations owed by it to the responsible State (ILC, 'Commentary to ARSIWA', p. 130, Commentary to Article 49, para. 6) [emphasis added].

258 *Ibid.*, pp. 128 f., Introductory remarks to Part Three, Chapter II, para. 4.

259 See the passage in ICJ, *Gabčíkovo-Nagymaros Project (Hungary/Slovakia)*, p. 63, para. 101 on the state of necessity, which also applies to countermeasures as another circumstance precluding wrongfulness (in this sense, ILC, 'Commentary to ARSIWA', p. 71, Introductory remarks to Part One, Chapter V, para. 3; Crawford, *State Responsibility*, pp. 683 f.): 'even if a state of necessity is found to exist, it is not a ground for the termination of a treaty. Even if found justified, it does not terminate a Treaty; the Treaty may be *ineffective* as long as the condition of necessity continues to exist; it may in fact be *dormant*, but – unless the parties by mutual agreement terminate the treaty – it

1.5.2.2 Liberties and Constraints in the Choice of Countermeasures

The fundamental difference from termination and suspension is clearly evidenced by the possibility, for the injured State adopting countermeasures, to withhold performance of obligations that neither correspond to nor are directly connected with the obligation breached.[260] Adopting so-called reciprocal countermeasures would make it easier to comply with the requirements of necessity and proportionality,[261] but is neither required of the injured State, nor necessarily the most advisable course of action to achieve the objective of the countermeasure. Given that the preference for countermeasures is prompted by the interest in a return to integral performance, the injured State will act instrumentally: in other words, it will be free to choose which obligation in its relationships with the responsible State not to perform, on the basis of the expected effect of compulsion.[262] As a result, the obligation breached by the original wrongful act might well not be affected at all by the countermeasure – if not in the sense of a positive externality when the defaulting State will resume compliance.

This refined understanding of how countermeasures operate helps explain an important limitation in the margin of action of an injured State. The norm entitling an injured State to adopt countermeasures can be seen as a secondary rule that derogates, in its quality as *lex specialis*, from the primary rule infringed by the measure.[263] Over time, different arguments have been advanced to limit this right. Already in 1928, in its award in the *Naulilaa* case, the arbitral tribunal stressed that resort to countermeasures is 'limited *by the experiences of mankind and good faith rules*';[264] decades later, this fundamental humanitarian concern has been formalized in the category of peremptory norms of international law.[265]

continues to exist. As soon as the state of necessity ceases to exist, the duty to comply with treaty obligation revives'.

260 ILC, 'Commentary to ARSIWA', p. 129, Introductory remarks to Part Three, Chapter II, para. 5; Politis, 'Rapport et projets de resolution', p. 10.

261 ILC, 'Commentary to ARSIWA', p. 129, Introductory remarks to Part Three, Chapter II, para. 5.

262 Simma, 'Reflections on Article 60', p. 21.

263 In this sense, Linos-Alexander Sicilianos, 'The Relationship between Reprisals and Denunciation or Suspension of a Treaty' (1993) 4 EJIL, p. 352.

264 Arbitration between Portugal and Germany, 'Award of 31 July 1928 (*Naulilaa* case)', in (1929) 2 *Reports of International Arbitral Awards*, pp. 1011 f. [translation by the author; emphasis in the original].

265 See Article 53 VCLT.

Now that a hierarchy of norms exists, derogation by way of countermeasures would no longer be permitted if the primary norm to be infringed were hierarchically superior: *lex superior derogat inferiori*.[266] Accordingly, Article 50(1) ARSIWA prohibits all countermeasures affecting obligations under peremptory norms of general international law: these also include, in line with the ICJ jurisprudence in the *Nuclear Weapons* and *Wall* advisory opinions,[267] obligations of a humanitarian character prohibiting reprisals.[268]

1.5.2.3 The Logic of Enforcement in the Functioning of Countermeasures

(1) The Coercive Nature of Countermeasures The enforcement paradigm at the roots of the law of countermeasures manifests itself in the fact that not only the obligation breached by way of countermeasures, but also the obligation affected by the original internationally wrongful act continue to exist. Within the framework of State responsibility, the legal consequences of an internationally wrongful act 'do not affect the continued duty of the responsible State to perform the obligation breached'.[269] In other words, neither the establishment of nor compliance with the obligations of cessation and reparation that form the content of international responsibility would cause the pre-existing legal relation to disappear.[270] Countermeasures act as an instrument that positively upholds, rather than negatively affects, the primary obligation and the norm by which it is established: giving new meaning to the expression coined by the ILC, they operate as a shield against those consequences of a wrongful act that could jeopardize the cogency of a norm, not as a sword that determines its termination.[271]

266 See Sicilianos, 'The Relationship between Reprisals', p. 352.

267 ICJ, *Legality of the Threat or Use of Nuclear Weapons*, p. 257, para. 79; ICJ, *Legal Consequences of the Construction of a Wall in the Occupied Palestinian Territory, Advisory Opinion*, I.C.J. Reports 2004, p. 199, para. 157.

268 Article 50(1)(c) ARSIWA. Also prohibited are those countermeasures that affect: the obligation to refrain from the threat or use of force and obligations for the protection of fundamental human rights.

269 Article 29 ARSIWA.

270 ILC, 'Commentary to ARSIWA', p. 88, Commentary to Article 29, para. 2. See also *ibid.*, para. 4: '[w]hether and to what extent that obligation [*scil.*, that has been breached] subsists despite the breach is a matter not regulated by the law of State responsibility but by the rules concerning the relevant primary obligation'.

271 The expression (which can be found *ibid.*, p. 71, Introductory remarks to Part One, Chapter V, para. 2) was originally used to indicate the differences between circumstances

This formalization of countermeasures reverberates across the specific purposes that the ARSIWA attach (or refuse to attach) to the adoption of countermeasures; in this sense, the enforcement paradigm informs, in different but complementary ways, each of the objectives that these measures can legitimately pursue. Article 49(1) ARSIWA states that countermeasures may be adopted by the injured State against the responsible State only in order to induce the latter to comply with its obligations under Part Two of ARSIWA.[272] In the Commentary, the ILC then clarifies that the obligations to be enforced are those of ceasing the internationally wrongful act, if it is continuing, and of providing reparation to the injured State.[273]

Therefore, the ILC defines the purpose of countermeasures on the basis of the content of State responsibility, endorsing and bringing to fruition a long trajectory of scholarly refinement that had analysed these measures. In its 1934 resolution on the *Régime des représailles en temps de paix*, the Institut de Droit International had already stressed that countermeasures had the objective of compelling the responsible State to comply with the law[274] – a formula which was specifically crafted to

precluding wrongfulness, on one side, and the termination of the obligation itself, on the other.

272 *Ibid.*, p. 129.

273 *Ibid.*, p. 130, Commentary to Article 49, para. 1. By so claiming, the Commentary implicitly excludes from the purview of countermeasures other consequences of an internationally wrongful act, such as the obligation to offer assurances and guarantees of non-repetition. A footnote to the ILC Commentary applies to this obligation considerations similar to those made with regard to the failure to provide satisfaction as demanded by the injured State (see *ibid.*, p. 131, Commentary to Article 49, para. 8, footnote 754). Article 37 ARSIWA had placed the State responsible for an internationally wrongful act under an obligation to 'give satisfaction for the injury caused by that act insofar as it cannot be made good by restitution or compensation', thus qualifying satisfaction as the third, subsidiary form of reparation (see *ibid.*, p. 105). Its allegedly 'symbolic or supplementary character' prompted the ILC to claim that 'it would be highly unlikely that a State which had ceased the wrongful act and tendered compensation to the injured State could properly be made the target of countermeasures for failing to provide satisfaction as well' (*ibid.*, p. 131, Commentary to Article 49, at para. 8). This affirmation is debatable not only on its own merits, but also with regard to its application to the obligation to provide assurances and guarantees of non-repetition. Satisfaction may well be the only viable remedy to the unlawful act when it is impossible to obtain the other forms of reparation (i.e., restitution and compensation). In such cases, excluding countermeasures on the ground of the inherently symbolic nature of satisfaction seems an unwarranted step, whereas dismissing them on the ground of the subsidiary character of the remedy seems to forget that satisfaction bears special importance exactly when the damage is otherwise irreversible.

274 See IDI (XXXIX Session), 'Résolution I. – Régime des représailles en temps de paix', in (1934) *Annuaire de l'Institut de Droit International*, p. 708.

include both the aim of putting an end to the violation, and that of securing reparation for the injury.[275] While authoritative scholars like Venezia and Brownlie would support this conclusion,[276] later authors (such as Zoller and De Guttry) emphasized the element of coercion,[277] thus indicating how countermeasures would find their *raison d'être* in the wider purposes associated with State responsibility. This aspect of countermeasures would eventually be upheld by the ICJ judgment in the *Gabčíkovo-Nagymaros* case;[278] just a few years later, the ILC would close the circle by stressing that countermeasures were 'instrumental ... to achieving ... compliance by the target State with its international obligations of cessation and reparation'.[279]

(2) Enforcement as the Element Structuring the Purpose of Countermeasures In serving as a form of 'inducement' to achieve compliance with these two obligations,[280] the logic of enforcement operates at various levels. For one thing, the instrumental link with the

275 Politis, 'Rapport et projets de résolution', p. 25. See *ibid.*, p. 8 for the formula proposed in the first draft of the resolution to describe the objective of reprisals adopted in peacetime (*scil.*, 'retour à la légalité'); see also IDI, 'Session de Paris', in (1934) *Annuaire de l'Institut de Droit International*, pp. 642–44, for the comments and amendments proposed by La Brière and De Visscher.

276 Jean-Claude Venezia, 'La notion de représailles en droit international public' (1960) 64 RGDIP, pp. 467 f.; Ian Brownlie, *System of the Law of Nations: State Responsibility* (Oxford: Clarendon Press, 1983), Part I, p. 34; Pierre-Marie Dupuy, 'Observations sur la pratique récente des "sanctions" de l'illicite' (1983) 87 RGDIP, p. 530.

277 Zoller, *Peacetime Unilateral Remedies*, p. 72; Andrea De Guttry, *Le rappresaglie non comportanti la coercizione militare nel diritto internazionale* (Milano: Giuffrè, 1985), p. 12; Christian Dominicé, 'Observations sur les droits de l'État victime d'un fait internationalement illicite', in *Droit international* (Paris: Pedone, 1982), vol. II, p. 55.

278 ICJ, *Gabčíkovo-Nagymaros Project (Hungary/Slovakia)*, pp. 56–57, para. 87 (whereby the purpose of countermeasures is 'to induce the responsible state to comply with its international obligations under international law').

279 Crawford, 'Third Report on State Responsibility, Addendum 3', p. 22; for similar conclusions, see Crawford, 'Second Report on State Responsibility, Addendum 2', p. 13, as well as Crawford, 'Third Report on State Responsibility, Addendum 4', UN Doc. A/CN.4/507/Add.4, in (2000) II(1) ILC Ybk, p. 9. The same construction can already be found in Draft Article 47 adopted on first reading (see ILC, 'Draft Articles on the Responsibility of States for Internationally Wrongful Acts, as Provisionally Adopted by the International Law Commission on First Reading', UN Doc. A/CN.4/SER.A/1996/Add.1 (Part II), in (1996) II(2) ILC Ybk, p. 66) and in the ILC Commentary to that provision (ILC, 'Text of Draft Articles 42 (Para. 3), 47, 48 and 51 to 53 with Commentaries thereto Provisionally Adopted by the Commission at Its Forty-Eight Session', in (1996) II(2) ILC Ybk, p. 67).

280 ILC, 'Commentary to ARSIWA', p. 131, Commentary to Article 49, para. 7.

obligation of cessation reveals that enforcement is primarily associated with the continued cogency of the norm *per se*. Countermeasures share with that obligation the intent 'to safeguard *the continuing validity and effectiveness* of the underlying primary rule',[281] thus upholding the interests both of the injured State(s) and of the wider international community 'in the preservation of, and reliance on, the rule of law'.[282] The protection of the juridical sphere of the injured State comes through the enforcement of the breached rule and through compliance with the ensuing obligations – not, as in the case of negative reciprocity, through their demise. At a second, complementary level, construing countermeasures as a tool to induce compliance with the obligation to repair also makes them a tool of enforcement in *practical* terms. Under Article 31 ARSIWA, the obligation to make full reparation requires the responsible State to 'wipe out all the consequences of the illegal act and reestablish the situation which would, in all probability, have existed if that act had not been committed';[283] if countermeasures represent a tool to compel observance with this obligation, they aim at enforcing a norm not only in purely abstract terms, but also in its actual consequences on the material situation of the injured State. Besides re-affirming the continued validity of a breached norm, countermeasures will provide the tool to ensure that those obligations be given full effect in practice.

The role of the enforcement paradigm in structuring the notion of countermeasures is evidenced not only by the purposes that these measures can pursue, but also by the objectives that they cannot legitimately seek to accomplish. Much of the debate about countermeasures, both within and outside of the ILC, had centred on whether they had punitive aims. In the first half of the twentieth century, authors like Kelsen,[284] La Brière[285] and Ago[286] would stress that countermeasures had a chiefly afflictive and repressive character that qualified them as a true form of

281 *Ibid.*, p. 89, Commentary to Article 30, para. 5 [emphasis added].
282 *Ibid.*
283 PCIJ, *Factory at Chorzów (Germany* v. *Poland)*, p. 47.
284 Quoted by Arangio-Ruiz as one the authors 'who conceive internationally wrongful acts as delicts of a predominantly "penal" or criminal nature [and] assign to reprisals an afflictive, punitive or retributive function' (Arangio-Ruiz, 'Third Report on State Responsibility', p. 15, referring in particular to Hans Kelsen, 'Unrecht und Unrechtsfolge im Völkerrecht' (1932) *Zeitschrift für öffentliches Recht*, pp. 571 f.).
285 La Brière, 'Évolution de la doctrine', p. 256.
286 Roberto Ago, 'Le délit international', in (1939) 68 *Recueil des cours de l'Académie de droit international de La Haye, 1939-II*, p. 527. See also Roberto Ago, 'Addendum to the Eighth Report on State Responsibility', p. 54.

penalty for international delicts. Long into the drafting of the ARSIWA, the ILC acknowledged that the aim of inflicting punishment could legitimately motivate the adoption of countermeasures.[287] In the final years of the century, and especially in the aftermath of the ICJ judgment in the *Gabčíkovo-Nagymaros* case,[288] the ILC eventually rejected with growing conviction that view, and ultimately stated in its Commentary to ARSIWA that countermeasures cannot be taken as a form of punishment for internationally wrongful acts.[289]

It is submitted that this exclusion is particularly relevant in demonstrating to what extent the concern for enforcement informs the law of countermeasures. Had these punitive features been recognized, an injured State could have had legitimate recourse to countermeasures even if the secondary obligations of cessation and reparation had been duly complied with: indeed, the thrust of the measure would have resided in stigmatizing the unlawful conduct, even when the internationally wrongful act had been remedied under all respects. In that scenario, countermeasures would have represented a form of additional but unnecessary "stress" to which the primary rule would have been subject – additional, because the norm had already been breached by the original illegality; unnecessary, because the legal relation had already been restored "upwards" by cessation and/or reparation. Enforcement of the breached norm could swiftly turn in the prelude of further violations. By eradicating all punitive traits from the notion, the ILC removed *ex ante* the risk of unwarranted threats to the cogency of the rule in cases where the secondary obligations of cessation and reparation had been respected, and ensured that the primary obligation not be threatened by further violations, no matter if they were justified or not.

The identification of the legitimate purposes attached to countermeasures has paved the way for the definition of the substantive and

[287] See ILC, 'Text of Articles 28 to 32, with Commentaries thereto, Adopted by the Commission at Its Thirty-First Session', UN Doc. A/34/10 and Corr. 1, in (1979) II(1) ILC Ybk, p. 115; Arangio-Ruiz, 'Fourth Report on State Responsibility', p. 7. States had conflicting views on the issue: see the statements by Denmark on behalf of the Nordic countries and France in ILC, 'State Responsibility: Comments and Observations Received from Governments', UN Doc. A/CN.4/488, in (1998) II(1) ILC Ybk, p. 114. The ILC even considered the opportunity of introducing a form of punitive damages for cases of gross or egregious breaches of obligations due to the international community as a whole (Crawford, 'Third Report on the State Responsibility, Addendum 4', pp. 9 f.).

[288] ICJ, *Gabčíkovo-Nagymaros Project (Hungary/Slovakia)*, pp. 56–57, para. 87.

[289] ILC, 'Commentary to ARSIWA', pp. 130–31, Commentary to Article 49, paras. 1 and 7.

procedural conditions that must accompany their adoption. As shown above, the requirement of termination, whereby countermeasures shall be brought to a halt as soon as the responsible State has complied with the obligations created by the internationally wrongful act,[290] stems from the refusal to confer on them a punitive function.[291] Similar considerations apply to the other requirements that have been traditionally associated with these measures. The requirement that the countermeasure be 'reversible'[292] is easily explained when one considers that the objective of restoring compliance with the breached norm by the responsible State must not come at the price of barring the injured State's ability to observe its own obligations. An analogous concern motivates the procedural conditions that must be implemented before adopting a countermeasure:[293] if cessation of the internationally wrongful conduct and full reparation for the injury can be obtained by means of simple threats, negotiation or third-party settlement, non-performance of an international obligation on the part of the injured State jeopardizes the very rule of law that it is designed to protect and accordingly loses all justification. With regard to the requirement of proportionality,[294] it has been observed that 'it provides a functional connection between the aims and the means of self-help measures':[295] in other words, it ensures that the *vulnus* inflicted to the legal order by countermeasures, however justified, does not exceed what is required in order to reach the objectives of cessation and reparation.[296]

1.6 At the Cross-roads: Choosing the Framework for Belligerent Reprisals

1.6.1 The Mutually Exclusive Features of Negative Reciprocity and Enforcement

Over the course of the twentieth century, international legal theory has drawn a sharp line of demarcation between, on one hand, measures

[290] Article 53 ARSIWA.
[291] ILC, 'Commentary to ARSIWA', p. 131, Commentary to Article 49, para. 7.
[292] ICJ, *Gabčíkovo-Nagymaros Project (Hungary/Slovakia)*, p. 57, para. 87; Article 49(3) ARSIWA, which introduces some temperament in the rigidity of the rule.
[293] Article 52 ARSIWA.
[294] ILC, 'Commentary to ARSIWA', p. 134, Commentary to Article 51.
[295] Crawford, *State Responsibility*, p. 698.
[296] ILC, 'Commentary to ARSIWA', p. 135, Commentary to Article 51, para. 7.

inspired by negative reciprocity under the law of treaties, and, on the other, countermeasures under the law of State responsibility. Even though both institutions constitute a form of reaction to breaches,[297] the two paradigms in which they are logically grounded (i.e., reciprocity and enforcement) bear specular characteristics and opposite aspirations. The distinction between the institutions is so clear in theory that scholars[298] and tribunals[299] alike have eventually recognized the 'parallel existence of countermeasures and reactions based on Article 60 [VCLT]',[300] notwithstanding fears that the availability of the former in all cases might result in easily circumventing the strict conditions provided for the latter.[301] As a result, termination (or suspension) on account of material breach and countermeasures have come to differ under all the aspects that relate to their formalization under international law: in the logic that they follow, the purpose that they serve, the way in which they affect legal norms and obligations, the interests that motivate them, and the scope of their action.

Termination of an agreement and suspension of its operation due to breach 'embody the negative side of the *do ut des* aspect of reciprocity',[302] and serve as a 'remedy' for an injured State that wishes to protect its juridical sphere from the effects of the counterpart's breach.[303] As Simma poignantly noted, a State following this strategy aims at 'restor[ing] the balance of rights and obligations in the sum total of its legal relationships with the violator on a lower level by getting rid of those contractual burdens whose corresponding advantages have ceased to exist'.[304] To reach this goal, these institutions function as a ground of permanent

[297] See Sicilianos, 'The Relationship between Reprisals', p. 341.

[298] Simma and Tams, 'Commentary to Article 60', pp. 1376 f., paras. 71–73; Crawford, *State Responsibility*, pp. 682–84.

[299] *Case concerning the Difference between New Zealand and France concerning the Interpretation or Application of Two Agreements, concluded on 9 July 1986 between the Two States and which Related to the Problems Arising from the Rainbow Warrior Affair*, arbitral award, 30 April 1990, in (1990) 20 *Reports of International Arbitral Awards*, pp. 251 f., para. 75; ICJ, *Gabčíkovo-Nagymaros Project (Hungary/Slovakia)*, p. 38, para. 47.

[300] Simma and Tams, 'Commentary to Article 60', p. 1377, para. 72.

[301] Donald W. Greig, 'Reciprocity, Proportionality, and the Law of Treaties' (1994) 34 *Vanderbilt Journal of International Law* (1994), p. 398.

[302] Simma, 'Reflections on Article 60', p. 20.

[303] See, in this regard, Crawford, *State Responsibility*, p. 684.

[304] Simma, 'Reflections on Article 60', pp. 20 f. See also Simma and Tams, 'Commentary to Article 60', p. 1354, para. 4.

or temporary extinction of the breached norm,[305] with the condition of reciprocity operating not in violation of the law but in conformity with it.[306] Since a State will decide to terminate a treaty or suspend its obligations only when it has lost interest in its performance,[307] it will only be entitled to cease performance of the '*same* treaty that has been breached by the defaulting State'.[308]

Countermeasures feature diametrically opposed characteristics on each of those points. As the modern expression of the *talio* principle,[309] the notion is driven by a logic of compulsion directed at the enforcement of a right[310] and, by implication, of the corresponding norm and of the wider legal system. Their purpose is that of inducing a State responsible of a wrongful act to discontinue its unlawful conduct and make full reparation for the injury caused: enforcement is achieved by removing the consequences of illegality and re-instating the consequences of legality. Restoration of the balance of rights and obligations occurs not by detraction (i.e., by reducing the scope of legal relationships between the parties through the extinction of the breached norm) – more comprehensively, that objective is achieved by addition, that is, by 'compelling the defaulting party to return to integral performance'[311] and to re-establish the situation that would have existed if the unlawful act had not been committed. In line with these purposes, countermeasures operate as 'justified violations of a still-binding norm',[312] with no prejudice for its continued existence.[313] With a view to maximizing the effect of compellence,[314] the State adopting the countermeasure is not required to withhold performance of the same or a closely related obligation;[315]

305 Politis, 'Rapport et projets de résolution', p. 10, as well as Simma and Tams, 'Commentary to Article 60', p. 1354, para. 4. See also René Provost, 'Reciprocity in Human Rights and Humanitarian Law' (1994) 65 BYIL, p. 399; Emmanuel Decaux, *La Reciprocité en droit international* (Paris: Librerie Générale de Droit et de Jurisprudence, 1980), p. 255.

306 Politis, 'Rapport et projets de résolution', p. 60.

307 Simma, 'Reflections on Article 60', p. 21.

308 Simma and Tams, 'Commentary to Article 60', p. 1371, para. 54.

309 Simma, 'Reflections on Article 60', p. 20.

310 Crawford, *State Responsibility*, p. 684.

311 Simma, 'Reflections on Article 60', p. 20.

312 Provost, 'Reciprocity in Human Rights', p. 399.

313 Simma and Tams, 'Commentary to Article 60', p. 1354, para. 4.

314 Simma, 'Reflections on Article 60', p. 21.

315 ILC, 'Commentary to ARSIWA', p. 129, Introductory remarks to Part Three, Chapter Two, para. 5.

subject to specific restrictions, it can choose which obligation it will derogate from.[316]

1.6.2 *Applying the Frameworks to Belligerent Reprisals: Determinants and Implications*

In formalizing the notion of belligerent reprisals, the international legal theory of the twentieth century had the opportunity of drawing inspiration from these two models, and the corresponding duty of deciding whether the phenomenon of retaliation in warfare should be framed within the paradigm of negative reciprocity or the framework of enforcement. If the idea behind belligerent reprisals was to provide parties to an armed conflict with a tool to ensure equality of chances, their purpose and function should be designed on the basis of mechanisms inspired by negative reciprocity. According to this alternative, the model of termination and suspension of a treaty due to breaches would render belligerent reprisals a mainly remedial mechanism: in presence of a breach, the legal relationships between the parties would be re-balanced at a lower level, but the contractual synallagma would ensure that retaliation affect the same rules as the ones originally violated. If, on the other hand, belligerent reprisals were to be seen as a tool of restoring compliance with a breached norm, their purpose and function should be shaped according to the model of countermeasures. This solution would uphold and re-affirm the integrity of the legal system in all its components, re-balancing the legal relationship between the parties at the higher edge and limiting justified violations of the laws of war to what was strictly necessary to repel the unlawful behaviour by the counterpart.

In this connection, it is important to address a potential objection. It could be argued that subsuming belligerent reprisals under provisions that limit recourse to both termination (or suspension) of a treaty and adoption of countermeasures would prevent either of these notions from acting as a model or paradigm for reference. As we have seen above, Article 60(5) VCLT shields from the effects of termination and suspension those provisions that prohibit any form of reprisals against persons protected by treaties of a humanitarian character.[317] Similarly, Article 50(1) ARSIWA rules out countermeasures that affect obligations of a

[316] Simma and Tams, 'Commentary to Article 60', p. 1354, para. 4.
[317] See Section 1.4.1.3(2)(a).

humanitarian character prohibiting reprisals.[318] In light of these provisions, one could have the impression that adopting these institutions as a paradigm of reference in the formalization of belligerent reprisals would be a logical short-circuit.

That impression is fallacious, because it misconstrues the relationship between the operation of these institutions, on one side, and the prohibitions of belligerent reprisals, on the other. Neither Article 60(5) VCLT, nor Article 50(1) ARSIWA are meant to confirm or to broaden the category of impermissible belligerent reprisals – what they do envisage is to avoid that the specific reactions to international breaches that they are concerned with nullify the effects of the already existing prohibitions on certain belligerent reprisals. In the sphere of the law of treaties, it is clear that rules outlawing certain belligerent reprisals could be easily circumvented if the whole convention in which they are written could be terminated or suspended.[319] Therefore, the rule contained in Article 60(5) VCLT wards off the possibility that, by extinguishing even in part the legal bond, a retaliatory conduct prohibited in a humanitarian convention be once again made legal; it does not, however, make other belligerent reprisals illegal in addition to those that have already been proscribed.[320] Similar considerations apply with regard to Article 50 ARSIWA, even if the ILC Commentary to the provision might create some confusion.[321] As a secondary rule, that provision is not concerned with the primary rules on belligerent reprisals established under the laws of war – neither in the sense of upholding, nor in the sense of expanding their reach. On its plain terms, Article 50 ARSIWA only prevents a belligerent from withholding performance of those primary rules that *already* prohibit belligerent reprisals against certain categories of persons and objects. The norm safeguards the internal coherence of the hierarchy

[318] See Section 1.5.2.2.

[319] As the Greek delegate at the Vienna Diplomatic Conference noted, this is particularly so if the humanitarian conventions go further than customary law in this regard (UN Doc. A/CONF.39/SR.21, pp. 113–14, para. 43).

[320] See, in this regard, Simma, 'Reflections on Article 60', p. 75, footnote 320: 'the [Vienna] Convention's limitation in scope to termination and suspension with their *sedes materiae* in the law of treaties has as its effect that paragraph 5 in no way affects the right of an injured party to suspend the operation of a humanitarian agreement as a measure of *reprisal*' [emphasis in the original].

[321] ILC, 'Commentary to ARSIWA', p. 132, Commentary to Article 50, para. 8, whereby Article 50(1)(c) ARSIWA '*reflects* the basic prohibition of reprisals against individuals, which exists in international humanitarian law' [emphasis added].

of norms – it does not purport to modify it by adding new obligations of a peremptory character.

Once we have clarified the relationship between these notions and norms, it appears that placing belligerent reprisals within the framework of reciprocity or enforcement would not run afoul of the conceptual tenets of termination (and suspension) or countermeasures. The fact that these three institutions might (or might not) interact across regimes and in the respective fields of operation does not exclude that one be modelled on the characteristics of the other. The problem, it is submitted, lay elsewhere: specifically, in the fact that the choice between the different paradigms of reciprocity and enforcement was not a neutral one, in a twofold sense. First, each of the two models appears internally consistent: their individual features are strictly connected to each other and can only be understood when taken together. As a consequence, the two models appear impervious to hybridization: attribution to belligerent reprisals of one of those features would entail the immediate application of the whole model of reference, and the corresponding exclusion of the other. Second, opting for one model instead of the other would establish a complex dynamic with the whole legal regime governing hostilities. On one hand, the relative weight attributed to equality of chances or compliance in motivating recourse to belligerent reprisals would significantly determine the place of negative reciprocity and enforcement in the laws of war. At the same time, the principles and forces that have determined the evolution of the legal regime in a certain direction would ensure that the chosen model be in line with the wider goals and imperatives pursued by the laws of war.

Understanding the implications as well as the constraints of this choice leads to the conclusion that there was nothing inherent, or necessary, or pre-determined in formalizing belligerent reprisals according to one paradigm or the other. The adoption of one framework at the expense of the other was determined by a myriad of factors, including historical contingencies, diplomatic manoeuvering, values underpinning the legal regime, and scholars' idiosyncrasies. The choice of which model belligerent reprisals would adopt, and therefore which *causa* would determine their characters, can only be understood in relation to the evolution of the notion over time. Therefore, while the present chapter has provided a static overview of the relevant notions, the following one will look at the dynamics of this interaction, uncovering how the institution of belligerent reprisals has related itself with negative reciprocity and countermeasures over time.

2

The Development of Belligerent Reprisals as an Enforcement Tool

2.1 The Long Path to Consensus

This chapter reconstructs the process that has led to the current formalization of belligerent reprisals under international law. By looking at the evolution of the concept throughout the twentieth century, it will show how belligerent reprisals have progressively taken on the features of a tool aiming at the enforcement of the laws of war, leaving behind those traits associated with negative reciprocity and undergoing a gradual assimilation with countermeasures. It will thus appear how the different actors that partake in the formation of international law have transformed retaliation, from an existential threat to *ius in bello*, into an instrument to uphold its continued validity amid breaches – in other words, how the belligerents' concern for equality of chances and parity of arms has been "sublimated" into a form of continued commitment to the cogency of the legal regime. In so doing, it reveals the seeming paradox of a legal order that permits the partial disapplication of its own rules with a view to enforcing them.[1]

In line with the two elements that have been construed as making up the notion of *causa* in Chapter 1, the following pages identify two, related trajectories that have brought the notion of belligerent reprisals within the paradigm of enforcement. Section 2.2 is concerned with the element of function, that is, with how belligerent reprisals have been understood to operate. Its main thrust is to demonstrate how the notion of belligerent reprisals has ceased to be identified with the retaliatory act only, and has been progressively associated with the complex and highly formalized procedure that governs its adoption. Section 2.3 will note that the main consequence of that "proceduralization" lies in its creating a regulatory

[1] Olivier Barsalou, 'The History of Reprisals up to 1945: Some Lessons Learned and Unlearned for Contemporary International Law' (2010) 49 *Military Law and the Law of War Review*, p. 359.

framework that bridges the notion of belligerent reprisals with that of countermeasures. Finally, Section 2.4 will reveal how such assimilation has detached the notion of belligerent reprisals from the sphere of negative reciprocity, and resulted in the attribution to belligerent reprisals of an enforcement function.

2.2 Proceduralizing Recourse to Belligerent Reprisals

2.2.1 The Odds of Legal Qualification: Word, Act and Process

One of the golden rules of law-making, already known at the time of Justinian, posits that 'words suit the things which they are used to denote' (*consequentia nomina rebus esse*).[2] Compliance with this instruction is far from straightforward even in domestic law, where central legislatures sometimes struggle to keep pace with social change. These difficulties are but exacerbated in a legal system such as the international one: in the absence of any central authority ensuring that names maintain a close connection with the practice that they had originally indicated, it is a common feature that new meanings develop over time, and different conducts are indicated by the same word.

The centuries-old concept of "reprisal" is one of the most notable examples in this regard. For centuries, reprisals have been interpreted as an *act*, that is, as a certain behaviour well-defined in time and clearly limited in its duration. The name of this notion finds its origin in the Latin *reprehendere* (which means "hold back" and "catch"). This clearly hints at the practice, common during the Middle Ages and the Renaissance, of 'the seizure, licensed by the authorities of a community, of the goods of a foreign community for the benefit of one or more members of the retaliating community who claimed to have suffered a loss through the failure of the community against which the reprisal was authorized to right a wrong committed by one or more of its members'.[3] Therefore, the accent was on the very act of capturing goods, rather than on the fairly complex set of conditions and rules that preceded it.

This remained the case even when, in the nineteenth and twentieth centuries, reprisals ceased to consist in the appropriation of property, and became a method of coercion used by one State against another.[4] Back

[2] Justinian, *Institutes* (tr. J. B. Moyle) (Oxford: Clarendon Press, 1913), p. 26, II.7.3.

[3] Colbert, *Retaliation in International Law*, p. 9.

[4] *Ibid.*, p. 60.

then just like now, the tools by which an international actor influences the conduct of another involve a series of positive and negative incentives of great complexity. Understanding these dynamics would soon give rise to new social disciplines, but was not the province and main interest of the international law of the epoch, which in many aspects was still in its formative phase. A nascent legal theory was there, not to analyse and comprehend those dynamics, but to reduce composite phenomena to a single occurrence, conceptualize it as a normatively relevant fact, and attribute legal consequences to it.

The regulation of war was no exception to this specific trait of legal thinking. When, in the second half of the nineteenth century, States began convening international conferences to define the laws and customs applicable in war, the term "*représailles*" appeared as a natural candidate to indicate '[a] means of bringing about the cessation of a violation of the law committed by the enemy'.[5] Adopting that word, however, also implied accepting all the traits and features that a centuries-old practice had attached to it: indeed, the fact that the first codifications of reprisals chiefly focused on their 'mode of exercise'[6] suggests that they were conceptualized as a single act. It comes as no surprise that even today, when an authoritative definition of the concept is still missing, belligerent reprisals are still said to consist in the '[otherwise unlawful] *action* … [taken] in reaction to unlawful acts of the adversary'.[7] Overall, the original features of this legal institution still shape our understanding of belligerent reprisals solely as the '*act* violating one or other rule of the laws of war'.[8]

And yet, it is equally possible, and arguably more correct, to construe belligerent reprisals as a *process*, where retaliatory non-compliance with the laws of armed conflict is but the final ring in the long chain of actions and warnings inaugurated by the original breach. Under this view, the *legal* concept of reprisal is not limited to the retaliatory act that is

[5] See the text of a proposed new article titled 'Des violations des lois et coutumes de la guerre' for Section IV of the second *Projet d'une convention internationale concernant les lois et coutumes de la guerre*, introduced by Baron Jomini, Russian delegate at the Brussels Conference of 1874 [translation by the author]. For the debate on the article (which was unanimously deleted from the final text of the Declaration of Brussels), see Charles Samwer and Jules Hopf (eds.), *Nouveau Recueil Général de Traités* (Gottingen: Dieterich, 1879), vol. II(3), pp. 138 ff.

[6] IDI, 'Oxford Manual', Articles 85–86 [translation by the author].

[7] Henckaerts and Doswald-Beck, *Customary IHL Study*, vol. I, p. 513 [emphasis added].

[8] Kalshoven, *Belligerent Reprisals*, p. 367 [emphasis added].

eventually taken. It also consists of all the procedural elements that shall be met to adopt lawfully a measure by way of reprisal, and that are, as such, worth of precise regulation under the law. This section will be devoted precisely to analysing how a more elaborate understanding of belligerent reprisals, now interpreted as a combination of procedure and action, has taken root in the modern regulation of the institution.

2.2.2 *Treaty-Law and the Difficulty in Proceduralizing Recourse to Belligerent Reprisals*

2.2.2.1 Early Codification Efforts

In a nutshell, the seeds for understanding belligerent reprisals as also comprising a complex procedure in addition to a single act were implicit in the highly ritualized requirements that accompanied private as well as public reprisals in the ancient practice. But the credits of consciously following this alternative path for the first time must be given to the negotiators entrusted with the codification of the laws of war in the late nineteenth century. When fifteen delegations met in Brussels in 1874 to discuss a *Projet d'une Convention internationale concernant les lois et coutumes de la guerre*, the Russian delegation headed by Baron Jomini submitted on two occasions a detailed regulation for belligerents to resort lawfully to reprisals. Section IV of the original draft distributed at the Conference set forth, among other things, that belligerent reprisals were only admitted 'when it will be irrefutably shown that the laws and customs of war have been violated by the enemy', and 'with the authorisation of the commander-in-chief'.[9] Similar procedural concerns inspired a second draft intended to replace the original Section IV, whereby the limits to reprisals require that 'they will never be taken unless under the formal order of the commander-in-chief of the army and under their responsibility'.[10]

Eventually, the Declaration of Brussels did not contain any provisions on belligerent reprisals,[11] preferring instead to leave the matter 'in the

[9] Samwer and Hopf (eds.), *Nouveau Recueil Général*, p. 14, paras. 69 and 71 [translation by the author].

[10] *Ibid.*, p. 139 [translation by the author].

[11] 'Project of an International Declaration concerning the Laws and Customs of War', 27 August 1874, Dietrich Schindler and Jiri Toman (eds.), *The Laws of Armed Conflicts* (Dordrecht: Martinus Nijhoff, 1988), pp. 22–34.

domain of unwritten law, under the sanction of public conscience'.[12] However, just a few years later, the IDI criticized the silence of the Declaration of Brussels on the topic, stressing 'the urgent need for a definition *and regulation* of belligerent reprisals, so long as their complete prohibition was unattainable'.[13] Faithful to its previous stance, the IDI in its 1880 Oxford Manual not only tackled the issue of belligerent reprisals directly, but also included and expanded the procedural requirements for their adoption. On one side, it was reiterated that these measures 'cannot be taken without the authorization of the commander-in-chief'; on the other, it was also added that 'reprisals are formally prohibited if the damage about which there are grounds for complaint has been repaired'.[14]

These rudimentary conditions are but distant precursors of the detailed rules that have been developed to proceduralize recourse to belligerent reprisals; however, these first proposals were placing the taking of such measures well beyond the immediate and limited logic of retaliatory acts that had characterized previous warfare. True, providing for a prior authorization by the commanding officer, as well as conditioning the adoption of the measure on the failure to repair the damage, served as additional words of caution. Still, the most important contribution of these procedural requirements lay in their acknowledging the manifold new dimensions that are inaugurated by the breach in the relationship between the belligerents. Asking the military commander to authorize the measure forced them to look at the violations of the laws of war (both the original and the retaliatory one) in the wider picture of the ongoing hostilities. Under this new light, belligerent reprisals ceased to be an act disconnected both from what had happened before and from what would happen after their taking: they were just another possible occurrence in a long thread of inimical acts. At the same time, the priority of reparation over retaliation meant that belligerents were now placed within a complex web of legal relationships, all of which affected (and would be affected by) the retaliatory measure. In this sense, the suggestion that certain steps and requirements condition the adoption of belligerent reprisals contributed to "proceduralizing" the mechanism: in a

12 Thus Baron Lambermont, representative of Belgium: see Samwer and Hopf (eds.), *Nouveau Recueil Général*, p. 139 [translation by the author].

13 Kalshoven, *Belligerent Reprisals*, p. 52. See also IDI, 'Conclusion IX', in (1877) I *Annuaire de l'Institut de Droit International*, p. 136.

14 IDI, 'Oxford Manual', Articles 85 and 86 [translation by the author].

way, they emphasized that the behaviours and attitudes that precede and follow the adoption of the measure – in a word, the *process* of reprisals – are as important as the act itself.

2.2.2.2 The Paradigm Shift Following the 1929 Prisoner of War Convention

Despite the goodwill of the IDI members, the call for a more precise identification of the steps to recur lawfully to belligerent reprisals went largely unheeded. The two Peace Conferences that took place at The Hague in 1899 and 1907, which resulted in a number of separate conventions purporting to codify the laws of war, shied away from discussing (let alone codifying) the rules on belligerent reprisals, for 'fear that express regulation might be interpreted as a legitimation of their use'.[15] The most significant change of paradigm only took place in the aftermath of World War I, when the adoption of the 1929 Geneva Convention Relative to the Treatment of Prisoners of War set a precedent that would determine the following evolution of the law.[16]

During the negotiations that led to the signature of this treaty, the British delegation proposed an amendment to the original draft tabled by the ICRC. The British provision would have allowed a belligerent, under a stringent procedure, to take belligerent reprisals against prisoners of war 'in the case of unlawful acts committed or endorsed by their own Government in relation to the treatment of prisoners of war'.[17] The British attempt at proceduralizing belligerent reprisals was as ill-fated as its nineteenth-century predecessors, but the 1929 Prisoners of War Convention stands out as it does indeed contain a provision on these measures. Quite simply, the negotiators gathered in Geneva chose a different strategy, and limited themselves to banning belligerent reprisals when taken against prisoners of war.[18] According to Des Gouttes, the success of the 1929 Conference in this regard shows at what price a

[15] Kalshoven, *Belligerent Reprisals*, p. 67. That addressing belligerent reprisals in a code on the laws of war should not be interpreted as a way of upholding their use was made clear by Baron Jomini, from the Russian delegation, already at the Brussels Conference in 1874: see Samwer and Hopf (eds.), *Nouveau Recueil Général*, pp. 139 f.

[16] Convention Relative to the Treatment of Prisoners of War, Geneva, 27 July 1929, in force 19 June 1931, no longer in operation following the universal acceptance of the Geneva Conventions of 1949, 47 Stat. 2021; T.S. No. 846; 118 L.N.T.S. 343; 130 BFSP 239.

[17] Paul Des Gouttes, *Commentaire de la Convention de Genève du 27 Juillet 1929* (Geneva: ICRC, 1930), p. 451 [translation by the author].

[18] Article 2(3) of the 1929 Geneva Convention on Prisoners of War.

provision on belligerent reprisals could be included in a multilateral treaty: a black-letter law on this highly divisive notion could only be created, not by outlining the procedural aspects of those measures that were considered as still acceptable, but by prohibiting those measures that 'humanity does not accept'.[19] As noted by Kalshoven, the new strategy would 'detach [the *régime* applicable to belligerent reprisals] from the Hague Regulations on Land Warfare and . . . make it the subject of a separate convention, thus turning it into a part of the "law of Geneva"'.[20] In the patent unwillingness of States to define a procedure for the adoption of belligerent reprisals, the only way of reaching an agreement on them was to outlaw in humanitarian treaties those measures that were no longer considered acceptable, and leave all the others subject to the limits set forth by customary law.

The approach successfully introduced by the 1929 Prisoners of War Convention can be seen at work throughout the arch of the modern humanitarian movement. The 1949 GCs only address belligerent reprisals in the sense of prohibiting their adoption against the categories of persons and objects that they protect.[21] The same is true for 1977 AP I, with some important insights from the *travaux préparatoires* confirming this impression.[22] In 1975, Main Committee I of the Geneva Diplomatic Conference (which was entrusted with discussing general questions) received a proposal by the French delegate to introduce a new Article 74 *bis* in the framework of AP I.[23] Similarly to a competing (and

[19] Des Gouttes, *Commentaire de la Convention de 1929*, p. 464 [translation by the author].

[20] Kalshoven, *Belligerent Reprisals*, p. 106.

[21] Geneva Conventions Relative to the Protection of the Victims of International Armed Conflicts, Geneva, 12 August 1949, in force 21 October 1950, 75 UNTS 31; UKTS 39 (1958), Cmd 550; 157 BFSP 229; 6 UST 3114; TIAS 3362; ATS 21 (1958).

[22] Protocol Additional to the Geneva Conventions of 12 August 1949, and relating to the Protection of Victims of International Armed Conflicts (Protocol I), Geneva, 8 June 1977, in force 7 December 1978, 1125 UNTS 3.

[23] CDDH/I/221/Rev.1, 22 April 1976, in Swiss Federal Political Department, *Official Records of the Diplomatic Conference on the Reaffirmation and Development of International Humanitarian Law Applicable in Armed Conflicts – Geneva (1974–1977)* (Bern: 1978), vol. III, p. 324 (hereinafter, *CDDH Official Records*). France had already submitted a proposed new Article 74 *bis* at an earlier stage: CDDH/I/221, 19 February 1975, in *CDDH Official Records*, vol. III, p. 323. It is worth quoting the text of the final version of the French amendment in full:

> New Article 74 *bis*. Reprisals
>
> 1. In the event that a party to a conflict commits serious, manifest and deliberate breaches of its obligations under this Protocol, and a party

'mutually exclusive')[24] new Article 70 *bis* introduced by the Polish delegation, the provision put forward by France 'aimed at introduction of a general clause on reprisals into the Protocol',[25] and set forth a very detailed procedure for taking them.

In the view of the French delegation, laying down a precise regulation for the recourse to belligerent reprisals had a well-defined objective: that is, caging retaliation in a procedure that would increase the number of steps and conditions necessary for the actual taking of the measure. Trying to strike a middle ground between two extremes (the lack of enforcement mechanisms to counter violations of the laws of armed conflict, on one hand, and negative reciprocity activated by breaches thereof, on the other), the French proposal aimed at 'avoid[ing] . . . not only the breach of the law but [also] the escalation of violence'.[26] Within this framework, paramount importance was given to the *threat* of resorting to belligerent reprisals, whose formal characteristics ('it must be formally proclaimed at the highest level')[27] are seen as necessary

victimized by these breaches considers it imperative to take action to compel the party violating its obligations to cease doing so, the victimized party shall be entitled, subject to the provisions of this Article, to resort to certain measures which are designed to repress the breaches and induce compliance with the Protocol, but which would otherwise be prohibited by the Protocol.

2. The measures described in paragraph 1 of this Article may be taken only when the following conditions are met:
   a) The measures may be taken only when other efforts to induce the adverse party to comply with the law have failed or are not feasible, and the victimized party clearly has no other means of ending the breach;
   b) The decision to have recourse to such measures must be taken at the highest level of the government of the victimized party; and
   c) The party committing the breach must be given specific, formal, and prior warning that such measures will be taken if the breach is continued or renewed.
3. If it proves imperative to take these measures, their extent and their means of application shall in no case exceed the extent of the breach which they are designed to end. The measures may not involve any actions prohibited by the Geneva Conventions of 1949. The measures must cease, in all events, when they have achieved their objective, namely, cessation of the breach which prompted the measure.

[24] Nahlik, 'Reprisals in Light of Diplomatic Conference', p. 49.
[25] *Ibid.*
[26] CDDH/I/SR.46, 28 April 1976, in *CDDH Official Records*, vol. IX, p. 59, para. 24.
[27] *Ibid.*

conditions for it to be 'sufficient to serve [its] purpose'.[28] Only if and when such threat had proved ineffective, the *act* of reprisal would be resorted to, but even in this case with the procedural hurdle that 'that formidable decision' be taken by the Government, no longer by military authorities.[29]

Even from this cursory overview of the French proposal, it appears that the emphasis was shifted from the act of adopting the measure to the whole process of belligerent reprisal, inaugurated by the original breach and consisting of a number of steps. In this stance, the threat of retaliating bears as much relevance as the final retaliation. The fact that the French proposal, while acknowledging the role of belligerent reprisals, significantly curtailed the availability thereof for a belligerent victim of a violation of the laws of war, did not go unnoticed by the Canadian delegation. Its representative noted that '[t]he draft of Article 74 *bis* submitted by France made it possible to bring such actions out into the open and to impose limits and conditions which would be both accepted and acceptable'.[30] Other delegations, however, were not convinced by the French proposal, fearful as they were that the notable expansion of the *ratio materiae* of the 1977 Additional Protocols would challenge the strict dichotomy between the laws of Geneva and The Hague. Thus, the delegate of Austria pointed out that his country 'had great difficulty with the idea of introducing into humanitarian law a legal sanction of the law of war always regarded as incompatible with the very principle of humanity'.[31] And after France and Poland announced that they would both withdraw their proposed amendments,[32] the French delegation could only acknowledge that 'the time has not yet arrived to place the problem of sanctions for grave violations of humanitarian law *inside a legal framework*'.[33]

Even more than it had occurred in Brussels fifty years before, it can be said, borrowing Baron Lambermont's words, that the regulation of belligerent reprisals had been 'sacrificed on the altar of humanity' when the

[28] *Ibid.*

[29] *Ibid.*, pp. 59–60, para. 25.

[30] *Ibid.*, p. 64, para. 46.

[31] CDDH/I/SR.47, 29 April 1976, in *CDDH Official Records*, vol. IX, p. 78, para. 52.

[32] CDDH/I/SR.72, 13 May 1977, in *CDDH Official Records*, vol. IX, p. 417, paras. 3–4, as well as p. 418, para. 11.

[33] CDDH/I/SR.73, 16 May 1977, in *CDDH Official Records*, vol. IX, p. 443 [emphasis added].

issue arose during the negotiation of multilateral treaties.[34] International conferences had been the cradle where the procedural aspects of belligerent reprisals were acknowledged and developed for the first time, but negotiations exacerbated the fear that opponents would ruthlessly take advantage of any limit imposed on these measures. This prevented States from going beyond the prohibition of belligerent reprisals taken against so-called victims of war, and from agreeing on any specific regulation of the mechanism even in the widespread understanding of its urgent need. For this reason, what we call the "proceduralization" of belligerent reprisals, that is, the development of its procedural aspects, would be carried on in large part through channels external to treaty law: that is, international case-law and the work of the ICRC.

2.2.3 The Role of International Tribunals and the ICRC in Sanctioning Proceduralization

2.2.3.1 The Post-WWII Case-Law in the *Hostage* and the *Rauter* Cases

In light of their judicial function, tribunals have been the first bodies to delve into customs and principles of international law and find or develop the main tenets regulating belligerent reprisals. During the war crimes trials that followed World War II, counsels repeatedly relied on the doctrine of belligerent reprisals as a defence for the unlawful conduct ascribed to their defendants, and therefore as a defence against allegations of criminal responsibility.[35] The judgments that openly dealt with

[34] Samwer and Hopf (eds.), *Nouveau Recueil Général*, p. 139.

[35] On the post-WWII case-law dealing with the defence of belligerent reprisals, see Arthur R. Albrecht, 'War Reprisals in the War Crimes Trials and in the Geneva Conventions' (1953) 47 AJIL, pp. 590–614; Kalshoven, *Belligerent Reprisals*, pp. 216–63. In the following pages, only the judgments related with the aspect of the "proceduralization" of belligerent reprisals will be addressed. It is however advisable to list here the judgments and proceedings that addressed belligerent reprisals: Nürnberg Military Tribunal II-A, *The United States of America* v. *Otto Ohlendorf and Others (The Einsatzgruppen Case)*, 8–9 April 1948, in *Trials of War Criminals before the Nuernberg Military Tribunals* (Washington: US Government Printing Office, 1950), vol. IV, pp. 1 ff.; Nürnberg Military Tribunal V-A, *The United States of America* v. *Wilhelm von Leeb and Others (The High Command Case)*, 27 October 1948, in *Trials of War Criminals before the Nuernberg Military Tribunals* (Washington: US Government Printing Office, 1950), vol. X–XI; British Military Court in Rome, *Trial of Generals Von Mackensen and Maelzer*, 18–30 November 1945, Case No. 43, VIII *Law Reports of Trials of War Criminals*, pp. 1 ff.; British Military Court in Rome, *Trial of Field Marshal Kesselring*, 17 February–6 May 1947, Case No. 44, VIII *Law Reports of Trials of War Criminals*, pp. 9 ff.; Military

these claims, albeit largely surpassed by following reflections and practice on the topic, had the merit of eventually 'transform[ing] the previously sketchy rules on [belligerent] reprisals into a more comprehensive and elaborate system of control'.[36] What is even more important for our purposes, this judicial effort on a European scale often resulted in the "invention"[37] of a rather complicated procedure for the adoption of belligerent reprisals: what could still be avoided by delegations negotiating treaties in Brussels, The Hague or Geneva, could no longer be bypassed by tribunals adjudicating on issues of criminal responsibility.

The most notable example in this regard is the 1948 judgment in the so-called *Hostage* case, which was tried in Nuremberg, in the American zone of occupation of Germany, under Control Council Law No. 10 by the United States Military Tribunal V.[38] The central question that the judges were called upon to decide, raised by Count One of the Indictment, was whether armed attacks by unlawful enemy resistance forces, acts of sabotage and injuries committed by unknown persons could entitle the German armed forces to kill by way of belligerent reprisal individuals taken from the civilian population of occupied territories.[39] Throughout the judgment, the judges insisted on drawing a clear distinction between the execution of hostages and that of reprisal prisoners: while the former category included 'those persons of the civilian population who are taken into custody for the purpose of guaranteeing with their lives the future good conduct of the population of the community from which they were taken',[40] the latter referred to 'those

Tribunal of Brussels (2nd Chamber), *In re Von Falkenhausen*, Judgment, 9 March 1951; US Military Commission in Rome, *In re Dostler*, Judgment, 12 October 1945, Case No. 2, I *Law Reports of Trials of War Criminals*, pp. 22 ff.

[36] Albrecht, 'Reprisals in War Crimes Trials', p. 590.

[37] The semantic richness of the term is particularly appropriate here: whereas the origin of the word (the Latin *invenire*) indicates the act of "finding" something, the modern meaning points instead to the act of creating something. This mirrors quite faithfully the reasoning in the judgments under review, given the difficulty in establishing to what extent the rules pertaining to belligerent reprisals identified therein reflected existing practice or were rather deduced by principles that inspired the laws of armed conflict.

[38] Nürnberg Military Tribunal V, *The United States of America* v. *Wilhelm List and Others (The Hostage Case)*, 19 February 1948, in *Trials of War Criminals before the Nuernberg Military Tribunals* (Washington: US Government Printing Office, 1950), vol. XI, pp. 757–1332. See also Control Council for Germany Law No. 10, 'Punishment of Persons Guilty of War Crimes, Crimes Against Peace and Against Humanity', 20 December 1945, in *Official Gazette of the Control Council for Germany*, No. 3, p. 12.

[39] *The Hostage Case*, p. 1248.

[40] *Ibid.*, p. 1249. See also *ibid.*, p. 1248.

individuals who are taken from the civilian population to be killed in retaliation for offenses committed by unknown persons within the occupied area'.[41] While the distinction was ultimately based on whether the individuals had been arrested before or after the commission of the act that led to their execution, the law that the Tribunal applied to the reprisal *killing* of the two categories was substantially the same.[42] It is within this framework that the judges, led by the conviction that '[t]he occupant is required to use every available method to secure order and tranquillity before resort may be had to the taking and execution of hostages',[43] set forth a number of procedural conditions that should accompany the threat and implementation of a measure of belligerent reprisal.[44]

Thus, the Tribunal concluded that hostages could be taken from the civilian population only if 'regulations of all kinds . . . imposed to secure peace and tranquillity'[45] had not effectively deterred attacks upon troops and military installations, and if 'it can be shown that the population generally is a party to the offense, actively or passively'.[46] For the measure to be lawful under customary law, it was also deemed necessary that 'proclamation be made, giving the names and addresses of hostages

[41] *Ibid.*, p. 1249. See also *ibid.*, p. 1251.

[42] Kalshoven, *Belligerent Reprisals*, p. 225.

[43] *The Hostage Case*, p. 1249.

[44] The judgment in the *Hostage* case has been criticized along various grounds, especially in light of the distinction that following case-law would make between belligerent reprisals (as acts directed against a State to which the alleged original breach can be attributed) and collective punishment (as injury inflicted on a population that is responsible *in solidum* for the criminal act committed by individuals that cannot be identified). See, for instance, Military Tribunal of Rome, *In re Kappler*, Judgment No. 631, 20 July 1948, analysed in Section 3.4.2.1. In the *Hostage* case, the exclusive focus of the judgment on the relationship between the occupying power and the civilian population under its control, without any enquiry into the connections between the latter and the ousted government, might well lead to interpret its findings as only relevant in the field of collective punishment (see especially *The Hostage Case*, p. 1248). But at the time of its adjudication, given the obscurity of black-letter law, contested State practice, and scholarly uncertainties, the judgment represented a major *déclaration d'intention* in the analytical effort to isolate the concept of belligerent reprisals from such concurrent mechanisms as collective punishment, and to regulate it by means of a detailed procedure. That both hostage-taking and reprisal executions were seen in the judgment as strategies taken by the occupation authorities with a view to *deterring* enemy's *violations* of the laws of war (two concepts traditionally associated with belligerent reprisals) already warns against reading the ruling as only addressing issues of collective punishment.

[45] *The Hostage Case*, p. 1249.

[46] *Ibid.*, p. 1250.

taken, notifying the population that upon the recurrence of stated acts of war treason the hostages will be shot'.[47] Finally, a military commander would only be able to order the shooting of the hostages 'upon the finding of a competent court martial that necessary conditions exist and all preliminary steps have been taken which are essential to the issuance of a valid order'.[48] A similar procedure was set forth for the execution of so-called reprisal prisoners: a proclamation must have previously warned that 'if a certain type of act is committed, a certain number of reprisal prisoners will be shot if the perpetrators cannot be found';[49] it must be shown that 'the population as a whole is a party to the offense, either actively or passively';[50] and the execution must be based on 'a judicial finding that the necessary conditions exist and the essential steps have been taken to give validity to such actions'.[51]

That such a detailed procedure was enshrined in a judicial decision stands out as an *unicum*, not only in the proceedings that followed World War II, but also in war crimes adjudications in following decades. Commentators have characterized the detailed procedure set forth in the *Hostage* judgment as an invention of the Tribunal and as a mere *obiter dictum*. For the proponents of the first argument, it would have been impossible to find in international law such a comprehensive and intrusive set of rules for the execution of hostages or reprisal prisoners;[52] and for the advocates of the latter, a finding of guilt could have been easily reached even without such an in-depth investigation of the rules governing the adoption of a reprisal.[53] Still, the actions and policies under scrutiny could not be legally evaluated outside of a framework setting out the law of belligerent reprisals, and no matter how easy to reach, the *ratio decidendi* for the judgment derives from the failure to meet the requirements for excluding criminal liability. What is more, these criticisms in no way invalidate the relevance of this judicial pronouncement for our purposes. The *Hostage* case represents the first official instance where a belligerent reprisal is unequivocally construed as comprising a complex procedure, in which the lawful adoption of the

[47] *Ibid.*
[48] *Ibid.*
[49] *Ibid.*, p. 1252.
[50] *Ibid.*
[51] *Ibid.*, p. 1253.
[52] Kalshoven, *Belligerent Reprisals*, pp. 228–29.
[53] *Ibid.*, p. 230.

measure is conditioned on the occurrence of a set of cumulative and burdensome requirements.

The readiness with which other post-war tribunals embraced the *Hostage* precedent bears witness to the desperate need for a stringent regulation of belligerent reprisals. The procedural requirements set forth therein would be recalled and applied even beyond the limited scope of American prosecutions grounded in Control Council Law No. 10, as demonstrated by the judgment of first instance in the *Rauter* case, rendered on 4 May 1948 by the Special Criminal Court of The Hague.[54] In this pronouncement, the Court was called upon to determine, *inter alia*, the criminal responsibility of the defendant for 'the numerous public executions of prisoners, whether suspected or not of a crime against the Occupant but not convicted according to the due process of law'.[55] The judges associated themselves with the "permissive" facets of the ruling in the *Hostage* case when they affirmed that 'reprisals against innocent persons for the purpose of maintaining order and tranquillity in occupied territory were permissible';[56] but they also deemed applicable, and not met in the case at hand, the procedural requirements that had been identified by their American counterparts. Even if the tribunal wished to highlight that it had recognized the faculty of the occupying authority to take belligerent reprisals in light of its desire to 'adopt the view most favourable to the accused',[57] the cumbersome procedure for the lawful taking of belligerent reprisals was evidently interpreted as a balancing factor that could adequately bind the action of the occupant.[58]

[54] Special Criminal Court in The Hague, *In re Rauter*, Judgment, 4 May 1948, Case No. 193, in (1949) 16 *Annual Digest and Reports of Public International Law Cases*, p. 531.

[55] *Ibid.*

[56] *Ibid.*, p. 532.

[57] *Ibid.*

[58] Kalshoven has noted that the Special Court in The Hague conceived of two types of retaliation against unlawful acts committed by the civilian population in occupied territory (that is, belligerent reprisals properly understood and collective punishment), but failed to clearly distinguish between the two (Kalshoven, *Belligerent Reprisals*, p. 249). On the other hand, in the judgment of second instance *in re Rauter*, the Special Court of Cassation set out clear boundaries between the two notions (Special Court of Cassation of the Netherlands, *In re Rauter*, Judgment, 12 January 1949, Case No. 193, in (1949) 16 *Annual Digest and Reports of Public International Law Cases*, pp. 538–41). The former category covers those cases 'when a State resorts, by means of his organs, to measures at variance with international law, on account of the fact that its opponent . . . had begun, through one or more of its organs, to commit acts contrary to international law' (*ibid.*, p. 538). The latter indicates 'retaliatory measures taken in time of war by the Occupant of

2.2.3.2 The Contribution of the ICRC

(1) ***The 1969 ICRC*** **Report on the Reaffirmation and Development of the Laws and Customs Applicable in Armed Conflicts** In the last decades, the ICRC has contributed decisively and with lasting impact to proceduralizing the adoption of belligerent reprisals. As the guardian and promoter of IHL, tasked by its Statutes with preparing any development of that body of rules,[59] the organization has attempted on different occasions to clarify the law applicable to belligerent reprisals: in all those instances, particular attention was devoted to identifying, either as a matter *de lege ferenda* or *de lege lata*, procedural yardsticks that had to be satisfied before taking such measures.

Already in May 1969, following an experts meeting held in Geneva, the ICRC published a *Report on the Reaffirmation and Development of the Laws and Customs Applicable in Armed Conflicts* (later submitted to the XXI International Conference of the Red Cross). After defining the field of belligerent reprisals as one where it was 'pressing to update and clarify the law',[60] the ICRC asked the experts whether, should complete prohibition of such measures appear impossible, 'certain limits should not be set to [them], in order to reduce their tragic consequences'.[61] Interestingly, procedural limits to belligerent reprisals only appeared in one of the suggestions put forward by the organization: more precisely, belligerent reprisals would be excluded 'unless the Party alleging violation ha[s] offered the possibility of an enquiry and impartial observation of the facts'.[62] In their reply, the experts did approve the procedural limit put

enemy territory as retaliation . . . against hostile acts of the population of the territory in question or of individual members thereof, which, in accordance with the rights of occupation, he is not bound to tolerate' (*ibid.*). While admitting that genuine belligerent reprisals of the first type could in theory be taken also against the civilian population in occupied territory, the Special Court of Cassation emphasized that they should be taken 'within certain limits' (*ibid.*, p. 539); however, it did not proceed to a specific description of these limits, as it concluded that the Netherlands had not committed any previous international offence against Germany (*ibid.*).

59 Article 5(2)(g) of the Statutes of the International Red Cross and Red Crescent Movement, adopted by the 25th International Conference of the Red Cross at Geneva in 1986, and amended in 1995 and 2006.

60 ICRC, *Reaffirmation and Development of the Laws and Customs Applicable in Armed Conflicts – Report Submitted by the ICRC at the XXI International Conference of the Red Cross (Istanbul, September 1969)*, Geneva 1969, p. 32.

61 *Ibid.*, p. 85.

62 *Ibid.* The other suggested limits were that: '(b) The scale of reprisals must not be out of proportion to that of the violation they aim at stopping; (c) They must be carried out, so far as possible, only in the same field as that of the violation'.

forward by the ICRC, but felt it necessary to voice out a word of concern: according to their view, it was highly doubtful that 'it would always be possible to apply [it]'.[63]

With all likelihood, the experts' hesitation was due to the difficulty in tracing the quasi-judicial process suggested in the 1969 ICRC Report to any instance of available State practice (as manifested, for instance, by the military manuals of States).[64] Already in criminal proceedings conducted in the aftermath of World War II, tribunals had relied extensively on those instructions that governed the conduct of armed forces and security services on the battlefield:[65] having been published by the ministries and departments entrusted with the conduct of combat operations, these documents could not afford to remain vague on issues as foundational as belligerent reprisals. Therefore, they contained detailed rules on the conditions and steps for taking such measures, and were construed by judges as the most authoritative source to discern the applicable law. In the absence of international treaties and uniform practice, the emphasis traditionally put by these national documents on the procedural aspects of belligerent reprisals had become a defining feature of the international regulation of the phenomenon.

Various and wide-ranging procedural requirements for the adoption of belligerent reprisals were indeed envisaged in military manuals drafted in the same years as the 1969 ICRC Report. By way of example, according to the 1956 *US Field Manual* belligerent reprisals could be resorted to only if: other remedies for securing compliance with the laws of war had been exhausted; appeals to the enemy for redress had failed; it had been determined, as a matter of policy, that 'the opposing forces are not more likely to be influenced by a steady adherence to the law'; careful enquiry into the alleged offence had been conducted; a commander had given direct orders to the effect of adopting the measure; and, 'unless immediate action is demanded', the highest accessible military authority had been consulted.[66] All of these requirements were restated and, on some

[63] *Ibid.*, p. 87.

[64] Henckaerts and Doswald-Beck, *Customary IHL Study*, vol. I, p. xxiii.

[65] For instance, the judgment in the *Hostage* case (quoted in this respect by the judgment of the Special Criminal Court in The Hague in *Rauter*, p. 532), cited the US Army's *Field Manual 27-10* containing the Rules on Land Warfare (p. 89, para. 358 *b*) and the British *Manual of Military Law* (para. 458).

[66] US Department of the Army, *Field Manual 27-10, The Law of Land Warfare*, 18 July 1956, as modified by Change No. 1, 15 July 1976, para. 497(d). As a way of tempering the rigidity of the rule, it was specified that prior exhaustion of other remedies

occasions, expanded by the 1976 *US Air Force Pamphlet*;[67] in similar terms, under the 1958 *UK Military Manual* recourse to belligerent reprisals was subjected to: a prior definite ascertainment that a violation of the laws of war has occurred; the impossibility to detect and punish the actual offenders; an evaluation that the facts warrant such reaction; a prior complaint with the enemy; a decision by a military commander.[68]

(2) ***The 2005 ICRC* Customary IHL Study** Differently from the 1969 Report, the ICRC has drawn heavily from such military regulations and instructions in drafting the rules applicable to belligerent reprisals in its *Customary IHL Study*.[69] The ensuing regulation, contained in the Commentary to Article 145 of the document, is largely premised on the assumption that the procedure that leads to a belligerent reprisal is the most important limitation for those cases where the measure has not been prohibited yet.[70] In the ICRC's view, these procedural hurdles consist in the fact that belligerent reprisals 'may only be taken in reaction to a prior serious violation of international humanitarian law'; that they 'may only be carried out as a measure of last resort'; that 'the decision to resort [thereto] must be taken at the highest level of government'; and that they 'must cease as soon as the adversary complies with the law'.[71]

As it appears from this cursory overview, the perspective of an 'enquiry and impartial observation of the facts' propounded in the 1969 ICRC Report differed considerably from the procedural hurdles provided for by contemporary military manuals and ultimately upheld by the 2005 *Customary IHL Study*. The quasi-judicial process under the 1969 Report might be seen as "slimmer", but it could have impinged on a belligerent's freedom of action to a much greater extent than the procedures envisaged under customary law: while the former would have likely allowed a third party (if not the very belligerent allegedly responsible for

should be pursued 'unless the safety of the troops requires immediate drastic action and the persons who actually committed the offences cannot be secured' (*ibid.*).

67 US Department of the Air Force, *Air Force Pamphlet 110-31, International Law – The Conduct of Armed Conflict and Air Operations*, 1976, para. 10–7(c)(3)–(8).

68 UK War Office, *The Law of War on Land being Part III of the Manual of Military Law*, HMSO, 1958, paras. 645 f.

69 Henckaerts and Doswald-Beck, *Customary IHL Study*, vol. I, p. 515: '[m]ost of these conditions [for lawful recourse to belligerent reprisals] are laid down in military manuals and are supported by official statements'.

70 *Ibid.*

71 *Ibid.*, pp. 515–18.

the violation of the laws of war) to participate in the ascertainment of the facts, the latter were ultimately under the control of the belligerent that had allegedly suffered from the breach.

Different factors might account for this change of approach on the part of the ICRC. In 1969, the preference for a requirement potentially more intrusive of States' prerogatives could be justified by the ICRC Report's avowed purpose of '*develop[ing]* the laws and customs applicable in armed conflict'[72] – something that suggests a more progressive identification of the solutions to the challenges faced by belligerents. This explanation could also account for the contrast with the findings of the *Customary IHL Study*, whose scope *ratione materiae* sets a very high threshold for the practices that could be identified as having crystallized into custom. For these reasons, the most recent appraisal of the customary law of belligerent reprisals in the *Study* establishes, as a realistic substitute for a more impartial system of enquiry, a cumbersome procedure that is ultimately left in the hands of the belligerent allegedly victim of a violation of the laws of war. It would seem that some sort of procedure is the best alternative to truth – the same truth that, already in the fifth century BC, Aeschylus[73] recognized as the first casualty of war.

2.2.3.3 Procedural Elements of Belligerent Reprisals in the Case-Law of the ICTY

The importance of procedural requirements in structuring the notion of belligerent reprisals has been recognized by another body that operated around the same time as the ICRC was preparing its *Customary IHL Study*. Mandated to bring to justice those individuals responsible for serious IHL violations that had been committed in the former Yugoslavia since 1991, the International Criminal Tribunal for the former Yugoslavia (ICTY) has adjudicated different cases where the doctrine of belligerent reprisals constituted one of the main lines of defence. The most relevant proceedings in this regard are represented by the *Kupreškić* and the *Martić* cases. With its judgments, the ICTY has reaffirmed and shed light on those procedural elements that must precede the lawful adoption of a measure by way of belligerent reprisals: it thus picked up the baton that had been passed on by the post-WWII tribunals, and brought to fruition the trajectory of "proceduralization"

[72] ICRC, *Report on Reaffirmation and Development*, p. 1 [emphasis added].
[73] Also attributed to Samuel Johnson.

that had been inaugurated by the early codification efforts in the nineteenth century.

(1) *The* **Kupreškić** *Case* The trial in the case *Kupreškić et alii* commenced in August 1998 and was judged by Trial Chamber II of the ICTY in January 2000;[74] an appeal was immediately filed by the Prosecutor, and the Appeals Chamber released its judgment in October 2001.[75] Six defendants stood accused of nineteen counts, 'including persecution as a crime against humanity committed against the Bosnian Muslim population of Ahmici, Central Bosnia, from October 1992 to April 1993, and murder, inhumane acts, and cruel treatment for an attack on that village on 16 April 1993'.[76] In convicting five of the six accused for crimes against humanity,[77] the Trial Chamber had to deal with the Defence's allegation that 'similar attacks [to the one carried out in Ahmici] were allegedly being perpetrated by the Muslims against the Croat population'.[78] After rejecting as fallacious and inapplicable the *tu quoque* argument that it saw at the basis of this argument,[79] the Trial Chamber decided to address the closely related notion of belligerent reprisals[80] even if it had not been raised by the Defence counsel.[81] Accordingly, the tribunal focused on belligerent reprisals taken against civilians (or civilian objects) in the combat zones (which had been prohibited as a matter of treaty law by AP I) and inquired whether 'these provisions, assuming that they were not declaratory of customary international law, have subsequently been transformed into general rules of international law'.[82] The judges gave a positive answer to that question by relying on

[74] ICTY, *The Prosecutor* v. *Kupreškić et al.* (IT-95-16-T), Judgment, Trial Chamber II, 14 January 2000.
[75] ICTY, *The Prosecutor* v. *Kupreškić et al.* (IT-95-16-A), Appeal Judgment, Appeals Chamber, 23 October 2001.
[76] Darcy, 'Evolution of Reprisals', p. 235.
[77] ICTY, *Kupreškić* TC, pp. 324–27.
[78] *Ibid.*, p. 199, para. 511.
[79] *Ibid.*; see also *ibid.*, pp. 201–4, paras. 515–20.
[80] See *ibid.*, p. 201, para. 515. Interestingly, the Trial Chamber construed the notion of belligerent reprisals as coinciding to a large extent with a second meaning attributed to the *tu quoque* principle, whereby 'such breaches, having been perpetrated by the adversary, legitimise similar breaches by a belligerent in response to, or in retaliation for, such violations by the enemy' (*ibid.*).
[81] Darcy, 'Evolution of Reprisals', p. 235.
[82] ICTY, *Kupreškić* TC, p. 207, para. 527.

numerous considerations, including the role of *opinio iuris sive necessitatis* in compensating for the lack of State practice,[83] the inconsistency of such measures with 'fundamental rights of human beings',[84] and the presence of 'widely available' and 'fairly efficacious' means of inducing compliance with international law.[85]

Probably with a view to shielding its findings from future criticism,[86] the Trial Chamber backed up its analysis with two considerations. First, it noted that, 'whatever the content of the customary rules on reprisals, the treaty provisions prohibiting them were in any event applicable',[87] given the fact that both Croatia and Bosnia and Herzegovina had acceded to the four 1949 GCs in 1992[88] and ratified the APs in 1993.[89] Second, even if it did not expressly say that they had been violated in the case at hand, the court mentioned different principles restricting recourse to admissible belligerent reprisals. Beside and before the principle of proportionality and the elementary considerations of humanity, the Trial Chamber listed two requirements of a purely procedural type: that is, the principle whereby belligerent reprisals 'must be a last resort' to be adopted after an unsuccessful prior warning,[90] and 'the obligation to take special precautions before implementing them', including a decision at the highest political or military level.[91]

The issue of belligerent reprisals was not raised and discussed during the appeals proceedings (which reversed the convictions of three of the six defendants);[92] moreover, the discussion on belligerent reprisals in the

[83] *Ibid.*, p. 207, para. 527.
[84] *Ibid.*, p. 208, para. 529.
[85] *Ibid.*, pp. 208–9, para. 530. The Tribunal also listed the work of the ILC, the customary status of Common Article 3 GCs, and the ICJ judgment in the *Nicaragua* case: see pp. 211–12, para. 534.
[86] See, in this regard, the notable objections raised against this judgment by Frits Kalshoven, 'Two Recent Decisions of the Yugoslavia Tribunal', in Lal Chand Vohrah (ed.), *Man's Inhumanity to Man: Essays on International Law in Honour of Antonio Cassese* (The Hague: Kluwer, 2003), pp. 494–507; Christopher Greenwood, 'Belligerent Reprisals in the Jurisprudence of the International Criminal Tribunal for the Former Yugoslavia', in Horst Fischer, Clauss Kress and Sascha Rölf Luder (eds.), *International and National Prosecution of Crimes under International Law: Current Developments* (Berlin: Berliner Wissenschaftsverlag, 2001), pp. 549–56.
[87] ICTY, *Kupreškić* TC, p. 212, para. 536.
[88] *Ibid.*, p. 212, para. 536, footnote 796.
[89] *Ibid.*, p. 212, para. 536.
[90] *Ibid.*, p. 212, para. 535.
[91] *Ibid.*
[92] ICTY, *Kupreškić* AC, pp. 168–73.

judgment by the Trial Chamber has been regarded as *obiter dictum* with no binding precedent.[93] Even under these circumstances, the Trial Chamber considered that its conclusions with regard to the procedural requirements for the adoption of belligerent reprisals would still be vested with 'persuasive authority concerning the existence of a rule or principle'[94] – as demonstrated by the ICTY decisions in the *Martić* case.

(2) ***The* Martić *Case*** The trial against Milan Martić, leader of the Croatian Serbs, commenced in 2005, ten years after his initial indictment had been confirmed and an international arrest warrant had been issued.[95] The judgment released by Trial Chamber I in 2007 found Martić guilty under all but one count and sentenced him to thirty-five years' imprisonment,[96] but was appealed by both the Prosecution and the Defence. The Appeals Chamber reversed the convictions with regard to specific alleged crimes but did not revise the sentence.[97] In its indictment, the Prosecution had alleged that the Serb forces had committed persecutions in the Serbian Autonomous Region of Krajina and the Republic of Serbian Krajina between August 1991 and December 1995, intentionally destroyed or plundered public and private property in those regions, and carried out unlawful attacks on Zagreb and on undefended Croat and Muslim villages.[98] In relation to these counts, the Prosecution had alleged that Martić had participated in a joint criminal enterprise and that he was individually criminally responsible for various crimes against humanity and violations of the laws or customs of war.[99] Throughout the proceedings, however, the bombardment of Zagreb presented the Tribunal with

93 Darcy, 'Evolution of Reprisals', p. 243.

94 ICTY, *Kupreškić* TC, p. 215, para. 540.

95 ICTY, *The Prosecutor* v. *Martić* (IT-95-11-R61), Decision (Rule 61), Trial Chamber I, 8 March 1996. See also ICTY, *Rules of Procedure and Evidence*, IT/32/Rev. 7, 18 January 1996.

96 ICTY, *The Prosecutor* v. *Martić* (IT-95-11-TC), Judgment, Trial Chamber I, 12 June 2007, p. 185, paras. 517–19.

97 ICTY, *The Prosecutor* v. *Martić* (IT-95-11-A), Appeal Judgment, Appeals Chamber, 8 October 2008.

98 ICTY, *Martić* TC, pp. 7–8, para. 4. These acts of persecution were said to include 'the extermination and murder of hundreds of Croats, Muslims and other non-Serb civilians', their 'prolonged and routine imprisonment . . . in specified detention facilities', the 'torture and inhumane treatment of prisoners', and 'the deportation and forcible transfers of tens of thousands of non-Serb civilians' (*ibid.*).

99 *Ibid.*, pp. 8–9, paras. 6–8.

difficult questions, which related to the possibility of justifying that conduct as a form of belligerent reprisals.

Already in 1996, while confirming for a second time the indictment against Martić pursuant to Rule 61 of the Rules of Procedure and Evidence, a Trial Chamber had wondered whether 'the fact that the attack was carried out as a reprisal reverse the illegality of the attack'.[100] Relying on different sources,[101] the tribunal concluded that 'the rule which states that reprisals against the civilian population as such, or individual civilians, are prohibited in all circumstances, even when confronted by wrongful behaviour of the other party, is an integral part of customary international law and must be respected in all armed conflicts'.[102]

Undeterred by this finding, during the trial on first instance the Defence submitted that the shelling of Zagreb represented a reaction to Operation Flash, which had been carried out by the Croatian military and police forces in breach of the ceasefire agreement and 'without any respect to the norms of international humanitarian law'.[103] In analysing the argument,[104] Trial Chamber I stressed that belligerent reprisals, 'in order to be lawful, are subject to strict conditions [that] are well-established in customary law'.[105] Among these, the judges stressed the requirement that the measure be 'used only as a last resort and only when all other means have proven to be ineffective',[106] and that it be authorized 'at the highest political or military level'.[107] The court drew a connection between the existence of ongoing peace negotiations when Operation Flash took place, and the failure to adopt belligerent reprisals as a measure of last resort;[108] it also noted that the retaliating party had not

[100] ICTY, *Martić* Rule 61, p. 6, para. 15.

[101] These include the 'opinion of the great majority of legal authorities', Common Article 1 to the GCs, the judgment of the ICJ in the *Nicaragua* case, General Assembly Resolution 2675 (i.e., UN Doc. A/RES/2675(XXV), *Basic Principles for the Protection of Civilian Populations in Armed Conflicts*, 9 December 1970), as well as the 1977 APs: see ICTY, *Martić* Rule 61, pp. 6–7, paras. 15–16.

[102] *Ibid.*, p. 7, para. 17.

[103] ICTY, *Martić* TC, pp. 166–67, para. 464.

[104] *Ibid.*, p. 168, para. 468.

[105] *Ibid.*, p. 167, para. 465.

[106] *Ibid.*, p. 167, para. 466. According to the Trial Chamber, '[t]his limitation entails that reprisals may be exercised only after a prior and formal warning has been given, which has failed to put an end to the violations committed by the adversary' (*ibid.*).

[107] *Ibid.*

[108] *Ibid.*, p. 168, para. 468.

given prior warning that it would take belligerent reprisals for the violations allegedly committed during Operation Flash.[109] On the basis of these elements, Trial Chamber I dismissed the Defence argument based on the doctrine of belligerent reprisals.[110]

These procedural requirements played a prominent role in excluding the qualification of the bombardment of Zagreb as a lawful belligerent reprisal. Accordingly, the Defence counsel challenged the Trial Chamber's findings in its grounds for appeal. Martić argued that all other remedies had been exhausted and the shelling was a measure of last resort, since the Croats had rejected peace negotiations.[111] While acknowledging that there had been no specific warning, he claimed that an equivalent effect had been obtained through 'the repeated warning that Zagreb would be shelled in the case of "aggression" against the RSK [*scil.*, the Republic of Serbia Krajina], the context of peace negotiations, and the practice of announcing military targets to save civilians'.[112] However, the Appeals Chamber first upheld the Trial Chamber's determination of the law applicable to belligerent reprisals, including the procedural requirements that the latter had identified;[113] then, it rejected the arguments advanced by Martić,[114] stating that they 'failed to show that the Trial Chamber erred in concluding that the two conditions justifying reprisals had not been met'.[115]

The judgments delivered by the ICTY Trial and Appeals Chamber in the *Martić* case provide clear evidence of the paramount role assigned to procedural requirements in determining the lawfulness of belligerent reprisals. The principles demanding that such measures be adopted as a last resort and only after prior warning represented *the* decisive criterion in ruling out the legality of the indiscriminate shelling of Zagreb as a belligerent reprisal.[116] In this sense, the ICTY case-law, together with the almost contemporary ICRC *Customary IHL Study*, represent the culmination of the trajectory of "proceduralization" that has been identified in

[109] *Ibid.*
[110] *Ibid.*
[111] ICTY, *Martić* AC, p. 86, para. 237.
[112] *Ibid.*, p. 86, para. 238.
[113] *Ibid.*, p. 95, para. 263.
[114] *Ibid.*, p. 96, paras. 264–66.
[115] *Ibid.*, p. 96, para. 267.
[116] ICTY, *Martić* TC, p. 168, para. 468.

this first section.[117] It remains to be seen what the implications of this process have been, and what drivers have made it possible.

2.3 The Assimilation between Belligerent Reprisals and Countermeasures

2.3.1 Possible Explanations for the "Proceduralization" of Recourse to Belligerent Reprisals

In spearheading the effort to clarify and establish the procedural requirements for the adoption of belligerent reprisals, judges, officials and scholars have achieved the most durable and successful feature in the development of the notion. After decades of theoretical refinement and consolidation, belligerent reprisals do not consist only in the final retaliatory act, but also comprise a complex series of behaviours. The relevance of elements such as last resort, prior warning and authorization does not lie exclusively in their contributing to the lawfulness or unlawfulness of the measure, but relates to their being part and parcel of the institution of belligerent reprisals. Once we understand their importance, the question immediately arises of *why* the notion of procedure has played such a prominent role in determining the traits of belligerent reprisals.

A possible answer would argue that emphasizing the procedural requirements of belligerent reprisals has compensated for the difficulty in giving precise contours to the more substantive requirements that the measure must observe. In this regard, one would be immediately

[117] For a recent confirmation of this trend, see the judgment delivered by the German Federal Court of Justice on 25 October 2010 in the *Italian Partisans* case (translated and quoted in ICRC, *Customary IHL Database*, Practice related to Section F of Rule 145 – available at https://ihl-databases.icrc.org/customary-ihl/eng/docs/v2_rul_rule145_sectionf). The defendant in the case had been 'convicted on ten counts of murder and attempted murder and sentenced to life imprisonment' (*ibid.*, para. 4) for having killed or seriously injured ten Italian civilians in alleged retaliation for the killing, at the hands of the partisans, of two German soldiers and injury of a third one (*ibid.*, paras. 2–3). In confirming the finding of the lower criminal court that 'the objective requirements for a permissible war reprisal were not fulfilled' (*ibid.*, para. 44(c)), the Federal Court of Justice affirmed: '*[t]he least controversial condition* for the lawfulness of a war reprisal in this context was the so-called notification, i.e., the public declaration of the event. … The purpose of the notification was, on the one hand, to repel future repetitions of attacks against the occupying power … and, on the other hand, to demonstrate "that the measures taken were in the interest of enforcing the law"' (*ibid.*, para. 43) [emphasis added].

prompted to consider the difficulties encountered in articulating the principle of proportionality, one of the bedrock principles applicable to belligerent reprisals. International law has long required that the execution of any such measure 'be done with adherence to the principle of proportionality',[118] but has been much less clear 'as to what that belligerent reprisal must be proportionate to'.[119] As noted in Chapter 1, the scholarship is still divided on whether proportionality should be assessed on the basis of the original unlawful act, the damage that has been suffered, the objective that the retaliatory act pursues, or a combination of all these elements.[120] This *impasse* is exacerbated by the fact that judgments on the matter have largely refrained from defining proportionality in positive terms, preferring instead to demand that the belligerent reprisals be 'not . . . excessive compared to the precedent unlawful act of warfare'.[121] Even the commentary to the ICRC *Customary IHL Study* is not immune from ambiguity in this regard, and acknowledges the difference in opinions on the matter.[122]

The argument stressing the "compensatory" character of the procedural requirements would apply with equal force with regard to the principle of humanity, whose application to belligerent reprisals has long divided international legal theory. This principle was first applied to belligerent reprisals by the Oxford Manual, which stated in Article 86 that these measures 'shall comply, at any rate, with the laws of humanity and morality'.[123] However vague, the principle addressed the concern that the remedy for violations of the laws of armed conflict should not be worse than the disease it purported to heal. Still, it was clearly felt that the adoption of the principle masked a fundamental dilemma: to the extent that 'inhumanity . . . is more or less by definition a characteristic of

118 Darcy, 'Evolution of Reprisals', p. 194.

119 *Ibid.*

120 See Section 1.2.1.3.

121 ICTY, *Kupreškić* TC, p. 212, para. 535. For earlier uncertainty on the matter, see *Naulilaa* case, pp. 1026 and 1028.

122 The ICRC appears to spouse the view requiring that 'reprisal measures be proportionate to the original wrong': Henckaerts and Doswald-Beck, *Customary IHL Study*, vol. I, p. 517. However, in another passage it affirms that '[r]eprisal action must be proportionate to the violation *it aims to stop*', which could be taken to re-introduce the factor associated with the purpose to be achieved through the belligerent reprisal in the assessment of proportionality (*ibid.* [emphasis added]). Finally, the ICRC admits that 'only a few pieces of practice specify that proportionality must be observed with regard to the damage suffered' (*ibid.*, p. 518).

123 IDI, 'Oxford Manual', Article 86 [translation by the author].

belligerent reprisals',[124] how could such measures ever comply with the principle of humanity?

This foundational short-circuit in the interpretation of belligerent reprisals was clearly perceived by criminal tribunals, whose pronouncements strive to re-concile these conflicting facets of the mechanism. The *Hostage* case tried to avoid the conceptual hurdle by claiming that belligerent reprisals were not inhuman per se, but only when their implementation was 'tortured beyond recognition':[125] by means of a very formalistic approach, compliance with the principle of humanity was therefore maintained.[126] For their part, the judges in the *Rauter* case acknowledged much more straightforwardly their difficulties in bringing to a coherent synthesis the practice of belligerent reprisals and the principle of humanity. In the judgment, they hide neither that they subscribe to the *Hostage* precedent only in light of the principle of criminal law *in dubio pro reo*, nor that the policy of killing innocent citizens in occupied territory for the purpose of maintaining peace and order, however justified under certain conditions, represents a practice 'contrary to the most elementary conceptions of humanity and justice'.[127] In the *Martić* case, the judges of the Trial Chamber also stated that 'acts of reprisal must respect "the laws of humanity and the dictates of public conscience"'.[128] The principle of humanity was even given a precise meaning: according to the judges, 'reprisals must be exercised, to the extent possible, in keeping with the principle of the protection of the civilian population in armed conflict and the general prohibition of targeting civilians'.[129] But in assessing the facts of the case, the court contented itself with concluding that the procedural requirements for the adoption of belligerent reprisals had not been satisfied, and did not consider compliance with other, non-procedural conditions such as the principle of humanity.[130]

Probably, the most telling demonstration of the inadequacy of the principle of humanity in constraining the practice of belligerent reprisals

[124] Frits Kalshoven, 'Human Rights, the Law of Armed Conflict, and Reprisals' (1971) 121 IRRC, p. 189. The author sowed the seeds for the tension when he acknowledged the principle of humanity as one of 'the fundamental principles governing justifiable recourse to belligerent reprisals' (*ibid.*).

[125] *The Hostage Case*, p. 1253.

[126] *Ibid.*

[127] *In re Rauter* (Special Criminal Court), pp. 531 f.

[128] ICTY, *Martić* TC, p. 167, para. 467.

[129] *Ibid.*

[130] *Ibid.*, p. 168, para. 468.

is given by the marginal attention devoted to it by the experts meeting convened in Geneva in 1969 by the ICRC and described above. When asked whether belligerent reprisals 'should in any case not be contrary to the laws of humanity', they refrained from treating the principle of humanity as an autonomous rule, preferring to interpret it as a facet of the clearer and less debated rule of proportionality.[131] Based on this evidence, Kalshoven has argued that the requirement of humanity 'is not a legal requirement of the law of reprisals, not even a flexible one, that would of itself suffice to render particular retaliatory measures illegal';[132] more modestly, it should be considered instead as 'a principle of law, which in any particular case should be carefully balanced against other principles, such as necessity and effectiveness'.[133]

2.3.2 *Rejection of the "Compensatory" Account of Proceduralization*

While capturing important dynamics in how the notion of belligerent reprisals has evolved over time, this "compensatory" account of proceduralization is not fully explanatory. With regard to the principle of proportionality, difficulties in defining its precise content in theory have not hindered its implementation in practice – quite the contrary, oftentimes a given recourse to belligerent reprisals has been considered unlawful by criminal tribunals because of its failure to comply with the principle of proportionality.[134] Likewise, the scholarship has been able to re-cast the parameters to assess the principle, shifting from a requirement of strict proportionality to the more flexible notion of 'absence of obvious disproportionality',[135] and restricting the belligerents' freedom of action with the requirement of reasonableness.[136] As opposed to its abstract formulation, the actual application of the principle of proportionality has been seen as 'far from [being] an insurmountable task'.[137]

With regard to the principle of humanity, difficulties in upholding it as a substantive requirement hardly account for the "proceduralization" of

[131] ICRC, *Report on Reaffirmation and Development*, pp. 86 f.

[132] Kalshoven, *Belligerent Reprisals*, p. 344.

[133] *Ibid.*

[134] See, for instance, Shane Darcy, 'Reciprocity and Reprisals', in Rain Liivoja and Tim McCormack (eds.), *Routledge Handbook on the Law of Armed Conflict* (London/New York: Routledge, 2016), p. 499, discussing the judgment in *The Einsatzgruppen Case*.

[135] Kalshoven, *Belligerent Reprisals*, p. 341.

[136] *Ibid.*, p. 342.

[137] Darcy, 'Evolution of Reprisals', p. 194.

the law applicable to belligerent reprisals, for two reasons. First, considering belligerent reprisals as necessarily inhumane measures not only takes for granted that the measure will necessarily impinge on the most fundamental values of the human person protected by the legal order – it also assumes that the belligerent reprisals will invariably be taken. In so doing, that explanation fails to appreciate one of the most important consequences of that "proceduralization": namely, the understanding that belligerent reprisals constitute a process rather than act, and that their aims could be reached by means of a simple threat rather than through the actual adoption of the retaliatory behaviour. Second, the explanation premised on the compensatory value of the procedural requirements overlooks a decisive element. At the same time as the ICRC *Customary IHL Study* and the ICTY case-law were endorsing the proceduralization of belligerent reprisals, different national tribunals reinstated the principle of humanity as a fundamental requirement for the adoption of belligerent reprisals. Judging upon different cases concerned with belligerent reprisals during World War II, Italian and German courts affirmed that the taking of such measures was subject to notions such as 'the fundamental and primary requirements of humanity'[138] and the 'so-called barrier of humanity'.[139] As a consequence, interpreting the creation of a rigid procedure as a form of compensation for the principle of humanity would run foul of the fact that the principle to be compensated for has gained increased backing.

Overall, the fundamental problem with the "compensatory" explanation is that it downplays the importance of proceduralization. It assumes that, compared to limits of a procedural character, the substantive requirements embodied in the principles of proportionality and humanity would be more effective in constraining resort to belligerent reprisals, and worthy of more consideration from a value-laden perspective. By so doing, it creates a sort of hierarchy between requirements, whereby the

[138] Military Tribunal of Rome, *In re Hass and Priebke*, Judgment, 22 July 1997, para. 4 (see also Section 3.4.2.2).

[139] German Federal Court of Justice, *Italian Partisans* case, para. 40(2). The Court later gave specific meaning to the notion of *Humanitätsschranke* with regard to the facts of the case in the following terms: '[t]he way in which the killing was carried out is often considered a central aspect in determining the "humanity" of a killing in the context of a reprisal. . . . The destruction of a building by explosion in which the victims, unaware of their fate, were detained, is considered a humiliating and degrading and therefore inhumane way of killing which is not justified under the laws of war. The same is true for the subsequent and additional killing by firing machine guns' (*ibid.*, para. 42(3)).

procedural ones largely serve the purpose of making up for the uncertainties associated with the substantive ones. To overcome the shortcomings of this view, I submit that the procedural requirements should be seen, not in relation to the other elements in the definition of belligerent reprisals, but in connection with the wider battle for defining the very essence, or *causa*, of the institution.

2.3.3 Procedure as a Common Denominator between Belligerent Reprisals and Countermeasures

It is submitted that the main thrust of the "proceduralization", motivating at once its origin and its success, lies in its consequences on the formalization of belligerent reprisals. By emphasizing the nature of these measures as a tool of 'last resort',[140] judges, officials and scholars have shaped an understanding of how belligerent reprisals operate that is largely modelled on the example of countermeasures. The clearest example of this attitude is to be found in the relationship between the articles devoted to countermeasures in the 2001 ILC ARSIWA, on one side, and the rules on belligerent reprisals contained and commented in the 2005 ICRC *Customary IHL Study*, on the other.

As noted above, Rule 145 of the ICRC *Study* states that '[w]here not prohibited by international law, belligerent reprisals are subject to stringent conditions'.[141] According to the commentary to the norm, the ICRC describes the rule as a norm of customary law applicable in international armed conflicts,[142] and sets out to identify the conditions that 'must be met in order for belligerent reprisals against permitted categories of persons and objects not to be unlawful'.[143] In this endeavour, the ICRC constantly refers to the articles on countermeasures codified in the ARSIWA as evidence of the customary aspects of (and requirements for) belligerent reprisals. Thus, Article 52 ARSIWA, setting forth the conditions relating to resort to countermeasures, is explicitly mentioned by the ICRC as fundamental proof of a customary rule obliging States to adopt belligerent reprisals only as a measure of last resort and only after giving reasonable notice to the enemy.[144] More generally, the ICRC

140 ICTY, *Kupreškić* TC, p. 167, para. 466; Henckaerts and Doswald-Beck, *Customary IHL Study*, vol. I, p. 516.

141 *Ibid.*, p. 513.

142 *Ibid.*

143 *Ibid.*, p. 515.

144 *Ibid.*, p. 516, as well as vol. II, Part 2, pp. 3328 f., para. 161.

commentary makes abundant use of the ARSIWA while discussing the rules on the purpose of belligerent reprisals as well as the applicability of the principles of humanity, proportionality and termination.[145] It is important to note that all the customary conditions set forth in Rule 145 of the ICRC *Customary IHL Study* had been included in national legislation, military manuals, and international as well as national case-law.[146] In this connection, continuous reference by the ICRC to the ARSIWA can hardly be seen as an attempt at filling specific *lacunae* in the customary law of belligerent reprisals by way of analogy; it rather mirrors a deeply rooted conviction that, notwithstanding their different fields of application, the notions of belligerent reprisals and countermeasures operate in almost identical terms and share a common formalization under international law.

A similar view was also shared by the ILC. It is true that the commentary to the ARSIWA excludes in explicit terms belligerent reprisals from the notion of countermeasures examined in the Articles. The ILC acknowledges that the term "reprisals" originally covered different types of 'otherwise unlawful action, including forcible [one], taken by way of self-help in response to a breach';[147] it stresses, however, that that term has become a synonym of belligerent reprisals, while the term "countermeasures" has been referred to reprisals not associated with armed conflict.[148] The very fact that the ILC felt the need to carve the notion of countermeasures out of the wider category of reprisals (including forcible ones adopted in peace-time) testifies for the close similarity that it was detecting in the functioning of these different self-help measures, and most evidently between countermeasures and belligerent reprisals.

This view is also confirmed by some previous reflection of the ILC on Article 14(d) ARSIWA as adopted on first reading, which represents the precursor to what is now Article 50 ARSIWA.[149] The provision prevented an injured State from resorting, by way of countermeasures, to

[145] *Ibid.*, p. 3303, para. 66 (purpose); p. 3337, para. 209 (proportionality); p. 3357, para. 338 (humanity).

[146] *Ibid., passim.*

[147] ILC, 'Commentary to ARSIWA', p. 128, Introductory remarks to Part Three, Chapter II, para. 3.

[148] *Ibid.*

[149] ILC, 'Report of the Commission to the General Assembly on the work of Its Forty-seventh session', UN Doc. A/CN.4/SER.A/1995/Add.1 (Part 2), in (1995) II(2) ILC Ybk, p. 66.

'[a]ny conduct which derogates from basic human rights'.[150] In the commentary, the ILC interpreted that provision as simply reflecting existing prohibitions against certain belligerent reprisals:[151] as a consequence, the notion of belligerent reprisals was ultimately seen as an instance of countermeasure, identical and indistinguishable from it. As demonstrated in Chapter 1, the final amended version of Article 50 ARSIWA as adopted on second reading made an important clarification: the (prohibited) countermeasure with which the Article is concerned consists, not in the actual taking of a prohibited belligerent reprisal, but in the with-holding of performance of the primary rules prohibiting belligerent reprisals against certain protected targets.[152] Even so, the work of the ILC (which was quoted twice by the ICTY Trial Chamber I in the *Kupreškić* judgment)[153] bears witness to the tight interconnections identified by legal theory between the two institutions of belligerent reprisals and countermeasures.

At the roots of both the ICRC's and the ILC's understanding lies the implicit assumption that the notion of reprisals is 'twofold'[154] and designates both 'the historical basis of the notion of countermeasures' and 'countermeasures in times of war'.[155] According to this account, countermeasures and belligerent reprisals would all derive from the Medieval institution of the *lettres de marque* – a form of 'public endorsement for private enforcement action [that was] issued by higher instances in the feudal system'.[156] The fact that these two self-help mechanisms share a common "genetic" background would, in this sense, justify the fact that their formalization (including the procedure governing their adoption) is largely coincident. It would also validate those cases where documents that were concerned exclusively with peace-time reprisals, whether forcible (such as the arbitral award in the *Naulilaa* case)[157] or not (such as the American Law Institute's *Restatement Third of the Foreign Relations*

150 *Ibid.*
151 *Ibid.*, pp. 71 f., paras. 17 f.
152 See Section 1.6.2.
153 ICTY, *Kupreškić* TC, p. 208, para. 529, as well pp. 211–12, para. 534.
154 Matthias Ruffert, 'Reprisals', in *Max Planck Encyclopaedia of Public International Law*, para. 7 (available at https://opil.ouplaw.com/display/10.1093/law:epil/9780199231690/law-9780199231690-e1771?prd=EPIL).
155 *Ibid.*
156 *Ibid.*, para. 4.
157 Henckaerts and Doswald-Beck, *Customary IHL Study*, vol. II, Part 2, p. 3336, para. 203; Kalshoven, *Belligerent Reprisals*, pp. 7–8.

Law of the United States)[158] would be extensively relied upon to craft the notion of belligerent reprisals.

In conclusion, the main thrust and consequence of the "proceduralization" lies in its fundamental contribution to the understanding of the *function* of belligerent reprisals, that is, of the way by which they operate. First, belligerent reprisals now appear as a procedure aimed at attributing a specific legal meaning to the act of retaliation; second, the assimilation with the notion of countermeasures leads to construing that specific legal meaning on the basis of the framework provided by the law of State responsibility and, therefore, the enforcement paradigm. Investigating the respective implications of these two findings will reveal the *purpose* of belligerent reprisals – the second, fundamental element in defining the *causa* of the institution.

2.4 The Inclusion of Belligerent Reprisals within the Enforcement Framework

2.4.1 Re-affirming the Cogency of the Breached Rule: Belligerent Reprisals as Sanctions

The previous section has concluded that belligerent reprisals function by attributing to a retaliatory violation of the laws of war a specific legal meaning: by means of a well-determined procedure, the retaliatory act is made qualitatively different from the unlawful act that originated it. On the basis of these features, international legal theory has long approached the notion of belligerent reprisals from a particular viewpoint, wondering whether they constituted a *sanction* of international law and, more specifically, of the laws of war. This discussion, which occupied the scholarship for a significant part of the twentieth century, resulted in a growing sophistication of the notion of self-help under international law. It is hardly a coincidence that, on the wave of that discussion, international practice disentangled the opposite poles of reciprocity and enforcement that were still combined in the earlier scholarship on belligerent reprisals. The ground for choosing the paradigm that would guide the formalization of belligerent reprisals was laid.

[158] See ICRC, *Customary IHL Database*, Practice relating to Rule 145 – Section A, XII (available at https://ihl-databases.icrc.org/customary-ihl/eng/docs/v2_rul_rule145_sectiona).

Writing in 1935 (i.e., just a few years after the fundamental contributions on belligerent reprisals by Le Fur and La Brière analysed in Chapter 1),[159] Morgenthau provided a comprehensive theory of international sanctions, which he defined as 'the measure[s] of coercion that are resorted to in case a norm is violated'.[160] Morgenthau broke the norm (construed as 'a prescription of will') in two elements: on one side, the 'normative provision', that is, 'the expression of will that aims at achieving a particular result';[161] on the other, the 'validity',[162] which is 'the abstract ability to bring about that will'.[163] Following this distinction, Morgenthau was then able to describe the function of a sanction as that of 'provid[ing] a norm with the element of validity, of reality, that is to say, transforming the idea of a norm into a valid, real norm'.[164]

Following this characterization, legal scholarship thoroughly debated the presence and notion of sanctioning mechanisms under international law – a debate that was seen as a pre-requisite to demonstrate the legal nature of the international system. Apart from a handful of scholars claiming that norms need not be sanctioned to maintain their legal character,[165] the doctrine was largely united in asserting that 'the sanction is essential for the existence for a norm'.[166] Therefore, controversies have insisted on the question 'whether reprisals constitute irremediably unlawful (though perhaps in some cases tolerated), justifiable, or even entirely lawful acts'.[167] But all these debates were based on a single, paramount assumption: namely that, however closely connected, the norm and its sanction were two, clearly distinguished elements. Kelsen bluntly described this fundamental difference by arguing that under international law 'norms prescribe or permit a certain conduct for states',[168] whereas reprisals are defined as 'sanctions of international

[159] See Section 1.3.2.2.

[160] Hans Morgenthau, 'Théorie des sanctions internationales' (1935) 3 *Revue de droit international et de législation comparée*, pp. 482–83 [this and following translations by the author].

[161] *Ibid.*, p. 478.

[162] *Ibid.*

[163] *Ibid.*

[164] *Ibid.*, p. 479.

[165] *Ibid.*, p. 477, footnote 10.

[166] *Ibid.*, p. 477.

[167] Kalshoven, *Belligerent Reprisals*, p. 23 (also for a general overview of the positions taken by the scholarship).

[168] Hans Kelsen, *Principles of International Law* (New York: Rinehart and Co., 1952), p. 17.

law [taken as] a reaction against ... international delicts'.[169] The (violation of the) norm is the logical pre-condition for adopting a reprisal – but the sanction is not to be confused either with the 'primary obligation to refrain from the behaviour causing the damage', nor with the 'substitute obligation to refrain from the behaviour causing the damage in case of nonfulfillment of the primary obligation'.[170]

This construction has a fundamental consequence: being a condition for the existence of the norm, the sanction (and, therefore, the belligerent reprisal) is inextricably linked to the continued validity of the breached rule. The adoption of a belligerent reprisal is no longer grounded in a condition of reciprocity that severs the *vinculum iuris*, as stated in the earlier reflections on the measure: if that were the case, the logic of the sanction would be flipped over, since belligerent reprisals would extinguish a norm while trying to determine its reality. Under the new construction, belligerent reprisals both presuppose and envisage the continued existence of the underlying obligation. Even if 'they are aimed directly to affect one or the other value of the offending State',[171] they will not affect the cogency of the norm per se – on the contrary, it will only be the adoption of a belligerent reprisal that will manifest the existence of that norm. Overall, belligerent reprisals cease to operate as prescribed by negative reciprocity – that is, as a means of direct execution whose value lies in removing a violated rule and in bringing about an immediate re-balancing of the legal relationship. In their novel formalization, they operate according to the logic of enforcement, that is, indirectly and in order to give validity and effectiveness to a prescription of will.[172]

Framing belligerent reprisals as a sanction of international law resulted in them being emancipated from the logic of negative reciprocity, and being vested with the purpose of enforcing the laws of war. Incidentally, the potential benefits of this doctrinal shift had just appeared in the field of practice, as suggested by the *travaux préparatoires* of the League of Nations Conference for the Reduction and Limitation of Armaments that took place in Geneva from 1932 to 1934. In Kalshoven's analysis, the lengthy discussions on the consequences of a breach of the rules on the means and methods of warfare bear witness to the growing sophistication

[169] *Ibid.*, pp. 21–22.
[170] *Ibid.*, p. 19.
[171] Kalshoven, *Belligerent Reprisals*, p. 26.
[172] See *ibid.*, whereby reprisals constitute 'imperfect, reactive, indirectly operating and non-final sanctions of international law'.

in the debate about the framework applicable to belligerent reprisals.[173] Indeed, belligerent reprisals could provide negotiators (especially those led by a genuine interest in the progressive development of *lex lata*) with a window of opportunity to craft different solutions for instances where a party was confronted with violations of the applicable rules. In the case of the Disarmament Conference, practical considerations led practitioners to conceive of reprisals as a way of 'steering a middle ground'[174] between, on one side, institutionalized sanctions (such as monitoring mechanisms and joint police force) and, on the other, the disappearance of the *vinculum iuris* under the traditional doctrine of negative reciprocity. Being the lesser of two evils, belligerent reprisals were seen as effective tools to counter breaches without taking the corresponding rule out of the field. Even if largely as a by-product of a practical move to obtain consensus, the role of belligerent reprisals as a sanction of breached rules was upheld; this separated the mechanism from the rationale and the operationalization of negative reciprocity, and brought it closer and closer to the logic and the mechanisms of enforcement.

2.4.2 *Protecting the Breached Rule from the Risks Associated with Self-Help*

As noted above, the second implication of "proceduralizing" belligerent reprisals relates to the assimilation of the latter notion with countermeasures. Specifically, recourse to belligerent reprisals has been regulated by a set of procedural requirements that largely coincide with those applicable to countermeasures; in turn, this dynamic has prompted scholars and practitioners to draw analogies between the two institutions, conceiving of them as strictly related notions governed by a similar logic. However, that assimilation has also had a lasting impact on the identification of the *purpose* of belligerent reprisals, insofar as it has determined the place of the measure in the complex web of legal relationships set up by the breach of the primary rule.

Curiously, this topic is almost absent in the scholarship on belligerent reprisals, which has mainly focused on the scope of the prohibitions set forth in humanitarian treaties while leaving largely aside the questions associated with the conceptual features of the measure. Conversely,

173 *Ibid.*, pp. 90–104.
174 *Ibid.*, p. 102.

debates on the formal placement of the instrument have served as the stage (if not as the very battlefield) for most of the scholarly debate on countermeasures. Not differently from what had happened in the field of the procedural requirements, the formalization developed with reference to countermeasures has been an omni-present point of reference in ascertaining the objectives of belligerent reprisals.

It will be recalled from Chapter 1 that, under the law of State responsibility sanctioned by the ARSIWA, the commission of an internationally wrongful act establishes a new legal relationship between the responsible and the injured State: the former is thus placed under an obligation to cease the internationally wrongful conduct, if it is continuing, and to make full reparation for the injury provoked. Within this framework, countermeasures may be adopted by the injured State only in order to induce compliance by the responsible State with the secondary obligations of cessation and reparation; consequently, they would not be justified when undertaken with a view to exacting punishment.

The system developed by the ILC differs considerably from previous formalizations of the consequences of international wrongful acts. In Kelsen's view, the breach of an international obligation engendered, as a '*unique* and *immediate* consequence',[175] the recourse to measures of self-help: the sanction was therefore seen as stemming directly from the breach.[176] Embracing Anzilotti's theory, another strand of the scholarship accepted that the only consequence of a wrongful act consists in 'the establishment of a new legal relationship between the State to which the relevant act is attributable (which has an obligation to repair) and the State towards whom the obligation that was not complied with was due (which can demand reparation)';[177] but even under a theory that stressed the distinction between the primary and the secondary obligation, authors like Ago maintained that self-help measures represent one of the *immediate* consequences of the wrongful act – one meeting the definition of sanction under international law and having a chiefly

[175] Benedetto Conforti, *Diritto Internazionale*, 7th ed. (Napoli: Editoriale Scientifica, 2006), p. 340 [translation by the author]; see also Kelsen, *Principles*, pp. 20–22.

[176] Conforti, *Diritto Internazionale*, p. 340.

[177] Dionisio Anzilotti, *Cours de droit international*, 3rd ed. (Paris: Librairie du Recueil Sirey, 1929), vol. I, p. 467. Importantly, in Anzilotti's view self-help measures lack any autonomous role under this construction: indeed, the function of punishing the wrongdoer that still characterized reprisals was attributed by Anzilotti to the reparation due under the new relationship. See Anzilotti, *ibid.*, p. 468; Anzilotti, *Teoria generale della responsabilità*, pp. 96 f., footnote 2.

punitive function.[178] The common denominator of all these different theories is that the faculty to adopt self-help measures *flows directly from the violation of the primary norm.*

In their final form, the ARSIWA brought about significant changes in the paradigm inherited from the jurisprudence. By conditioning the adoption of countermeasures on the responsible State's failure to comply with the secondary obligations of cessation and reparation, the ARSIWA completely *disconnected self-help measures from the primary norm.* The attribution to countermeasures of a purely coercive purpose emphasizes that self-help only operates as a function of the secondary obligations established by the wrongful act: their justification derives from non-compliance with the new set of legal relations established by the breach, no longer from the original unlawful behaviour. In equal terms, the rejection of the punitive purpose (which Ago still considered 'an undeniable character')[179] highlights that countermeasures cease to be an autonomous consequence of the breach: their link with the primary obligation, and therefore their role as immediate sanction of the primary rule, is irremediably severed.

This move has been criticized on the grounds that, under the construction upheld by the ILC, the obligation created by the secondary norm does not differ, in the last instance, from the obligation created by the primary norm breached; in this sense, the solution endorsed by the ARSIWA would unwisely complicate the mechanism of State

[178] In Ago's view, international law attaches two distinct consequences to a wrongful act: on one side, the obligation to provide (and the corresponding right to demand) reparation for the damage are established under customary law by the secondary norm (Roberto Ago, 'Le délit international', in (1939) 68 *Recueil des cours de l'Académie de droit international de La Haye, 1939-II*, p. 529); on the other, self-help measures 'bear all the features of a private penalty and represent under all respects the typical and well-defined form of the sanction' (*ibid.*, p. 529). In a two-step process, Ago first builds on Kelsen's theory by recognizing punitive features to the unilateral coercive action, and then combines these self-help mechanisms with Anzilotti's theory of a new juridical relationship arising from the unlawful act. Ago asked, but did not clearly answer the question whether the choice between the two consequences of the breach is left to the victim State, or if the repressive sanction can be applied 'only if it is manifestly impossible to obtain the reparation' (*ibid.*, p. 530 [translations by the author]).

[179] *Ibid.*, p. 527–28. The same author had warned against conceiving of self-help measures as simple coercive acts, as this would have detracted from their 'afflictive and punitive character' (*ibid.*). He forcefully claimed that 'it is wrong ... to consider [reprisals] as tools to coerce the responsible State into providing the reparation or the satisfaction that other means are not capable of bringing about' (*ibid.*) [translations by the author].

responsibility by duplicating without real necessity the obligations between the parties.[180] This criticism correctly identifies the core innovation brought about by the ARSIWA, but fails to understand its rationale and mistakenly qualifies it as a factor of weakness rather than strength. In reality, by linking the adoption of countermeasures exclusively to the secondary obligations, the primary norm is insulated from the risk that repeated non-compliance (whether unjustified or justified as a countermeasure) erodes its validity. It is true that, from a *material* point of view, things do not change significantly: even under this new construction, the adoption of the countermeasure might well entail an additional breach of the primary norm. But from a *formal* perspective, the change is substantial: countermeasures, and all the further breaches that might eventually follow, will be seen as affecting the new juridical relationship created by the secondary norm in the aftermath of the original breach. In other words, the risk of non-compliance is shifted from the obligation generated by the primary norm, to the obligations generated by the secondary norm.

It is now apparent that the criticism against an unnecessarily complicated formalization embraced by the ILC is largely misplaced. That formalization, as all other forms of *fictio iuris*, might well be 'a rather artificial way of representing reality'[181] – but for a precise reason. Shifting the theoretical base of countermeasures to the secondary obligations immunizes the primary norm from the risk that enforcement action be seen as delinquent behaviour. In a way, this strategy skilfully translates the old-fashioned idea of "sanction" in the language and *forma mentis* that characterize contemporary international law, which construes the wrongful act as generating a new legal relationship.

By refining their formalization in a decades-long process, international law has purged countermeasures of all those elements that could negatively affect the validity of the primary norm. Albeit governed by the logic of self-help, the resulting notion provides a model that clearly aims at upholding legal norms and strengthening international obligations in the face of wrongful acts that could challenge their standing. It is hardly a coincidence that such a formalization of the consequences of a breach has found fertile ground in the domain of the laws of armed conflict. Over the past few years, international as well as national tribunals have highlighted 'the

[180] Conforti, *Diritto Internazionale*, p. 341.
[181] *Ibid.*, p. 340.

fundamental nature'[182] of the 'intransgressible'[183] norms and principles that form that body of law; similarly, they have also understood the corresponding obligations as being 'absolute'[184] and of an *erga omnes* character[185] – if not the very 'translation into legal norms of the "categorical imperative" formulated by Kant in the field of morals'.[186]

In the ensuing effort to frame belligerent reprisals in line with this understanding of *ius in bello*, the concept of countermeasures has represented a natural point of reference in the identification of the purpose of belligerent reprisals. The manifold connections between the two notions had first revealed themselves in the similarity of the procedural requirements that governed their adoption, but the archetype embodied in countermeasures would also influence the purpose eventually attributed to belligerent reprisals. The following sections will outline how, in their most recent definition of the objectives pursued by belligerent reprisals, judges and scholars have come to embrace the enforcement paradigm.

2.4.3 *Belligerent Reprisals and the Purpose of Inducing Compliance*

2.4.3.1 The ICTY Decisions

The influence of the enforcement paradigm has been particularly pronounced in the case-law of the ICTY, whose wording and reasoning reveal a clear assimilation between belligerent reprisals and countermeasures. It will be remembered that the 1996 Decision pursuant to Article 61 in the *Martić* case represents the first pronouncement of that tribunal on the matter of belligerent reprisals: the notion was recalled and analysed by the Trial Chamber as a possible defence for the shelling of Zagreb, for which the defendant would face trial upon apprehension. To indicate the notion of belligerent reprisals, the tribunal used the expression 'circumstances which would exclude wrongfulness, in whole or in part'.[187] Instead of attempting to define belligerent reprisals on their own terms, the judges relied on a formula that was typically used in the framework of State responsibility to indicate, among other institutions,

[182] Constitutional Court of Colombia (Plenary Chamber), *Constitutional Case No. C-291/07*, Judgment, 25 April 2007, p. 61.

[183] Court of Bosnia and Herzegovina, *In re Lučić*, Judgment, 19 September 2007, p. 64.

[184] ICTY, *Kupreškić* TC, p. 202, para. 517.

[185] Constitutional Court of Colombia, *Constitutional Case No. C-291/07*, p. 61.

[186] ICTY, *Kupreškić* TC, pp. 202–3, para. 518.

[187] ICTY, *Martić* Rule 61, p. 6, para. 15.

countermeasures.[188] The Trial Chamber did not elaborate on the implications of such qualification of belligerent reprisals, as it was mainly concerned with the question whether belligerent reprisals against the civilian population or individual civilians were prohibited in all circumstances and conflicts.[189] Nonetheless, subsequent judgments kept to the course indicated by that seminal decision.

In its judgment in the *Kupreškić* case, the Trial Chamber contrasted the 'barbarous'[190] and somewhat anachronistic institution of belligerent reprisals with the 'more widely available and ... fairly efficacious' prosecution and punishment of war crimes and crimes against humanity.[191] In making that comparison, the judges explicitly construed belligerent reprisals as a 'means of compelling the enemy to abandon unlawful acts of warfare and to *comply in future with international law*'.[192] Even for the cases where the measure could be considered as still lawful, the tribunal demanded that it be adopted 'to impose compliance by the adversary with legal standards'.[193] Similar conclusions were reached a few years later by the Trial Chamber I in its judgment of first instance in the *Martić* case: the tribunal defined belligerent reprisals as 'drastic and exceptional measures employed by one belligerent for the *sole purpose of seeking compliance* with the law of armed conflict by the opposite party'.[194] In sum: by drawing an implicit connection with countermeasures, the ICTY was able to construe the purpose of belligerent reprisals as one of 'putting an end to the breach which provoked them'.[195] The objective of bringing about cessation of the unlawful act and, therefore, enforce future compliance with the laws of war was transferred from the field of countermeasure to that of belligerent reprisals.

2.4.3.2 The Scholarly Consensus on the Enforcement Paradigm

In the aftermath of World War II and the adoption of the 1949 GCs, only a handful of authors have adhered to the view grounding belligerent

[188] See ILC, 'Commentary to ARSIWA', Part One, Chapter V, p. 71.
[189] ICTY, *Martić* Rule 61, pp. 6–7, paras. 15–17.
[190] ICTY, *Kupreškić* TC, p. 208, para. 528.
[191] *Ibid.*, pp. 208–9, para. 530.
[192] *Ibid.* [emphasis added].
[193] *Ibid.*, p. 212, para. 535.
[194] ICTY, *Martić* TC, p. 167, para. 465 [emphasis added]. See also *ibid.*, para. 467: 'the reprisals must cease as soon as they have achieved their purpose of putting an end to the breach which provoked them'.
[195] *Ibid.*

reprisals in negative reciprocity. Stone, for instance, affirmed that '[t]he premise on which retaliation in war proceeds is, indeed, that a belligerent's duty to observe the laws of war is not absolute, but conditional on the enemy's reciprocation'.[196] Arguably, this limited strand has derived that conclusion more from a general appraisal of the foundational premises of the laws of war than from a specific analysis of the concept of belligerent reprisals – an approach that could well place the internal coherence of the notion under significant strain. By way of example, Schwarzenberger's theory of belligerent reprisals swings between the poles of enforcement and reciprocity without apparent difficulty: the measure aims at 'induc[ing] the enemy to comply with his duties under the laws of war,[197] but is said to operate by 'revers[ing] the operation of the chief working principles behind the laws of war from positive, to negative, reciprocity'.[198]

These few exceptions notwithstanding, the majority of the scholarship has not hesitated to place belligerent reprisals under the enforcement paradigm and attribute to them the purpose of inducing compliance with the laws of war. It is significant that, in one of the first articles analysing the war crimes trials, Albrecht worded the desired effect of belligerent reprisals in the very terms traditionally used with regard to countermeasures, that is, 'to provide restitution for the damage done by the enemy or to produce a change in his conduct or, preferably, both'.[199] Throughout the 1950s and 1960s, authoritative jurists such as Castrén,[200] Venezia,[201] and McDougal and Feliciano[202] maintained that the purpose of belligerent reprisals was to enforce respect for the laws of armed conflict, both by putting an end to existing

[196] Julius Stone, *Legal Controls of International Conflict: A Treatise on the Dynamics of Disputes- and War-Law* (New York: Rinehart, 1959), p. 354.

[197] Georg Schwarzenberger, *International Law as Applied by International Courts and Tribunals* (London: Steven and Sons, 1968), p. 453.

[198] *Ibid.*

[199] Albrecht, 'Reprisals in War Crimes Trials', p. 592. See also *ibid.*, p. 590 ('[w]ar reprisals may be defined as otherwise illegitimate acts of warfare which under certain conditions may legally be used by a belligerent against the enemy in order to deter the enemy from a repetition of his prior illegal acts and thus to *enforce compliance with the generally recognized rules of war*') and p. 591 ('[t]he function of the law of war reprisals is to provide a *sanction for the rules of war*') [emphasis added].

[200] Erik Castrén, *The Present Law of War and Neutrality* (Helsinki: Annales Academiae Scientiarum Fennicae, 1954), p. 69.

[201] Venezia, 'La notion de représailles', pp. 467–68. His definition was comprehensive enough as to cover a large variety of State behaviours, including both non-forcible and forcible reprisals (*ibid.*, p. 468) and belligerent reprisals (*ibid.*, pp. 484 ff.).

[202] McDougal and Feliciano, *Law and Minimum World Public Order*, p. 679.

violations and by deterring future infringements. The unequivocal rejection of the view whereby the notion would be based in negative reciprocity was stated by Greenspan, who defined belligerent reprisals as 'illegitimate acts of warfare, *not for the purpose of indicating abandonment of the laws of war*, but, on the contrary, *to force compliance to those laws*'.[203]

The theory of belligerent reprisals was greatly refined by the scholarly work of Kalshoven, who devoted to the topic the first comprehensive monograph in the early 1970s. By means of a thorough investigation of the notion, the eminent scholar was able to reach a more nuanced understanding of belligerent reprisals, which he skilfully systematized in a coherent and influent theory. From the outset, Kalshoven refused to conceive of belligerent reprisals as 'an interstate action merely serving to restore the disturbed synallagmatic relationship',[204] therefore detaching the notion from the sphere of negative reciprocity.[205] In his view, negative reciprocity is based in military necessity[206] and 'operates as an autonomous device';[207] belligerent reprisals, on the other hand, are characterized by 'the element of law enforcement',[208] which defines their purpose as one of 'coerc[ing] the addressee to change its policy and bring it into line with the requirements of international law, be it in respect to the past, the present or the future'.[209] As a species of public reprisals, belligerent reprisals are construed as 'sanctions of international law'[210] and characterized by the function of 'compel[ling] the offender to

[203] Morris Greenspan, *The Modern Law of Land Warfare* (Berkeley: University of California Press, 1959), p. 408 [emphasis added].

[204] Kalshoven, *Belligerent Reprisals*, p. 362.

[205] See on this *ibid.*, pp. 24–26.

[206] *Ibid.*, p. 33.

[207] *Ibid.*, p. 363.

[208] *Ibid.*, p. 362.

[209] *Ibid.*, p. 33. See also Kalshoven, 'Human Rights, the Law of Armed Conflict, and Reprisals', p. 208.

[210] Kalshoven, *Belligerent Reprisals*, p. 24. In concluding his analysis, Kalshoven wondered if belligerent reprisals could still function as sanctions of the laws of armed conflict, given that their field of application had been considerably restricted by the numerous prohibitions contained in humanitarian treaties (*ibid.*, pp. 375–76). In answering the question, the author considered States' reticence to invoke the notion as a justification in recent armed conflicts, as well as the development of weapons the use of which by way of reprisals could entail disastrous consequences for the civilian population and humanity in general (*ibid.*, p. 376). Based on these elements, he concluded that 'the idea of law enforcement has to give way to the sheer inhumanity inherent in such reprisals' (*ibid.*).

comply with the rules of warfare'.[211] Insightfully, Kalshoven noted that the abstract possibility of qualifying belligerent reprisals as sanctions of the laws of war does not detract from the fact that the measure will mostly operate as a form of 'self-help-*cum*-execution':[212] in other words, the decision-making process with regard to belligerent reprisals (i.e., which form to give them, but also whether to take them or not) will be ultimately influenced by a combination of public authority and private interest.[213] Even in acknowledging that enforcement of the law might not always be the *primary* objective, Kalshoven forcefully claimed that that purpose will necessarily be present and shape the decision to adopt belligerent reprisals.[214]

The attribution of an enforcement purpose to belligerent reprisals, as well as the distinction of the notion from the operation of negative reciprocity, became a point of little debate among the authors writing after Kalshoven (such as Meyrovitz,[215] Draper,[216] Nahlik,[217] Almond,[218] Bierzanek[219] and Hampson).[220] It was Greenwood, however, who built on Kalshoven's legacy and endeavoured to entrench the notion of belligerent reprisals in the enforcement paradigm by setting clear boundaries *vis-à-vis* negative reciprocity. The conceptual tenets of countermeasures acted as an important reference point in the formulation of Greenwood's definition of belligerent reprisals:[221] in his view, such measures can only be adopted 'for the purpose of putting an end to the enemy's unlawful conduct and preventing future illegalities and not for mere revenge'.[222] Like Kalshoven, Greenwood acknowledged that a State acting by way of reprisal will, with all likelihood, be guided by 'other motives in addition to those of securing a

211 *Ibid.*, p. 4.
212 *Ibid.*, p. 24.
213 *Ibid.*
214 *Ibid.*
215 Henri Meyrovitz, 'Review of *Belligerent Reprisals* by Frits Kalshoven' (1972) 66 AJIL, p. 648.
216 Gerald I. A. D. Draper, 'Implementation of International Law in Armed Conflict' (1972) 48 *International Affairs*, p. 49. See also Gerald I. A. D. Draper, 'Rules Governing the Conduct of Hostilities – The Laws of War and Their Enforcement' (1980) 62 *International Legal Studies Series of the US Naval War College*, p. 260.
217 Nahlik, 'Reprisals in Light of Diplomatic Conference', p. 37.
218 Almond, 'Reprisals: The Global Community', pp. 197–98.
219 Bierzanek, 'Reprisals in Armed Conflict', pp. 829 and 835.
220 Hampson, 'Reprisals and the 1977 Protocols', pp. 820 and 843.
221 Greenwood, 'Twilight of Reprisals', p. 38.
222 *Ibid.*, p. 40.

norm to legality':[223] yet, he did not consider this as problematic so long as the belligerent reprisal is taken with a view to bringing about cessation of the unlawful conduct and deterring its repetition in the future.[224] At the same time, Greenwood distinguished such ulterior motives from those instances where 'the need to respond and to prevent further violations becomes more than simply a matter of law enforcement, it may be essential to avoid defeat'.[225] In such cases, it is admitted that the notions of belligerent reprisals and negative reciprocity become necessarily entangled,[226] because the alleged violation of the laws of war not only disrupts the legal order, but also determines a significant military imbalance between the parties to the armed conflict. Greenwood resolves this deadlock by emphasizing the different extent to which the two notions affect the primary obligation,[227] and by depicting belligerent reprisals as 'a more limited form of response' governed by considerations of proportionality.[228]

2.5 The Enforcement Purpose of Belligerent Reprisals as Modern Dogma

In the past thirty years, the previous doctrinal consensus around the enforcement purpose of belligerent reprisals has solidified into a virtually unchallenged dogma. While former authors discussed at length the possibility and consequences of an overlapping between belligerent reprisals and negative reciprocity, contemporary contributions take almost for granted that the two institutions represent mutually exclusive mechanisms with diametrically opposed functions.[229] Cessation of the

223 *Ibid.*, p. 46.
224 *Ibid.*
225 *Ibid.*, p. 59.
226 *Ibid.*, p. 60.
227 *Ibid.*, p. 38: '[i]t is also necessary to distinguish belligerent reprisals from cases where a rule is so framed that its violation by one party to an armed conflict releases its adversary from its obligations'.
228 *Ibid.*, p. 61.
229 The only exception to this trend comes from the scholarship that focuses on negative reciprocity. The work by Watts is a notable example where the relationship between the two notions is discussed at length, but even in this case the author eventually sides with the majority of the scholarship (see Watts, 'Reciprocity and Law of War', pp. 384–86). For an understanding of belligerent reprisals (and of the laws of war in general) as a tool to resolve principal–agent problems, with a strong focus on the role of advance warning and authorization by the highest military echelons, see Eyal Benvenisti and Amichai Cohen, 'War Is Governance: Explaining the Logic of the Laws of War From a Principal-Agent Perspective' (2014) 112 *Michigan Law Review*, p. 1408.

wrongful conduct and future compliance with the laws of war are unanimously seen as the two defining objectives of recourse to belligerent reprisals.[230] On the basis of this, the ICRC could safely conclude in its *Customary IHL Study* that the purpose of belligerent reprisals consists in 'inducing the adversary to comply with the law'.[231]

The organization would further dispel any doubts about the nature of the institution as an enforcement measure in its updated *Commentaries* to the 1949 GCs. In the commentary to common Article 1, the ICRC has claimed that the wording 'in all circumstances' provides conclusive evidence for the non-reciprocal nature of the GCs.[232] Had belligerent reprisals been grounded in negative reciprocity, this interpretation of common Article 1 GCs would have logically prevented a belligerent from adopting such measures – but this conclusion would have been at odds with the view adopted in the *Customary IHL Study*, whereby as a matter of customary law certain belligerent reprisals could still be lawful.[233] To maintain the coherence with its previous work, the updated *Commentaries* immediately affirm that 'respect "in all circumstances" does not seem to imply, by itself, an absolute prohibition on reprisals beyond those prohibitions specifically provided for in the Conventions'.[234] In other words, the operation of belligerent reprisals is completely separated from negative reciprocity, and construed instead as an instance of enforcement of the laws of war. This is finally confirmed in the updated commentary to common Article 3 GCs, in which the ICRC makes clear that belligerent reprisals 'aim to put an end to the violation and to induce the adverse Party to comply with the law'.[235]

230 Kwakwa, 'Belligerent Reprisals', pp. 79–80; George H. Aldrich, 'Pour le respect du droit international humanitaire' (1991) 282 IRRC, p. 15; Steven Kuan-Tsyh Yu, 'The Development and Implementation of International Humanitarian Law' (1991–92) 11 *Chinese Taiwan Yearbook of International Law and Affairs*, p. 13; Darcy, 'Evolution of Reprisals', pp. 185 and 191; Philip Sutter, 'The Continuing Role for Belligerent Reprisals' (2008) 13 *Journal of Conflict and Security Law*, p. 94; Barsalou, 'The History of Reprisals', p. 337; Bílková, 'Reprisals in NIACs', p. 33.

231 Henckaerts and Doswald-Beck, *Customary IHL Study*, vol. I, p. 515.

232 ICRC, *Commentary on GC III*, 2nd ed., para. 221. For an earlier articulation of the position, see Pictet (ed.), *Commentary to the I Geneva Convention*, p. 25. On the formula 'in all circumstances' in AP I, see Sandoz, Swinarski and Zimmermann (eds.), *Commentary on the APs*, p. 37, para. 49.

233 Henckaerts and Doswald-Beck, *Customary IHL Study*, vol. I, p. 513, Rule 145: '[w]here not prohibited by international law'.

234 ICRC, *Commentary on GC III*, 2nd ed., para. 222. The ICRC noted, however, that the opposite conclusion had been reached by the ICTY: *ibid.*

235 *Ibid.*, para. 943.

In conclusion, a century-long trajectory has finally led to the formalization of belligerent reprisals as a legal concept firmly established in the enforcement framework. The development of a highly ritualized procedure for the adoption of such measures has led to their assimilation with the notion of countermeasures; as a result, it has been possible to construe belligerent reprisals as a sanction of the laws of war, and to identify the objective of enforcing compliance as their main purpose. At the same time, this process has progressively deprived the notion of belligerent reprisals of all the elements traditionally associated with the paradigm of negative reciprocity. In choosing which paradigm to apply to the notion of belligerent reprisals, international law has opted for the one that fulfilled the interest in the re-affirmation of the legal order, and sacrificed the one protecting formal equality and parity of arms of belligerents.

3

The Resilience of the Reciprocity Paradigm

3.1 Persistence and Influence of the Reciprocity-Based Paradigm

Chapter 2 has shown to what extent international tribunals, the authoritative interpretation of the ICRC, and the majority of the scholarship support the application to belligerent reprisals of the enforcement paradigm. At the same time, a deeper scrutiny in the national practice of States reveals that also the paradigm grounded in reciprocity continues to determine the purpose and function of belligerent reprisals – often in a decisive way. This subtle but steady influence, which challenges the predominant formalization of belligerent reprisals as an enforcement tool, manifests itself in several ways, to which we shall now turn. In this chapter, we will see it at play in different forms of *verbal* acts of States[1] – such as States' positions while negotiating international treaties or reacting to their adoption, the provisions of military manuals, and the pronouncements of national jurisdictions. In the next one, we will turn to *physical* acts of States:[2] by focusing on a specific armed conflict, we will appreciate the importance of the reciprocity framework in influencing the actual recourse to belligerent reprisals on the battlefield. All these instances of practice are particularly relevant because they relate to States that have long maintained their right to adopt belligerent reprisals, or that had to adjudicate on conducts labelled as retaliatory, or finally that resorted to such measures during armed conflict. In this sense, they could be characterized as emanating from specially affected States,[3] and be

[1] Henckaerts and Doswald-Beck, *Customary IHL Study*, vol. I, p. xxxviii; ILC, *Draft Conclusions on Identification of Customary International Law, with Commentaries*, in (2018) II(2) ILC Ybk, commentary to Conclusion 6, para. 2 (see however *ibid.*, Conclusion 10, para. 2 and related commentary at paras. 5–6, whereby such verbal expressions are treated as forms of evidence of acceptance as law (*opinio juris*)).

[2] Henckaerts and Doswald-Beck, *Customary IHL Study*, vol. I, p. xxxviii; ILC, *Identification of Customary International Law*, Conclusion 6, para. 2 and related commentary at para. 5.

[3] On this notion, see *ibid.*, Conclusion 6, para. 2; for a more nuanced approach, see Henckaerts and Doswald-Beck, *Customary IHL Study*, vol. I, pp. xliv–xlv.

given particular weight in the ascertainment of the features of belligerent reprisals and, most notably, of their purpose and function.

3.2 The Debates within the 1974–1977 Geneva Diplomatic Conference

3.2.1 Draft Provisions on Belligerent Reprisals

The Diplomatic Conference on the Reaffirmation and Development of International Humanitarian Law Applicable in Armed Conflicts (hereinafter, CDDH)[4] was convened in Geneva from 1974 to 1977, and led to the adoption of the First and Second Additional Protocols to the 1949 Geneva Conventions.[5] On that occasion, numerous States had the opportunity to elaborate on the set of objectives that they attached to the notion of belligerent reprisals. More specifically, these discussions focused on three provisions of draft AP I, and took place in two tranches.

The first cluster of statements was expressed with regard to draft Article 46 AP I, whose paragraph 4 prohibited attacks against the civilian population or civilians by way of reprisals.[6] The provision was adopted 'with almost no discussion'[7] by Main Committee III, but was later criticized by the French delegation during the Plenary Meetings of the CDDH,[8] and only adopted after a roll-call vote.[9] The vote explanations expressed in that context contain a wide array of statements about the purpose and characteristics associated with belligerent reprisals. An even franker debate occurred with reference to the second group of draft provisions. In front of Main Committee I, the Polish and the French

[4] Swiss Federal Political Department, *Official Records of the Diplomatic Conference on the Reaffirmation and Development of International Humanitarian Law Applicable in Armed Conflicts – Geneva (1974–1977)* (Bern: 1978) (hereinafter, *CDDH Official Records*).

[5] Protocol Additional to the Geneva Conventions of 12 August 1949, and relating to the Protection of Victims of International Armed Conflicts (Protocol I), Geneva, 8 June 1977, in force 7 December 1978, 1125 UNTS 3; Protocol Additional to the Geneva Conventions of 12 August 1949, and relating to the Protection of Victims of Non-International Armed Conflicts (Protocol II), Geneva, 8 June 1977, in force 7 December 1978, 1125 UNTS 609.

[6] *CDDH Official Records*, vol. I, Part Three, p. 16. In line with the precedent represented by the 1949 GCs, draft Protocol I contained no less than five articles prohibiting specific instances of belligerent reprisals: that is, draft Articles 20, 46, 48, 49, 66.

[7] Nahlik, 'Reprisals in Light of Diplomatic Conference', p. 48.

[8] CDDH/SR.41, 26 May 1977, in *CDDH Official Records*, vol. VI, pp. 161–62, paras. 110–16.

[9] *Ibid.*, p. 163: the article was adopted by seventy-seven votes in favour, sixteen abstentions and France against (*ibid.*).

delegations submitted two 'mutually exclusive'[10] amendments to draft AP I, each of them directed at complementing the specific prohibitions against belligerent reprisals with a general clause.[11] On the one hand, proposed new Article 70 *bis* AP I, submitted by Poland, prohibited belligerent reprisals against persons and objects protected by the Geneva Conventions and Additional Protocol I.[12] On the other hand, proposed new Article 74 *bis* AP I, suggested by France, entitled a party to an armed conflict that was victimized by serious, manifest and deliberate breaches of the Protocol to resort to reprisal measures, subject to a very detailed list of procedural and substantive requirements.[13] Eventually, both draft provisions were withdrawn in a spirit of compromise[14] and replaced by what would become Article 89 of the final text of AP I;[15] nevertheless, the debates that they aroused in front of Main Committee I, its Working Group B, and again Main Committee I explored at length the question as to the purpose of belligerent reprisals. By combining the discussions around Articles 46, 70 *bis* and 74 *bis* of draft AP I, it is possible to obtain a fairly comprehensive picture of how States conceived of belligerent reprisals at a fundamental stage in the development of IHL.[16]

During the debate on the French amendment, a first challenge to the enforcement paradigm came from a few delegations questioning that belligerent reprisals could ever aspire to invite compliance with the laws of war. Mr. Rechetniak (speaking on behalf of the Soviet Socialist Republic of Ukraine) claimed that, even if the purported purpose of belligerent reprisals was 'to oblige the party committing the breach to respect the law [,] in fact it would merely introduce the law of

[10] Nahlik, 'Reprisals in Light of Diplomatic Conference', p. 51.

[11] *Ibid.* See also Section 2.2.2.2.

[12] CDDH/III/103, 1 October 1974, in *CDDH Official Records*, vol. III, p. 313.

[13] CDDH/I/221/Rev. 1, 22 April 1976, in *CDDH Official Records*, vol. III, p. 324. The draft provision has been quoted in its entirety in Section 2.2.2.2, footnote 23.

[14] CDDH/I/SR.72, 13 May 1977, in *CDDH Official Records*, vol. IX, pp. 417–18, paras. 3–4 and 11.

[15] Article 89 AP I reads as follows: 'In situations of serious violations of the Conventions or of this Protocol, the High Contracting Parties undertake to act, jointly or individually, in co-operation with the United Nations and in conformity with the United Nations Charter.'

[16] For a comprehensive analysis, see also Nahlik, 'Reprisals in Light of Diplomatic Conference', *passim*; Bierzanek, 'Reprisals in Armed Conflict', *passim*; Darcy, 'Evolution of Reprisals', *passim*.

retaliation'.[17] On his part, Mgr. Luoni (from the Holy See) affirmed that 'respect for humanitarian law could not be assured by authorizing its violation, even in exceptional cases'.[18] Here, criticism of the enforcement paradigm mirrored a wide opposition to introducing a regulation of belligerent reprisals in the text of AP I.[19] At the same time, the placement of these measures within the enforcement paradigm was explicitly upheld by several delegations. Rebutting the Ukrainian argument, Mr. Partsch (of the Federal Republic of Germany) noted how the French amendment actually rejected the *lex talionis*;[20] similarly, in commending the proposed new Article 74 *bis*, the Swiss delegate, Mr. Bindschedler, referred to belligerent reprisals as 'measures of deterrence'.[21] Both the Spanish and the Dutch delegation defined belligerent reprisals as measures of last resort to induce cessation of the wrongful conduct and ensure respect for the law.[22] Finally, the delegation of Cameroon considered that the regulation of belligerent reprisals in the French proposal would have 'a deterrent aspect that would have made it more likely, [i]f not certain, to be effective'.[23]

3.2.2 The Tension between Enforcement and Negative Reciprocity in Statements by States

A second, stronger challenge to the enforcement paradigm came from a group of other States that, while looking with favour at the French amendment, manifested a different understanding of the objective and function of belligerent reprisals. Their statements still attached to the measure the purpose of obtaining compliance; at the same time, they also mentioned considerations that clearly pertain to the sphere of negative

[17] CDDH/I/SR.46, 28 April 1976, in *CDDH Official Records*, vol. IX, p. 62, para. 38.

[18] CDDH/I/SR.48, 30 April 1976, in *CDDH Official Records*, vol. IX, p. 91, para. 36. See also *ibid.*, para. 34, whereby it is 'incumbent on the international community to seek other legal and morally acceptable means of ensuring respect for humanitarian law', different from belligerent reprisals.

[19] See Nahlik, 'Reprisals in Light of Diplomatic Conference', p. 54.

[20] CDDH/I/SR.48, 30 April 1976, in *CDDH Official Records*, vol. IX, p. 84, para. 4.

[21] CDDH/I/SR.46, 28 April 1976, in *CDDH Official Records*, vol. IX, p. 65, para. 51.

[22] The Spanish delegate used the expression 'a last resort for putting an end to grave breaches and ensuring that observance of international law' (CDDH/I/SR.48, 30 April 1976, in *CDDH Official Records*, vol. IX, pp. 85–86, para. 10). The Dutch delegation, on its part, opted for the wording 'a measure of last resort by which to induce an enemy to respect the law' (*ibid.*, p. 86, para. 14).

[23] Annex to CDDH/I/SR.73, 16 May 1977, in *CDDH Official Records*, vol. IX, p. 454.

reciprocity. This is a particularly important tension in the definition of the measure, since it came from the very States that were more willing to uphold the right of a Party victimized by a serious, manifest and deliberate breach of the Protocol to react by way of reprisal.

Commenting on the French proposal of new Article 74 *bis*, Mr. Breucker (from the Belgian delegation) commenced by expressing his delegation's support for 'all measures designed to ensure respect for law'.[24] He noted that violations of the laws of war have often been committed on the field of battle in order to *gain an additional military advantage*;[25] in these cases, setting up instruments such as commissions of inquiries would have required considerable time – a delay which would have '*weighed heavily in the balance of the fortunes of war*'.[26] In the view of the Belgian delegation, the French proposal had the merit of addressing this fundamental concern: the recognition of a limited right to react by way of belligerent reprisals would clearly dissuade an enemy belligerent from violating the laws of war, but it would also help establish 'a legitimate right of self-defence in the last resort, in the face of a ruthless act of violence'.[27] Analogous considerations were expressed by the Afghan delegation, during the discussions in the plenary meetings on draft Article 46(4). While agreeing fully with the substance of the provision, Mr. Naoroz recorded his delegation's reservations 'when the consideration of the preservation of civilian lives and objects conflicted with the demands of a nation's legitimate defence'.[28]

A similar dialectic between enforcement and reciprocity appears in the statements expressed by the delegation of the United Kingdom. The first perspective is evident in all the different references that Mr. Draper made to the purpose of belligerent reprisals: the French proposal was seen as a serious 'attempt to make [international humanitarian] law a living reality rather than a series of hopeful aspirations that had no effect in binding the parties at war'.[29] The delegate explicitly referred to the measures envisaged by the French proposal as 'counter-measures',[30] and emphasized the parallelism with that notion by stating that their purpose would be neither punishment nor retaliation, but 'to repress breaches and

[24] CDDH/I/SR.46, 28 April 1976, in *CDDH Official Records*, vol. IX, p. 65, para. 53.
[25] *Ibid.*
[26] *Ibid.* [emphasis added].
[27] *Ibid.*, p. 66, para. 54.
[28] CDDH/SR.41, 26 May 1977, in *CDDH Official Records*, vol. VI, p. 165, para. 126.
[29] CDDH/I/SR.47, 29 April 1976, in *CDDH Official Records*, vol. IX, p. 73, para. 33.
[30] *Ibid.*, para. 34.

induce compliance with the Protocol'.[31] Notwithstanding the strong emphasis put on the enforcement purpose of belligerent reprisals, at the roots of the British intervention stood the deeply held conviction that the behaviour of parties to an armed conflict is determined by considerations of reciprocity. The delegation expressed support for the French proposal '[i]n view of the nature of the exchange of armed force in conflict'[32] – or, in the even clearer terms of the French version, '[é]tant donné la *nature de l'action réciproque* des forces armées en cas de conflit'.[33] Moreover, the preoccupation with maintaining the equality of opportunities is implicit in the fundamental objective that the British delegation attached to the mechanism, that is, 'to restrain the type of excesses that were familiar to all'.[34]

Similarly to the British delegation, Canada expressed different understandings about the purpose of belligerent reprisals. On one hand, its delegation construed the measure as 'the only action open to the victim of a breach ... aimed at the termination of the wrongdoing',[35] and 'designed to repress the breaches and to induce compliance with the Protocol'.[36] In discussing the prospect of an enemy bombing civilian population centres, the Canadian representative predicted however that 'no Government would stand idly when the only way of stopping the bombing was to do the same to the other side'.[37] The French version of the statement, which reads '*rendre la pareille* à l'adversaire',[38] conveys clearly the interest in parity of arms that underlies recourse to belligerent reprisals in those cases. This is all the more so if one considers that the delegate was not necessarily suggesting strictly symmetrical retaliation, but a more limited entitlement to strike at civilian objects in exchange for attacks on civilians or the civilian population.[39]

[31] *Ibid.* See also *ibid.*, p. 74, para. 38, whereby belligerent reprisals are seen as 'a method of recalling the parties to a conflict to observance of humanitarian law'.

[32] *Ibid.*, p. 73, para. 37.

[33] CDDH/I/SR.47, 29 April 1976, in Swiss Federal Political Department, *Actes de la Conférence Diplomatique sur la réaffirmation et le développement du Droit international humanitaire applicable dans les conflits armés* (Bern: 1978), p. 80, para. 37 [emphasis added] (hereinafter, *Actes de la CDDH*).

[34] CDDH/I/SR.47, 29 April 1976, in *CDDH Official Records*, vol. IX, p. 73, para. 37.

[35] Annex to CDDH/I/SR.73, 16 May 1977, in *CDDH Official Records*, vol. IX, pp. 436–37.

[36] CDDH/I/SR.46, 28 April 1976, in *CDDH Official Records*, vol. IX, p. 64, para. 47.

[37] CDDH/III/SR.7, 18 March 1974, in *CDDH Official Records*, vol. XIV, p. 55, para. 38.

[38] CDDH/III/SR.7, 18 March 1974, in *Actes de la CDDH*, vol. XIV, p. 61, para. 38 [emphasis added].

[39] CDDH/III/SR.7, 18 March 1974, in *CDDH Official Records*, vol. XIV, p. 55, para. 38.

The most evident tensions within the construction of belligerent reprisals are manifested in the various statements by the French delegation. Throughout their speeches, the French delegates took care to place belligerent reprisals within the enforcement paradigm: they stressed that the very threat of the measure would dissuade the enemy from committing or continuing violations, and oblige it to respect the laws of war.[40] They again subscribed to that framework by saying that the proposed new Article 74 *bis* would avoid the escalation of breaches,[41] and by qualifying the measure as a form of sanction for grave violations of humanitarian law.[42] At the same time, the French position was undeniably premised on the need to ensure equality of opportunities between belligerents and grounded in considerations pertaining to negative reciprocity. Already in criticizing draft Article 46(4), the French representative affirmed that prohibiting reprisals on the civilian population would 'seriously hamper the conduct of defensive military operations against an invader and prejudice the exercise of the inherent right of legitimate defence recognized in Article 51 of the Charter of the United Nations'.[43] This position was manifested with even more strength during the debates on the new Article 74 *bis*, which France itself had submitted. Its delegations remarked that, during a period of armed conflict, a breach of the laws of war 'could cause a *serious and perhaps decisive upset in the balance of forces*'.[44] The need to provide for a limited right to retaliate against enemy violations of the laws of war stemmed, in the French view, from the injustice of 'plac[ing] the combatant who respected the law *in a position of inferiority* to the combatant who violated it'.[45] Therefore, remedying the imbalance created by the violation is explicitly qualified as the function of

[40] See CDDH/I/SR.46, 28 April 1976, in *CDDH Official Records*, vol. IX, p. 59, para. 24 and p. 60, paras. 26–27. See also CDDH/I/SR.48, 30 April 1976, in *CDDH Official Records*, vol. IX, pp. 93–94, para. 49.

[41] CDDH/I/SR.46, 28 April 1976, in *CDDH Official Records*, vol. IX, p. 59, para. 24.

[42] CDDH/I/SR.73, 16 May 1977, in *CDDH Official Records*, vol. IX, p. 443.

[43] CDDH/SR.41, 26 May 1977, in *CDDH Official Records*, vol. VI, p. 162, para. 111. See also *ibid.*, para. 114: 'the French delegation considered that Article 46 [. . .] was likely seriously to impair the inherent right of legitimate defence'.

[44] CDDH/I/SR.46, 28 April 1976, in *CDDH Official Records*, vol. IX, p. 58, para. 19 [emphasis added]. It was on this basis that the French delegation claimed the insufficiency of the enforcement mechanism premised on penal sanctions, which only intervenes 'after the event', and not 'at the time when the rule was broken' as it would be required (*ibid.*).

[45] *Ibid.*, p. 58, para. 22 [emphasis added].

belligerent reprisals.[46] The co-existence of the competing paradigms of enforcement and negative reciprocity is ideally captured by a late statement of the French delegation: while commenting on the withdrawal of the proposed new Article 74 *bis*, its delegate remarked that belligerent reprisals constituted 'the only measures which a Government can take to *put a stop* to such violations and *safeguard the very survival of the nation* in the exceptional circumstances that may arise'.[47]

3.3 Declarations and Reservations to AP I

The same ambiguity that characterized the position of various States *vis-à-vis* the purpose and function of belligerent reprisals during the CDDH also influenced their attitude toward the final text of AP I. Upon ratification or accession to that treaty, five States formulated declarations or reservations with regard to certain provisions contained in Part IV, Section I of the Protocol (dedicated to the general protection of the civilian population against the effects of hostilities). As seen above,[48] these articles included some of the most important and innovative prohibitions against belligerent reprisals to be found in AP I, and some of those reserving statements were explicitly directed at interpreting or modifying the scope of a party's obligations with regard to those measures. If carefully considered, those declarations and reservations will reveal the same patterns identified with regard to the Diplomatic Conference. On one hand, some States fully embraced the enforcement paradigm in their understanding of belligerent reprisals. Upon their respective ratifications, Italy[49] and the Federal Republic of Germany[50]

[46] CDDH/I/SR.48, 30 April 1976, in *CDDH Official Records*, vol. IX, p. 94, para. 50: '[i]t was easy enough, no doubt, to uphold humanitarian ideals with high-sounding phrases, but the French delegation could not agree that humanitarian law should result in protecting those who violated it *at the expense of* those who respected it' [emphasis added].

[47] CDDH/I/SR.73, 16 May 1977, in *CDDH Official Records*, vol. IX, p. 443 [emphasis added].

[48] See Section 1.2.1.1.

[49] Italy, *Declaration made at the time of ratification of AP I*, 27 February 1986: 'Italy will react to serious and systematic violations by an enemy of the obligations imposed by Additional Protocol I and in particular its Articles 51 and 52 with all means admissible under international law in order to prevent any further violation' (available at https://ihl-databases.icrc.org/applic/ihl/ihl.nsf/Notification.xsp?action=openDocument&documentId=E2F248CE54CF09B5C1256402003FB443).

[50] Germany, *Declaration made at the time of ratification of the 1977 APs*, 14 February 1991, para. 6: 'The Federal Republic of Germany will react against serious and systematic violations of the obligations imposed by Additional Protocol I and in particular its

appended very similar declarations, whereby they would react against serious and systematic violations of the obligations imposed by AP I, and in particular its Articles 51 and 52, 'with all means admissible under international law in order to prevent any further violation'.[51] The common reference to prevention of future breaches unmistakably places these declarations under the enforcement paradigm.[52]

3.3.1 *The Egyptian Declaration and the British Reservation*

The reserving statements formulated by other States were not equally clear, as they oscillated constantly in their understanding of the measure between the poles of enforcement and negative reciprocity. Upon ratification of AP I and II on 9 October 1992, Egypt appended the following declaration:

> *The Arab Republic of Egypt, while declaring its commitment to respecting all the provisions of Additional Protocol I and II, wishes to emphasize,* on the basis of reciprocity, *that it upholds the right to react against any violation by any party of the obligations imposed by Additional Protocols I and II with all means admissible under international law* in order to prevent any further violation.[53]

While the final words clearly attach an enforcement purpose to belligerent reprisals in their mirroring the Italian and German emphasis on deterrence, the reference to reciprocity in the earlier part of the declaration seems to re-locate the basis of the measure in the opposite

Articles 51 and 52 with all means admissible under international law in order to prevent any further violation' (available at https://ihl-databases.icrc.org/applic/ihl/ihl.nsf/Notification.xsp?action=openDocument&documentId=3F4D8706B6B7EA40C1256402003FB3C7).

[51] *Ibid.*

[52] A different question is the uncertainty as to the actual measures that will be open to the victim willing to react by way of reprisal. The formula 'with all means admissible under international law' features a high degree of ambiguity, but it has been interpreted as indicating that 'those States view customary international law as permitting the use of reprisals against those targets which Protocol I seeks to protect' (Darcy, 'Evolution of Reprisals', pp. 226–27). Pointing in that direction, see Italian Chiefs of Defence Staff, *Manuale di Diritto umanitario*, SMD-G-014, 1991, vol. I, paras. 25–26; but seeming to offer a contrary view, German *Law of Armed Conflict Manual*, para. 490. See also Haque, 'Renouncing Reprisals'.

[53] Egypt, *Declaration upon ratification of the 1977 APs*, 9 October 1992 (available at https://ihl-databases.icrc.org/applic/ihl/ihl.nsf/Notification.xsp?action=openDocument&documentId=AF3791A0FF167FFDC1256402003FB393) [emphasis added].

paradigm. It would be hard to interpret that reference as indicating that negative reciprocity would operate as an autonomous device, leading to the termination or suspension of the treaty: the non-reciprocal nature of the obligations established by the 1949 GCs and the 1977 APs, long recognized in the practice and scholarship,[54] would militate against that conclusion. By mentioning it, Egypt could only signify that negative reciprocity represented the mechanism governing the functioning of belligerent reprisals. Therefore, the basis and the purpose of belligerent reprisals are referred to two different paradigms.

A similar conclusion must be reached with regard to the reservation appended by the United Kingdom upon ratification of AP I, on 28 January 1998.[55] For the case an adverse party launched serious and deliberate attacks on civilian individuals and objects protected under Articles 51–55 AP I, the United Kingdom reserved for itself the right to 'take measures otherwise prohibited by the Articles in question to the extent that it considers such measures necessary *for the sole purpose of compelling the adverse party to cease committing violations* under those Articles'.[56] The objective of inducing cessation of an unlawful behaviour

[54] See discussion in Sections 1.4.1.3(2)(a) and 2.5.

[55] United Kingdom, *Reservation (m) regarding Articles 51–55 AP I*, 28 January 1998:

> The obligations of Articles 51 and 55 are accepted on the basis that any adverse party against which the United Kingdom might be engaged will itself scrupulously observe those obligations. If an adverse party makes serious and deliberate attacks, in violation of Article 51 or Article 52 against the civilian population or civilians or against civilian objects, or, in violation of Articles 53, 54 and 55, on objects or items protected by those Articles, the United Kingdom will regard itself as entitled to take measures otherwise prohibited by the Articles in question to the extent that it considers such measures necessary for the sole purpose of compelling the adverse party to cease committing violations under those Articles, but only after formal warning to the adverse party requiring cessation of the violations has been disregarded and then only after a decision taken at the highest level of government. Any measures thus taken by the United Kingdom will not be disproportionate to the violations giving rise thereto and will not involve any action prohibited by the Geneva Conventions of 1949 nor will such measures be continued after the violations have ceased. The United Kingdom will notify the Protecting Powers of any such formal warning given to an adverse party, and if that warning has been disregarded, of any measures taken as a result.

(available at https://ihl-databases.icrc.org/applic/ihl/ihl.nsf/Notification.xsp?action=openDocument&documentId=0A9E03F0F2EE757CC1256402003FB6D2).

[56] *Ibid.* [emphasis added].

is not the only piece of evidence of the qualification of belligerent reprisals as an enforcement mechanism; also the requirements to which adoption of the measure is subject (i.e., formal warning, authorization at the level of government, proportionality and termination) reflect the "proceduralization" of belligerent reprisals and their assimilation with the notion of countermeasures outlined above.[57] These elements notwithstanding, the reservation is opened by an introductory formula that is strongly reminiscent of negative reciprocity: '[t]he obligations of Articles 51 and 55 are accepted *on the basis that* any adverse party against which the United Kingdom might be engaged will itself *scrupulously observe those obligations*'.[58] Just as in the case of Egypt, a reservation that would interpret the relationships under AP I as being of a strictly synallagmatic character would likely be incompatible with the object and purpose of the treaty. As a consequence, here as well the notion of reciprocity is mentioned to underlie recourse to belligerent reprisals – a conclusion which is also in line with the position occupied by the reference to reciprocity at the very beginning of the reservation on these measures.

3.3.2 *The French Declaration*

In the declaration made by France upon accession to AP I on 11 April 2001, the tension between the paradigms of enforcement and reciprocity is less patent, but still present. The statement reads as follows:

> The Government of the French Republic declares that it will apply the provisions of Article 51, paragraph 8, in such a way that the interpretation of those will not be an obstacle to the employment, in conformity with international law, of those means which it estimates are indispensable for protecting its civilian population from serious, manifest and deliberate violations of the Geneva Conventions and this Protocol by the enemy.[59]

[57] See Chapter 2.

[58] UK, *Reservation (m) regarding Articles 51–55 AP I* [emphasis added].

[59] France, *Reservation upon accession to AP I*, 11 April 2001, para. 11 [English translation in Darcy, 'Evolution of Reprisals', p. 226]. The French original reads as follows: 'Le gouvernement de la République Française déclare qu'il appliquera les dispositions du paragraphe 8 de l'article 51 dans la mesure ou l'interprétation de celles-ci ne fait pas obstacle à l'emploi, conformément au droit international, des moyens qu'il estimerait indispensables pour protéger sa population civile de violations graves, manifestes et délibérées des conventions de Genève et du Protocole par l'ennemi' (available at https://ihl-databases.icrc.org/applic/ihl/ihl.nsf/Notification.xsp?action=openDocument&documentId=D8041036B40EBC44C1256A34004897B2).

The text of the French declaration refers to the application of Article 51, *paragraph 8*. This provision states that '[a]ny violation of these prohibitions shall not release the Parties to the conflict from their legal obligations with respect to the civilian population and civilians, including the obligation to take the precautionary measures provided for in Article 57'.[60] As the ICRC *Commentary* to AP I noted on the basis of the *travaux préparatoires*, the provision constitutes 'an attempt to safeguard the population even when the appropriate authorities do not take the required measures of protection with regard to them'[61] (for instance, by using them as human shields or putting them in harm's way).[62] By enforcing the protection of enemy civilians even in the presence of a party to the conflict that disregards its obligations, Article 51(8) AP I provides for an explicit rejection of negative reciprocity. With respect to this article, the French declaration intervened with a scope and with effects that need clarification.

With regard to its scope, even if the declaration does not give a precise qualification to the 'means' mentioned therein, three elements suggest that it is concerned with the institution of belligerent reprisals as understood under the enforcement paradigm. First, the documents in the *travaux préparatoires* recalled in the previous paragraphs clearly demonstrate that France was envisaging belligerent reprisals when carving a space for retaliation in AP I;[63] the declaration would thus represent the back-up option for the French government in light of its failure to have a regulation of belligerent reprisals agreed upon in the treaty. Second, in the widely held belief that the victim party would be precluded from seeking release from the obligations under the Protocol on the basis of negative reciprocity, the formula 'in conformity with international law' would only make sense with regard to belligerent reprisals. Third, the fact that recourse to these means is restricted to what is indispensable for the protection of the civilian population introduces a quantitative limitation that recalls the requirement of proportionality of belligerent reprisals under the assimilation with countermeasures.

[60] Article 51(8) AP I reads as follows: '[a]ny violation of these prohibitions shall not release the Parties to the conflict from their legal obligations with respect to the civilian population and civilians, including the obligation to take the precautionary measures provided for in Article 57'.

[61] Sandoz, Swinarski and Zimmermann (eds.), *Commentary on the APs*, p. 628, para. 1990.

[62] See Article 51(7) AP I.

[63] See Section 3.2.

If all these elements seem to place the notion of belligerent reprisals under the enforcement paradigm, the way in which the measures would actually operate under the French declaration seems, once more, to mirror the functioning of negative reciprocity. According to the declaration, recourse to belligerent reprisals will potentially *affect the scope of application* of Article 51(8) AP I.[64] By so doing, the belligerent reprisal ceases to operate as a circumstance precluding wrongfulness, and starts to control to what extent and in which way a norm determines *in concreto* the obligations between the parties. This renders the qualification of belligerent reprisals as enforcement measures less straightforward, insofar as the measure becomes a tool to re-balance the system of legal relationships between belligerents. This is also confirmed by the fact that the parameter guiding the recourse to belligerent reprisals is no longer represented by the enforcement of a norm, but by the actual protection of the civilian population of the victim State. Overall, the peculiar conceptualization of belligerent reprisals under the French declaration re-instates within the functioning of Article 51(8) AP I the elements of negative reciprocity that the provision purported to eliminate.

3.4 Military Manuals and the Case-Law

3.4.1 Ambiguity in the Applicable Framework as Reflected in the Practice of the United States

A few instances of State practice from the United States will demonstrate to what extent the discussions on belligerent reprisals during the drafting of AP I still influence today's formalization of the mechanism. After the United States signed both the 1977 APs at the close of the Diplomatic Conference, and as late as the early 1980s, 'the submission of Protocol I to the Senate for advice and consent to ratification seemed merely a matter of time';[65] yet, the question whether certain rights of reprisal action should be reserved was one of the few contentious issues debated within the US government.[66] Therefore, it is little surprising that the

[64] In this regard, the distinction in the French declaration between the application and the interpretation of Article 51(8) AP I might be valid from a formal point of view, but very tenuous in practice. If the objective is to remove obstacles to the adoption of a belligerent reprisal, interpretation will most of the times equal complete disapplication of the norm.

[65] George H. Aldrich, 'Prospects for United States Ratification of Additional Protocol I to the 1949 Geneva Conventions' (1991) 85 AJIL, p. 2.

[66] *Ibid.*

innovative prohibitions on belligerent reprisals in Articles 51–56 AP I represented one of the reasons that ultimately led US President Reagan to decide not to ratify the instrument.[67] On that occasion, the US Department of State referred to belligerent reprisals as 'an important sanction against violations of those [*scil.*, the 1949 Geneva] Conventions' that had been eliminated by AP I.[68] This view aligned with the stance taken during the Diplomatic Conference by the US delegation, which had supported the French proposal.[69]

Even though belligerent reprisals were straightforwardly qualified by the Department of State as sanctions of the laws of war in the document that lamented their prohibition, the military manuals adopted in those same years by the United States featured fundamental uncertainties with regard to the conceptual tenets of the notion. As recently as 1976, the US Department of the Air Force had stressed in its *Air Force Pamphlet* that belligerent reprisals could only be taken 'for the purpose of compelling the adversary to observe the law of armed conflict'.[70] The same document, however, explicitly pointed to negative reciprocity as the basis for belligerent reprisals.[71] In looking at the requirements for the adoption of such measures, even the 1997 *Annotated Supplement to the Naval Handbook* (prepared by the US Naval War College) displayed a similar concern for the equality of opportunities protected by negative reciprocity. It is true that the document demanded that a careful inquiry into the alleged illegality be carried out by the injured belligerent, before belligerent reprisals could be authorized.[72] However, the injured belligerent could dispense with the procedure and adopt immediate belligerent reprisals, if 'the safety of his armed forces would clearly be endangered by a continuance of the enemy's illegal acts'.[73] The central concern underlying the exception is not the abstract enforcement of the breached norm,

[67] US Department of State, *Report Annexed to Message from the President of the United States*, 100th Congress, 1st Session, Treaty doc. 100-2 (Washington, DC: US Government Printing Office, 1987).

[68] *Ibid.*

[69] CDDH/I/SR.48, 30 April 1976, in *CDDH Official Records*, vol. IX, p. 94, para. 54.

[70] US Department of the Air Force, *Air Force Pamphlet 110-31*, para. 10-7(c)(2). See also *ibid.*: '[belligerent reprisals] are directed against an adversary in order to induce him to refrain from further violations of the law of armed conflict'.

[71] *Ibid.*, para. 10-1(b).

[72] US Naval War College, Oceans Law and Policy Department, Centre for Naval Warfare Studies, *Annotated Supplement to the Commander's Handbook on the Law of Naval Operations*, November 1997, para. 6.2.3.1, footnote 38.

[73] *Ibid.*

but the victim's entitlement to pursue the military effort without being unduly harmed by the unlawful conduct of hostilities on the part of the enemy. As had been the case with various statements made during the CDDH, the position of inferiority to which a compliant belligerent would be relegated by the enemy breach brings the concept and regulation of belligerent reprisals closer and closer to the paradigm of negative reciprocity.

Ambiguity as to the framework to which belligerent reprisals are subject also vitiates the provisions devoted to these measures by the recent US Department of Defense *Law of War Manual*. The Manual emphasizes on different occasions that belligerent reprisals are coercive measures that seek to enforce the laws of war by persuading the enemy to cease violations at present and in the future.[74] However, the inclusion of belligerent reprisals within the enforcement paradigm is challenged in the part of the Manual dedicated to the function of reciprocity in the laws of war regime. In this regard, the *Law of War Manual* affirms that 'the principle of reciprocity is reflected in the concept of reprisals'.[75] The connection of the two mechanisms is also witnessed by the different definition of belligerent reprisals adopted in that section: the measure is here seen as a means of '*remedy[ing]* an enemy's breach of the law'[76] – a wording that hints at the logic of re-balancing the legal relationship between belligerents that is typical of reciprocity.[77] The Manual pushes the link between belligerent reprisals and negative reciprocity to the point of suggesting that prohibitions of the former in humanitarian treaties 'may be understood to reflect important limitations on the principle of reciprocity' in the operation of modern *ius in bello*.[78] The tension

[74] See US DoD, *Law of War Manual*, paras. 18.18 ('[r]eprisals are extreme measures of coercion used to help enforce the law of war by seeking to persuade an adversary to cease violations'), 18.18.1 ('Definition of Reprisal. Reprisals are acts taken against a party: (1) that would otherwise be unlawful; (2) in order to persuade that party to cease violating the law'), and 18.18.1.3 ('[r]eprisals are intended to influence a party to cease committing violations at present and in the future. Reprisals are not revenge or collective punishment').

[75] *Ibid.*, para. 3.6.2.

[76] *Ibid.* [emphasis added].

[77] The relationship between the various mechanisms (enforcement, reciprocity, belligerent reprisals) becomes extremely hard to disentangle here: paradoxically, the *Law of War Manual* considers that, in structuring the notion of belligerent reprisals, the principle of reciprocity operates 'in the enforcement of the law of war' (title of para. 3.6.2)!

[78] *Ibid.*

between enforcement and reciprocity in structuring belligerent reprisals, evident in the debates at the CDDH, continues to trouble the modern reflection on the notion.

3.4.2 *The Italian Case-Law on World War II Atrocities*

Some recent judgments by Italian courts in relation to atrocities committed during World War II offer an important litmus test to assess the resilience of the reciprocity paradigm. Germany had occupied the northern and central portions of the Italian peninsula in the last phases of the war, following the armistice of 8 September 1943;[79] in the following months, thousands of civilians were killed as a result of operations that were justified by the military authorities as reprisals but which ultimately aimed at hindering civilian support for the *Partigiani* (i.e., Resistance) forces.[80] In the immediate aftermath of the conflict, only a handful of German members of the Wehrmacht and the Schutzstaffel (S.S.) were tried by Allied and Italian tribunals for their role in the mass killings[81] – but in 1994, Italian military courts inaugurated a second wave of proceedings that continues to this day. Belligerent reprisals have thus been the object of several judgments, rendered at a considerable distance in time and, more importantly, in very different stages of the legal formalization of the notion. As a consequence, the latest Italian case-law is an ideal setting to understand if (and to what extent) the grounding of belligerent reprisals in negative reciprocity has left room for an interpretation based on enforcement.

[79] Military Tribunal of Rome, *In re Kappler*, Judgment, 20 July 1948, Case No. 631, under 'Facts', p. 2 [on file with, and following translations by, the author]; Military Court of Appeals of Rome, *In re Albers et al.*, Judgment No. 25/08, 7 May 2008, Case No. 1/2008 R.G., section 8(4), p. 97; Supreme Court of Cassation, *Germany* v. *Milde*, Judgment, 13 January 2009, Case No. 1072/2009, 92 Riv Dir Int 618, ILDC 1224 (IT 2009), under 'Motives', para. 3; Military Tribunal of Verona, *In re Winkler et al.*, Judgment No. 43/2011, 6 July 2011, Case Nos. 172/08 and 80/09, pp. 418–19.

[80] Military Tribunal of La Spezia, *In re Sommer et al.*, Judgment, 22 June 2005, Case No. 45/2005, paras. 8(2)-(3).

[81] For detailed information on the first wave of proceedings, as well as the reasons of the following oblivion, see Paolo Pezzino, 'Crimini fascisti e crimini tedeschi nell'Italia occupata: la difficile strada della giustizia di transizione (1945–2015)', Presentation at Fondazione per la Formazione Forense dell'Ordine degli Avvocati di Firenze, 10 April 2017 (available at www.fondazioneforensefirenze.it/eventi_view.aspx?cat=7&id=1515).

3.4.2.1 *In re Kappler*

The unavoidable touchstone for all the recent cases on belligerent reprisals is represented by the trial on the Cave Ardeatine massacre that took place soon after the end of the conflict. Defendants in that case included six S.S. officers serving at the Rome *Außenkommando* of the security police (SiPo) and security service (S.D.) (including Herbert Kappler, former head of the Gestapo in Rome) for their role in the killing of 335 individuals (for the biggest part Italian citizens, both military and civilians, who were not participating in military operations). The executions were carried out at a quarry near Rome on 24 March 1944, in reaction to a bomb attack by a group of Italian *Partigiani* that had killed thirty-three German policemen in Via Rasella the day before. The Military Tribunal of Rome concluded that 320 individuals were executed pursuant to a superior order by General Maeltzer (military commander of the city), ten on the initiative of Lt. Kappler, and the remaining five out of mistake.[82] Even though it found that the executions could not be justified either as belligerent reprisal or as collective punishment,[83] the court was not conclusively convinced that the defendants were aware and willing to implement an unlawful order.[84] As a consequence, the court held Kappler responsible only for the killing of the last two groups of victims and acquitted the other five defendants on the grounds that they were acting under superior orders.[85]

Beyond the merits of the case, this first judgment on the Cave Ardeatine massacre is notable for the formalization of belligerent reprisals that it advances. Certain elements in the decision point to an understanding of reprisals as an enforcement mechanism, such as their stated objectives of bringing about the cessation of an unlawful activity and avoiding repetition of a harmful act, or the requirement that the reprisal be proportional to, but not necessarily of the same nature as, the original unlawful act.[86] The general notation that reprisals can be adopted both in time of peace and in time of war suggests that the notion was assimilated with countermeasures, and that the judges were placing the notion in the framework of State responsibility.[87]

[82] Military Tribunal of Rome, *In re Kappler*, under 'Law', p. 18.
[83] *Ibid.*, pp. 18–20 and 22–23.
[84] *Ibid.*, pp. 22 and 24.
[85] *Ibid.*, pp. 22–24.
[86] *Ibid.*, p. 17.
[87] *Ibid.*

At the same time, the tribunal refrains from submitting a precise formalization of belligerent reprisals. Stating that the principle of proportionality applies to reprisals 'no matter how they are formalized in any given theory of law',[88] the tribunal concedes that they can be construed as 'a means of self-help, of sanction or of self-defence'.[89] In a judgment characterized by a broad understanding of the notion of reprisals, the reference to self-defence can still be explained as an allusion to measures of redress short of war in the sphere of *ius ad bellum*, while the idea of sanction would reaffirm a formalization under the enforcement paradigm. If this is the case, the additional reference to self-help (in the first place of the list, no less) conveys the impression that reprisals are chiefly interested in the safeguard of the juridical position of the belligerents and in the maintenance of the balance of rights and obligations – in other words, that they are grounded in reciprocity.

The possibility of formalizing the mechanism outside of the enforcement paradigm emerges even more starkly when one considers the element on which the very idea of belligerent reprisals is premised. In the opinion of the tribunal, the paramount criterion distinguishing reprisals from other forms of reaction to a wrong (e.g., collective punishment) lies in the imputability of the original illegality to a State. Only when a wrongful act can be attributed (directly or indirectly) to the activity of a State, the victim is entitled, as of right, to adopt a reprisal.[90] According to Provost, requiring imputability of the original violation to the State targeted by way of reprisal is a strong signal 'indicat[ing] the reciprocal nature of the obligations of both states under humanitarian law'.[91] In other words: if only the State that is responsible for the initial breach can be the addressee of a reprisal, this implies that the measure is justified by the infringement of the contractual synallagma and is

[88] *Ibid.*, p. 18.

[89] *Ibid.*

[90] *Ibid.*, p. 16. In the present case, the tribunal concluded that, in principle, Germany was entitled to resort to reprisal action (*ibid.*, p. 18). On the one hand, it concluded that 'the attack in Via Rasella, whatever its concrete features, is an unlawful act of warfare insofar as it has been carried out by individuals belonging to a volunteer corp that, by March 1944, did not fulfil any of the conditions' set forth in Article 1 of the 1907 Hague Convention; on the other hand, those individuals 'belonged to a military organization that formed part of the *Giunta Militare* (Military Junta) ... which acted as a lawful organ, at least de facto, of the Italian State' (*ibid.*, p. 16).

[91] Provost, *International Human Rights and Humanitarian Law*, p. 190.

directed at restoring the balance of rights and obligations.[92] By stressing that the very rationale of the reprisal lies in the international responsibility of the target State, the judgment downplays the coercive function of the measure and identifies its legal basis ('*fondamento*' in the Italian original)[93] in the disruption of the legal relationship caused by the original breach.

Such grounding of belligerent reprisals in the reciprocity paradigm was confirmed in the appeals judgment rendered by the Supreme Military Tribunal in 1952. Even though the judges ruled out imputability to the Italian State for the bomb attack in Via Rasella,[94] the Tribunal followed in the formalization of belligerent reprisals suggested by the court of first instance in two respects. By dropping the categories of sanction and self-defence, and by choosing to qualify the measure as a 'right of self-help' ('*potestà di autotutela*'),[95] it explicitly used the definition that was most reminiscent of negative reciprocity.[96] It then held that reprisals are 'premised on the failure by the enemy belligerent to comply with an obligation flowing from international law [which] must be the effect of an action or omission attributable to the State'.[97] In so doing, the

[92] *Ibid.*, pp. 185–86. Writing in 2002, Provost argues that such a strict requirement of imputability finds scarce support in State practice (*ibid.*, pp. 190–91); preferring a test based on 'the solidarity between the target and the group whose policy is sought to be changed', the author concludes that the function of belligerent reprisals is that of 'a lever to force a return to compliance with humanitarian law' (*ibid.*, p. 192). However, his treatise actually preceded most of the judgments rendered by Italian tribunals on World War II atrocities. As we shall see, the latest case-law still demands attribution of the original wrong to the target State and, in so doing, signals the persistence of the reciprocity paradigm.

[93] Military Tribunal of Rome, *In re Kappler*, p. 17.

[94] Supreme Military Tribunal, *In re Kappler*, Judgment, 25 October 1952, Case No. 1714, section B.3, p. 69 [translations by the author]. The Tribunal relied on the fact that the authors of the bomb attack did not belong to the Italian army, and excluded that external help by the Italian State to the activity of the *Partigiani* in occupied territory sufficed to qualify them as State organs (*ibid.*). After the Supreme Military Tribunal rejected the appeal by Kappler, the Supreme Court of Cassation declared his subsequent recourse inadmissible (as quoted *ibid.*, p. 91): see Supreme Court of Cassation, *In re Kappler*, Judgment, 19 December 1953, Case No. 26.

[95] Supreme Military Tribunal, *In re Kappler*, section B.3, p. 69.

[96] Interestingly, the judgment made reference to reactions that (in the quoted words of Rolin) could be adopted in extreme occurrences and could therefore be assimilated with a sort of self-defence – but it limited such justified behaviours to the actions that could have been taken at the very moment of the original attack, and immediately distinguished them from those situations that justify the following adoption of a reprisal: *ibid.*, pp. 68–69.

[97] *Ibid.*

Tribunal reiterated once more how the requirement of imputability establishes an intimate connection between belligerent reprisals, on one side, and the bundle of rights and obligations, on the other.

3.4.2.2 *In re Hass and Priebke*

The two early pronouncements in the proceedings against Kappler represented an important precedent when, nearly fifty years later, Italian tribunals re-focused their attention on World War II atrocities in the peninsula. Picking up the thread that had long been abandoned, the trial signalling the opening of this second wave of war crimes proceedings related, once more, to the Cave Ardeatine massacre. Before the Military Tribunal of Rome stood accused Erich Priebke, an S.S. captain with a key role in the preparation of the onslaught, and Karl Hass, an S.S. major who participated in the executions.[98] In its judgment, the Tribunal considered belligerent reprisals as a possible 'just cause' ('giustificato motivo') that must be absent for the conditions of the ascribed crime of violence with continued mass murder to be met.[99] The judges concluded that the massacre did not constitute a lawful reprisal because it did not satisfy the requirements of proportionality and necessity,[100] held the two defendants accountable for the killing of all the 335 individuals, and condemned them to several years of imprisonment.[101]

In reaching this verdict, the Tribunal made some important notations that confirm an ambiguous position regarding the formalization of belligerent reprisals. At the outset, the court defines such measures as a type of sanction, insofar as 'the unlawfulness of the act prompting the reaction ... determines the lawfulness of the sanctioning action'.[102] As we have seen, characterizing retaliation as a tool to re-affirm the breached rule is in line with an understanding of reprisals as an enforcement mechanism. At the same time, the judges hint unmistakably at the reciprocity paradigm when they quote the definition of belligerent reprisals from the Italian *Law of War* promulgated with Royal Decree

[98] Military Tribunal of Rome, *In re Hass and Priebke*, Judgment, 22 July 1997, p. 1 and section 3, p. 8.

[99] *Ibid.*, section 7, p. 19 [this and following translations by the author].

[100] *Ibid.*, section 4, pp. 9–10. With regard to the latter, the Tribunal noted that a reprisal is lawful only when all possible investigations to identify and apprehend the authors of an unlawful act prove unsuccessful: *ibid.*

[101] *Ibid.*, section 7, pp. 19–20; p. 36.

[102] *Ibid.*, section 4, p. 9.

No. 1415 of 1938, whereby the measure *suspends* the observance of obligations flowing from international law.[103]

This ambivalence is confirmed when the judgment identifies 'the twofold function of reprisals', seen as means of enforcing compliance or obtaining compensation, but also of punishing the wrongdoing.[104] This formulation seems to re-call the theories on the purpose of countermeasures discussed by authors such as Anzilotti and Ago,[105] signalling perhaps a belief in the assimilation of reprisals with that mechanism. And yet, various factors would militate once more in the opposite direction. We have seen above that the rejection of the punitive purpose is one of the main tenets in the most recent interpretation of countermeasures;[106] therefore, any admission of an afflictive function would automatically rule out a full identification of reprisals under the enforcement paradigm. Moreover, in the wording of the judgment the punitive purpose brings about an 'injury to the juridical sphere' of the target State.[107] It will be re-called that countermeasures affect the factual interests of the responsible State, without impinging on the substance and extent of the underlying legal relationship. Conversely, reprisals are seen here as having a bearing primarily on the web of rights and obligations connecting the belligerents, in a way that is more akin to the functioning of reciprocity.

These considerations reveal that the notion of sanction must not be taken here in its strong meaning, which would interpret belligerent reprisals as a re-affirmation of the violated norm and exclude from the notion all aspects of reciprocity. It should rather be understood in a more limited sense – as 'a reaction to a suffered breach'[108] that does not curtail *a priori* the breadth of the possible purposes associated with a reprisal. By re-introducing the notion of punitive sanction, this judgment admits the idea of a reprisal that flows directly from the primary norm; in so

103 *Ibid.* The reference is to Article 8(1) of the *Legge di Guerra*, promulgated with Regio Decreto No. 1415, 8 July 1938-XVI, 'Approvazione dei testi della legge di guerra e della legge di neutralità', in (1938) 211 *Supplemento ordinario alla Gazzetta Ufficiale*, Allegato A, p. 3 (for the full text of the law, see Section 3.4.2.4, footnote 141).

104 Military Tribunal of Rome, *In re Hass and Priebke*, section 4, p. 9. Interestingly (and somewhat tautologically), the Tribunal considers that the distinction between the two functions is purely . . . functional: *ibid.*

105 See Sections 1.5.1 and 2.4.2.

106 See Section 1.5.2.3(2).

107 Military Tribunal of Rome, *In re Hass and Priebke*, section 4, p. 9.

108 *Ibid.*

doing, however, it also forfeits the most important consequence of deriving retaliatory action from the violation of the secondary norm – that is, the protection of the primary norm and its continuing validity even in the face of retaliatory non-compliance. In conclusion, this formalization re-surrects those components of reciprocity that had been discarded since belligerent reprisals began their long trajectory of assimilation with countermeasures.

This "de-coupling" from the paradigmatic example of the enforcement paradigm is so profound that it also affects the very mechanism by which that assimilation had taken place – that is, the "proceduralization" of belligerent reprisals. It is hardly a coincidence that the judgment does not include prior warning among the requirements for a lawful reprisal – quite the contrary, it explicitly admits that the victim State react to a breach 'immediately or at any rate expeditiously' ('tempestivamente' in the Italian original).[109] Here, the urgency of remedying an injury of the rights, and even of the interests of a State outweighs the benefits of considering retaliation as a last resort (including post-poning recourse to reprisals, signalling their meaning, and potentially avoiding their adoption). This is a further, extremely revealing proof that, in the opinion of the Tribunal, belligerent reprisals operate as tools to safeguard the equilibrium in the legal relationship, more than as means to enforce compliance with the law.

Against this backdrop, it could seem surprising that the Tribunal departs significantly from the *Kappler* precedents with regard to the question of imputability. The present judgment considers any analysis concerning the legality of the bomb attack carried out by the *Partigiani* not only beyond the scope of the charges, but also potentially misleading.[110] This implies that, once the 'just cause' for the killings is ruled out because of the disproportionate and unnecessary nature of the reprisal, the judges refrain from deciding whether the original attack was imputable to the Italian State. Attribution of the original attack to the Italian State had been the premise upon which the judgments *in re Kappler* of 1948 and 1952 had developed their theory of reprisals – if this foundational requirement is removed from the analysis, should we then conclude that those other aspects of reprisals that the judgment associates with reciprocity would not stand any longer?

[109] *Ibid.*
[110] *Ibid.*, section 4, p. 10.

Various elements militate against this conclusion. First, the decision not to address the legal qualification of the attack by the *Partigiani* can be explained by rationales that are hardly connected with the formalization of reprisals. The judges had already been able to determine the lack of the substantive and procedural requirements that must accompany the adoption of a reprisal. Probably, delving further and assessing if the very conditions for recourse to such measure existed not only appeared unnecessary, but would have required the Tribunal to judge on issues (the legality of the attack by the *Partigiani*) with highly political implications. If, on the other hand, the reprisal had appeared legitimate under all other respects, an inquiry into the responsibility of the target State could not have been avoided: the Tribunal itself holds that reprisals are directed against 'any rights or juridical interests of a State *that is responsible of an international offense*'.[111]

Second, the appeals decision in this case by the Military Court of Appeals of Rome shows that, far from being removed, the imputability requirement takes on additional functions.[112] At the outset, this judgment reiterates that the action in Via Rasella would not be assessed either from the legal or from the political and military viewpoint.[113] And yet, as soon as the issue of reprisals is addressed, the judges quote at length those passages in the 1952 *Kappler* opinion that exclude attribution of the Via Rasella attack to the Italian State.[114] The Court re-affirms that the authors of the attack were not State organs and that the responsibility of the Italian State was not engaged either by its action (external help to the Resistance movement) or its omission (failure to take measures against voluntary corps in its territory that do not fulfil the conditions for lawful belligerency).[115] But it also goes one step further by saying that, absent such imputability, 'the civilian population of the Italian State could under no circumstance be considered a legitimate target of the alleged reprisal'.[116]

[111] *Ibid.*, section 4, p. 9 [emphasis added].
[112] Military Court of Appeals of Rome, *In re Hass and Priebke*, Judgment, 7 March 1998. Having excluded the mitigating circumstances that had been recognized by the Military Tribunal (including that of superior orders), the Military Court of Appeals sentenced both defendants to life imprisonment: *ibid.*, p. 75. This sentence was confirmed a few months later by the Supreme Court of Cassation, *In re Hass and Priebke*, Judgment, 16 November 1998, p. 18.
[113] Military Court of Appeals of Rome, *In re Hass and Priebke*, section 3.3.2, p. 51.
[114] *Ibid.*
[115] *Ibid.*
[116] *Ibid.*

Here, the imputability requirement further re-inforces the link between reciprocity and belligerent reprisals. In the *Kappler* case-law analysed above, imputability to a State had the purpose of distinguishing reprisals from other forms of reaction to a wrong (e.g., collective punishment)[117] – but it was not explained which State could be the addressee of a reprisal. Now, the appeals judgment in *Hass and Priebke* clarifies that there must exist an identity between the responsible and the target State. Not only does imputability operate upwards, by attributing an internationally wrongful act to the responsible State and justifying a reprisal (as opposed to other reactions) by the victim thereof – it also runs downwards, by determining which subjects with a meaningful legal relationship with the responsible State can be the addressee of the measure. It is only the juridical sphere of the responsible State that can be affected by the reprisal, whereas it is immaterial if the measure would be more effective should it be directed at other targets that do not bear responsibility for the original wrong. As a result, the synallagmatic character of the reprisal is reinforced at the expenses of its sanctioning features.

As a final notation, a passage of the appeals judgment in *Hass and Priebke* could be rich in implications for the formalization of reprisals. The Court considers that the proportionality of a reprisal should be measured against the original wrongful act; it also explains that, if the alternative criterion based on the dissuasive effect of the measure were adopted, there would be potentially no limits to a reprisal directed at the civilian population in occupied territory.[118] Normally, the purpose of preventing the repetition of unlawful acts is associated with the enforcement scenario. The fact that it is explicitly rejected in a judgment highlighting the reciprocal features of reprisals should then come as no surprise, but it also raises a fundamental question: Would it not be possible to read proportionality also in a formalization of reprisals that is based on the reciprocity paradigm?

A tempting answer would be in the negative, based on the common understanding that the mechanisms based on reciprocity bring about a cessation of the *vinculum iuris* and therefore release the victim from any obligation to subject their reaction to a proportionality test. And yet, already in the 1948 *Kappler* judgment the Military Tribunal of Rome had held that 'the proportionality principle characterizes the content of a

[117] See Section 3.4.2.1.

[118] Military Court of Appeals of Rome, *In re Hass and Priebke*, section 3.3.2, p. 51.

reprisal, *no matter how the mechanism is formalized in legal theory*'.[119] Now, the *Hass and Priebke* case-law links reprisals with suspension in the observance of legal obligations. Compared to termination, the latter notion is equally based on reciprocity, but does not rule out the possibility of resuming the legal obligations and restraining the scope of the retaliation. Seen from this perspective, the formalization of belligerent reprisals under the framework of reciprocity is not *ipso facto* incompatible with the ideas of limit and proportionality; consequently, requiring proportionality in the adoption of the measure does not necessarily mean an interpretation of reprisals as an enforcement mechanism. A dialogue between judgments nearly fifty years apart reveals unexpected osmosis in the interpretation of key tenets that are traditionally associated with one or the other paradigm structuring belligerent reprisals.

3.4.2.3 *In re Saevecke* and *In re Engel*

If the judgments in *Hass and Priebke* picked up the threads of an early reflection on belligerent reprisals by Italian tribunals, the following two pronouncements stand out for their originality. In the first case, Theodor Emil Saevecke, an S.S. captain who had been in charge of SiPo and S.D. in Lumbardy, was tried for the 1944 shooting of fifteen Italians detained in the San Vittore prison in Milan.[120] The executions had been ordered as a reprisal against a series of bomb attacks carried out by a *Partigiani* group called Patriotic Action Group (G.A.P.) in and around Milan between 21 July and 10 August 1944, one of which resulted in the explosion of a German truck and the death of several Italian civilians.[121] Having excluded that the reprisal killings could be justified, the Military Tribunal of Turin held Saevecke responsible and condemned him to life imprisonment.[122] The material facts of this case bear many similarities with the Cave Ardeatine massacre, which was at the centre of both the *Kappler* and the *Hass and Priebke* cases. But even if the *Saevecke* judgment borrows several features of belligerent reprisals from those precedents,[123] it also gives them new and unexpected shades of meaning.

[119] Military Tribunal of Rome, *In re Kappler*, p. 18 [emphasis added].

[120] Military Tribunal of Turin, *In re Saevecke*, Judgment, 9 June 1999, Cases No. 1619/96 R.N.R. and 0409/97 R.G.U.D., p. 14 [on file with, and translations by, the author].

[121] *Ibid.*, pp. 2–3 and 5–6.

[122] *Ibid.*, p. 14.

[123] For instance, both the definition of and the requirements for belligerent reprisals (listed *ibid.*, p. 8: prior harm to a State right or interest; proportionality with the damage suffered; respect for elementary considerations of humanity) are almost identical to

At the outset, the ruling seems to move away from an interpretation of belligerent reprisals based on reciprocity. The imputability requirement, which played such a prominent part in the earlier case-law, is affirmed at best implicitly, that is, inasmuch as it is posited that both the actor and the victim of reprisal must be a State.[124] For the rest, the judgment only stresses that the G.A.P. was not internationally recognized, without even broaching the question of possible grounds for attribution of its conducts to the Italian State.[125] Moreover, it is reaffirmed that the requirement of proportionality must be measured against the damage suffered, but the latter notion is interpreted very narrowly: even if the evidence indicates that the Germans intended to retaliate against a string of attacks by the *Partigiani*, the Tribunal only measures the reprisal against the latest attack in Viale Abruzzi.[126]

And yet, other elements in the judgment reveal how deeply belligerent reprisals are grounded in reciprocity. Interestingly, the ruling adopts a very limited understanding of what type of harm can justify a reprisal. Germany is not considered injured either from a qualitative viewpoint (because the victims only comprised Italian civilians) or from a quantitative one (because its own assets had suffered only minor damage).[127] By choosing this standard, the Tribunal makes the important determination that a violation of *ius in bello* is not sufficient to justify recourse to reprisals where it does not result in some material loss. Put differently, the harm justifying a reprisal cannot consist only in the abstract violation of a norm, as it also needs to negatively affect the victim State. This necessarily implies that the purpose of reprisals lies not so much in the re-affirmation of the legal order through an enforcement perspective, as in the safeguard and maintenance of the equilibrium between the rights and obligations of the parties to the conflict.

This concern with the concrete consequences of a breach for the victim resonates loudly in the judgment. For instance, by distinguishing between harm to German assets and to the Italian population, the Tribunal de-couples the interest of the occupying belligerent to protect the security of its armed forces from its responsibility to ensure public order and

those listed in the judgment of first instance in Military Tribunal of Rome, *In re Hass and Priebke*, section 4, p. 9.

124 Military Tribunal of Turin, *In re Saevecke*, p. 8.

125 *Ibid.*

126 *Ibid.*, pp. 5–6 and 9.

127 *Ibid.*, pp. 8–9.

safety in the occupied territory. Reprisals are considered justified only when unlawful conducts jeopardize the military interest of the belligerent, but not when they hinder the performance of its duties towards the civilian population. Similarly, the judgment conflates the familiar requirement of necessity (whereby a reprisal is lawful only if all possible investigations to identify and apprehend the authors of the unlawful attack have failed) with the notion of 'military necessity' (arising from the 'grave difficulties' encountered by the German occupying forces in the period under scrutiny).[128] In all these instances, the primary purpose of belligerent reprisals is that of balancing the undue advantage obtained by means of unlawful means and methods of warfare.

For all this emphasis on military expediency, a comparison of the ruling in *Saevecke* with the appeals judgment in *Hass and Priebke* shows that the attribution to reprisals of features inspired by reciprocity (as opposed to enforcement) can practically limit the risk of inaugurating an endless cycle of violence. As we have seen, in *Hass and Priebke* the Court had resorted to a particular interpretation of the proportionality requirement to avoid the potentially boundless implications of a dissuasive purpose. Here, a similar objective is achieved by re-calibrating the substantiative conditions for reprisals: by raising the threshold of the notion of harm, the *Saevecke* judgment only allows belligerent reprisals when the violence that they unleash (and the ensuing damage) remedies a damage from a material (not only a legal and symbolic) viewpoint.

Similar dynamics can be seen at play in the following judgment, rendered just a few months later by the same Military Tribunal of Turin in the trial against Siegfried Engel. As officer in command of the *Aussenkommando* of Genoa, the defendant in this case was accused for his role in four events occurred between April 1944 and March 1945, including the so-called Benedicta massacre. In that instance, German troops had executed several dozens of surrendering *Partigiani* and young deserters from the Italian Social Republic after a six-day attack against their base.[129] The Tribunal describes the occurrence as 'the first, great

[128] *Ibid.*, p. 9.

[129] Military Tribunal of Turin, *In re Engel*, Judgment, 15 November 1999, Case Nos. 2046/96 R.N.R. and 0111/99 R.G.U.D., section 2(A), p. 4 and section 3, p. 6. The other incidents were the Turchino slaughter (fifty-nine hostages were shot after five German soldiers were killed and fifteen wounded by a bomb attack organized by the G.A.P. in a cinema in Genoa), the Portofino massacre (twenty-two Italian citizens were shot and their bodies jettisoned for unknown reasons), and the Crevasco killings (twenty Italian citizens executed after an ambush by the G.A.P. resulted in the death of eight German

intimidating operation ... to safeguard the lines of communication between the Ligurian Riviera and the Po Valley',[130] and is ready to acknowledge that the first requirement for a lawful recourse to reprisals (i.e., injury to a right or interest of the State) 'can be considered satisfied' for the Benedicta massacre.[131] However, the judgment turns away from a construction where preventive self-help would allow reprisals even in the face of merely potential breaches of the laws of war. True, the Tribunal relies on the disproportionate number of individuals killed after the round-up to rule out the legality of the executions – but the decisive element in its analysis is the complete absence up to that point of any criminal attack by the *Partigiani* of that zone. The hypothetical risks flowing from the establishment of a Resistance camp, the abstract possibility that it becomes a source of sabotage and attacks, is contrasted with the bare fact that no actual harm had yet arisen from it.[132]

Admittedly, the *Engel* judgment is far from a model of judicial clarity. The conditions for the adoption of a belligerent reprisal are treated indistinctly; moreover, it is doubtful whether the recurrence of some requirements is granted only *ex hypothesi*, with the legality of reprisals being discarded on other grounds. However, if looked through the analytical lenses offered by the precedents in *Hass and Priebke* and *Saevecke*, the ruling confirms the centrality of actual damage for a remedy to make sense and, therefore, for a reprisal to be justified. Whether it is called intimidation or enforcement, a purely forward-looking rationale that is not equally grounded in substantial injury fails to provide a valid reason for reprisal action. Conversely, judges juggle with the requirements of reprisals, sometimes separately (as in *Hass and Priebke* or *Saevecke*), sometimes in a combined way (as in *Engel*), but always with a similar objective in mind. By stressing that the core of the measure lies not only (and not so much) in the violation of the legal order and its re-affirmation, as in the disruption of the legal relationship between belligerents and its re-establishment, they aim to link reprisals with the notion of harm and reciprocity, as opposed to that of breach and enforcement.

soldiers): *ibid.*, sections 2(B)-(D), pp. 4–5. The Tribunal held that none of them met one or the other requirement for a lawful reprisal and could be justified on those grounds: see *ibid.*, section 3, p. 10.

130 *Ibid*, section 2(A), p. 4 [this and following translations by the author].

131 *Ibid.*, section 3, p. 9. The abstract definition of, and requirements for, belligerent reprisals in this judgment follow closely the precedent in *Saevecke.*

132 *Ibid.*, section 3, p. 10.

3.4.2.4 *In re Sommer et al.*

The following judgment in this overview of the Italian case-law contains a most detailed analysis of belligerent reprisals. Under many respects, the decision in *Sommer et al.* signals the beginning of a new, mature phase in the reflection on the notion, with its passages being often quoted even in the latest pronouncements concerning World War II atrocities. The case concerns the operation carried out in August 1944 by the 16. S.S. Panzergrenadier Division "Reichsführer-S.S." in Sant'Anna di Stazzema: on that occasion, between 457 and 560 individuals who were not participating in military operations – mostly elderly, women and children – were rounded up and executed.[133] The ten defendants were all officers and petty officers accused of having determined and, in one case, even participated in the killings.[134]

In this judgment, the legal analysis of belligerent reprisals benefits from a careful appraisal of the historical background and tactical significance of the military operation. Noting that the events of Sant'Anna represented 'the first mass killing of civilians carried out in Italy on a large scale and with the cruellest means',[135] the judgment goes to great lengths to re-construct the succession of orders by the German authorities to govern their fight against the *Partigiani*.[136] What is more, the Tribunal approaches the critical question concerning the rationale behind the massacre. The judges rule out several reasons that had been submitted over time, including the wounding of a German soldier, the willingness to avenge the killing of members of the Italian Social Republic by a member of the Resistance, and failure to comply with the order to evacuate the village.[137] Instead, the Tribunal concludes that the operation was motivated by the 'substantial equivalence' postulated by the Germans between the *Partigiani* forces and the civilian population, and that it aimed at discouraging all support to the Resistance forces in a region of fundamental strategic importance.[138]

As the decision clarifies, understanding the reasons behind the massacre has important consequences from a legal viewpoint, including the

[133] Military Tribunal of La Spezia, *In re Sommer et al.*, Judgment, 22 June 2005, Case No. 45/2005, 'List of Charges'.
[134] *Ibid.*
[135] *Ibid.*, section 8(3) [this and following translations by the author].
[136] *Ibid.*, section 7(3).
[137] *Ibid.*, section 8(2).
[138] *Ibid.*

possibility of justifying the conduct as belligerent reprisal.[139] Indeed, the judgment contrasts the "self-standing" purpose of the massacre (i.e., emptying the territory of its inhabitants) with the "relational" nature of a lawful reprisal (which exists insofar as it is preceded by a violation of the laws of war). The judges rely on doctrinal writings to ground this understanding of reprisals as a sequence of action and reaction[140] – but as they try to give legal vest to this sequence of retaliatory events, the resulting formalization shifts constantly from reciprocity to enforcement.

This ambivalence appears in different sections of the judgment, starting from the legal basis that is found for belligerent reprisals. Contrary to the judges of first instance in the *Hass and Priebke* case, this Tribunal quotes *in full* Article 8 of the Italian *Law of War* from Royal Decree No. 1415 of 1938.[141] A comprehensive reading of this instrument re-inforces the original impression that reprisals are grounded in reciprocity, since the idea of a suspension in the observance of international obligations appears both in paragraph 1 and in paragraph 3 of Article 8.[142] At the same time, the statement in paragraph 2 whereby reprisals aim to 'induce the enemy belligerent to comply' with international obligations surprises for its clear reference to the logic of enforcement.[143] Therefore, regulations in force at the time of the conflict included aspects traceable to *both* paradigms of belligerent reprisals.

[139] *Ibid.*

[140] See the cited definition of reprisals by Pau, according to whom they are 'a tool of self-help whereby a State reacts to a violation of the laws of war by infringing the same or another norm of the same laws of war': *ibid.*, section 12.

[141] *Legge di Guerra*, in Regio Decreto No. 1415 (1938) (also quoted in Military Tribunal of La Spezia, *In re Sommer et al.*, section 12). The decree reads as follows [translation by the author]:

> *Art. 8 (Reprisals)*
>
> *The observance of obligations flowing from international law can be suspended, by way of reprisal, even in derogation from this or another law,* vis-à-vis *the enemy belligerent who does not comply, in full or just in part, with those obligations.*
>
> *Reprisals aim at prompting the enemy belligerent to comply with the obligations flowing from international law. They can take place both with acts identical to those committed by the enemy belligerent, and with acts of a different nature.*
>
> *The observance of provisions enacted to execute international conventions that explicitly exclude reprisals cannot be suspended according to paragraph 1.*

[142] *Ibid.*

[143] *Ibid.*

Also the conditions associated by the judgment with the taking of reprisals push the notion in different directions. On the one hand, the judgment re-affirms the requirement that the original unlawful act be attributed to the enemy belligerent – which we have often seen associated with reciprocity.[144] On the other, for the Tribunal the requirement of necessity means the impossibility for the injured belligerent to obtain 'any . . . form of reparation', and is met when protests and negotiations have failed to provide 'satisfaction' for the harm unlawfully caused.[145] These two notions recall the content of international responsibility, compliance with which can be induced through countermeasures: they therefore place the notion of reprisals under the enforcement framework.

Finally, different interpretations can be given for the very language used in the judgment to describe the legitimate purpose of reprisals, that is, to be 'used to restore the breached order' (in Italian, 'servi[re] per ripristinare l'ordine violato').[146] "Order" could be interpreted in a general sense, as a reference to the whole set of rules governing the conduct of hostilities – the legal order in an abstract and all-encompassing sense. In this reading, the accent is on re-stating compliance with the norms, as in the enforcement paradigm dominated by the example of countermeasures. But the first part of the sentence ('used to restore') conveys the idea that reprisals *themselves* bring about such restoration of the law. Unlike countermeasures, they are not coercive, mediate acts that weigh on the wrongdoer to induce it to comply. Instead, they are direct, immediate means of re-instating order, understood this time as the concrete legal relationship between the belligerents – as in the reciprocity framework. Both interpretations are equally valid, and there is no textual basis to privilege one over the other.

In sum, all mentions of reprisals in this judgment are characterized by elements that can be linked partially with reciprocity and partially with enforcement. A possible explanation for this ambivalence is that the chief preoccupation of the Tribunal lay elsewhere, that is, in distinguishing lawful reprisals from 'crude vengeance' or 'manifestation of brute force'.[147] As seen above, the key difference is that only reprisals are characterized by a dynamic relation with the original wrongdoing. Insofar as both enforcement and reciprocity obeyed this "relational"

[144] Military Tribunal of La Spezia, *In re Sommer et al.*, section 12.
[145] *Ibid.*
[146] *Ibid.*
[147] *Ibid.*

logic, it was not strictly necessary to make a stark choice between the two.[148]

Unfortunately, this explanation is hard to re-concile with the lasting influence that the judgment in *Sommer* has exerted on the following case-law by Italian tribunals,[149] including the cases of *Albers* and *Winkler*. The former dealt with the Marzabotto massacre between 29 September and 5 October 1944, when around 800 Italian civilians were killed by the 16th Panzergrenadier Division of the Waffen-S.S. during an anti-*Partigiani* operation.[150] In the latter, twelve defendants from the Panzerdivision "Hermann Göring" were accused of several mass killings that occurred in the Appennine region of Italy between March and May 1944.[151] The analysis of reprisals in these two judgments follows *Sommer* closely, and sometimes quotes it word by word. They re-affirm the relational aspects of reprisals and their regulation in the Italian Royal Decree No. 1415 of 1938; find the chief motivation of the mass killings in the desire to rid strategic areas of any human presence; and exclude that the requirements of imputability, previous violation, necessity, proportionality and humanity were met in the case at hand.[152]

[148] The Tribunal states that, since it had not been possible to ascertain in what consisted the allegedly unlawful act, it was 'consequently' barred from assessing the lawfulness of the ensuing reprisal: see *ibid.*

[149] The judgment in first instance in *Sommer et al.* was confirmed by the following levels of judgment, which however were not called upon to pronounce on the issue of reprisals. See Military Court of Appeals of Rome, *In re Sommer et al.*, Judgment No. 65, 21 November 2006 (especially sections 2(1)-(3) on the purpose to hinder support to the *Partigiani* forces and on the absence of a state of necessity); Supreme Court of Cassation, *In re Sommer et al.*, Judgment No. 1362/07, 8 November 2007 (especially section 10, p. 31 on state of necessity).

[150] Military Tribunal of La Spezia, *In re Albers et al.*, Judgment No. 1, 13 January 2007, under 'Facts'.

[151] Military Tribunal of Verona, *In re Winkler et al.*, Judgment No. 43/2011, 6 July 2011, Case Nos. 172/08 and 80/09, pp. 1–5.

[152] Military Tribunal of La Spezia, *In re Albers et al.*, under 'Juridical qualification of the facts'; Military Tribunal of Verona, *In re Winkler et al.*, pp. 423–24. The idea that reprisals must be 'used to restore the breached order' is re-stated in the former judgment but absent from the latter. Arguably, the interest in this question was mooted by the absence of any indication as to the original violation calling for reprisals: as the judges note, 'the confrontation between the *Partigiani* units and the German troops took place in the context of military operations and [involved] casualties on both sides': Military Tribunal of Verona, *In re Winkler et al.*, p. 424 [translation by the author]. The issue of reprisals was touched upon only incidentally in the following levels of these cases: see Military Court of Appeals of Rome, *In re Albers et al.*, Judgment No. 25/08, 7 May 2008, Case No. 1/2008 R.G., section 8(4), pp. 94–98 (on the killings as a measure of terrorism);

3.4.2.5 Assessment of the Italian Case-Law

As *Sommer* keeps exerting its influence as a precedent, there is a possibility that reluctance to untangle its conceptual knots is intended, and that the judiciary is actually willing to recognize the influence of both paradigms in the logic of belligerent reprisals. The pervasiveness and importance of aspects associated with reciprocity in the Italian case-law on World War II atrocities is hardly accidental or unintended. According to these judgments, features linked with reciprocity govern the two initial (and decisive) requirements of reprisals, that is, (i) damage (as in *Engel*) and (ii) attribution of the original unlawful conduct to the enemy belligerent (as in *Kappler* and in *Sommer*). Moreover, this case-law demonstrates that requirements of reprisals that are traditionally related with the enforcement paradigm can also sustain a reciprocity-inspired formalization of the mechanism (such as proportionality in *Hass and Priebke*). Finally, the purpose of reprisals is mostly construed in connection with the past (i.e., the notions of violation and harm predominant in *Saevecke*) and with a view to re-establishing the bilateral relationship between the belligerents (see again *Kappler* and *Hass and Priebke*). Although the aim of the measures is also read with reference to the future (as return to compliance) and could be interpreted holistically (as a tool to re-create the legal order), these aspects do not prevail over the ones inspired by reciprocity – at best, they stand side-by-side at the same hierarchical level. Perhaps the Italian judges must be reproached, not for confusion in construing reprisals, but for not attempting to integrate these different inputs in a coherent framework.

3.5 Reciprocity Out of the Shadows

It is possible to draw several conclusions from the instances of State practice analysed above. First of all, they are powerful indicators of the resilience of the reciprocity paradigm in structuring the purpose and function of belligerent reprisals. Reciprocity still defines the purposes that belligerent reprisals are construed as pursuing (such as equality of rights and obligations, or equality of arms); it accounts for how belligerent reprisals are operationalized (as a form of suspension rather than circumstance precluding wrongfulness); it gives concrete content to the

Supreme Court of Cassation, *In re Winkler et al.*, Judgment No. 23288, 19 March 2014, section 5 (in relation to the aggravating circumstance of odious motives).

parameters that must accompany the adoption of the measure (such as immediacy and proportionality).

Second, this practice also demonstrates that the support for the reciprocity-inspired understanding of belligerent reprisals cannot be explained exclusively on the basis of the higher propensity of certain States to retaliate. For sure, the fact that certain States were historically victims of acts of aggression and serious IHL violations could have contributed to their interpretation of belligerent reprisals as acts meant to level the playing field with a non-compliant enemy. However, the Italian case-law demonstrates two important elements. Firstly, even a State that has been the victim of acts qualified as belligerent reprisals could provide elements supporting the reciprocity-inspired interpretation of belligerent reprisals. Secondly, construing the measures under that paradigm does not necessarily imply broadening the scope of the governing standards – as we have seen with respect to proportionality and harm, it might actually curtail them. Therefore, whatever policy concern might accompany the interpretation of belligerent reprisals, it will nonetheless have to be pursued on the basis of, and adjusted to, the wider legal landscape in which the legal notion is framed.

Still, in many of these instances both the reciprocity and the enforcement paradigms concur in structuring the notion of belligerent reprisals. The purpose of re-establishing equality of rights and obligations is mentioned alongside that of securing cessation of the wrongful conduct, and the reference to suspension of obligations is predicated together with the belief in the continued cogency of the breached norm – with no concern for the supposedly mutually exclusive character of the two frameworks of reference. At the same time, there is no patent attempt at combining them in a coherent picture. This would seem rather surprising, since the form in which some of this practice is articulated (particularly the case-law) is apt for careful systematization of legal concepts.

We sometimes re-trace a similar incoherence if we compare States' positions when structuring their international obligations, with those that they adopt when drafting domestic documents. Whereas both reciprocity and enforcement underlie the reservation and declaration appended respectively by the UK and France to AP I,[153] their latest military manuals characterize belligerent reprisals in ways that pull in opposite

[153] See Sections 3.3.1–3.3.2.

directions and muddy waters even further. The UK MoD *Joint Service Manual* re-affirms the country's reservation,[154] but stresses by now the enforcement aspects of belligerent reprisals.[155] On its part, the French *Manuel de droit des opérations militaires* re-calls the interpretive declaration only in relation to the AP I provisions on the natural environment,[156] but defines belligerent reprisals somewhat ambiguously as measures that '*derogate from* the law of armed conflict'.[157] Conversely, even if Italy had fully embraced the enforcement paradigm in its declaration in relation to AP I, its *IHL Manual* re-surrects the idea (also inspiring its legislation and recent case-law[158] and, as we saw above in even clearer terms, the UN Conference on the Law of Treaties)[159] whereby belligerent reprisals lead to a suspension in the observance of international norms (in line with the reciprocity model).[160]

Against this backdrop, an opportunity for conceptual elucidation is presented by the actual occurrence of armed conflicts. This is less surprising than it seems at first sight, if one considers that such situations call for a detailed classification, presentation and justification in legal terms of battlefield conducts. It is to this type of legal arguments and practices that we shall now turn, with a view to clarifying the interplay of reciprocity and enforcement in defining belligerent reprisals.

[154] UK MoD *Joint Service Manual*, paras. 16.19.1–2 and footnote 62 thereto.

[155] *Ibid.*, paras. 16.16 and 16.17(b). See however *ibid.*, para. 5.18, with the more ambiguous reference to 'suppress[ing] illegitimate acts of warfare'.

[156] French Ministry of the Armies, *Manuel de droit des opérations militaires*, para. 4.4.2.4 and the table 'Focus' at p. 137. Conversely, it does not draw from it any inferences in relation to the civilian population and objects, objects indispensable to the survival of the civilian population, and works and installations containing dangerous forces, against which belligerent reprisals are considered as prohibited: *ibid.*, paras. 3.2, 4.3.1.1 and 4.5.1.1.

[157] *Ibid.*, para. 4.4.2.4.

[158] See Section 3.4.2.

[159] See Section 1.4.1.3(2)(a); Simma, 'Reflections on Article 60', p. 57 (noting how the Swiss oral amendment implied that the draft provision on termination and suspension in the VCLT would have 'generally authoriz[ed] the application of specific reprisals').

[160] Italian Chiefs of Defence Staff, *Manuale di Diritto umanitario*, vol. I, para. 25 (but see also *ibid.*, paras. 23 and 26).

4

Belligerent Reprisals in International Armed Conflict

A Case-Study in Chemical Attacks and the "War of the Cities" during the Iran–Iraq War (1980–1988)

4.1 The Importance of the Iran–Iraq War

This chapter will turn to battlefield practice in an international armed conflict to test the validity of the dominant formalization of belligerent reprisals as an enforcement mechanism modelled on the notion of countermeasures. To reach this objective, we will focus on how belligerents have articulated in legal terms their recourse to belligerent reprisals, and therefore how they have formalized the purposes and functions that they were attaching to their retaliatory conducts. This analysis will show all the limits of interpreting belligerent reprisals as a tool based in enforcement: The objective of enforcing compliance proves unable to capture the number and complexity of the purposes associated with the measure, and the dynamics by which the mechanism plays out will prove much more akin to those governing reciprocity than countermeasures.

The chapter will delve into the Iran–Iraq War (1980–1988) – one of the longest, deadliest and bitterest armed conflicts of the twentieth century. Since the beginning of the war, the scale and gravity of the breaches of the laws of war was such as to 'plac[e] in jeopardy the very essence of principles of international humanitarian law'.[1] However, two aspects are particularly relevant for our purposes. First, the Iran–Iraq War stands out for the extent and depth of discussions surrounding alleged violations: both belligerents sent the UN Security Council thousands of letters and communiqués to denounce alleged IHL breaches committed by the enemy and to defend their own actions. Second, in a scenario where rules were breached, and breaches were the rule, the

[1] ICRC, *Annual Report 1984* (Geneva: ICRC, 1985), p. 60.

parties to the conflict saw their behaviours (especially unlawful ones) as a direct response to the counterpart's.

Conducts consisting of a *prima facie* breach of the laws of war, but justified on account of their retaliatory character, affected several norms – including those on the treatment of prisoners of war.[2] This inquiry, however, will focus on two sets of conducts (and corresponding violations): the reciprocal use of chemical weapons (both on the armed forces and the civilian population of the enemy), and the retaliatory bombing of enemy civilians and civilian population centres (oftentimes dubbed "war of the cities"). Consideration of these specific occurrences is justified not only by their pervasiveness throughout the armed conflict and the innovative (and bewildering) character of the weapons through which such attacks were carried out.[3] Rather, these two aspects of the Iran–Iraq War allow us to test the enforcement or reciprocal basis of belligerent reprisals in a unique way.[4]

The first part of our analysis will rely on chemical warfare during the Iran–Iraq War as a sort of litmus paper for the purpose and function of belligerent reprisals. As we shall see, resort to chemical weapons was traditionally interpreted as a domain permeated by negative reciprocity – therefore, we would expect it to operate also during the Iran–Iraq War in ways, and according to logics, markedly different from those governing belligerent reprisals as understood under the enforcement paradigm. In reality, the analysis of this practice will corroborate a much more nuanced finding, whereby the two paradigms of enforcement and reciprocity contributed in equal measure to shaping the adoption of belligerent reprisals. In the second part of the chapter, we will approach the

[2] See UN Doc. S/16962, 22 February 1985, paras. 64 and 127; UN Doc. S/20012, 13 July 1988, p. 3; UN Doc. S/20754, 2 August 1989, pp. 3–4; UN Doc. S/21104, 24 January 1990, p. 2. For a legal analysis of the conflict, see Ige F. Dekker and Harry H. G. Post (eds.), *The Gulf War of 1980–1988: The Iran–Iraq War in International Legal Perspective* (Dordrecht: Martinus Nijhoff, 1992) and, in the domain of naval warfare, Andrea De Guttry and Natalino Ronzitti (eds.), *The Iran–Iraq War (1980–1988) and the Law of Naval Warfare* (Cambridge: Grotius Publications, 1993).

[3] See David Segal, 'The Iran–Iraq War: A Military Analysis' (1988) 66 *Foreign Affairs*, especially pp. 955–60; Thomas L. McNaugher, 'Ballistic Missiles and Chemical Weapons: The Legacy of the Iran–Iraq War' (1990) 15 *International Security*, pp. 5–34. Specifically on chemical weapons, see Javed Ali, 'Chemical Weapons and the Iran–Iraq War: A Case Study in Noncompliance' (2001) 8 *The Nonproliferation Review*, pp. 43–58. Specifically on ballistic missiles, see also US Central Intelligence Agency, *Iran–Iraq: Ballistic Missile Warfare and Its Regional Implications. An Intelligence Assessment*, March 1986, *passim*.

[4] Importantly, the belligerent reprisals addressed below will not be analysed in their legality (or not), but only with a view to ascertaining their purpose(s).

purpose and function of belligerent reprisals straight on, by analysing the objectives pursued through retaliatory conducts during the "war of the cities". This inquiry will highlight how belligerent reprisals were employed for aims that exceeded by far the simple enforcement of norms, and that resonated with reciprocity both in its negative dimension (as a way to re-establish parity of arms) and in its positive aspect (as a form of law-making that clarifies, or even brings about, the applicability of norms). Taken together, these two pieces of practice will demonstrate how a purely enforcement-based interpretation of belligerent reprisals fails to capture the deepest essence of retaliation in international armed conflict, and show to what extent reciprocity provides a better lens to discern the traits of the mechanism.

4.2 Chemical Warfare during the Iran–Iraq War

4.2.1 The Applicable Legal Framework

4.2.1.1 The 1925 Geneva Protocol

It is generally acknowledged that both Iraq and (although to a lesser extent) Iran used chemical weapons during the armed conflict that they fought between 1980 and 1988.[5] Alleged (and later confirmed) instances of chemical warfare ushered in multilateral efforts that would lead, in 1992, to the adoption of the Chemical Weapons Convention,[6] with its robust verification regime.[7] But as hostilities were ongoing, those incidents shed light on the gaps in the conventional law then in force,[8] and on 'the technical challenges in enforcing, monitoring, and verifying compliance' with it.[9]

The only instrument applicable *qua* treaty law to the armed conflict between Iran and Iraq in the domain of chemical warfare consisted of the Protocol for the Prohibition of Asphyxiating, Poisonous or Other Gases, and of Bacteriological Methods of Warfare, signed in Geneva in 1925

[5] McNaugher, 'Ballistic Missiles and Chemical Weapons', p. 16.

[6] Convention on the Prohibition of the Development, Production, Stockpiling and Use of Chemical Weapons and on their Destruction, Geneva, 3 September 1992, in force 29 April 1997, 1975 UNTS 45.

[7] Ali, 'Chemical Weapons and Iran–Iraq War', p. 45.

[8] Paul Tavernier, 'La Guerre du Golfe: Quelques aspects de l'application du droit des conflits armés et du droit humanitaire' (1984) 30 *Annuaire français de droit international*, p. 56.

[9] Ali, 'Chemical Weapons and Iran–Iraq War', p. 44.

(hereinafter, the Geneva Protocol).[10] This convention re-affirmed the prohibition against the use in war of asphyxiating, poisonous or other gases and of all analogous liquids, materials or devices, and extended it to the use of bacteriological methods of warfare.[11] The Geneva Protocol marked a substantive advancement compared to previous instruments, insofar as it outlawed actual recourse to chemical and bacteriological agents during war *irrespective* of the targets affected or the mode of delivery.[12]

On the other hand, the Geneva Protocol did not also prohibit the production and stockpiling of chemical and bacteriological weapons, nor did it provide for any form of enforcement or supervision for compliance with its provisions. The humanitarian concerns underpinning the adoption of the Geneva Protocol[13] were accompanied since the beginning (and outpaced shortly after) by the concern for symmetry and the interest in crystallizing parity of arms. McNaugher has highlighted how the belief in the character of chemical weapons as a game-changer in the conduct of military operations permeated the strategic thinking of much of the twentieth century.[14] This is reflected in the reservations that several States appended to the Protocol, whereby it would cease to be binding *vis-à-vis* those States whose armed forces or allies did not respect

[10] Protocol for the Prohibition of the Use in War of Asphyxiating, Poisonous or Other Gases, and of Bacteriological Methods of Warfare, Geneva, 17 June 1925, in force 8 February 1928, 94 LNTS 65; UKTS 24 (1930), Cmd 3604; 126 BFSP 324; 26 UST 571; TIAS 8061. Iran acceded to it on 5 November 1929, Iraq on 8 September 1931. On the applicability of the Geneva Protocol not only in cases of 'use *in war*' (see the Preamble of the Geneva Protocol, emphasis added), but also in cases of international armed conflict, see the last operative paragraphs of UN Doc. A/RES/2603(XXIV) A, 16 December 1969, as well as Baxter and Buergenthal, 'Legal Aspects of Geneva Protocol', pp. 868 f. Arguing for its applicability also in cases of 'a mixed civil-international conflict ... if it involved Parties to the Protocol as opposing belligerents', see John Norton Moore, 'Ratification of the Geneva Protocol on Gas and Bacteriological Warfare: A Legal and Political Analysis' (1972) 58 *Virginia Law Review*, pp. 470–72.

[11] Geneva Protocol, first operative paragraph.

[12] Compare with Declaration IV (2) concerning Asphyxiating Gases, The Hague, 29 July 1899, in force 4 September 1900, Schindler and Toman (1988) 105, which only obliged States Parties to 'abstain from the use of projectiles *the sole object of which* is the diffusion of asphyxiating or deleterious gases' (first operative paragraph, emphasis added). For a comparison between the two instruments, see James Molony Spaight, *Air Power and War Rights* (London: Longmans, 1947), p. 189 and Boothby, *Weapons and the Law*, p. 109.

[13] See the Preamble of the Geneva Protocol and its aim of 'binding alike the conscience and the practice of nations'.

[14] McNaugher, 'Ballistic Missiles and Chemical Weapons', *passim*.

its provisions.[15] Also the practice subsequent to the adoption of the Geneva Protocol confirmed that the belligerent attacked with chemical or bacteriological weapons would consider itself as dispensed from the obligations set forth in that text[16] – an interpretation vastly embraced by the scholarship.[17]

4.2.1.2 The Iraqi Reservation: An Enhanced Condition of Negative Reciprocity

Looking specifically at the relationship between the two belligerents in our case, this interpretation of the Geneva Protocol as a ban only on first use resulted from the operation of a reservation made by Iraq upon accession in 1931. According to it, Iraq would 'cease to be bound by the [Geneva] Protocol towards any Power at enmity with him whose armed forces, or the armed forces of whose allies, do not respect the Protocol'.[18] This wording subjects the treaty obligations flowing from the Geneva Protocol to a particular and enhanced condition of negative reciprocity.

For one thing, this Iraqi reservation cannot be interpreted as a simple re-affirmation of the right to adopt (symmetrical) belligerent reprisals. The discontinuance of the *vinculum iuris* as a result of the breach, as set forth in the reservation, is not compatible with the continued cogency of the violated norm presupposed by belligerent reprisals, nor is any of the substantive or procedural requirements traditionally associated with belligerent reprisals mentioned here.[19] At the same time, the scope of

[15] A comprehensive list can be found in Bunn, 'Banning Poison', pp. 417–20.

[16] See the declarations by the Governments of Britain, France, Germany and Italy during World War II recalled by Frederic J. Brown, *Chemical Warfare: A Study in Restraints* (Princeton, NJ: Princeton University Press, 1968), pp. 210 f. and 231 f., as well as the US policies in World War II and the Korean War mentioned in Moore, 'Ratification of Geneva Protocol', p. 438. See also the template reservation recommended by the Council of the League of Arab States in its resolution 2676 adopted on 15 September 1970, and the explanations for the rejection of a Philippines amendment at the CDDH that would have included the use of asphyxiating, poisonous and other gases among the list of grave breaches (especially the declarations of the US, the UK, Jordan, Iraq and Canada in CDDH/SR.44, 30 May 1977, in *CDDH Official Records*, vol. VI, pp. 280–84 and 298). See also UN Doc. A/RES/32/77, 12 December 1977, paras. 1 and 3.

[17] Moore, 'Ratification of Geneva Protocol', p. 454; Boothby, *Weapons and the Law*, p. 124.

[18] Schindler and Toman, *The Laws of Armed Conflicts*, p. 123.

[19] On the former aspect, it is worth remembering that, once released from the obligations set forth in the Protocol, the victim would still be subject to the generally applicable rules governing the conduct of hostilities, including those on targeting and on the means and methods of warfare. On the latter aspect, compare Baxter and Buergenthal, 'Legal Aspects

the Iraqi reservation also exceeds the consequences traditionally associated with the *exceptio inadimpleti contractus* and the termination or suspension of treaty obligations on account of breach as set out in the VCLT.[20] Indeed, the only condition for the Iraqi reservation to exert its effect is that the enemy side 'do not respect the Protocol': in this sense, it does not require that the breach be material, nor that the victim State be specially affected by it.[21] What is more, the silence on any form of procedural requirement for the victim State to be released from its obligations suggests that the legal bond would be discontinued, if not by the very fact of the breach, at least *ad nutum*.[22] Arguably, the only point of convergence with the rules set forth in the VCLT is that the Iraqi reservation would result in a temporary suspension (not in the termination) of the Geneva Protocol.[23] Indeed, both textual, practical and

of Geneva Protocol', p. 872 with Bunn, 'Banning Poison', p. 393, footnote 82, for whom suspension of the Protocol by means of this reservation would not remove those steps preliminary to retaliation demanded by the rules on belligerent reprisals. Arguably, this blurring of the lines between reciprocity and reprisals is due to Bunn relying on a slightly different translation of the Iraqi reservation, whereby Iraq '*shall not be bound* by the Protocol' when it suffers from a violation thereof (*ibid.*, p. 418). In reality, this difference is not of the essence and only implies a shift in perspective: whereas the 'cease to be bound' formula looks at the dynamic result of discontinuing the *vinculum iuris*, the 'shall not be bound' wording only looks at the static outcome of that modification of the legal position of the parties. Overall, the effects of the reservation are not different under the two versions.

20 Baxter and Buergenthal, 'Legal Aspects of Geneva Protocol', p. 872; see also Moore, 'Ratification of Geneva Protocol', p. 452 for the more qualified view that the Iraqi reservation and the general treaty rule on suspension of the operation of a treaty 'might sometimes allow roughly the same result'. Admittedly, the VCLT was not applicable *qua* treaty between the two belligerents when the armed conflict broke out (Iran had only signed it in 1969, whereas Iraq had not taken that step either). Yet, the principle *inadimplenti non est adimplendum* had been recognized as a general principle of international law long before the entry into force of the VCLT (Simma and Tams, 'Commentary to Article 60', p. 1355, paras. 6 f.). As we saw in Section 1.4.1.3(2)(a), doubts subsist with respect to the customary status of Article 60(5) as well as Article 65 VCLT. But even if Article 60(5) VCLT were considered as declaratory of customary international law, on its very terms it would *not* affect the scope of Article 60(4) VCLT, which safeguards the ability to craft special rules on termination and suspension (such as the Iraqi and similar reservations to the Geneva Protocol), subject to the limitations provided for under peremptory norms of international law.

21 Baxter and Buergenthal, 'Legal Aspects of Geneva Protocol', pp. 871–72.

22 On breaches giving a *faculty* of abrogation, see Simma, 'Reflections on Article 60', p. 26; for an earlier and minority argument that a breach would *ipso facto* render the legal bond inoperative, see Aladar Goellner, *Pré-caducité, caducité et desuetude en matière de droit international public* (Paris: Rousseau, 1939), pp. 27 and 45.

23 Articles 60 and 65–68 VCLT and Section 1.4.1.3(1)(a) in Chapter 1.

teleological considerations militate in favour of an interpretation whereby the Geneva Protocol would be suspended *until, but not beyond* the cessation of active hostilities and the termination of military operations.[24]

In sum, the Iraqi reservation set up a *sui generis* mechanism to suspend the Geneva Protocol in case of enemy non-compliance that escaped rigid categorization, but also aligned with State practice in the field of chemical warfare up until the outbreak of the Iran–Iraq War. By not objecting to such reservation, Iran (which had already acceded to the Protocol in 1929) manifested a form of implicit acceptance that constituted Iraq a party to the Geneva Protocol in relation to Iran without further ado, since the treaty had already entered into force.[25] At the same time, the Iraqi reservation modified, to the extent provided therein, the provisions of the Geneva Protocol – and this, not only for Iraq in its relations with Iran, but also for Iran in its relations with Iraq.[26] In virtue of the contractual *synallagma*, the meaning as well as the scope of the obligations undertaken by the two parties were equally affected by the reservation formulated by Iraq and accepted by Iran.[27]

With its chief concern for parity of arms, the Iraqi reservation to the Geneva Protocol is characterized by conditions that are even less restrictive than the ones associated with the *exceptio inadimpleti contractus* – let alone those regulating recourse to belligerent reprisals. Therefore, we would expect instances of retaliatory use of chemical weapons during the Iran–Iraq War to be characterized by a strong polarization: The working hypothesis would envisage a recourse to belligerent reprisals as a limited reaction chiefly aimed at restoring compliance with the prohibition to use chemical weapons, whereas the activation of the Iraqi reservation to suspend the operation of the Protocol would represent a last resort to

[24] For the textual element, the suspension (which occurs *vis-à-vis* States 'at enmity') would be superseded by the physiological cessation in the application *ratione temporis* of the Geneva Protocol, which, on its very own terms, applies 'in war' (or, in subsequent parlance, armed conflict). From a practical point of view, it is doubtful that an earlier resumption of the Protocol, after it has already been violated once, would give sufficient assurances of non-repetition to the victim State. But teleologically speaking, the fundamental interest in the maintenance of treaty relationships discourages a solution that extends the suspension even after the end of the armed conflict.

[25] Article 20(4)(b) VCLT.

[26] Mirrored in Article 21(1)(a)-(b) VCLT.

[27] Kalshoven, 'Prohibitions or Restrictions on the Use of Methods and Means of Warfare', in Dekker and Post (eds.), *The Gulf War of 1980–1988*, p. 101, footnote 27.

guarantee symmetry of rights and obligations.[28] In this sense, we should have all reasons to believe that an analysis of the Iran–Iraq War will uphold the aforementioned dogma whereby belligerent reprisals have an enforcement function, whereas reciprocity (in the form of termination or suspension of obligations) acts as a guarantee of symmetry in rights and obligations. In reality, we shall see how chemical warfare in that conflict falls way short of confirming a strict separation between belligerent reprisals and reciprocity – it will point instead to a progressive convergence of the two mechanisms and, more importantly, to belligerent reprisals taking on several aspects normally associated with negative reciprocity.

4.2.2 *Analysis of Chemical Warfare*

4.2.2.1 Iranian Self-restraint and Belligerent Reprisals

The first Iranian reactions to the documented use of chemical weapons in its territory were characterized by self-restraint.[29] Iranian officials refrained from invoking the Iraqi reservation and suspending the Geneva Protocol,[30] and simply called on the UN to take action and prevent Iraq from carrying out further chemical attacks.[31] Iranian President Ali Khamenei went so far as to reply positively to a humanitarian appeal by the UN Secretary-General that, had it also been accepted by Iraq, would have prevented the use of chemical weapons 'of any kind for any reason' – thereby shielding the Geneva Protocol from both suspension and belligerent reprisals even in case of first use by the enemy.[32]

28 In this sense, see Kalshoven, 'Prohibitions or Restrictions', pp. 101–2.

29 In March 1984, the first of several fact-finding missions dispatched by the UN Secretary-General reached the unanimous conclusion that mustard gas and tabun had been delivered through aerial bombs in the Shatt-e-Ali, Hoor-el-Huwaizeh and Jofair areas, but could neither determine the extent of such use nor attribute responsibility therefor: UN Doc. S/16433, 26 March 1984, pp. 11–12, paras. 35–36.

30 UN Doc. S/16380, 29 February 1984, p. 1; UN Doc. S/16408, 9 March 1984, p. 1.

31 UN Doc. S/16446, 28 March 1984, p. 1.

32 The text of the appeal can be found in UN Doc. S/16663, 6 July 1984, pp. 1–2 ('[e]xcept for requiring a reciprocal commitment, these undertakings, by their very nature, are unconditional'), whereas the Iranian response in UN Doc. S/16664, 6 July 1984, p. 2 ('fully committed to continue with its policy not to use chemical weapons'). The Iranian Government interpreted the Iraqi failure to react to the proposal as a rejection: UN Docs. A/39/374-S/16690, 3 August 1984, p. 1 and A/40/118-S/16941, 5 February 1985, pp. 2–3.

The Iranian position underwent a first important shift when, in April 1985, a second fact-finding mission dispatched by the UN confirmed that Iranian soldiers had been affected by yperite.[33] Through its Permanent Representative at the UN, the Iranian Government threatened on various occasions the adoption of 'effective retaliation in kind in spite of its own desire and values'.[34] By using this lexicon, the Iranian officials did not clarify the scope of their intended reaction – in other words, they did not specify whether the operation of the Geneva Protocol would be suspended pursuant to the Iraqi reservation, or if it would remain in force and retaliation would take the more limited form of a belligerent reprisal in kind. At the same time, these statements also reveal that the threatened measure was conditioned on the failure by the international community to take action, and chiefly intended to prevent further chemical attacks[35] – two characteristics suggesting a qualification as belligerent reprisal under the enforcement paradigm.

It can be argued that this early approach, which stopped short of suspending the *vinculum iuris* created by the Geneva Protocol, was in line with the strategic interests of the Islamic Republic: given that Iran had not developed an adequate chemical arsenal yet,[36] the suspension of the contractual bond would have allowed Iraq to employ chemical weapons on a much greater scale (subject to the constraints set forth by other humanitarian treaties, customary law, and possibly general principles of the laws of armed conflict), while leaving Iran unable to respond effectively. Given this factual background, recourse to belligerent reprisals was arguably menaced to attain the same strategic objective as negative reciprocity (i.e., re-installing parity of arms by preventing recourse to chemical weapons), without also engendering

33 UN Doc. S/17127, 24 April 1985, p. 4. While suggesting (albeit with caution) that the attacks had been carried out 'by means of bombs dropped by aircraft', and that hydrocyanic gas might also have been used, 'alone or in combination with yperite' (*ibid.*), once more the mission was not able to attribute responsibility to one or the other belligerent.

34 UN Docs. A/40/189-S/17046, 21 March 1985, p. 1 and S/17059, 26 March 1985, p. 1.

35 UN Docs. A/40/118-S/16941, p. 3 and A/40/189-S/17046, p. 1.

36 Accounts as to the moment when the Iranian arsenal of chemical weapons was ready range from 1985 (J. Anderson and D. Van Atta, 'Iran May Turn Chemical Tables on Iraq', *The Washington Post*, 2 October 1985, p. F-11), March 1986 (C.I.A., *Iran–Iraq: Ballistic Missile Warfare*, p. 15), somewhere between1986 and 1988 (Ali, 'Chemical Weapons and Iran–Iraq War', p. 51), or 1987 (Segal, 'Iran–Iraq War', p. 956; P. E. Tyler, 'Both Iraq and Iran Gassed Kurds in War, U.S. Analysis Finds', *The Washington Post*, 3 March 1990, quoted in UN Doc. S/21329, 23 May 1990, p. 4). See also McNaugher, 'Ballistic Missiles and Chemical Weapons', p. 16.

the same negative effects (i.e., allowing Iraq to launch a full-blown chemical warfare).

4.2.2.2 Ambiguity as to the Form of Retaliation

This blurring of the lines between belligerent reprisals and negative reciprocity flows not only from the failure to expressly qualify the form of retaliation – it also emerges in a more apparent way from the statements of several Iranian officials. This is especially the case after two UN fact-finding missions published their reports on the use of chemical weapons against Iranian positions and forces during the offensive on the Al-Faw peninsula in early 1986.[37]

On the one hand, various elements suggest that the Iranian threat of 'effective and practical means unlike what it had previously employed' be interpreted as a reference to belligerent reprisals.[38] This is chiefly the case for the subsidiary nature of the measure, to be resorted to in light of the 'passive reactions' of the international community;[39] the enforcement objective underlying its avowed objective of 'stop[ping] the Iraqi chemical attacks';[40] and the implicit re-affirmation of the uninterrupted cogency of the 1925 Geneva Protocol.[41]

On the other hand, those same statements also feature elements that point rather unequivocally to suspension of treaty obligations. This is particularly the case with the threat of 'reciprocal measures on both the international and regional levels',[42] the re-affirmation of the 'capability to cope with Iraqi violations accordingly' (in French: 'répondre comme il convient'),[43] and the reminder of the 'possible consequences of these chemical attacks which are in violation of ... the 1925 Geneva Protocol'.[44] In the opinion of the Iranian Minister for Foreign Affairs, the 'unconditional' nature of the prohibitions in the Geneva Protocol was only meant to exclude reliance on 'the geographical or military situations

[37] UN Docs. S/17911, 12 March 1986, pp. 17–18, paras. 55–58 (particularly notable for its unanimous conclusion that '[o]n many occasions, Iraqi forces have used chemical weapons against Iranian forces') and S/18852, 8 May 1987, p. 11, paras. 28–30.

[38] UN Doc. S/17829, 14 February 1986, p. 2.

[39] *Ibid.*; see also UN Doc. S/17849, 19 February 1986, p. 3.

[40] UN Doc. S/17829, p. 2.

[41] UN Doc. S/18028, 22 April 1986, p. 1.

[42] UN Doc. S/17829, p. 2.

[43] UN Doc. S/17849, p. 4, para. 5. Note the Iranian availability to consider alternative 'constructive and valid proposals' by the UN out of 'its strong commitment to humanitarian principles and rules of international law' (*ibid.*).

[44] UN Doc. S/18028, p. 1.

of the war' to excuse first use of chemical weapons – it did not have an express bearing on the right for the victim of chemical attacks to retaliate.[45]

Admittedly, the simultaneous presence of references to belligerent reprisals and reciprocity in the very same statements could still be accounted for along traditional lines. In a phase of the conflict where Iran had shied away from employing chemical weapons, its officials seemed to be maintaining a wide margin of action *vis-à-vis* enemy breaches of the Geneva Protocol.[46] Along this spectrum, belligerent reprisals might appear as a step of lesser gravity than the *extrema ratio* represented by suspension of the Geneva Protocol. However, the fact that considerations grounded in reciprocity permeate the lexicon of belligerent reprisals creates an osmosis between the two mechanisms that defies strict lines of demarcation – a phenomenon that would become even more pronounced in the following months of the war.

4.2.2.3 The Invocation of the Iraqi Reservation by Iran

The Iranian position underwent a marked shift in the summer of 1987, after Iraq was accused of adding a new and worrisome dimension to the conflict by subjecting civilians to chemical attacks.[47] The UN Security Council had reacted to such allegations by adopting Resolution 598, which stood out as the first binding resolution in the conflict and demanded that the belligerents discontinue all military actions.[48]

45 UN Docs. S/17829, p. 2 and A/42/306-S/18878, 26 May 1987, p. 2.

46 After a UN fact-finding mission confirmed in its report to the UN Secretary-General that mustard gas had been used in the Basra operational sector (UN Doc. S/18852, p. 11, paras. 28–30), the Iranian Minister for Foreign Affairs declared that 'non-resort to the legitimate right of retaliation cannot be considered as a permanent and unchangeable policy on the part of the Islamic Republic of Iran' (UN Doc. A/42/306-S/18878, p. 3). A few weeks earlier, another UN fact-finding mission had concluded, for the very first time, that Iraqi forces had also been affected by mustard gas and a pulmonary irritant (possibly phosgene), without however being able to determine either the weapons used or the party employing them (UN Doc. S/18852, 8 May 1987, pp. 18–19, paras. 65(d) and 66 (c)). On a previous occasion, the Iranian Ministry for Foreign Affairs had categorically denied allegations as to the use of chemical agents by its armed forces (UN Doc. A/42/238-S/18820, 21 April 1987, p. 2).

47 UN Docs. A/42/375-S/18956, 30 June 1987, p. 1 and A/42/467-S/19029, 10 August 1987, p. 2.

48 UN Security Council, Resolution 598 (1987), 20 July 1987, para. 1. With regard to chemical weapons, the resolution only deplored in an introductory paragraph their use 'contrary to obligations under the 1925 Geneva Protocol' (*ibid.*). This had two consequences. First, it failed to clarify whether and to what extent, according to the Security

However, the Iranian Government expressed its dissatisfaction with such initiative by considering that it was not a 'balanced, impartial, comprehensive and practical resolution'.[49] Instead, on 10 August 1987 the Iranian Minister for Foreign Affairs registered his country's 'temporary reservation on the Geneva Protocol of 1925, reserving for itself the right of retaliation as long as practical measures to prevent Iraq from further chemical attacks have not materialized'.[50] Behind its ostensible simplicity, the statement hides the progressive convergence of treaty suspension and belligerent reprisals, and therefore of reciprocity and enforcement.

Let us start with some established points. First of all, the sentence manifests in unmistakable terms the Iranian willingness to seek release from the obligations of the Geneva Protocol in light of enemy non-compliance. Couched in language markedly different from earlier references to retaliation, it reveals an escalation in the scope of the Iranian response to Iraqi use of chemical weapons. Second, this statement could not be interpreted as the formulation of a new reservation – something that, under both treaty and customary law, could only be appended when a State manifests its intention to be bound.[51] Rather, in formulating its new policy Iran relied on the Iraqi reservation of 1931, which entitled the victim of a breach of the Geneva Protocol to suspend without further ado the operation of that treaty until (but not beyond) the cessation of active hostilities and the termination of military operations.

This being said, one should not conclude that the invocation of the Iraqi reservation would pave the way for an unchecked resort to chemical warfare. Several limitations to this outcome could be spotted, embedded both in the general regime governing reciprocity and in the terms of the Iranian invocation. At the outset, it should be recalled that, in light of the principle *pacta sunt servanda* and the obligation of performance in

Council, belligerents were entitled, as a matter of *lex lata*, to employ such weapons by way of retaliation. Second, in light of the operative part of resolution 598, their use became prohibited only as a result of the obligation to cease military operations, and only to the extent that the ceasefire between the two belligerents would, first, enter into force, and second, hold in the long term (consider, in this respect, the grounding of this resolution on, inter alia, Article 40 UN Charter, whereby 'provisional measures shall be without prejudice to the rights, claims or positions of the parties concerned'). For a stronger stance whereby the use of chemical weapons was prohibited 'whenever and wherever this may occur', see the report by the UN Secretary-General in UN Doc. S/18852, 8 May 1987, p. 2, para. 6.

49 UN Doc. S/19031, 11 August 1987, p. 2, para. 2.

50 UN Doc. A/42/467-S/19029, p. 4.

51 Article 19 VCLT; Villiger, *Commentary on VCLT*, p. 268, para. 9.

good faith, suspension in the operation of the treaty (as opposed to termination thereof) would prohibit all act tending to obstruct its resumption – something that would arguably exclude large-scale resort to chemical weapons by either party to the conflict.[52] Second (and as a bolster to the previous point), the regime created by the Iraqi reservation was invoked by Iran only partially and selectively. The underlying contractual bond was removed only provisionally: not necessarily until the end of the conflict (as the Iraqi reservation would have entitled to do), but only for 'as long as practical measures to prevent Iraq from further chemical attacks have not materialized'. The suspension was seen less in relation to the military equilibrium between belligerents, and more with a view to effectively enforce the Geneva Protocol. Third and finally, Iran only claimed a right to retaliate, implying that it would only employ chemical weapons in response to a previous use by Iraq.

We are thus confronted with three elements (the persistence – albeit tenuous – of the underlying *vinculum iuris*, the desire to see the Geneva Protocol ultimately re-affirmed and implemented, and the circumscribed scope for retaliation) that strongly echo the working of belligerent reprisals. However, it would be incorrect to conclude that the new Iranian policy was but a recourse to belligerent reprisals under the travesty of (or poorly classified as) suspension of the Geneva Protocol. Should it occur, recourse to retaliatory chemical attacks would be necessarily characterized, from now on, by its taking place against the backdrop of such suspension. As the Iranian statement made clear, the prospect of effective enforcement of the Geneva Protocol would represent just *one* element in the definition of the strategy against the continued use of chemical weapons by Iraq; recourse to 'retaliatory measures' would hardly be disjunct from considerations of a military nature and, therefore, from alterations to the military balance that such weapons engendered.[53]

In sum, the new Iranian policy took a mechanism grounded in negative reciprocity (such as the invocation of the Iraqi reservation and the suspension of the Geneva Protocol), gave it actual operationalization in the form of belligerent reprisals, and coloured the adoption of the latter measures with traits that flow from the over-arching suspension of the

[52] Article 72(2) VCLT; Villiger, *Commentary on VCLT*, p. 890, para. 11.

[53] UN Doc. A/42/467-S/19029, p. 4 – compare the English original version ('in its final military decision or retaliatory measures') with the French translation ('sa décision finale sur le plan militaire, voire des mesures de rétorsion').

treaty operation. Here, we are not confronted with the co-existence of two mechanisms that are oftentimes framed as mutually exclusive – it is rather one institution that gives concrete application to the other and is, in turn, determined by the wider (legal as well as strategic) context in which it takes place. Taken together, the two mechanisms curb and broaden at once the retaliatory action, in ways that each of them could not achieve separately. The suspension in the operation of the Geneva Protocol stops short of interrupting the *vinculum iuris*, but has the effect of (i) creating a perimeter for authorized reaction without opening the door to an all-out chemical warfare, and (ii) determining the conditions and content of such reaction. At the same time, the vindication of a right to retaliate in the form of belligerent reprisals fits in the legal space opened by the suspension, offering a viable tool to pursue the aims of reciprocity beyond the limited scope of enforcement action. Whereas reciprocity (in the form of the suspension) dictates the strategic outlook, retaliation (in the form of belligerent reprisals) provides the working tool.

4.2.2.4 The Convergence of Belligerent Reprisals and Negative Reciprocity

The final phases of the conflict upheld the dynamic identified in the previous section. Albeit accusing Iran of resorting to chemical weapons several times throughout 1988, the Iraqi government refrained from invoking the maximalist model of unrestricted response embedded in its reservation to the Geneva Protocol.[54] Declarations by high-ranking Iraqi officials on this topic in the last year of the war are difficult to reconcile, but none of them goes so far as to claim an unbounded right to wage chemical warfare in the face of Iranian conduct (be it the use of chemical weapons or the suspension of the Geneva Protocol).[55] This seems to suggest that, in the conduct of chemical warfare, Iraq bought into the Iranian offer of considering limited retaliation through

[54] UN Docs. S/19695, 28 March 1988, p. 3 and S/19730, 5 April 1988, p. 2; see also UN Docs. S/19982, 5 July 1988, p. 2; S/20013, 13 July 1988, p. 1; S/20077, 1 August 1988, p. 1.

[55] In a press interview brought to the attention of the UN Secretary-General by Iran but swiftly denied by the Iraqi Mission to the UN, the Foreign Minister of Iraq acknowledged the Iraqi use of chemical weapons but argued that 'Iran started its use' (UN Docs. S/20074, 29 July 1988, p. 1 and S/20076, 1 August 1988, p. 1). Two UN fact-finding missions confirmed that Iraqi forces had carried out chemical attacks against Iranian positions in the Hamid area (UN Doc. S/20060, 20 July 1988, pp. 15–16, para. 46(a)-(e)) and against civilians during an air attack on the city of Oshnaviyeh (UN Doc. S/20134, 19 August 1988, pp. 10–11, paras. 22(a) and 23(a)-(c)).

belligerent reprisals as a more acceptable course of action than seeking the release from the underlying treaty commitments. The same holds true for Iran: although its actual use of chemical weapons by way of retaliation is a matter of debate,[56] its officials continued to re-affirm the 'legitimate right . . . to employ all facilities at [Iran's] disposal in order to put an end, once and for all, to such Iraqi atrocities'.[57]

At the same time, the concern for symmetry and equilibrium of rights and obligations that is at the core of negative reciprocity (also in its form of treaty suspension) emerges from the consistent emphasis on the in-kindness of the envisaged retaliation. Both the Iraqi and the Iranian threats in these last phases of the war are more concerned with the qualitative aspect of retaliation (i.e., the breach of the same rule) than with the quantitative one (i.e., the number of the targets and their qualification as combatants or civilians).[58] Reliance on belligerent reprisals alone would have offered the opportunity to react by violating a norm different from the one originally breached; however, the normative stigma and the military implications associated with chemical warfare made it important to respond in kind.[59] Hence the passage through the suspension of the Geneva Protocol as a preliminary step in

[56] Iran has denied allegations of resort to chemical weapons both during and after the war: see respectively the letter by the Minister for Foreign Affairs of Iran in UN Doc. A/43/288-S/19741, 5 April 1988, p. 2 and the 1997 press conference by the outgoing President of Iran (and former commander-in-chief of Iran's armed forces during the conflict) Rafsanjani, Teheran, 25 May 1997, quoted in Robert Fisk, *Cronache Mediorientali* (Milano: Saggiatore, 2009; it. tr. from *The Great War for Civilization*, Fourth Estate, 2005), p. 271. In 1988, two UN fact-finding missions concluded that Iraqi military personnel had been injured by chemical agents, but were not able to allocate specific responsibility therefor: UN Docs. S/19823, 25 April 1988, pp. 16–17, para. 54(c)-(e) and S/20063, 25 July 1988, pp. 11–12, para. 32(a)-(b) and (e).

[57] UN Doc. S/19967, 27 June 1988, pp. 2–3; see also UN Doc. S/19639, 17 March 1988, p. 1 ('the agony of considering retaliatory measures').

[58] In April 1988, Iraq threatened to 'choose a number of large Iranian cities to be the targets of chemical weapons as a deterrent and punitive measure' (see the declaration by an Iraqi government spokesman gathered by the Iraqi News Agency, taken up by *The Washington Post*, and ultimately reproduced in UN Doc. A/43/282-S/19734, 4 April 1988, p. 1); this came immediately after a letter by the Minister for Foreign Affairs of Iraq lamenting chemical attacks by Iran 'a number of times at the battlefronts and in towns' (UN Doc. 19695, p. 3). As for Iran, the threat of reprisal action followed accusations of Iraqi use of chemical weapons in the theatre of military operations as well as against civilians (both Iraqi Kurds and Iranians): UN Docs. S/19639, p. 1 and S/19967, p. 2.

[59] This also explains why Iran menaced chemical retaliation since the early phases of the war, even if it seems that it did not have the technical means to follow up on such threat (see Section 4.2.2.1).

the adoption of belligerent reprisals: the precise mirroring between action and reaction highlighted the concern for the parity of arms that could be jeopardized by the very recourse to a prohibited means of warfare.

4.2.3 *Conclusion on Chemical Warfare*

This overview has clarified the progressive convergence of belligerent reprisals and negative reciprocity in the practice surrounding resort to chemical warfare during the Iran–Iraq War. The belief in belligerent reprisals as an enforcement tool, alternative to (and of lesser impact than) instances of negative reciprocity, holds true only for the initial phases of the military confrontation. Later on, the qualified invocation of the Iraqi reservation on the part of Iran started a dynamic where belligerent reprisals and negative reciprocity acted almost osmotically, influencing (rather than excluding) each other. On the one hand, the reciprocity-inspired suspension of the Geneva Protocol did not result in the farthest-reaching consequences heralded by the belligerents' rhetoric – instead, it was operationalized in the threat (and, potentially, the adoption) of belligerent reprisals. On the other hand, the legal perimeter drawn by the suspension resulted in belligerent reprisals taking up some of the features normally associated with negative reciprocity, especially the in-kind character of retaliation and the objective of re-establishing the equality (both formal and substantive) upset by the breach of the Geneva Protocol. In practical terms, belligerent reprisals sustained a new equilibrium between belligerents, providing a form of governance of chemical warfare that pursued the objectives (but not the more extreme implications) of negative reciprocity.

4.3 The "War of the Cities"

4.3.1 *Applicable Law*

In Section 4.2, we have seen how belligerent reprisals could take on certain elements of negative reciprocity due to the broader context of treaty suspension in which they were situated and that they contributed to operationalize. In another sense, belligerent reprisals can also be seen as assuming certain elements of negative reciprocity autonomously, because of the inner logic that governs their adoption and unfolding.

It is to this feature that we shall now turn, by analysing the so-called "war of the cities" that characterized much of the Iran–Iraq War.

Since the first years of the conflict, both belligerents accused the counterpart of carrying out attacks against the civilian population in enemy territory, especially by airstrikes, artillery fire, and ground-to-ground missiles. Several actors (including the ICRC) asked for the immediate cessation of these conducts,[60] but a clear-cut assessment of their lawfulness was complicated by the paucity of conventional undertakings applicable *qua* treaty law. Even though AP I (which entered into force in 1978) had introduced a comprehensive framework for the general protection of the civilian population against the effects of hostilities,[61] neither Iraq nor Iran had become a party to it.[62] Interestingly, it did occur on a handful of occasions that one party assessed the counterpart's conduct in the "war of the cities" by reference to certain AP I provisions, including those governing the conduct of hostilities[63] – but in the absence of a clear elaboration on the legal title for the application of that instrument, such scattered statements should be interpreted, at best, as reflecting the belief in the customary status of certain AP I provisions on the means and methods of warfare.

[60] ICRC, *Memorandum from the International Committee of the Red Cross to the States Parties to the Geneva Conventions of August 12, 1949 Concerning the Conflict between Islamic Republic of Iran and Republic of Iraq*, Geneva, 7 May 1983; *Second Memorandum from the International Committee of the Red Cross to the States Parties to the Geneva Conventions of August 12, 1949 Concerning the Conflict between Islamic Republic of Iran and Republic of Iraq*, Geneva, 10 February 1984. See also the press release of 13 January 1988 and the solemn written appeal of 11 February 1987 addressed by the ICRC to the two parties to the conflict (mentioned in ICRC, *1987 Annual Report* (Geneva: ICRC, 1988), p. 76). See also the 'vigorous representations' made on 28 February 1988 by the ICRC to the Governments of Iran and Iraq, and the press release of 10 March 1988 by the same organization (mentioned in ICRC, *Annual Report 1988* (Geneva: ICRC, 1989), p. 78.

[61] Part IV, Section I (Articles 48–67) of Protocol Additional to the Geneva Conventions of 12 August 1949, and relating to the Protection of Victims of International Armed Conflicts (Protocol I), Geneva, 8 June 1977, in force 7 December 1978, 1125 UNTS 3.

[62] Kalshoven emphasizes the fact that, since Iran had signed AP I in 1977 and had not made clear its intention not to become a party to it, it was under an obligation (set forth under Article 18(a) VCLT) to refrain from acts which would defeat its object and purpose (Kalshoven, 'Prohibitions or Restrictions', p. 98). It should be noted, however, that Iran had . . . only signed the VCLT, therefore it was not, strictly speaking, bound by the latter provision.

[63] See, for instance, the February 1983 document compiled by the Iranian Ministry for Foreign Affairs quoted in Tavernier, 'La Guerre du Golfe', p. 58.

4.3.1.1 Applicable Customary Safeguards

In relation to the "war of the cities", this is primarily the case for several rules in Article 51 AP I that 'give effect' to the general principle whereby '[t]he civilian population and individual civilians shall enjoy general protection against dangers arising from military operation'.[64] First, the prohibition of attacks specifically directed against the civilian population[65] had crystallized into a rule of customary law as a result of the progressive convergence of two trajectories in the realms of land[66] and air warfare,[67] which culminated in a string of UN General Assembly resolutions between the 1960s and 1970s.[68] The same holds true for the prohibition against all acts or threats of violence the primary purpose of which is to spread terror among the civilian population,[69] which had made its first appearance in the form of a crime of 'systematic terrorism' in the aftermath of World War I:[70] after appearing in all the draft conventions trying to grapple with new forms of warfare,[71] the norm featured prominently in both GC IV[72] and in a 1969 resolution by the Institut de Droit International on the distinction between military

[64] Article 51(1) AP I.

[65] Article 51(2) AP I.

[66] See, especially, the Preamble of the Declaration Renouncing the Use, in Time of War, of Explosives Projectiles Under 400 Grammes Weight (Saint Petersburg, 11 December 1868, in force 11 December 1868, Schindler and Toman (1988) 102) and Article 25 of the Regulations annexed to Hague Convention No IV on the Laws and Customs of Warfare on Land (The Hague, 18 October 1907, in force 26 January 1910, 205 CTS 277; USTS 539; 100 BFSP 338; 2 US Treaties 2269; UKTS 9 (1910), Cd 5030).

[67] See Declaration XIV Prohibiting the Discharge of Projectiles and Explosives from Balloons, The Hague, 18 October 1907, in force 27 November 1909, UKTS 15 (1910); Draft Rule 14(3) in Hague Commission of Jurists, *Draft Rules of Aerial Warfare*, The Hague, 19 February 1923, 17 AJIL Supp. 245, 32 AJIL Supp. 1; Article 1(1) in Assembly of the League of Nations, *Resolution on Protection of Civilian Populations against Bombing from the Air in Case of War*, 30 September 1938, Schindler and Toman (2004) 329.

[68] See especially UN Doc. A/RES/2444(XXIII), *Respect for Human Rights in Armed Conflict*, 19 December 1968, letter (c), and UN Doc. A/RES/2675(XXV), *Basic Principles for the Protection of Civilian Populations in Armed Conflict*, 9 December 1970, para. 4.

[69] Article 51(2) AP I.

[70] Commission on the Responsibility of the Authors of the War and on Enforcement of Penalties, *Report Presented to the Preliminary Peace Conference*, 29 March 1919, in (1920) 14 AJIL, p. 114.

[71] Hague Commission, *Draft Rules of Aerial Warfare*, Article 22; Article 4 of International Law Association, *Draft Convention for the Protection of Civilian Populations against New Engines of War*, Amsterdam, 2 September 1938, Schindler and Toman (1988) 223.

[72] Article 33 of Geneva Convention Relative to the Protection of Civilian Persons in Time of War (Geneva Convention IV), Geneva, 12 August 1949, in force 21 October 1950, 75 UNTS 287; 157 BFSP 355; UKTS 39 (1958), Cmd 550; TIAS 3365; 6 UST 3516.

objectives and non-military objects.[73] A similar finding applies to another obligation of particular import to the present case – that is, the issuance of effective warning of attacks that may affect the civilian population, unless circumstances do not permit.[74] Provisions to that effect had been included in the 1899 and 1907 Hague Regulations, and reflected in the practice of World War II.[75]

4.3.1.2 Unsettled Customary Norms

A more nuanced finding is warranted for other rules of great relevance to the "war of the cities": that is, the norms governing the distinction between civilian objects and military objectives, and those prohibiting indiscriminate attacks. There is little doubt that the *general tenets* underlying these sets of norms had crystallized into custom by the time the Iran–Iraq War started; however, the ensuing obligations were not necessarily settled under general international law, or as developed and specific under that source of law as those set forth in the more recent conventional undertakings.

Thus, although the paramount norm whereby only military objectives could be lawfully subjected to attack had appeared in virtually all treaties governing the conduct of hostilities, the very definition of what a military objective was had undergone significant shifts and developments by the time the Iran–Iraq War began. Previously, the long-standing practice had been that of enumerating in detail what could be made the object of attack,[76] or in any case that of regarding some immediate military characteristic as an essential component of the very idea of military objective.[77] This paradigm began to shift in the 1960s, as objectives no

[73] IDI, 'Resolution on the Distinction between Military Objectives and Non-military Objects in General and Particularly the Problems Associated with Weapons of Mass Destruction', 9 September 1969, in (1969) 53 *Annuaire de l'Institut de Droit International*, para. 6.

[74] Article 57(2)(c) AP I.

[75] See Article 26 of the Regulations annexed to Hague Convention No II with respect to the Laws and Customs of War on Land, The Hague, 29 July 1899, in force 4 September 1900, 32 Stat. 1803; T.S. No. 403; 91 BFSP 988. Article 26 of the Regulations annexed to the 1907 Hague Convention No IV. Article 6 of Hague Convention IX respecting Bombardment by Naval Forces in Time of War, The Hague, 18 October 1907, in force 26 January 1910, 100 BFSP 401; 2 US Treaties 2314; UKTS 13 (1910); 205 CTS 345. See also ICRC, *Customary IHL Study*, vol. II, pp. 686 f., para. 2224.

[76] Articles 1(1) and 2(1) of 1907 Hague Convention IX; Hague Commission, *Draft Rules of Aerial Warfare*, Article 24.

[77] ICRC, *Draft Rules for the Limitation of the Dangers Incurred by the Civilian Population in Time of War*, 15 October 1956 (Geneva: ICRC, 1956), Article 7.

longer needed to 'exhibit a generally recognized military significance' to count as military, as long as they could, 'by their very nature or purpose or use, make an effective contribution to military action'.[78] Article 52(2) AP I made a further detachment from the traditional tenets of the notion, first by doing away with the requirement that military objectives be recognized to be of military interest,[79] then by introducing the element of location as a criterion from which the effective contribution of the object could be inferred.[80] Therefore, it seems questionable that AP I reflected customary law when it entered into force; it is more correct to conclude that, by the time the Iran–Iraq War started, general international law still required that an object exhibited some intrinsic military characteristic to count as a military objective and be lawfully targeted.

Also the general prohibition of indiscriminate attacks must have attained a customary status by the time of the Iran–Iraq War,[81] since it had been formulated in several informal codification efforts both before and after World War II (at least in the area of air warfare).[82] A more nuanced finding, however, is warranted for the *specific* typologies and examples of indiscriminate attacks set forth in Article 51(4)-(5) AP I. Out of the highly sophisticated norms enshrined in those treaty norms, only the prohibition of attacks that are not directed at a specific military objective and of those that employ a method or means of combat that cannot be directed at a specific military objective could be found to be customary.[83]

[78] IDI, 'Resolution on the Distinction between Military Objectives and Non-military Objects', Article 2.

[79] Importantly, the original ICRC proposal had maintained such a condition: Sandoz, Swinarski and Zimmermann (eds.), *Commentary on the APs*, p. 635, para. 2019.

[80] *Ibid.*, p. 636, para. 2021.

[81] Article 51(4) AP I, which defines indiscriminate attacks as those that 'are of a nature to strike military objectives and civilians or civilian objects without distinction'.

[82] Hague Commission, *Draft Rules on Aerial Warfare*, Article 24(3); ILA, *Draft Convention for the Protection of Civilian Populations against New Engines of War*, Article 5(2); 20th International Conference of the Red Cross (1965), *Resolution XXVIII on the Protection of Civilian Populations against the Dangers of Indiscriminate Warfare*, in (1965) 56 IRRC, pp. 589 f.

[83] The norm enshrined in Article 51(4)(a) AP I flows logically from the principle of distinction between civilian objects and military objectives, and represents the negative formulation of the obligation to direct attacks only at the latter. The norm set forth in Article 51(4)(b) AP I derived from long-standing bans on chemical and bacteriological weapons, and had featured in most codification efforts (see ICRC, *Draft Rules for the Limitation of the Dangers Incurred by the Civilian Population in Time of War*, Article 14; IDI, 'Resolution on the Distinction between Military Objectives and Non-military

On the other hand, it would probably go too far to argue that, by the 1980s, the *entirety* of the detailed prohibitions of area bombardment and of attacks with excessive incidental effects in relation to the concrete and direct military advantage anticipated (enshrined in Article 51(5)(a)-(b) AP I) reflected existing custom. Only if and when considered at a higher level of abstraction, could those rules be considered as forming part and parcel of general international law applicable at the time. For instance, previous codification efforts had re-stated a looser proscription of carpet bombing, revolving around the prohibition to 'attack without distinction, as a single objective, an area including several military objectives at a distance from one another where elements of the civilian population, or dwellings, are situated in between the said military objectives'.[84] The same goes for the principle forbidding the launching of attacks that could be expected to entail incidental loss to civilian life, damage to civilian objects, or a combination thereof, to an extent disproportionate to the military advantage anticipated.[85] Deprived of its more progressive elements (such as the specification that the military advantage anticipated be 'concrete and direct', as in Article 51(5)(b) AP I), the prohibition of disproportionate attacks was seen as flowing from the duty to spare as much as possible the civilian population,[86] as well as from the application of the general principle of proportionality forming 'an integral part of the modern law of warfare'.[87] To that (more limited) extent could such norms be considered as forming part of the customary IHL applicable to the Iran–Iraq War.

4.3.1.3 Breaches and Belligerent Reprisals

This overview of applicable customary law could provide a plausible basis for the frequent finding (expressed both by the belligerents, in

Objects', para. 4; 24th International Conference of the Red Cross (1981), *Resolution XIII on Disarmament, Weapons of Mass Destruction and Respect for Non-combatants*, in (1981) 225 IRRC, p. 330, para. 1.

84 ICRC, *Draft Rules for the Limitation of the Dangers Incurred by the Civilian Population in Time of War*, Article 10; see also Sandoz, Swinarski and Zimmermann (eds.), *Commentary on the APs*, p. 624, paras. 1969–1972.

85 On this formulation, compare Article 15 of the *Lieber Code* with Article 24(4) of the Hague Commission of Jurists' *Draft Rules on Aerial Warfare* and with draft Article 46(3)(b) of the original ICRC draft for AP I submitted to the Diplomatic Conference (in *CDDH Official Records*, vol. I, Part III, p. 16).

86 Kalshoven, 'Prohibitions or Restrictions', p. 103.

87 Rainer Lagoni, 'Comments: Methods or Means of Warfare, Belligerent Reprisals, and the Principle of Proportionality', in Dekker and Post (eds.), *The Gulf War of 1980–1988*, pp. 117–18 and 122.

international fora and by the scholarship writing at the time of the Iran–Iraq War) whereby 'the attacks carried out on either side against the civilian population and civilian objects in enemy territory violated basic precepts of the law of war'.[88] However, concluding for the *prima facie* unlawfulness of the conducts underlying the "war of the cities" cannot exhaust the analysis. The peculiarity of the Iran–Iraq War is that in the majority of cases, each belligerent threatened (and even acknowledged) attacks on civilian targets in enemy territory as a 'means of retaliation',[89] a 'reciprocal measure',[90] or a form of 'strike back'.[91]

Being an instance of non-compliance with the laws-of-war norms identified above, such retaliatory attacks were construed (and explicitly qualified) as a form of belligerent reprisal, justified to the extent that its adoption did not infringe any other prohibitions.[92] Given the inapplicability of the reprisals provisions in Articles 51–56 AP I to the Iran–Iraq War (either *qua* treaty or as an expression of customary law), most of the scholars writing at the time concluded that belligerent reprisals could in principle be adopted against civilians, civilian populations and civilian objects during the conduct of hostilities.[93] In this sense, it is incorrect to conclude that such references to the lexicon of reprisal were 'rhetorical and propagandistic rather than ... really meant to justify their [*scil.*, belligerents'] attacks against or affecting the enemy civilian population'.[94] As we shall see in the following sections, a careful analysis of the belligerents' practice attests the wide range of functions and purposes attributed to belligerent reprisals during the "war of the cities".

88 Kalshoven, 'Prohibitions or Restrictions', p. 105. See also, for instance, the message from the UN Secretary-General to the Presidents of Iran and Iraq in UN Doc. S/16611, 11 June 1984, p. 1; the statements by the President of the UN Security Council in UN Docs. S/18538, 22 December 1986, p. 1, and S/19626, 16 March 1988, p. 1; and UN Security Council resolution 598 (1987), 20 July 1987. For the ICRC's position, see the documents mentioned in footnote 60 in this chapter.

89 UN Doc. S/15962, 9 September 1983, p. 1.

90 UN Doc. A/39/870-S/16967, 20 February 1985, p. 1.

91 UN Doc. A/38/763-S/16225, 19 December 1983, p. 2.

92 See, for instance, UN Docs. S/19551, 29 February 1988, pp. 1–2, and S/19611, 13 March 1988, p. 2.

93 Greenwood, 'Twilight of Reprisals', p. 63; Kalshoven, 'Prohibitions or Restrictions', pp. 104–5; Kwakwa, 'Belligerent Reprisals', p. 72. For the contrary view, see Eric David, 'La Guerre du Golfe et le droit international' (1987) 23 *Revue Belge de Droit International*, p. 163; see also the ICRC's memoranda of 1983 and 1984 (see footnote 60 in this chapter), as well as ICRC, *Bombing of Iraqi and Iranian Cities*, Press Release No. 1489, 7 June 1984.

94 Kalshoven, 'Prohibitions or Restrictions', p. 105.

4.3.2 Belligerent Reprisals in the "War of the Cities"

4.3.2.1 Enforcement and Punishment

During the initial phases of the conflict, conducts characterized as belligerent reprisals featured elements reminiscent of the enforcement paradigm. For instance, when describing its strikes on Iraqi population centres (especially the one on Basra in March 1985), Iran repeatedly highlighted three aspects: the restrained and limited nature of the retaliatory action; its stated aim of ensuring the cessation of enemy attacks on civilian areas; and the adoption of procedural steps before the adoption of the measures (such as warnings to the population and formal notice to the authorities).[95] The same holds true for Iraq: its military spokespersons described strikes against selected targets in Iranian towns as a deterrent against, and a response to, the bombardment of civilian targets in Iraq, and stressed the prior warnings communicated to the Iranian leadership.[96] These features of retaliatory action bear all the characteristics traditionally associated with an enforcement-inspired understanding of belligerent reprisals: their purpose, extent and procedure reflect the idea that belligerent reprisals were chiefly interested with bringing about compliance with applicable norms.

However, as the war dynamics developed over the years, so did the meaning(s) attributed to belligerent reprisals by the parties to the conflict. Especially in the first rounds of the "war of the cities", it is easy to identify a markedly punitive character in the adoption of retaliatory action. On one occasion in early February 1984, Iraq and Iran exchanged a series of increasingly menacing communiqués that announced retaliation for the bombing of civilian targets in the respective territories. Faced with the alleged shelling of a dozen towns, an Iraqi military spokesman communicated that its government had decided to strike at selected targets in seven Iranian cities.[97] The Foreign Minister of Iran categorically denied the accusations and requested the dispatch of a fact-finding mission, but also reserved the right to 'protect[] its people and vital interests through all possible means', should Iraq carry out those raids.[98] This statement had the effect of exacerbating the tension, with

[95] UN Docs. S/15962, p. 1; A/39/870-S/16967, p. 1; S/17002, 5 March 1985, pp. 2–3; S/17017, 10 March 1985, p. 2.

[96] UN Docs. A/38/763-S/16225, p. 2; A/38/787-S/16345, 16 February 1984, p. 2; A/38/790-S/16350, 17 February 1984, p. 2.

[97] UN Doc. A/38/784-S/16335, 10 February 1984, p. 3.

[98] UN Doc. S/16314, 6 February 1984, pp. 2–3.

Iraq adding four cities to its initial list,[99] and with Iran singling out three Iraqi cities and announcing that it would henceforth retaliate against Iraqi attacks.[100]

An identical pattern characterized the events of early June 1984, following allegations that Iraqi warplanes had attacked four neighbourhoods in the Iranian city of Baneh and killed hundreds of civilians celebrating a festivity.[101] Although Iraq maintained that its attack had actually targeted a camp of troops,[102] the Iranian government threatened to respond by launching air and ground attacks on eleven Iraqi towns.[103] Here as well, the cycle of threatened reprisals continued as Iraq promised to 'reciprocate' by 'strik[ing] back very forcefully' at fifteen Iranian cities.[104]

Throughout these exchanges, the punitive element does not flow from the qualification of enemy attacks on civilian targets as criminal acts worthy of sanction (an aspect that was nonetheless repeatedly raised by Iran).[105] Nor would it be warranted to interpret these statements as proof of an uncontrolled escalation, if only one considers that both parties called on civilian populations to keep away from listed cities in an effort to minimize casualties.[106] In reality, the willingness to punish emerges from the speed at which an increased number of cities came in the crosshairs of retaliatory action. The absence of a clear proportion between enemy action (whether actual or just potential) and the envisaged reaction highlights the symbolic nature of the belligerent reprisal, irrespective of any concern for the impact that the measure would have on the prospects for future compliance. This disproportion underlines the stigmatizing aspect of retaliation, which is coherent with a punitive, but not an enforcement, function.

4.3.2.2 Negative Reciprocity: Parity of Arms and Symmetry

(1) Symmetry Governing Escalation Whereas the punitive purpose characterized early examples of retaliatory action, following rounds in the "war of the cities" would emphasize the role of belligerent reprisals in

99 UN Doc. A/38/784-S/16335, p. 4.
100 UN Doc. S/16331, 9 February 1984, p. 2.
101 UN Doc. S/16604, 6 June 1984, p. 1.
102 UN Doc. S/16610, 19 June 1984, p. 2.
103 UN Doc. S/16607, 7 June 1984, p. 1.
104 *Ibid.*, p. 2.
105 UN Docs. S/16314, p. 2; S/16331, p. 2; and S/16604, p. 1.
106 UN Docs. A/38/784-S/16335, pp. 3–4; S/16331, p. 2; and S/16607, p. 2.

re-establishing the parity of arms altered by unlawful conduct. This peculiar aspect emerges from at least three instances of reciprocal attacks on cities and towns that took place in different phases of the conflict.

(a) Levelling the Score First, in February 1984, the permanent representative of Iran to the UN announced that its country had been 'forced . . . to take retaliatory measures' in reaction to the repeated attacks by the enemy on civilian targets.[107] According to Iraq, the Iranian reprisal consisted in the shelling of fifteen Iraqi towns for a period of five days, until the Chief of Staff of the Iranian Army called an end to it on 18 February 1984.[108] The Iranian statement mentioned that the measures had been taken with 'all the precautions', and only in order to 'save [its] innocent people' after 'many significant cases of violations of international humanitarian law' and the inaction of the international community.[109]

However, several elements suggest that the concern for enforcing future compliance might not have been the main driving force behind the Iranian conduct. First, the Iranian reprisal started precisely on the day that Iraq had selected and announced as an end to its own attacks on targets situated in Iranian towns;[110] therefore, it could be questioned whether any further incentive to prevent misconduct on the part of Iraq was warranted. Second, the Iranian response mirrored the unlawful actions blamed on Iraq, both in terms of duration (five and four days, respectively) and scope (fifteen Iraqi cities and villages targeted versus ten Iranian towns). Third, in explaining why it would not take action following the Iranian attacks, Iraq stated it was not willing to engage in a course of conduct that would have resulted in 'shelling . . . until we have killed as many people in Iran as have been killed in Iraq over the past five days'.[111] All these elements clarify that, in this phase of the "war of the

107 UN Doc. S/16346, 17 February 1984, p. 2. Just a few days earlier, the ICRC had mentioned that the regular indiscriminate bombing by the Iraqi air force of Iranian built-up areas was 'sometimes designated as reprisals', but 'contravene[d] the laws and customs of war, in particular with regard to the basic principle that a distinction must be made between military objectives and civilian persons and property' (ICRC, *Second Memorandum Concerning the Conflict between Islamic Republic of Iran and Republic of Iraq*, para. c). However, this notation misses the point that it is in the very essence of belligerent reprisals to breach an IHL obligation.

108 UN Doc. S/16363, 24 February 1984, pp. 1–2.

109 UN Doc. S/16346, pp. 1–2. See also UN Doc. S/16352, 17 February 1984, p. 2.

110 UN Doc. S/16363, p. 2.

111 *Ibid.*, p. 3.

cities", levelling the score of civilian bombardment with the enemy was an important concern of reprisal action, whether taken (as in the case of Iran) or not (as for Iraq).

(b) Mirroring Effect A second example of this particular aspect of belligerent reprisals took place in the spring of 1985. Upon denouncing Iraqi attacks on civilians in several towns, including Tehran and Isfahan,[112] Iran launched in retaliation a land-to-land missile against the Central Bank of Rafidin in Baghdad.[113] Iranian officials stressed that the measure had been adopted only to stop Iraqi attacks against civilians; to that end, they had warned the population of Baghdad of the intention to strike at certain economic and industrial centres in the capital, and opted for a late night attack with a view to minimizing the rate of civilian casualties.[114] It would then seem that this particular instance of belligerent reprisal falls squarely in the enforcement paradigm, both for its purpose and its modalities of adoption – but as soon as we consider the pattern of action inaugurated by the raid on the Central Bank of Rafidin, we understand that the thrust of the Iranian response was rather that of mirroring very closely the course of conduct allegedly followed by its Iraqi counterpart.

In the following weeks, any time (and as long as) Iraq suspended its attacks on civilian targets, Iran would also refrain from shelling enemy towns; but as soon as the former resumed indiscriminate bombings, the latter immediately retaliated in kind (most often by launching ground-to-ground missiles on Baghdad).[115] Although Iran stressed the limited and defensive nature of its belligerent reprisals, its statements would typically end with an offer to cease reprisal attacks on Iraqi towns on condition that (and as soon as) Iraq cease its unlawful actions. The paradigm shift is minimal but of the essence: compliance with IHL remains central, but it

[112] UN Docs. S/17025, 12 March 1985, p. 1 and S/17029, 14 March 1985, p. 1.

[113] UN Doc. S/17029, p. 1.

[114] *Ibid.*

[115] UN Doc. S/17058, 26 March 1985, p. 2 (Iran launching a missile on Baghdad, claiming that Iraq had renewed its attacks on civilian population centres and commercial vessels in the Persian Gulf after two days of interruption); UN Doc. S/17073, 1 April 1985, p. 2 (Iran launching two missiles on Baghdad in retaliation for the attacks on Iranian cities and civilian areas on 31 March); UN Doc. S/17078, 3 April 1985, p. 1 (Iran ordering its forces to cease all retaliatory measures against Iraqi cities on 2 April, reciprocating the pause in Iraqi attacks against the civilian quarters of the larger Iranian cities); UN Doc. S/17083, 5 April 1985, p. 1 (Iran threatening the adoption of retaliatory actions after Iraq resumed its attacks against civilian targets following a two-day interruption).

is understood more as a condition for stopping belligerent reprisals, than as a purpose for their adoption. The capacity of the retaliatory measure to influence the enemy's willingness to respect norms is supplanted by a focus on the symmetry between the belligerents' actions and reactions.

(c) Normalizing Reprisals A third example of the recourse to belligerent reprisals to re-establish a disturbed parity of arms took place in the final year of the war. On 10 March 1988, the Iraqi President chaired a meeting of the Revolution Command Council and the Regional Command of the Arab Baath Socialist Party. The long statement issued as a result of that consultation recalled many occasions when Iraq replied in kind to Iranian attacks on the civilian population with the avowed objective of inflicting punishment on the enemy and giving it a 'harsh' or 'extensive and clear lesson'.[116] Its most important feature, however, was the Iraqi promise to halt the "war of the cities" as of the following day. Such an undertaking to refrain from bombing Iranian cities in the future was subject to a set of conditions, two of which highlight the interest in re-establishing military equality between the belligerents that underlies the adoption of (or the refraining from) belligerent reprisals.[117]

One condition was that Iran does not resume the bombardment of Iraqi cities and villages through weapons directed against the civilian population and purely residential centres.[118] Belligerent reprisals are, so to say, "normalized": they are no longer conceived of as a pathological exception justified by its limited purpose, but as a physiological reaction to illegality that the victim of a breach can forfeit if the enemy renounces the advantages reaped from its unlawful conduct. It is not simply that recourse to the measure is seen from a different perspective – much more fundamentally, the underlying question transforms from "why adopting reprisals?", to "why not adopting reprisals?". The concern for equality of

[116] UN Doc. S/19598, 10 March 1988, pp. 2 and 5.

[117] *Ibid.*, p. 6, points 1–2. As for points 3 and 4, they are more concerned with retaliation in relation to *ius ad bellum* violations. This aspect was oftentimes conflated with *ius in bello* during the Iran–Iraq War (see for instance UN Doc. S/17097, 12 April 1985, p. 3, para. 9; UN Doc. S/PV.2663, 18 February 1986, pp. 32–33). On this occasion, it is distinguished from belligerent reprisals as a reaction to *ius in bello* violations by means of a differentiated proportionality ratio: 'retaliate *comprehensively* ... by bombarding *all* Iranian cities' for the former (emphasis added), versus 'resume the bombardment of Iranian cities' (implying a more restrained reaction) in the latter. As regards point 5, see Section 4.3.2.3(2)(d).

[118] UN Doc. S/19598, p. 6, point 2.

arms had become so entrenched, that on the following day even Iran expressed the position whereby '[i]t has been prepared to stop its limited retaliatory strikes against Iraq, if the international community compels Iraq to halt its bombardments of civilian areas'.[119]

The second relevant condition in the Iraqi commitment affirmed that, '[s]ince it was Iran that began the war of the cities, . . . the last bombardment operation must be Iraqi, before the cease-fire goes into effect at the [envisaged] time'.[120] To make the point even stronger, the statement went on to say that, should Iran bomb any Iraqi city 'in retaliation for the last Iraqi bombardment operation, [Iraq] shall continue the bombardment' of Iranian cities.[121] Here, the role of belligerent reprisals as a tool of re-establishing military parity with a law-violating enemy is evident. Not only is recourse to such measure completely indifferent to whether the enemy will comply with its IHL obligations – actually, it is precisely the idea that there would be no more violations by the other belligerent that underlies the retaliatory measure and gives it its true meaning and function. This statement reveals the artificiality of the traditional *fictio iuris* whereby belligerent reprisals represent tools to enforce the laws of war; instead, they appear as the chief instrument guaranteeing the substantial symmetry between parties to an armed conflict.

(2) **Symmetry Governing De-escalation** An important element behind the offer of 10 March 1988 was Iraq's recently acquired capacity to launch ground-to-ground missiles on important Iranian cities, including Tehran.[122] Previously, Iraq had relied on bombardment by fighter jets to retaliate against Iranian missiles, jeopardizing a scarce resource to achieve comparatively little results. The ability to retaliate through the new Al-Hussein missiles cemented a new and fuller form of symmetry between the belligerents, with the pace and type of Iraqi attacks reflecting precisely Iranian ones. This dynamic had already appeared in early 1988, with both parties targeting the enemy capital, but became evident after the March 1988 proposal failed to restrain the belligerents' behaviour. For instance, the Iraqi announcement that it would respond to alleged Iranian attacks on cities and settlements near the frontier by hitting Tehran[123] was

[119] UN Doc. S/19603, 11 March 1988, p. 2.
[120] UN Doc. S/19598, p. 6, point 1.
[121] *Ibid.*
[122] *Ibid.*, p. 4.
[123] UN Doc. S/19611, 13 March 1988, p. 2.

immediately met by a statement of the Iranian Government stressing its capacity to 'transform Baghdad into a hell the likes of which has never been seen before'.[124] This deep concern for symmetry, of both a symbolic, qualitative and quantitative character, emerges forcefully in a letter addressed by the Deputy Prime Minister and Minister for Foreign Affairs of Iraq to the UN Secretary-General, whereby 'in attacking Tehran, Iraq is merely responding in kind to the firing of missiles on Baghdad'.[125]

Although the "mirroring" effect of belligerent reprisals resulted in the repeated retaliatory bombing of the parties' capitals and main cities in the spring of 1988,[126] this escalation did not necessarily equate a spiralling-out of control. In the final weeks of the Iran–Iraq War, this interest in parity of arms actually worked as a tool to govern de-escalation in the level of IHL violations. On 20 April 1988, the Iraqi Government re-iterated its offer to halt the bombardment of Iranian cities as of midnight of that day.[127] The terms of this commitment traced precisely those appended to the earlier document of 10 March – including the request that the last bombardment be carried out by Iraq. At first sight, this newer Iraqi offer did not bear more fruits than its predecessor, as both parties continued denouncing attacks on their own towns in the following month. However, their statements also reveal that all the bombardments on civilian targets that allegedly took place after the Iraqi document of 20 April refrained from hitting major towns in Iran (such as Tehran or Isfahan) and Iraq (such as Baghdad or Mosul), focusing instead on the proximity of the frontlines.[128]

By offering a tool to interpret the meaning of retaliatory action as a form of strict symmetry in the conduct of the parties, the Iraqi commitment of 20 April played a key role in controlling and ultimately de-escalating one of the most intense rounds in the "war of the cities", initiated in February 1988. Although this outcome did represent a form

[124] UN Doc. S/19622, 15 March 1988, p. 2.

[125] UN Doc. S/19695, 28 March 1988, pp. 3–4. See also UN Doc. S/19618, 15 March 1988, p. 2.

[126] See, *passim*, UN Docs. S/19732, 4 April 1988; S/19743, 6 April 1988; S/19756, 11 April 1988; S/19760, 12 April 1988; S/19761, 12 April 1988; S/19785, 15 April 1988; S/19792, 18 April 1988; S/19801, 19 April 1988; S/19805, 20 April 1988; S/19817, 21 April 1988; S/19821, 22 April 1988; S/19825, 25 April 1988.

[127] UN Doc. S/19805, pp. 3–4.

[128] See, *passim*, UN Docs. S/19827, 25 April 1988; S/19847, 28 April 1988; S/19848, 28 April 1988; S/19852, 1 May 1988; S/19866, 5 May 1988; S/19876, 11 May 1988; S/19884, 16 May 1988; S/19888, 16 May 1988; S/19893, 19 May 1988; S/19897, 24 May 1988; S/19898, 25 May 1988; S/19907, 26 May 1988; S/19914, 31 May 1988.

of negotiated settlement, it was not accomplished by explicit agreement nor achieved by *dictum* of a third authority. Rather, it was reached by modulating the intensity, the scope and the targets of reprisal action. Recourse to retaliatory conducts that were similar in both type and measure to the lamented violation ensured that the material as well as the symbolic parity between belligerents be sustained over time.

4.3.2.3 Positive Reciprocity: Law-Making

The previous analysis has shown that belligerent reprisals were used to *maintain* the *material* equality between belligerents. As we have seen, this feature can have positive effects, insofar as it can lead to a decrease in the overall amount of IHL breaches; at the same time, those aspects of symmetry governing reciprocal conduct reveal a rather rudimentary manifestation of the logic of (*negative*) reciprocity in the adoption of belligerent reprisals. In the next sections, we will see that recourse to belligerent reprisals during the "war of the cities" could be characterized by a much more ambitious purpose. Such measures were at times used in a way echoing the dynamics of *positive* reciprocity, that is, with a view to *re-negotiating* the *formal* equality of belligerents by clarifying, debating, and ultimately agreeing on the content of the IHL obligations binding the two parties to the armed conflict. This feature appears more clearly in two distinct occurrences of the "war of the cities", where the coercive character of belligerent reprisals was chiefly targeted at making new law, rather than enforcing existing norms.

(1) The Protection of Civilians

(a) Re-affirming and Strengthening Applicable Standards The first instance took place in the initial years of the Iran–Iraq War, with a view to agreeing on a clearer framework for the protection of civilians from attacks. As noted above, the inapplicability *qua* treaty of the recently entered into force AP I complicated the task of determining the scope of obligations governing the conduct of hostilities, which had to be elucidated in light of customary law.[129] Tellingly, in the early phases of the war the UN Security Council could condemn 'all *violations* of international humanitarian law, in particular, the provisions of the Geneva Conventions of 1949 in all their aspects'[130] – but when it came to military operations against civilian targets, including cities and residential areas, it

[129] See Sections 4.3.1.1–4.3.1.2.
[130] UN Security Council Resolution 540 (1983), 31 October 1983, para. 2 [emphasis added].

could only 'call for the immediate cessation' thereof, without an explicit classification as illegal.[131] Seen from this perspective, the question as to the validity, specificity and viability of the customary norm prohibiting deliberate and indiscriminate attacks on the civilian population was by no means a moot one. At a time when the innovations brought about by the adoption of AP I were still recent, the scale and frequency of attacks affecting civilians could be taken as evidence that the underlying norms had not crystallized with sufficient cogency or precision.[132]

Against this backdrop, recourse to belligerent reprisals could attain two objectives. The more immediate one consisted in the re-affirmation of the cogency of the norm(s) breached: insofar as the belligerent reprisal is justified by (and consists of) a breach of the laws of war, its threat or adoption reiterates, in the eyes of the counterpart as well as the international community, that such norms continue to bind the parties to the conflict. Beyond that, belligerent reprisals could offer the other party incentives to (i) build on the scope of the obligations underlying the legal relationship, and (ii) provide a more solid grounding for applicable norms. In this sense, belligerent reprisals would operate not only by re-stating existing rules, but also by weaving new legal bonds – in a way typical of positive reciprocity.

This is precisely the path allegedly followed by Iraq between 1983 and 1984. Reacting to Security Council Resolution 540, Iraq welcomed the paragraph therein calling for the immediate cessation of all military operations against civilian targets, declared its willingness to be bound by it, but conditioned such acceptance on a reciprocal commitment on the part of Iran.[133] The implications of this position became even clearer a few months later, when Iraq denounced the alleged shelling of Basra and other cities by Iranian forces. While reiterating its intention to 'accord such an act the response that it deserves', a statement by the Iraqi military spokesman called on 'the peoples of Iran … to exert

[131] *Ibid.*

[132] In his reflections on the Gulf War, Kalshoven attributed an undisputed customary status to those rules on methods and means of warfare 'embodied mainly though not exclusively in Section I (Methods and Means of Warfare) of Part III (Methods and Means of Warfare, Combatant and Prisoner-of-War Status) of Protocol I of 1977' ('Prohibitions or Restrictions', p. 99); as regards 'the customary law character of some of the pertinent *basic* rules', such as the principle of distinction and the prohibition of disproportionate attacks, it was derived primarily from the unanimous adoption of a soft law instrument such as General Assembly resolution 2444 (XXIII): *ibid.*, pp. 102–3 [emphasis added].

[133] UN Doc. A/38/560-S/16120, 3 November 1983, p. 2, para. 1.

pressure on their rulers to *consent to the conclusion of an agreement* concerning non-aggression against cities and towns'.[134] Then, in mid-February 1984, just a few days after Iraq promised to cease attacks on targets situated in Iranian towns, the Chief of Staff of the Iranian Army announced that they would stop attacking civilian targets.[135] Although the international community continued to denounce attacks on civilian targets in the following weeks,[136] it is possible to discern (at least in the short term) a marked decrease in the intensity of the "war of the cities". Belligerents limited themselves to *threatening* the adoption of retaliatory attacks on cities, without carrying them out or acknowledging their use as done in the past;[137] instead, they preferred to emphasize the need to develop effective mechanisms to ensure international supervision to protect civilian centres.[138]

(b) The June Moratorium Eventually, this long process reached its culmination with the entry into force of the so-called June moratorium, whereby both Iraq and Iran undertook to the UN Secretary-General 'that all deliberate military attacks by any means on purely civilian population centres in either country w[ould] cease, effective 0001 GMT on 12 June 1984'.[139] The two belligerents accepted these terms on the conditions that the counterpart also commit thereby, and that an effective supervision and implementation of the agreement be guaranteed.[140]

The actual implications of the June moratorium are twofold. First, by means of this undertaking, the two belligerents committed in explicit terms to the prohibition on intentional attacks against civilian populations in the context of the Iran–Iraq War. This resolved all potential questions left open by the absence of applicable treaty rules, the previous conduct of the parties, and the vagueness of customary norms. Therefore, recourse to belligerent reprisals prompted the definition of a mutually agreed standard of conduct, which secured until the spring of 1985 a

[134] UN Doc. A/38/786-S/16344, 16 February 1984, p. 2 [emphasis added].
[135] UN Doc. S/16363, pp. 1–3.
[136] See the Declaration of the Presidency of the European Economic Community adopted on 28 February 1984 at the Ministerial Meeting on European Political Co-operation and reproduced in UN Doc. A/39/123-S/16389, 6 March 1984, p. 3.
[137] UN Doc. S/16372, 24 February 1984, p. 2.
[138] UN Doc. S/16361, 23 February 1984, p. 2.
[139] UN Docs. S/16614, 12 June 1984, p. 1, and S/16615, 12 June 1984, p. 1.
[140] UN Docs. S/16609, 10 June 1984, p. 2, and S/16610, p. 2.

significant reduction in attacks on civilians and civilian centres denounced by the parties.[141]

In addition to this categorical re-statement of the principle of distinction, the June moratorium represented an instance of proper law-making, insofar as Iran and Iraq gave up the right to adopt belligerent reprisals, at least against purely civilian population centres and as long as effective mechanisms of verification were put in place. The original proposal by the UN Secretary-General had only called on Iran and Iraq to commit to refrain in the future from *initiating* attacks on civilian targets – arguably, this did not demand of belligerents to renounce also the right to retaliate.[142] However, no such restrictive reading can be found in the answers of Iran and Iraq,[143] nor in the final terms of the moratorium communicated by the UN Secretary-General, which rule out 'all' attacks.[144] As seen above, this was undoubtedly a considerable advance over customary prohibitions ruling at the time – one that would have brought the obligations applicable to the Iran–Iraq War very close to the prohibition of attacks by way of reprisals against the civilian population set forth in Article 51(6) AP I.[145] The capacity of belligerent reprisals to provide incentives for the negotiation and adoption of new legal settings is here taken to the extreme result of ... leading to the renunciation of those very measures!

The prohibition to carry out deliberate attacks on civilians re-affirmed in the June moratorium remained an unavoidable yardstick to assess the parties' conduct for the rest of the conflict.[146] In this sense, belligerent reprisals proved effective in clarifying the scope of existing obligations. On the other hand, the surrender of the right to adopt belligerent reprisals against civilians could not be sustained over the long period, due to the shortcomings in the fundamental condition for its

[141] In late June 1984, the UN Secretary-General expressed its gratefulness for the good faith implementation of the June moratorium by both parties: UN Doc. S/16663, 6 July 1984, p. 1.

[142] UN Doc. S/16611, 11 June 1984, p. 1.

[143] In UN Doc. S/16609 and S/16610. In the former document, the fact that the Iranian acceptance was premised on the total ending of Iraqi bombardment of Iranian cities should be interpreted as a condition for the entry into force of the moratorium, rather than as a condition for its continued cogency – if claimed otherwise, the Iranian insistence in the same document on the creation of adequate monitoring mechanisms would lose its *raison d'être*.

[144] See UN Doc. S/16614 and S/16615.

[145] See Section 4.3.1.3.

[146] See, for instance, UN Doc. S/19071, 24 August 1987, p. 2.

success – that is, the setting up of mechanisms under the UN aegis to monitor compliance with the June moratorium.[147] To be sure, in the second half of 1984 two teams stationed in Baghdad and Tehran carried out missions to inspect specific allegations of violations of the moratorium denounced by both parties. However, the lapse of time between the attacks and the investigations, coupled with the limited scope of the teams' powers, often prevented the inspectors from finding unequivocally that a purely civilian population centre had been deliberately attacked.[148] When, in March 1985, the UN Secretary-General sponsored a renewed agreement to counter a further exacerbation in the "war of the cities",[149] only Iran accepted the proposal.[150] However, besides the previous conditions that also Iraq withhold its attacks on civilians and that serious and effective monitoring measures against violations be adopted, Iran reserved for itself the right to retaliate against Iraqi violations of the agreement.[151] This signalled the resumption of the "war of the cities", but it also paved the way for another demonstration of the law-making function of belligerent reprisals.

(2) **Economic Objects and Military Objectives** Despite its sweeping language, the June moratorium left unaddressed several issues. On its terms, the agreement only prohibited *deliberate* military attacks on *purely* civilian *population* centres.[152] As such, it did not cover instances where civilian persons and objects were hit incidentally as a result of attacks on legitimate targets.[153] Nor did it explain how to assess attacks aimed at

[147] See the proposal by the UN Secretary-General in UN Doc. S/16627, 15 June 1984, p. 1, accepted by the Security Council in UN Doc. S/16628, 15 June 1984, p. 1.

[148] See UN Doc. S/16750, 19 September 1984, p. 3, para. 11; UN Doc. S/16897, 16 January 1985, p. 5, para. 17 (conclusion on Alavaneh); UN Doc. S/16920, 30 January 1985, p. 3, para. 11(c). For a positive conclusion, see UN Doc. S/16897, p. 5, para. 17 (conclusion on Bardieh and Dehlavieh).

[149] UN Doc. S/17018, 10 March 1985, p. 1.

[150] UN Doc. S/17020, 10 March 1985, p. 2. As for Iraq, its Deputy Prime Minister and Minister for Foreign Affairs did not consider this enough, and urged the UN Secretary-General to establish direct contacts with the belligerents' representatives to 'draw up clear and agreed principles, rules and guarantees for an agreement to prevent the deliberate bombardment of purely civilian population centres': see UN Doc. S/17019, 10 March 1985, pp. 3–4.

[151] UN Doc. S/17020, p. 2.

[152] UN Docs. S/16614, p. 1, and S/16615, p. 1. Compare with the original proposal by the UN Secretary-General, which also used the arguably wider term 'civilian areas' (UN Doc. S/16611, p. 1).

[153] In its positive reply to the UN Secretary-General, Iraqi President Saddam Hussein hinted precisely at this issue by stating that 'both parties should refrain from placing military

targets that, while not harbouring the civilian population, did not have military significance either. The answer to both questions depended, in large part, on the definition of what a military objective was. As we saw above, however, the general international law ruling at the time was far from settled on this issue, since the traditional criteria based on the intrinsic military characteristics of an object were being slowly supplanted by the functional element of effective contribution to military action.[154] In the final years of the Iran–Iraq War, the need to reach a common understanding of what constituted a military objective became particularly pressing with regard to a particular set of objects, that is, economic installations. Here as well, belligerent reprisals served as a tool to negotiate a shared understanding and forge an agreement as to whether economic facilities could be considered or not as permissible targets. What is more, it was precisely by justifying and explaining their recourse to reprisal measures, that the positions of the two belligerents on the qualification of economic objects as military objectives were developed, refined, expressed, and debated.

(a) First Move and Countermove The process developed as a game of chess, where each move by one party was followed and matched by a countermove from the opponent. Initially, Iraq put forward the view that the notion of purely civilian population centres protected under the June moratorium did not include economic and industrial facilities, which could therefore be targeted.[155] The Iraqi position equated economic installations with military targets on the basis of the presumption (for which no rebuttal seemed to be accepted) that both categories of objects were used 'for the continuation of [the Iranian] aggression againt Iraq'[156] and in support of the Iranian war effort.[157]

Confronted with these arguments, Iran consistently qualified its attacks on economic and industrial targets as 'retaliatory measures'[158]

concentrations in or near towns so that there will be no intermingling between them during military operations' (UN Doc. S/16610, p. 2) – something that Iranian President Khamenei denounced as 'merely an excuse to avoid implementing [the] commitments and to renew attacks on our civilian areas' (UN Doc. S/16630, 15 June 1984, p. 2).

[154] See Section 4.3.1.2.

[155] See the statement by Deputy Prime Minister and Minister for Foreign Affairs of Iraq before the Security Council in UN Doc. S/PV.2663, pp. 28–29/30.

[156] UN Doc. S/18243, 28 July 1986, p. 2.

[157] UN Doc. S/18484, 26 November 1986, p. 2.

[158] UN Doc. S/18284, 18 August 1986, p. 1.

vis-à-vis unlawful Iraqi conducts (such as alleged attacks on purely civilian areas,[159] an Iranian passenger plane in Shiraz airport,[160] and non-military and residential centres).[161] Insofar as belligerent reprisals involve by definition the breach of a rule of the laws of war, the Iranian statements insisted implicitly on the illegality of attacks on economic objectives. To boost its argument, Iran drew an explicit link between, on the one hand, an appeal by the UN Secretary-General to refrain from attacks on civilian areas,[162] and, on the other, its own interruption of retaliatory strikes on economic and industrial targets.[163] By so doing, economic facilities were explicitly qualified as civilian objects, and excluded from the purview of legitimate military objectives.

(b) Second Move and Countermove In their next move, Iraq reacted to these Iranian arguments by advancing two claims. On the one hand, they reaffirmed that attacks on 'economic objectives supporting the Iranian war effort [were] in full accordance with the rules governing the conduct of hostilities'.[164] By so doing, Iraqi officials pursued a twofold objective, that is, asserting the legality of their own conduct *vis-à-vis* 'vital economic installations deep inside Iranian territory' while depriving Iran of the justification to take retaliatory conducts and re-ignite the "war of the cities".[165] This move, however, had a serious downside: if Iraqi attacks on economic targets were legal under international law, so had to be those carried out by Iran – even without the need to recur to a reprisal-based argument. This is why Iraq complemented the first part of its argument with a novel prong. In several communications to the UN, Iraqi officials complained that Iranian attacks purportedly directed at economic targets (and therefore *prima facie* lawful according to Iraq) were carried out through weapons that made it impossible, by their very nature, to target selectively and that 'could therefore be used only to wreak random havoc among the civilian

159 *Ibid.*
160 See the communiqué by the Iranian military information centre quoted by Iraq in UN Doc. S/18407, 16 October 1986, p. 1, as well as UN Doc. S/18410, 16 October 1986, p. 1.
161 UN Doc. S/19550, 29 February 1988, p. 2.
162 Quoted in (1990) 40 *Yearbook of the United Nations 1986* (Dordrecht: Martinus Nijhoff, 1990), p. 225.
163 UN Doc. S/18284, p. 1.
164 UN Doc. S/18484, 26 November 1986, p. 2.
165 UN Doc. S/18412, 17 October 1986, p. 2.

population in strictly residential areas'.[166] This claim entailed a complete reversal of the earlier arguments raised by Iran: the right to adopt reprisals was no longer vested on Iran (because of the Iraqi attacks on economic targets), but on Iraq (because of the indiscriminate attacks carried out by Iran).[167] In sum, this elaborate argumentative strategy gave Iraq the upper hand by (i) defending the legality of its attacks on economic targets, (ii) excluding the legality of similar Iranian ones (either on their own terms or as allegedly justified retaliation), and (iii) reclaiming a right to adopt belligerent reprisals against Iran.

This prompted Iranian authorities to further refine their position. Previously, Iran had considered attacks on economic targets as unlawful, but less grave than attacks on the civilian population. Still at the end of 1986, its officials understood the adoption of retaliatory measures against strategic and industrial targets as a form of self-restraint, if compared to the original bombardments of purely civilian centres that Iraq was allegedly carrying out.[168] Their arguments evolved at the turn of that year, as they started to consider Iraqi attacks on 'non-military installations' together with, and on the same footing as, those on residential and civilian quarters.[169] This implied that the protection of economic objects from attack was seen as flowing from the failure to identify in them some clear military characteristics, in line with the long-standing understanding of military objectives indicated above.[170] Resuming the lexicon adopted by the UN Secretary-General,[171] attacks on civilian populations and on economic targets were given the unitary label of attacks on 'civilian areas',[172] and were stigmatized comprehensively as the breach of 'one of the most important humanitarian rules pertaining to the protection of civilian persons and populations in time of war'.[173] Coherently with this qualification, from that moment onwards Iran considered itself legitimized to threaten retaliation in kind on cities and purely civilian areas, instead of recurring to the more

[166] UN Docs. S/18412, p. 2; S/18476, 24 November 1986, p. 2; S/18484, p. 2; and S/19551, 29 February 1988, p. 1.

[167] For a comprehensive example of this sequence, see UN Doc. S/19551, pp. 1–2. See also UN Docs. S/18476, p. 2, and S/18484, p. 2.

[168] UN Doc. S/18423, 24 October 1986, p. 1.

[169] UN Docs. S/18537, 22 December 1986, p. 2; S/19071, 24 August 1987, p. 2.

[170] See Section 4.3.1.2.

[171] See footnote 162 in this chapter.

[172] UN Doc. S/18488, 28 November 1986, p. 1.

[173] UN Doc. S/18537, p. 2.

limited form of 'token [retaliatory] measures' to which it had adhered in the past.[174]

(c) The Iraqi Offer of February 1987 The following move in this exchange marked an initial *rapprochement* in the positions of the two belligerents. In February 1987, a meeting of the Iraqi Revolution Command Council and regional leaders chaired by President Saddam Hussein announced a two-week halt in the 'bombardment of Iranian towns', subject to a series of conditions.[175] The document specified that '[t]his suspension of bombing naturally does not extend to military targets, concentrations of troops or *targets bearing a direct or indirect relationship to the war effort* of the Iranian régime'.[176] Although the broad wording of the last category of targets could be interpreted to include economic and industrial objects, other elements in the announcement go against such a broad interpretation. First, the communiqué represented the first time that Iraq did not *explicitly* classify such facilities as legitimate targets of attack, mentioning instead only the relation with the war effort. Second, by giving up on the overtly restrictive notion of "purely civilian residential centres" adopted in previous communications, Iraq signalled a willingness to enlarge the class of protected objects, and to refrain from hitting economic targets at least when they were placed in "Iranian towns". Iraq was therefore moving closer to the Iranian construction whereby the economic or industrial character of an object did not *necessarily* imply its relevance in sustaining the enemy economy and, as a consequence, its classification as a military objective. In conclusion, the announcement represents an example of constructive ambiguity that leaves the door open for a shared understanding on this element of the conduct of hostilities.

Unfortunately, the Iranian counterpart did not take full advantage of this opportunity. Iran refused to accept the Iraqi proposal (for reasons that did not relate to the interpretation of the notion of military objectives)[177] and Iraq considered that it was released from its commitment to

[174] UN Docs. S/18507, 7 December 1986, p. 2; S/18537, p. 2; and S/18540, 23 December 1986, p. 1.

[175] UN Doc. S/18704, 18 February 1987, p. 2. This is not to be confused with the later proposal of March 1988, discussed in Section 4.3.2.2(1)(c).

[176] *Ibid.* [emphasis added].

[177] UN Doc. S/18725, 26 February 1987, p. 1. According to Iran, the Iraqi communiqué subjected the suspension of attacks on civilians (a *ius in bello* question) upon the

halt bombarding enemy cities.[178] In the following months, the two parties reverted to their previous positions, with Iran denouncing attacks on economic targets as unlawful[179] while Iraq continued to claim the right to strike the Iranian 'war machine [including] economic, industrial, oil and logistic areas and facilities'.[180]

(d) The Statement of March 1988 Yet, the understanding of economic objects as a protected category – propounded by Iran and accepted (to a certain extent) by Iraq in its announcement of February 1987 – gained momentum in the final phases of the war. Reference has already been made above, while discussing attacks on civilian populations,[181] to the statement of March 1988 where the Iraqi military spokesman offered to halt the bombardment of Iranian cities, subject to Iran accepting a series of terms. In an important proviso, the document distinguished between 'the bombardment of economic targets which serve the aggressor war machine [from] the bombardment of purely civilian centres';[182] only the latter would be suspended as per the offer, whereas Iraq maintained the right to 'strike at the targets which *serve and supply* the machinery of aggression and war, as provided in international law'.[183]

At first sight, and insofar as economic targets are explicitly mentioned as lawful targets, this passage seems to backtrack from the February 1987 communiqué. At a more careful reading, however, it appears that the announcement of March 1988 provides economic targets with a higher scope of protection than its predecessor. Indeed, the criterion of "serving and supplying" demands a stricter nexus with the war effort than the "direct or indirect relationship" mentioned in the February 1987 communiqué. The contribution of economic objects to the pursuance of the conflict is no longer presumed, as had occurred in the past, but

discontinuance of military operations (a *ius ad bellum* issue) – see *ibid.* and points 1 and 2 in the Iraqi proposal (UN Doc. S/18704, p. 2).

[178] UN Docs. S/18719, 24 February 1987, pp. 2–3; S/18730, 2 March 1987, p. 1.

[179] See especially UN Doc. S/19072, 25 August 1987, p. 2, but also UN Docs. S/19070, 24 August 1987, pp. 1–2; S/19116, 9 September 1987, p. 1; and S/19205, 13 October 1987, p. 2.

[180] UN Doc. S/19108, 4 September 1987, p. 2.

[181] See Section 4.3.2.2(1)(c).

[182] UN Doc. S/19598, p. 6, point 5.

[183] *Ibid.* [emphasis added].

now needs to be based on a positive, instrumental correlation.[184] Having entered the war with an understanding of economic installations as a category of objects inextricably linked to the military effort, Iraq was brought by means of retaliatory action to soften its position and embrace an alternative construction of economic facilities as being in principle civilian.

Ultimately, the threat and adoption of belligerent reprisals resulted in a bargaining process through which the parties to the conflict developed, negotiated and eventually agreed upon standards for the conduct of hostilities *vis-à-vis* economic objects. The initial positions of the two belligerents were extremely polarized: whereas Iraq was interested in expanding the category of military objectives by also including economic objects, Iran strived to keep the class of permissible targets as restricted as possible, and upheld the customary criterion based on inherent military characteristics. By the end of the war, the positions of the two belligerents had come closer: a new form of mutual understanding had solidified, which was shaped and re-inforced by recourse to unilateral measures. Admittedly, under Iraqi pressure the classification as military objectives was now dependent on the military *significance* of an economic object, and no longer on its inherent military *characteristics* – a development that outpaced customary standards, but was perfectly in line with contemporary trends. However, due to the Iranian opposition, that qualification of economic objects as military objectives was still dependent on a very high threshold and stringent test, whereby their civilian status would only be forfeited if the instrumental character vis-à-vis the waging of war was direct and positively established. Beyond the terms of this mutual understanding, what strikes is the fact that this bargaining process was mostly conducted through the invocation of belligerent reprisals and the legal justifications that accompanied them over time.

4.3.3 *Conclusion on the "War of the Cities"*

The trajectory of rules protecting civilians and economic objects from intentional attacks during the Iran–Iraq War highlights the law-making

[184] This new construction might also contribute to explaining why, in following communications to the UN, both belligerents emphasized civilian casualties of enemy attacks, whereas their impact on economic and industrial targets (previously a highly recurrent topic of denunciation) almost vanished: see UN Docs. S/19611, 13 March 1988, pp. 1–2 and S/19612, 13 March 1988, p. 2.

function of belligerent reprisals. Retaliatory measures could hardly aim at upholding this set of norms, because their applicability to the conflict was not settled, or because their contours were uncertain, evolving and debated. Instead, belligerent reprisals represented a flexible tool to react to affirmative stances put in place by the counterpart, express satisfaction or dissatisfaction for a given legal construct, and eventually fine-tune an equilibrium that could be accepted by both parties. They did not undermine a legal framework whose traits were fully settled – quite the opposite, they contributed to sustaining it and to filling gaps in protection that had been left open by the bundle of obligations linking the parties to the conflict. In a new and specific sense, the symmetry between belligerents was something to craft and adjust, rather than just enforce and maintain.

4.4 Concluding Remarks on Belligerent Reprisals in the Iran–Iraq War

Writing in the closing stages of the Iran–Iraq War, David hinged on an interesting paradox of that conflict. He noted that, although the applicable rules were simple and did not raise any complex legal issues, some of them (at times among the most simple and elementary) were violated by one, or the other, or both parties.[185] He concluded his analysis by saying that the lawyer's task is limited to taking stock of this simple acknowledgement, and that the rest belongs to the factual or the political domain.[186]

I respectfully disagree with David's opinion. Assessing the IHL breaches that occurred during the Iran–Iraq War in isolation one from the other does not pay sufficient heed to the fact that applicable norms allowed for retaliation, and that parties explicitly qualified their actions as a legitimate response to the counterpart's behaviour. What is more, such a compartmentalized approach to IHL violations fails to understand the meaning that belligerents attributed to their retaliatory behaviours. The lawyer's task cannot be reduced to highlighting the non-conformity of an action to the controlling norm; much more ambitiously, it must encompass the difficult job of articulating in legal terms the purpose(s) that belligerents attributed to such retaliatory conducts.

[185] David, 'La Guerre du Golfe', p. 182.
[186] *Ibid.*

As the Iran–Iraq War demonstrates, belligerent reprisals escape the rigid contours drawn by the enforcement paradigm. Their logic and their operationalization are much more similar to those governing reciprocity. On the one hand, instances of chemical retaliation during that conflict refute the traditional view of belligerent reprisals as an enforcement tool clearly distinguished from, and of more limited import than, mechanisms inspired by negative reciprocity. When the parties threatened or adopted belligerent reprisals in the field of chemical weapons, negative reciprocity inspired both the purpose associated with such measures (i.e., preventing the enemy from maximizing the military advantages reaped from its unlawful behaviour) and their specific traits and features (in-kind violations of the 1925 Geneva Protocol).

This convergence between belligerent reprisals and reciprocity found further support in our analysis of the "war of the cities". Throughout the conflict, retaliatory attacks on enemy civilians and civilian objects took on a much wider set of purposes and functions than those associated with the enforcement paradigm. The interest in inducing compliance with a breached norm was but one – and by no means the most recurrent – objective of retaliation. The "war of the cities" highlighted that belligerent reprisals were threatened and carried out with a panoply of purposes in mind – that is, stigmatizing and punishing enemy breaches; remedying the consequences of violations that had placed a party in a position of military inferiority; and, most importantly, making law, either by strengthening applicable standards of conduct or by enacting and agreeing on new ones. All of these purposes reveal a strong interest in maintaining the equality between belligerents, both in a formal sense (equality of rights and obligations) and in a material one (parity of arms). This brings the functioning of belligerent reprisals much closer to a paradigm inspired by reciprocity, seen both in its negative aspects (as a way of seeking release from obligations *vis-à-vis* a non-compliant enemy) and in its positive ones (as a tool to increase the range of applicable norms).

One could argue that these reciprocity-inspired features are not inherent to belligerent reprisals, and that they can be accounted for in light of the relative paucity of treaty or customary norms applicable to the Iran–Iraq War. Although tempting, this explanation is not convincing. At a closer inspection, the purposes attached to belligerent reprisals became increasingly ambitious as the interaction between the parties to the conflict deepened. As each belligerent grew more and more aware of the counterpart's strategies, rationales and behaviours, and as the purview and content of norms grew more and more apparent, it became possible to attach ever-refined objectives to the threat or adoption of retaliatory conducts. In this sense, belligerent reprisals should not be seen as meaningful only in legal contexts characterized by unclear or rudimentary norms – quite the contrary, the sophistication of their functioning seems directly proportional to the depth of the belligerents' interaction and to the robustness of the legal framework.

Belligerent reprisals would then function as a highly flexible tool through which parties to an armed conflict bargain, approve or refuse, and ultimately police the concrete legal framework governing war-time interactions. As we have seen, their grounding in reciprocity is inextricably linked with the ideas of equality of rights and obligations, of symmetry and parity of arms. These aspects do not pose challenges insofar as we are confronted with international armed conflicts, which pit against each other entities (i.e., States) having the same status under international law. But what about non-international armed conflicts, where parties to an armed conflict do not necessarily enjoy the same status, and where their equality before the law is a matter of contention? Is a reciprocity-inspired understanding of belligerent reprisals tenable in that context as well? It is this important question that we will now address.

5

Belligerent Reprisals in Non-international Armed Conflict

Conceptual Issues

5.1 Belligerent Reprisals in NIAC: New Features for the "Altar of Humanity"

5.1.1 Black Letter Law: Saying Too Much, or Saying Too Little?

The topic of Chapters 5 and 6 could be described with Churchill's quote, as 'a riddle wrapped in a mystery inside an enigma'.[1] The preceding chapters have shown how elusive is the concept of belligerent reprisals, and how demanding the task of determining their purpose and function – but these difficulties are magnified when the mechanism is analysed in relation to non-international armed conflicts (NIACs).[2] When reprisals are taken against, or even by, a non-State armed group (NSAG), a range of new questions – all involving some foundational aspects of the laws of armed conflict – adds to the usual complexities. International and non-international armed conflicts differ both in the dynamics at play and in the applicable law. It is therefore legitimate to wonder if belligerent reprisals operate in much the same way in the two fields – even prior to that, if the very concept is transposable from inter-State wars to conflicts where at least one party does not have the prerogatives of a sovereign.

[1] Attributed to Winston Churchill, BBC broadcast, 1 October 1939.

[2] According to the ICTY, 'conflicts not of an international character' (common Article 3 to the 1949 GCs) exist 'whenever there is ... protracted armed violence between governmental authorities and organized armed groups or between such groups within a State': ICTY, *The Prosecutor* v. *Tadić* (IT-94-1-AR72), Decision on the Defence Motion for Interlocutory Appeal on Jurisdiction, Appeals Chamber, 2 October 1995, para. 70; ICTY, *The Prosecutor* v. *Tadić* (IT-94-1-T), Judgment, Trial Chamber, 7 May 1997, para. 562.

Treaty law offers contradictory indications in answering these questions. Neither Article 3 common to the 1949 Geneva Conventions,[3] nor the 1977 Additional Protocol II in its final form[4] contains a provision on reprisals in NIAC. Other treaties do prohibit reprisals in provisions that textually apply to both types of conflict: this is the case for the 1954 Hague Convention[5] and the II Protocol to the 1980 Convention on Certain Conventional Weapons (either in its amended form of 1996,[6] or through joint application of its original text with the 2001 amendment to its umbrella convention).[7] However, Bílková has argued that this ostensible regulation of reprisals in NIAC 'may be more a product of disordered drafting than of any intentional decision'.[8] Also the revised African Convention on the Conservation of Nature and Natural Resources prohibited 'using the destruction or modification of the environment as a means of combat or reprisal', without distinguishing between IAC and NIAC.[9] But here as well, the text does not allow

[3] Geneva Conventions Relative to the Protection of the Victims of International Armed Conflicts, Geneva, 12 August 1949, in force 21 October 1950, 75 UNTS 31; UKTS 39 (1958), Cmd 550; 157 BFSP 229; 6 UST 3114; TIAS 3362; ATS 21 (1958).

[4] Protocol Additional to the Geneva Conventions of 12 August 1949, and relating to the Protection of Victims of Non-international Armed Conflicts (Protocol II), Geneva, 8 June 1977, in force 7 December 1978, 1125 UNTS 609.

[5] Hague Convention for the Protection of Cultural Property in the Event of Armed Conflict, The Hague, 14 May 1954, in force 7 August 1956, 249 UNTS 215, Article 4(4) in conjunction with Article 19(1).

[6] Protocol on Prohibitions or Restrictions on the Use of Mines, Booby-Traps and Other Devices as amended on 3 May 1996 (Protocol II, as amended on 3 May 1996) annexed to the Convention on Prohibitions or Restrictions on the Use of Certain Conventional Weapons which may be deemed to be Excessively Injurious or to have Indiscriminate Effects, Geneva, 3 May 1996, in force 3 December 1998, 2048 UNTS 93, Article 3(7) in conjunction with Article 1(2).

[7] Article 3(2) of the 1980 version of Protocol II (Protocol on Prohibitions or Restrictions on the Use of Mines, Booby-Traps and Other Devices annexed to the Convention on Prohibitions or Restrictions on the Use of Certain Conventional Weapons which may be deemed to be Excessively Injurious or to have Indiscriminate Effects, Geneva, 10 October 1980, in force 2 December 1983, 1342 UNTS 137) in conjunction with Article 1 of the CCW as amended in December 2001 (Amendment to Article 1 of the Convention on Prohibitions or Restrictions on the Use of Certain Conventional Weapons Which May Be Deemed to Be Excessively Injurious or to Have Indiscriminate Effects, Geneva, 21 December 2001, in force 18 May 2004, 2260 UNTS 82).

[8] Bílková, 'Reprisals in NIACs', p. 48; Kalshoven, *Belligerent Reprisals*, pp. 276–77.

[9] Revised African Convention on the Conservation of Nature and Natural Resources, Maputo, 11 July 2003, in force 23 July 2016, Article XV(1)(c). In its original version, the Convention did not address military and hostile activities, including reprisals (African Convention on the Conservation of Nature and Natural Resources, Algiers, 15 September 1968, in force 16 June 1969, 1001 UNTS 1).

conclusive inferences. Arguably, the reference to 'Parties' bound by the provision indicates the States parties to the treaty rather than the parties to an armed conflict – which leaves any question as to the implications for non-State actors unresolved. To sum up, the place of belligerent reprisals in the law of NIAC is not elucidated by these treaties: the 'ordinary meaning to be given to the[ir] terms' suggests that reprisals are envisaged and regulated also outside of inter-State conflicts, but this inference is not confirmed if recourse is had to the supplementary means of interpretation.[10]

As for recent manuals on international law applicable during armed conflict, their lack of provisions on reprisals in relation to NIAC can be interpreted in several ways. Despite its comprehensive scope, the *San Remo Manual on the Law of Non-international Armed Conflict* makes no mention of reprisals, but significantly acknowledges that 'violations by one side are likely to encourage reciprocal misconduct by the other'.[11] The Commentary on the *Manual on International Law Applicable to Air and Missile Warfare* lists belligerent reprisals as a particular form of '*[i]mplementation and enforcement* of the law in the relations *between States*';[12] but since such issues are expressly excluded from the scope of the Manual, there is no indication whether the corresponding rule would also apply (and to what extent) in NIAC.[13] On its part, the *Tallinn Manual 2.0 on the International Law Applicable to Cyber Warfare* maintains the position (already expressed in its first edition on the basis of the work of the ICRC) whereby '[t]he concept of belligerent reprisal does not exist in non-international armed conflict'.[14] In sum, the absence of black-letter norms on the topic could either (i) remain unaccounted for;

[10] Vienna Convention on the Law of Treaties, Vienna, 23 May 1969, in force 27 January 1980, 1155 UNTS 331, Articles 31–32.

[11] International Institute of Humanitarian Law, *The Manual on the Law of Non-international Armed Conflict, with Commentary*, San Remo, 2006, Preface, p. 1. The statement is made in relation to the advantages of compliance with the Manual.

[12] Harvard Program on Humanitarian Policy and Conflict Research, *Manual on International Law Applicable to Air and Missile Warfare* (Cambridge: Cambridge University Press, 2013), p. xvi, para. D(c) (emphasis added).

[13] *Ibid.*

[14] Michael N. Schmitt (ed.), *Tallinn Manual 2.0 on the International Law Applicable to Cyber Warfare* (Cambridge: Cambridge University Press, 2017, 2nd ed.), p. 464, Commentary 3 on Rule 109 and, similarly, p. 461, Commentary 1 on Rule 108. See also Michael N. Schmitt (ed.), *Tallinn Manual on the International Law Applicable to Cyber Warfare* (Cambridge: Cambridge University Press, 2013), p. 150, Commentary 1 on Rule 46 and p. 153, Commentary 3 on Rule 47.

(ii) flow from a (at all times reversible) delimitation of the scope of research; or (iii) reflect a deliberate choice of substance.

We are thus confronted with two, seemingly opposed trends: on the one hand, the textual elements of treaties that foresee reprisals in NIAC are seen as going beyond the intentions of the drafters; on the other, the mechanism keeps re-surfacing even in those manuals that are particularly reticent to acknowledge it outside inter-State conflicts. How can we reconcile the fact that the law seems to say too much in one case, and too little in another?

5.1.2 Presuming Intended Language: The ILC Practice

As a first step, we should exercise considerable caution before concluding that references to the application of belligerent reprisals in NIAC are the side effect of negligent or unintended drafting. The burden of proof for such an argument is particularly heavy in a field – the law of armed conflict – where every treaty clause is meticulously crafted (as we shall see while discussing the *travaux préparatoires* of AP II). Besides running against the plain meaning of the text, this argument appears less and less tenable as the number of instruments that address reprisals even in intra-State conflicts grows incrementally.

What is more, in some contexts the notion of reprisals is applied to NIACs *with full knowledge* (if only by way of progressive development). The evolving practice of the ILC is a particularly telling example. Back in 2001, in its Commentary on the chapter on countermeasures in the ARSIWA, the Commission had defined belligerent reprisals as 'action taken in time of *international* armed conflict'.[15] A few years later, the issue came up again during work on the 'Protection of the Environment in relation to Armed Conflicts'. In a footnote to her Second Report of 2015, the Special Rapporteur Jacobsson endorsed (without further elaboration) the idea that 'the concept of reprisals does not exist in non-international armed conflict'.[16] And yet, the draft principles adopted on first reading in 2019 supported an altogether different conclusion: whereas draft principle 16 prohibited '[a]ttacks against the natural

[15] ILC, 'Commentary to ARSIWA', p. 128, Commentary 3 on Part III, Chapter II.

[16] Marie G. Jacobsson, 'Second Report on the Protection of the Environment in relation to Armed Conflicts', UN Doc. A/CN.4/685, 28 May 2015, p. 62, footnote 280.

environment by way of reprisals',[17] the ILC Commentary informed us at the outset that '[n]o distinction is generally made' in the work between IACs and NIACs.[18]

At first sight, this formulation raises the same interpretive problems as the treaties mentioned above: the provision on reprisals is separate from the definition of the scope *ratione materiae*, and the final text does not seem to reflect the original intentions of the drafters. But in this case, the inference that (the prohibition of) reprisals applies in both types of conflict is explicitly defended by the ILC. The opportunity of extending the prohibition of reprisals to NIACs had been discussed (and sometimes criticized) during the ILC meetings,[19] in comments by Governments[20] and before the 6th Committee of the UN General Assembly.[21] The ILC Commentary does reflect these debates: it recalls the objection of some members that 'by not differentiating between the position in international armed conflicts and non-international armed conflicts, draft principle 16 would attempt to create a new international law rule';[22] it also concedes that its inclusion 'can be seen as promoting the progressive development of international law'.[23] But in the end, the provision was seen as 'particularly relevant and necessary' and the decision was taken to retain it without modifications.[24] And in their final 2022 version, the ILC's 'Draft Principles on Protection of the Environment in relation to Armed Conflicts' take an even stronger stance. After recalling the divergent views on the applicability of belligerent reprisals in NIACs, the ILC Commentary stresses that draft Principle 15 (whereby '[a]ttacks against the environment by way of reprisals are prohibited')[25] is 'intended to

[17] ILC, 'Report of the ILC on the Work of Its Seventy-First Session', UN Doc. A/74/10, p. 213, Principle 16.

[18] *Ibid.*, p. 216, Commentary 3 on draft principle 1.

[19] ILC, 'Report of the ILC on the Work of Its Sixty-Seventh Session', UN Doc. A/70/10, para. 158; ILC, 'Report of the ILC on the Work of Its Sixty-Eighth Session', UN Doc. A/71/10, pp. 336–39.

[20] See Switzerland, 'Observations concernant la pratique et les instruments de la Suisse visant à protéger l'environnement en relation avec un conflit armé ainsi que des observations additionnelles sur le projet de principes', 68th session of the ILC (2016).

[21] UN Doc. A/CN.4/689, 28 January 2016, para. 65; Marie G. Jacobsson, 'Third Report on the Protection of the Environment in relation to Armed Conflicts', UN Doc. A/CN.4/700, 3 June 2016, paras. 40 and 49; UN Doc. A/CN.4/703, 22 February 2017, para. 44.

[22] UN Doc. A/74/10, p. 259, Commentary 8 on draft principle 16.

[23] *Ibid.*, p. 260, Commentary 10 on draft principle 16.

[24] *Ibid.*

[25] ILC, 'Draft principles on protection of the environment in relation to armed conflicts', UN Doc. A/77/10, in (2022) II(2) ILC Ybk, draft principle 15.

apply in *all* armed conflicts *irrespective of classification*',[26] and 'seems to be consistent with *lex lata* in non-international armed conflicts'.[27]

As this episode demonstrates, relying on preparatory work to restrict and potentially invalidate the implications of a legal instrument overlooks a fundamental aspect. Being the product of an evolving process as well as the basis for future practice, such text has more to it than the recollection of its drafting history. "Original intentions" and "intentional decisions" can shed light on the dynamics that have led to a given outcome, but do not necessarily determine it. They neither circumscribe the scope of possible results during a negotiation, nor do they exhaust the range of possible meanings that will be attributed to such results once the negotiation is over.

Seen under this light, the treaties and the manuals mentioned at the beginning of this chapter no longer give the impression of pushing in opposite directions – quite the contrary, they appear as different expressions of a similar uneasiness. Whether they say too much or too little, they all reveal the same difficulty to articulate in international legal terms the place and role of belligerent reprisals in NIAC. The familiar dilemma before the 'altar of humanity' felt by Baron Lambermont 150 years ago[28] is thus conjugated in the practice of the early twenty-first century. Back then, the impasse was between tackling reprisals (which could appear as a form of approval of the mechanism) or glossing over them (which could be felt as a culpable relinquishment of the humanitarian mandate). Today, the alternative is fundamentally the same, but the rationales for choosing one option over the other could be much less altruistic than in the past. A law-maker (or a law-interpreter) might wish to leave reprisals out of the regulation of NIAC for fear of legitimizing, not the mechanism as such, but the non-State actor that is granted the ability to invoke it; equally so, remaining silent over the issue might be a way of limiting recourse to reprisals, but also of having more liberty in deciding if, when and how to adopt them. Because of the nature of conflicts involving non-sovereign entities, what was born as a lose-lose scenario has become (i) from the viewpoint of policy, a tug-of-war between actors with vested interests, and (ii) from a normative perspective, a *vexata quaestio* that challenges the prescriptive ability of international law.

[26] *Ibid.*, p. 148, Commentary on draft principle 15, para. 8 [emphasis added].

[27] *Ibid.*, p. 149, para. 10.

[28] See Section 2.2.2.2.

5.1.3 Devising the Methodological Approach to the Question of Reprisals in NIAC

Given these high stakes and conceptual hurdles, it is hardly surprising that the question of reprisals in NIAC has not been answered once and for all in a univocal way.[29] But neither those elements, nor the loopholes and shortcomings in black-letter law could fully account for such a plurality of voices. It is rather the way in which the question is asked, as well as the perspective from which the problem is analysed, that play a huge role in determining the answer. Therefore, this section will look at the methodological approaches that can be found in two of the most quoted contributions to the study of belligerent reprisals in NIAC. By understanding their key assumptions and determining the standpoint of their analysis, it will be possible to calibrate a precise methodological lens to look at the issue of reprisals in NIAC.

5.1.3.1 The ICRC's Inductive Methodology

Rule 148 is the provision in the ICRC's *Customary IHL Study* that deals specifically with reprisals in NIAC. Its first sentence states that '[p]arties to non-international armed conflicts do not have the right to resort to belligerent reprisals'.[30] The second phrase, on its part, prohibits '[o]ther countermeasures against persons who do not or who have ceased to take a direct part in hostilities'.[31] Judging from the ICRC commentaries on both the *Customary IHL Study* and the 1949 GCs, the notion of 'other countermeasures' is not used here in its technical meaning, but should be interpreted as '[a]cts of so-called "reprisals" allegedly committed in non-international armed conflicts'.[32] This is revealing in two respects. First, using the notion of countermeasures as a substitute for reprisals underscores once more the assimilation operated by the scholarship between these two mechanisms, even in relation to NIACs.[33] Second, Rule 148 appears as incoherent: in the context of NIACs, reprisals are at once

29 See Bílková, 'Reprisals in NIACs' and Sivakumaran, *Law of NIAC*, chapter 10, section 3 – discussed extensively in this and Chapter 6. See also Andrew Clapham, *War* (Oxford: Oxford University Press, 2021), p. 510.

30 Henckaerts and Doswald-Beck, *Customary IHL Study*, vol. I, p. 526. See also ICRC, *Commentary on GC III*, 2nd ed., para. 943.

31 Henckaerts and Doswald-Beck, *Customary IHL Study*, vol. I, p. 526.

32 *Ibid.*, pp. 526–27; ICRC, *Commentary on GC III*, 2nd ed., para. 944.

33 See Section 2.3.

said to be: (i) inapplicable *tout court* as a concept (first sentence), (ii) explicitly prohibited in some cases and (iii) permitted (albeit implicitly) in others (second sentence). This inconsistency might be solved, up to a certain point, by saying that something is prohibited precisely because it does not apply – but it would still be impossible to argue for the permissibility of something that does not exist.

To resolve the contradiction, scholarly appraisals of Rule 148 downplay the importance of the second sentence (shunned as an 'apparent logical gap'[34] or at best accounted for as 'a subsidiary safety net')[35] while endorsing the first one (seen as a 'probably' correct conclusion to sympathise with).[36] Stressing the inapplicability of reprisals at the expense of the other findings, however, deflects attention from a serious deficit in the ICRC's analysis. To back up its conclusion, the Study states that '[t]here is insufficient evidence that the very concept of lawful reprisal in non-international armed conflict has ever materialized in international law'.[37] The underlying assumption is that reprisals are not (at least in NIAC) a legal "given":[38] their existence cannot be presumed and it must be proven on the basis of material evidence. This approach is coherent with the general methodology to assess customary international law, with its emphasis on the plastic moments of formation and crystallization of rules. But it is problematic insofar as it purports to answer a normative question (i.e., the existence of the very concept of reprisals in NIAC) with a purely inductive enquiry (i.e., the search for the evidence of a "material" practice). Inadvertently, the reasoning becomes a circular one. Evidence is invoked to demonstrate the existence and applicability of a concept – but absent such concept, the practice is necessarily "mute": the legal interpreter has no tool to identify and interpret the material before it; more importantly, the actor has no formula to attribute a legal meaning to its actions.

[34] David Turns, 'Implementation and Compliance', in Elizabeth Wilmshurst and Susan Breau (eds.), *Perspectives on the ICRC Study on Customary International Humanitarian Law* (Cambridge: Cambridge University Press, 2007), p. 372.

[35] Bílková, 'Reprisals in NIACs', p. 40.

[36] Turns, 'Implementation and Compliance', p. 371.

[37] Henckaerts and Doswald-Beck, *Customary IHL Study*, vol. I, p. 527.

[38] As it seems to be the case for reprisals in relation to IAC – see the comment by the United Kingdom in ILC, 'Protection of the Environment in relation to Armed Conflicts – Comments and Observations Received from Governments, International Organizations and Others', UN Doc. A/CN.4/749, 17 January 2022, p. 93 ('[t]he UK maintains that the doctrine of *allowing* belligerent reprisal is part of customary international law').

A recent example of this methodological short-circuit can be found in the 2020 ICRC's *Guidelines on the Protection of the Natural Environment in Armed Conflict*. Rule 4.B thereof prohibits reprisals against objects that are part of the natural environment, in case they constitute, among other things, cultural property protected by the 1954 Hague Convention. The rule is said to be of a customary nature (valid '[f]or all States') in IAC; as for NIAC, the application of reprisals is ruled out on the basis of the *Customary IHL Study*.[39] What is interesting (and somewhat baffling) is that the same treaty norm (i.e., Article 4(4) of the 1954 Hague Convention) is mentioned as evidence of the customary status of the prohibition of reprisals in IAC, but is not quoted at all in relation to NIAC (even if, as seen above, Article 19(1) of the same convention extends the applicability of Article 4 to that context).[40] Therefore, international practice is weighed differently, for reasons that cannot depend on its characteristics. It is rather the (presupposed) unavailability of a theoretical framework for reprisals in NIAC that prevents from identifying as relevant a practice that is nonetheless available.

Reference to the work of the ICRC demonstrates that an inductive approach *alone* cannot provide a satisfactory answer to the question of reprisals in NIAC. It needs to be complemented with a wider, more theoretical analysis, designed to comprehend the placing of the mechanism in the legal architecture governing NIAC and its relations with the fundamental tenets of that regime. Only at that point will we be equipped with the interpretive tool to interrogate the practice and attribute a legal meaning to the material that it offers.

5.1.3.2 Bílková's Deductive Methodology

A 2014 article by Bílková provides the most accomplished example of what could be termed a deductive methodology based on ideal-types. The author identifies from the outset 'three ways of conceptualizing the relationship between belligerent reprisals and non-international armed conflicts from a legal perspective' (the extralegal, the permissive and the restrictive approach);[41] international and national practice are then seen as an articulation of one or the other view. This methodology has several merits: it departs from an exclusively inductive approach and tackles the

39 ICRC, *Guidelines on the Protection of the Natural Environment in Armed Conflict*, 25 September 2020, pp. 46–47, Commentary on Rule 4.B, paras. 91 and 94.
40 See Section 5.1.1.
41 Bílková, 'Reprisals in NIACs', p. 36.

issue under scrutiny from a more systemic perspective; it captures the (com-)presence of various stances on the question of reprisals in NIAC; most importantly, it interprets this variety of mutually exclusive positions not as a dead end precluding analysis, but as a starting point to build a theory.

The problem with this taxonomy of approaches is that it is not as abstract and a-prioristic as it looks. Being largely modelled on the debates at the 1974–1977 Diplomatic Conference on Humanitarian Law in Geneva (CDDH), ultimately it is also an inductive effort, and there are few assurances that it remains valid irrespective of the context to which it is applied. Once more, the work of the ILC on the 'Protection of the Environment in relation to Armed Conflicts' provides evidence for this. In its commentary on the draft principles adopted on first reading, the ILC considers the inclusion of a prohibition of reprisals (restrictive approach) as a way of 'promoting the progressive development of international law'.[42] However, it is unclear what this progressive development refers to: Is it the creation of a prohibition that did not exist beforehand (which assumes as a baseline a permissive approach)? Or is it rather the novel inclusion in the NIAC framework of the previously inapplicable legal category of reprisals, bringing it closer with the IAC regime (therefore moving from an extralegal approach)?[43] Bílková's ideal-types do not clarify this point: they give us a precise instrument to "read" the result of the negotiation, but hardly shed light on the dynamics leading thereto.

Even more than the ILC work itself, comments by governments to the Draft principles reveal how fluid these ideal-types of inapplicability, prohibition and permissibility actually are. Only few States supported the extension to NIAC of the prohibition of reprisals against the environment, if only by way of progressive development.[44] Stances by the other States on the issue of reprisals defy the rigid categories identified by Bílková. They could rather be placed on a spectrum with varying overlaps, where the position on reprisals is ultimately a function of other elements – that is, the convergence (or not) between the laws of IAC and NIAC,[45] the relationship between treaty and customary

42 UN Doc. A/74/10, p. 260, Commentary on draft principle 16, para. 10.

43 UN Doc. A/71/10, p. 338, Commentary on draft principle 12 [II-4], para. 8.

44 See the comments by Germany, Switzerland and arguably Ireland in UN Doc. A/CN.4/749, pp. 91–92.

45 See the comments by France (*ibid.*, pp. 10–11 and 91). See also Kingdom of the Netherlands, 'Comment' during the 73rd Session of the ILC, 2022, paras. 2 and 8 and p. 6 of the advisory report reproduced therein.

norms,[46] or the easiness in developing one legal regime compared to another. Insofar as Bílková's taxonomy to map the legal approaches to reprisals depends on outside elements, their hermeneutical potential is seriously impaired.

5.1.3.3 The Third Way: A Systemic Perspective Illuminated by the Practice

To sum up, neither a purely inductive approach (such as the one of the ICRC), nor one by abstract types (such as the one proposed by Bílková) can address all the legal problems raised by this issue. The former has the merit of spotting the light on the practice of States, but in so doing leaves the questions of principle as to the very applicability of reprisals in NIAC in the background; as regards the latter, it tries to rationalize and put order into the disordered practice characterizing this field, but the categories that it relies on are not self-standing. To remedy these shortcomings, a systemic approach should be combined with an inductive one. First, the issue of reprisals will be addressed in relation to some of the fundamental problems underlying the legal regime governing NIAC. The question as to whether and how the notion of reprisals plays out in this context cannot be seen in isolation – it needs to be re-connected with other, wider concerns that cut across the law of NIAC. It is only by examining the legal context in which reprisals would be called to operate, that an answer as to their place and role in NIAC can be broached. Second, inputs from the practice of NIAC will be analysed to assess the concrete dynamics of belligerent reprisals in this context. The inductive approach will thus be recuperated, but this time within a framework that is capable of accommodating and interpreting the conduct of State (as well as non-State) actors. This two-pronged methodology will result in a richer understanding of reprisals in NIAC: in the ever-evolving sketching of IHL, this mechanism will act as a "point of escape" to which are directed most of the problems raised by the law of NIAC.

In line with this approach, the remainder of this chapter is dedicated to the systemic component of our analysis and will be articulated in two parts. The first part will address the question whether the concept of belligerent reprisals is applicable in NIAC at all. The question is a familiar one, but this time it will be tackled in light of the characteristic feature of NIAC (i.e., the non-sovereign quality of at least one of the

[46] See the comment by Canada in UN Doc. A/CN.4/749, pp. 90–91.

parties to the conflict) and of the contrasting pulls that it exerts on the notion of reprisals. The second part will inquire into the purpose and function of belligerent reprisals in the context of NIAC. If this issue tends to be overlooked for reprisals in IAC, it is completely neglected in relation to NIAC. At times it is conflated with the question of the (in)applicability of reprisals – something that fails to acknowledge the logical priority of existence over aim. On other occasions, the enforcement purpose seems to be taken for granted, which is paradoxical if only one considers that the application of (and therefore the assimilation with) countermeasures is not straightforward outside of inter-State relationships.

These two plans of analysis will cast a new light on the statements and proceedings at the Geneva Diplomatic Conference of 1974–1977.[47] The negotiations leading to the adoption of AP II remain an irreplaceable reservoir of ideas and practice on the notion of reprisals in NIAC, and the unavoidable point of departure for any discussion on the topic. However, their heuristic value is limited if they are not put in relation with (i) other provisions discussed at the Conference (and ultimately excluded from AP II), and (ii) the most recent trends and reflections on the law applicable to NIAC. From a methodological viewpoint, even the debates on reprisals that took place in Geneva will undergo a systemic re-interpretation aimed at placing them in the wider landscape of the negotiations behind AP II.

5.2 The Applicability of Belligerent Reprisals in NIAC

5.2.1 Belligerent Reprisals in the Build-Up to AP II

Our inquiry about the applicability of belligerent reprisals in NIAC will start from the *travaux préparatoires* of AP II. In stark contrast with the final text of this instrument (which does not mention belligerent reprisals at all), the vast diplomatic effort that led to its adoption contains countless reflections and views on the topic. In this context, the notion of belligerent reprisals first appeared in the draft Second Protocol prepared by the ICRC in June 1973: three provisions thereof (draft Articles 8(4), 19 and 26(4)) prohibited recourse to '[m]easures of reprisals' or

[47] Several scholars have retraced the trajectory of the provisions on reprisals during the drafting of AP II: Nahlik, 'Reprisals in Light of Diplomatic Conference', pp. 63–64; Bílková, 'Reprisals in NIACs', pp. 44–47; Darcy, *Collective Responsibility and Accountability*, pp. 167–71.

'[a]ttacks ... by way of reprisals' against specific categories of persons and objects.[48] In the words of the ICRC, including these provisions was either an indispensable acknowledgement of a traditional principle of international law,[49] or an effort to mirror corresponding provisions in the 1949 GCs and draft AP I.[50] What is more, before the beginning of the CDDH, several States submitted amendments to actually increase the categories of persons and objects protected from reprisals.[51] But as soon as the provisions on reprisals in draft AP II came before the three Committees of the CDDH, the delegations started to battle fiercely on them.

At the beginning, there was an attempt at exorcising disagreement by looking for an alternative wording to indicate these measures.[52] However, as the delegations of Brazil and Iraq noted, divergence stemmed from questions of substance rather than mere drafting.[53] A Working Group within Committee I 'failed to reach agreement either on the substance of that idea [i.e., of prohibiting reprisals] or on its form, or even on the position that such a provision should occupy in Part II, or even in

[48] *CDDH Official Records*, vol. I, Part III, pp. 35–36, 38 and 40. These were: 'all persons whose liberty has been restricted by capture or arrest for reasons in relation to the armed conflict'; 'the wounded, the sick, and the shipwrecked as well as ... medical personnel, medical units and means of medical transport'; 'the civilian population or civilians'.

[49] CDDH/II/SR.28, 3 March 1975, in *ibid.*, vol. XI, p. 291, para. 63 (with reference to draft Article 19 of AP II).

[50] CDDH/III/SR.5, 14 March 1974, in *ibid.*, vol. XIV, p. 37, para. 14, and CDDH/I/SR.32, 19 March 1975, in *ibid.*, vol. VIII, p. 339, para. 68 (with reference to draft Articles 26(4) and 8(4) respectively).

[51] The first round of amendments to the ICRC draft aimed at extending protection from reprisals not only to specific categories of objects, such as those containing dangerous forces (amendments by Romania and Finland – *ibid.*, vol. IV, pp. 88–89) or those indispensable for the survival of the civilian population (amendments by Finland and Sweden, and by Egypt, Iraq and Syria – *ibid.*, vol. IV, pp. 84–85), but also to the general category of civilian objects (amendments by Romania and later the German Democratic Republic – *ibid.*, vol. IV, pp. 84 and 80). It also purported to fill the lacuna in the protection from reprisals for 'all persons who do not take a direct part or who have ceased to take a part in hostilities, whether or not their liberty has been restricted' (amendment to Article 6 by Finland – *ibid.*, vol. IV, p. 18). However, already at this stage other States began questioning the opportunity of having the same amount of protection in AP I and AP II: see the comments by the representatives of the United States and USSR, countered by Norway and Italy (CDDH/III/SR.8, 19 March 1974 and CDDH/III/SR.9, 20 March 1974, in *ibid.*, vol. XIV, pp. 67 and 72–74).

[52] These include 'actions similar to those of reprisals', 'actions of extreme retaliation', 'measures in the nature of reprisals' (CDDH/II/SR.32, 7 March 1975, in *ibid.*, vol. XI, p. 336, paras. 53–55); or 'measures of retaliation comparable to reprisals', 'retaliation', 'vengeance' (CDDH/I/SR.32, in *ibid.*, vol. VIII, p. 325, para. 11 and p. 327, para. 21).

[53] CDDH/II/SR.33, 10 March 1975, in *ibid.*, vol. XI, pp. 345–46, paras. 33–34 and 42).

Protocol II'.[54] Shortly afterwards, the idea of entrusting a Joint Working Group with the task of drafting a less divisive wording (originally approved by both Committee I and Committee II) foundered because of the lack of clarity as to what its terms of reference would be.[55] The debate on the terminology to indicate reprisals subtended a more serious disagreement on the notion and its place in the framework of NIACs.

Given this stalemate, it was decided at the outset of the third session (1976) that 'the problem of reprisals as a whole, as presented in the two draft Protocols' would be assigned to Committee I of the CDDH.[56] In the following weeks, several versions of a new provision on reprisals (Article 10 *bis* of draft Protocol II) were submitted by the ICRC,[57] the Sub-group on reprisals established by Working Group B of Committee I,[58] and Working Group B itself.[59] Moving away from the initial preference for several specific prohibitions, all these new versions provided for a single, general protection from retaliatory conduct. At the beginning of the fourth session of the CDDH (1977), Committee I adopted Article 10 *bis*, but the vote was split both on the enumeration of the categories of objects to be protected from reprisals, and on the opportunity of including the provision as a whole.[60]

A similar divergence of opinions characterized the discussions during the final Plenary, which had to assess the proposal of the Pakistani delegation to delete, among other articles and 'as a [form of] compromise', Article 10 *bis*.[61] When it was finally put to the vote, the provision was

[54] CDDH/I/287/Rev.1 (Report to Committee I on the proceedings of Working Group B), in *ibid.*, vol. X, p. 108. The Working Group even established a Sub-group on reprisals, but its proposal did not prevent delegations from submitting a number of new proposals (*ibid.*, pp. 108–10).

[55] CDDH/I/SR.33, 20 March 1975, in *ibid.*, vol. VIII, p. 343; CDDH/II/SR.49, 8 April 1975, in *ibid.*, vol. XI, pp. 561–62; CDDH/III/SR.38, 10 April 1975, in *ibid.*, vol. XIV, pp. 414–16.

[56] CDDH/SR.31, 21 April 1976, in *ibid.*, vol. V, p. 375, para. 22.

[57] CDDH/I/302, 23 April 1976, in *ibid.*, vol. IV, p. 37. The ICRC also submitted two proposals for an amended version of draft Article 6(3): *ibid.*, p. 19.

[58] CDDH/405/Rev.1, in *ibid.*, vol. X, pp. 234–35.

[59] *Ibid.*, pp. 233–34 and CDDH/234/Rev.1, in *ibid.*, vol. X, p. 133, paras. 96–98.

[60] CDDH/I/SR.73, 16 May 1977, in *ibid.*, vol. IX, pp. 428–30 and 435–59, and CDDH/405/Rev.1, in *ibid.*, vol. X, p. 202, paras. 125–30. Article 10 *bis* was adopted by Committee I by thirty-three votes to fifteen, with twenty-eight abstentions. Article 10 *bis* as adopted by Committee I read as follows: 'The provisions of Parts II and III and of Articles 26, 26 *bis*, 27 and 28 shall not, in any circumstances or for any reason whatsoever, be violated, even in response to a violation of the provisions of the Protocol' (CDDH/405/Rev. 1, in *ibid.*, vol. X, p. 283).

[61] CDDH/SR.51, 3 June 1977, in *ibid.*, vol. VII, pp. 107–9, 114 and 119–23.

rejected by forty-one votes to twenty, with twenty-two abstentions.[62] The deletion was welcomed by some delegations and criticized by others,[63] but for the biggest part States tried to minimize it – although their arguments clashed under significant respects.[64] Moreover, the rejection of Article 10 *bis* did not result in the re-introduction of those specific prohibitions of reprisals that had featured in the earlier versions of draft Protocol II. In the later stages of the CDDH, the corresponding provisions had been either re-drafted or deleted on the understanding that a general norm would deal with the issue of reprisals comprehensively. Yet, an elimination that was meant to be conditioned on the adoption of Article 10 *bis*, became a definitive one with the simplification of the Protocol brought about by the Pakistani draft.[65]

In the end, failure to adopt Article 10 *bis* resulted in the complete absence of any reference to reprisals in the final version of AP II – one of the elements that led the delegation of the Holy See to lament that the plenary had removed from the newly adopted instrument 'much of its humanitarian marrow'.[66]

5.2.2 *Sovereignty and Equality: Complementary or Competing Principles?*

In considering the *travaux préparatoires* of AP II, the literature has purported to determine the applicability of the concept of reprisals in NIAC by looking exclusively at the provisions and debates centred on that topic. Framing the analysis in these terms has not provided conclusive answers, and this can certainly be imputed to the variety of positions expressed by Governments and the political constraints under which the final text was adopted.[67] But on closer scrutiny, this approach reveals the same misunderstanding that animated those negotiators at the CDDH

62 *Ibid.*

63 See Nigeria for the former attitude, Finland and the Holy See for the latter (*ibid.*).

64 For instance, the idea of Sweden that Article 10 *bis* is a development of IHL clashes with the idea that it derives from (and builds on) Common Article 3 GCs (Italy) or that it is implicit in other primary norms (Belgium); the idea (again by Italy) that the prohibition of reprisals has an intransgressible nature contrasts with the claim that such prohibition is unacceptable with the States with more experience (thus New Zealand): see *ibid.*

65 CDDH/221/Rev.1, in *ibid.*, vol. XIII, pp. 132–33; CDDH/407/Rev.1, in *ibid.*, vol. XV, p. 467, paras. 70–72.

66 CDDH/SR.58, 9 June 1977, in *ibid.*, vol. VII, p. 321.

67 Darcy, *Collective Responsibility and Accountability*, pp. 170–71; Bílková, 'Reprisals in NIACs', pp. 46–47.

who believed that the stalemate on reprisals could be unlocked by a simple change of wording.[68] All of them fail to recognize that in drafting AP II, the notion of reprisals was not, however problematic, a point of contention in and of itself. It rather represented a faultline where the tension was accumulated (and released when an equilibrium was not found), a further crack dug by the divergent forces that animated (and still animate) the regulation of NIAC: that between the principle of sovereignty, on the one hand, and the principle setting forth the equality of rights and obligations between parties to the armed conflict, on the other. Back in the 1970s, it was the way these two principles were approached during the drafting of AP II that ultimately determined the fate of the reprisals provisions; similarly today, their current balance can reveal what are the prospects for the inclusion of reprisals in the law governing NIAC.

Both these principles had a place in the draft AP II prepared by the ICRC. Draft Article 3 reassured States that their sovereignty would not be unduly encroached by Protocol II, which only 'assure[d] fundamental guarantees to the human person'[69] and could not be used by non-State armed groups to obtain political recognition.[70] Building on paragraph 4 of Article 3 common to the 1949 GCs, the provision 'establish[ed] clearly that the application of international humanitarian law in case of non-international armed conflict would have no effect on the legal status of relations' between parties to the conflict.[71] As the ICRC explained, applying Protocol II (or other applicable IHL provisions) would not in itself imply recognition of belligerency by the established Government, nor confer on an insurgent party any wider authority or immunity.[72] As regards the principle of equality, draft Article 5 elaborated on paragraph 1 of Common Article 3 GCs and provided that '[t]he rights and duties of the parties to the conflict under the present Protocol are equally

[68] See Section 5.2.1.

[69] ICRC explanation in CDDH/I/SR.23, 17 February 1975, in *CDDH Official Records*, vol. VIII, p. 227, para. 68. Draft Article 3 read as follows (*ibid.*, vol. I, Part III, p. 34):

> Article 3. – Legal status of the parties to the conflict
>
> The legal status of the parties to the conflict or that of the territories on which they exercise authority shall not be affected by the application of the provisions of the present Protocol, or by all or part of the provisions of the Geneva Conventions of August 12, 1949, and of the Additional Protocol relating to the protection of victims of international armed conflicts brought into force in accordance with Article 38 or by the conclusion of any agreement provided for in the Geneva Conventions and their Additional Protocols.

[70] Canada (CDDH/I/SR.23, in *ibid.*, vol. VIII, p. 227, para. 71).

[71] ICRC (*ibid.*, para. 70).

[72] ICRC (*ibid.*, para. 68).

valid for all of them'.[73] In the ICRC's view, also this provision found its rationale in the 'unswerving principle of absolute and unconditional respect for the enemy *hors de combat*, the wounded, the prisoner or the civilian – who was no longer an enemy, but only a human being'.[74] This time, however, the purpose of the norm was to clarify that 'draft Protocol II should be applied by all the Parties to a conflict, whether established Governments or rebels'.[75]

The draft AP II suggests that the difference of status between State and non-State armed group could co-exist with the equality of rights and obligations under IHL. According to the ICRC's original idea, the two principles were not mutually exclusive but operated at two different levels. For one thing, even if a NSAG could conclude certain agreements and enjoy a legal relation with the State it was fighting against, this did not mean that these two actors were on the same footing under international law: recognition of a (limited) legal personality did not bring about parity of status. At the same time, rights and obligations of States and NSAGs were not necessarily different or uneven – they were actually identical, because neither draft AP II, nor *a fortiori* Article 3 common to the 1949 GCs had discriminatory provisions.[76] Certain agreements could be concluded between a State and a NSAG, and their substantive content would not be predetermined as unbalanced by the difference in status (if it were, NSAGs would not have much interest to enter into a legal relation with disadvantageous terms).[77] So, even if limited legal personality did not lead to parity of status, difference in status did not necessarily exclude equality of rights and obligations.

Articles 3 and 5 of draft AP II met with favour and were approved with only minor drafting changes by Committee I during the second session of the CDDH.[78] However, both provisions were deleted pursuant to the

[73] *Ibid.*, vol. I, Part III, p. 34.

[74] ICRC (CDDH/SR.1, 20 February 1974, in *ibid.*, vol. V, p. 11, para. 22).

[75] ICRC (CDDH/I/SR.24, 18 February 1975, in *ibid.*, vol. VIII, p. 239, para. 55).

[76] For a detailed discussion of this issue, see Section 5.2.4.

[77] Canada: '[i]t should be possible to draft Protocol II in such a way as to be beneficial both to the Government and to the insurgents' (CDDH/I/SR.23, in *CDDH Official Records*, vol. VIII, p. 215, para. 71).

[78] Text of draft Article 3 as adopted by Committee I (CDDH/219/Rev.1, in *ibid.*, vol. X, p. 42, para. 103):

> The application of the provisions of the present Protocol, or of all or part of the provisions of the Geneva Conventions of August 12, 1949, and of the Additional Protocol relating to the protection of victims of international armed conflicts brought into force in accordance with Article 38 or by the conclusion of any agreement provided for in the Geneva Conventions and

shortened version of AP II submitted by Pakistan, in a move that sparked a lively debate in the Plenary.[79] These discussions reveal that, far from treating the questions of difference of status and equality of rights and obligations as separate (as the ICRC did), most delegations at the Conference did see the two issues as mutually exclusive. For some delegations, NSAGs could not claim equality of rights and obligations because they did not have an international legal footing equal to that of the armed forces of a State: 'rebels . . . devoid of the recognised attributes of sovereign States' did not (and should not) have 'the same rights as the national Government, which was the embodiment of State sovereignty and which held general responsibilities'.[80] Other delegations took the opposite approach, giving priority to the principle of equality of rights and obligations, and objecting to changes in the Protocol that would 'place[] the Parties to a conflict on an unequal footing'.[81] In their view, questions of legitimacy linked with international status should not have called into question or jeopardized the pivotal principle of equality in rights and duties.

In the Plenary, States took the view that the principles of difference in status and of equality in rights and obligations could not co-exist. So, even if they differed on the principle to be given priority, delegations by and large agreed in rejecting the ICRC's fundamental belief that the two principles could complement each other harmoniously. This had direct and important consequences on the fate of the reprisals provisions in the final text of AP II. Arguably, the mention of reprisals in the first formulations of draft Articles 8 (4), 19 and 26(4) had only been made possible by the co-existence of those two principles in the original ICRC draft of AP II.[82] By virtue of the principle

> their additional Protocols shall not affect the legal status of the parties to the conflict.

Text of draft Article 5 as adopted by consensus by Committee I (*ibid.*, p. 44, para. 116):

> The rights and duties which derive from the present Protocol apply equally to all the Parties to the conflict.

The Chairman of Working Group B confirmed that the capital letter used for 'Parties' was 'a mere typographical error' (CDDH/I/SR.30, 18 March 1975, in *ibid.*, vol. VIII, p. 309, para. 57).

[79] CDDH/SR.50, 3 June 1977, in *ibid.*, vol. VII, pp. 85–86.

[80] Zaire (CDDH/SR.56, 8 June 1977, in *ibid.*, vol. VII, p. 219, para. 125); see also Saudi Arabia (CDDH/SR.49, 2 June 1977, in *ibid.*, vol. VII, p. 65, para. 33).

[81] Cuba (CDDH/SR.56, 8 June 1977, in *ibid.*, vol. VII, p. 224, para. 153).

[82] It is true that the ICRC considered neither 'the conditions for the application of humanitarian law [nor] its reciprocity' (i.e., neither positive nor negative reciprocity) as pertinent for the protection of enemies *hors de combat*, the wounded, the prisoners or the civilians (CDDH/SR.1, in *ibid.*, vol. V, p. 11, para. 22). However, this view stood in stark

of equality in rights and obligations, any suggestion that reprisals were applicable in NIAC would have equalled entitling also NSAGs to adopt them – something that States could swallow only if re-assured that the armed groups' status under international law would not be affected. It is no coincidence that, when draft Article 3 on the legal status of the parties to the conflict was dropped, all the provisions on reprisals (and, *a fortiori*, draft Article 5 on equality of rights and obligations) encountered the same fate.[83] As both the Federal Republic of Germany and Italy noted, from a political point of view, use of the word 'reprisal' could have given the impression of placing NSAGs on the same footing as established governments.[84]

5.2.3 *Belligerent Reprisals and Inequality of Status*

Looking at the question of belligerent reprisals in NIAC from the perspective of status led to rejection of that notion. Admittedly, such 'sovereignty reflex of States'[85] could be impossible to dispense with in a process as State-centric as the negotiation of a multilateral treaty, and it proved ultimately useful in ruling out a mechanism that would have

contrast with the organization's previous work: as Moir reminds us, the effort to give a legal vest to the practice of reciprocity for the case of internal armed conflict ran through all the preliminary work and the *travaux préparatoires* that led to the adoption of Article 3 common to the 1949 GCs (Lindsay Moir, 'The Historical Development of the Application of Humanitarian Law in Non-international Armed Conflicts to 1949' (1998) 47 ICLQ, pp. 354–61). See especially the draft provision at the 1946 Preliminary Conference of National Red Cross Societies: 'In case of armed conflict in the interior of a State, the Convention shall be *equally applied* by each of the adverse Parties, *unless one of these expressly declares its refusal to conform* thereto' (Resolution XIV of the 16th International Red Cross Conference (London, 1938), quoted *ibid.*, p. 354; emphasis added). See also the draft provision submitted to the 1949 Diplomatic Conference: 'In all cases of armed conflict not of an international character which may occur in the territory of one or more of the High Contracting Parties, each of the Parties to the conflict shall be bound to implement the provisions of the present Convention, *subject to the adverse Party likewise acting in adherence thereto*. The Convention shall be applicable in those circumstances, whatever the legal status of the Parties to the conflict and without prejudice thereto' (quoted *ibid.*, p. 355; emphasis added).

83 CDDH/SR.50, in *CDDH Official Records*, vol. VII, pp. 85–86; CDDH/SR.51, in *ibid.*, vol. VII, pp. 107–9. This also led to the disappearance of any reference to the notion of 'parties to the conflict' that featured in several draft articles: see discussion in Plenary on draft Articles 6 and 8 (CDDH/SR.50, in *ibid.*, vol. VII, pp. 86–92), 24 (CDDH/SR.52, 6 June 1977, in *ibid.*, vol. VII, pp. 129–35), 27 (*ibid.*, pp. 135–37), 28 (*ibid.*, p. 138), 29 (CDDH/SR.53, 6 June 1977, in *ibid.*, vol. VII, pp. 143–44).

84 Federal Republic of Germany (CDDH/I/SR.32, in *ibid.*, vol. VIII, p. 325, para. 11); Italy (CDDH/SR.52, in *ibid.*, vol. VII, p. 129, para. 30).

85 Egypt (CDDH/I/SR.73, 16 May 1977, in *ibid.*, vol. IX, pp. 442).

created political difficulties. But this bias also led to overlooking a series of important implications. First, if the risks for sovereignty that are implicit in the question of status take precedence over all other considerations (including equality in rights and obligations and entitlement to adopt reprisals), the dimension is closer to a human-rights framework than a law-of-war one.[86] In other words, the "vertical" relationship between the established government and the alleged rebels (and the corresponding regulation under domestic law) prevails over the "horizontal" one establishing equal rights and obligations between the parties to the conflict (and the resultant regulation under *ius in bello*).[87]

Second, from a systemic viewpoint this formalization of the law applicable to NIAC challenges the very value of AP II. The final text of the Protocol left deep dissatisfaction: it was too little for those delegations who wanted 'a real legal instrument' to control 'the most cruel and most pitiless of all conflicts',[88] and too much for those wishing to keep the management of internal rebellion beyond the reach of international norms.[89] But with specific regard to reprisals, framing the issue only as a problem of equal footing overlooks the particular material field of application of AP II. A difference in status between parties to a NIAC exists by definition only in the type of NIACs to which AP II applies – that is, those that, among other conditions, take place between the armed forces of a State party to AP II and 'dissident armed forces or other organized armed groups which, under responsible command, exercise … control over a part of its territory'.[90] However, other types of NIAC are envisageable (and often take place) where the issue of difference in status does not arise – for instance, because both parties to the armed conflict are NSAGs. In these cases, the prejudicial obstacle to reprisals does not exist any longer, because neither group can claim a higher standing under international law than its opponent.

Seen from this wider perspective, the legal rationales that are largely responsible for the exclusion of reprisals from AP II do not impose

[86] Egypt (CDDH/I/SR.24, in *ibid.*, vol. VIII, p. 234, para. 29).

[87] For a similar discussion, see ICRC, *International Humanitarian Law and the Challenges of Contemporary Armed Conflicts*, Report, 31st International Conference of the Red Cross and Red Crescent (2011), p. 14.

[88] Holy See (CDDH/SR.52, in *CDDH Official Records*, vol. VII, p. 136, para. 81). AP II is described as 'a statement of good intentions which in terms of humanitarian law came down to a "legal ectoplasm"' (*ibid.*). See also CDDH/SR.58, in *ibid.*, vol. VII, pp. 320–22.

[89] Uganda (CDDH/SR.56, in *ibid.*, vol. VII, p. 251): 'Protocol II is quite unnecessary'.

[90] Article 1 AP II.

themselves outside the boundaries of that particular instrument. First, prioritizing the human rights dimension over the law-of-war one fails (and willingly so) to formalize the full scope of the legal implications of NIAC. Second, drawing any definite conclusion as to the (in-) applicability of reprisals in NIAC from their absence in the final text of AP II or from the *travaux préparatoires* thereof overlooks the black-letter limitations in the material scope of application of that treaty. The concern with status led to the elimination of various concepts from the text of AP II, but not necessarily from the wider edifice of IHL. States and NSAGs continue to be 'parties to the conflict' even if that formula was deleted from several articles of AP II;[91] similarly, reprisals cannot be ruled out of NIAC on the simple basis of the Protocol's silence over them, when both the practice preceding the CDDH and the *opinio iuris* of various States during the negotiations of AP II did not object to them.[92]

5.2.4 *Belligerent Reprisals and Equality in Rights and Obligations*

If looking at the question of reprisals in NIAC from the perspective of difference in status is not conclusive, it is appropriate to approach this issue from the viewpoint of equality in rights and obligations. Also in this case, the fact that the latter principle was not included in the final text of AP II does not end the discussion. As seen above, draft Article 5 affirming the equality in rights and obligations foundered not on its own merits, but only because of the unwillingness of most States to keep it separate from the issue of status. Several delegations actually supported the

[91] See in this chapter, footnote 83.

[92] For practice preceding the 1949 GCs, see Sivakumaran, *Law of NIAC*, pp. 449–50. At the CDDH, several States expressed themselves in favour of the applicability of the notion in NIAC, and therefore of the use of the term in AP II: Sweden (CDDH/III/SR.20, 14 February 1975, in *CDDH Official Records*, vol. XIV, p. 178, para. 50, and CDDH/I/SR.32, in *ibid.*, vol. VIII, p. 331, para. 45); Federal Republic of Germany (*ibid.*, p. 325, para. 11); New Zealand (*ibid.*, p. 331, para. 43); Finland (*ibid.*, p. 324, para. 8). France voted against the retention of draft Article 10 *bis* but specified that it was not, 'by so doing, expressing any views on [its] substance' (CDDH/SR.51, in *ibid.*, vol. VII, p. 120). The Holy See 'deplore[d] the disappearance of purely humanitarian provisions – adopted, after all, in Committee – such as … [the] prohibition of reprisals' in draft Article 10 *bis* (CDDH/SR.58, in *ibid.*, vol. VII, p. 321). Several other States in the Plenary voted in favour of draft Article 10 *bis* with its mention of reprisals, including the German Democratic Republic, Poland and Byelorussia (CDDH/I/SR.73, in *ibid.*, vol. IX, pp. 428–29). See also ICRC (CDDH/II/SR.28, in *ibid.*, vol. XI, p. 291, para. 63).

principle[93] – and even if the provision was not adopted in the end, the text of AP II (either in its draft or in its final form) did not contain any norms discriminating between the governmental and the insurgent forces.[94] Differences in terms of substantive protection existed (and still exist) if the legal regime governing NIAC is compared to that of IAC, but they are not written into the rights and obligations established for parties to a NIAC by IHL (as opposed to domestic law).[95] This is the reason why the principle of equality in rights and obligations in NIAC is still endorsed by both the ICRC[96] and several scholars.[97]

Besides upholding the equality in rights and obligations for NIAC, the *travaux préparatoires* of AP II reveal an important correlation between that principle and the subject of our enquiry. Those States that supported the equality in rights and duties were keener on acknowledging the existence of reprisals (or of measures akin to them) in the legal

93 Amendment submitted by Australia (*CDDH Official Records*, vol. IV, p. 17); statements by USSR (CDDH/III/SR.18, 12 February 1975, in *ibid.*, vol. XIV, p. 151, para. 3), New Zealand (CDDH/II/SR.33, in *ibid.*, vol. XI, p. 340, para. 6); Report on the Work of Working Group B of Committee I (CDDH/I/238/Rev.1, in *ibid.*, vol. X, p. 97); adoption of draft Article 5 by Committee I with very little discussion (CDDH/I/SR.30, in *ibid.*, vol. VIII, p. 309); amendment concerning Protocol II as a whole submitted by Canada (*ibid.*, vol. IV, pp. 191 f.); explanation of vote by the Netherlands (CDDH/SR.50, in *ibid.*, vol. VII, p. 101).

94 *Ibid.*, vol. I, Part III (see draft Article 8(3): 'within the limits of their capabilities'); on the passage from 'regularly constituted court' in Common Article 3 GCs, to 'a court offering the essential guarantees of independence and impartiality' in Article 6(2) AP II, see Sandoz, Swinarski and Zimmermann (eds.), *Commentary on the APs*, p. 1398, paras. 4600-07, and ICRC, *Commentary on GC III*, 2nd ed., paras. 714 and 728–29.

95 Thus, if members of insurgent forces can be convicted even for acts of violence committed in the course of the armed conflict that comply with IHL, this is a fundamental difference from the combatant privilege applicable in IAC; however, this difference flows from the application of domestic law criminalizing acts of violence and rebellion, not from the implementation of an international norm that discriminates between the armed forces of a State and the forces fighting against them. See ICRC, CDDH/I/SR.32, in *CDDH Official Records*, vol. VIII, pp. 323–24, paras. 2–6; ICRC, *International Humanitarian Law and the Challenges of Contemporary Armed Conflicts*, Report (2011), p. 50.

96 ICRC, *International Humanitarian Law and the Challenges of Contemporary Armed Conflicts*, Report, 28th International Conference of the Red Cross and Red Crescent (2003), p. 19; ICRC, *International Humanitarian Law and the Challenges of Contemporary Armed Conflicts*, Report (2011), p. 14; ICRC, *International Humanitarian Law and the Challenges of Contemporary Armed Conflicts*, Report, 32nd International Conference of the Red Cross and Red Crescent (2015), pp. 17–18.

97 Marco Sassòli, 'Taking Armed Groups Seriously: Ways to Improve Their Compliance with International Humanitarian Law' (2010) 1 *Journal of International Humanitarian Legal Studies*, pp. 16–17 and 35; Sivakumaran, *Law of NIAC*, pp. 245–46. For a contrary opinion, see Louise Doswald-Beck, 'The Right to Life in Armed Conflict: Does International Humanitarian Law Provide All the Answers?' (2006) 88 IRRC, p. 903.

framework governing NIAC. For New Zealand, draft Article 5 was the main guarantee against any threat that a mention of the word 'reprisals' would pose to State sovereignty.[98] The Canadian proposal on the 'Question of prohibiting reprisals' was the only one that, in case of persistent violations of AP II by 'a Party to the conflict' (therefore, both State and non-State) actually *authorized* 'measures which are in breach of the Protocol' against non-protected targets.[99] Similarly, in proposing the wording 'acts of retaliation comparable to reprisals', a Working Group of Committee II remarked that ensuring compliance with humanitarian law 'by *all* Parties to the conflict' was as necessary as respecting the sovereignty and legislation of States.[100]

This correlation between the two notions is not unique to the 1974–1977 CDDH – it is actually reinforced by the increasing alignment of the law applicable in IAC and NIAC. The above-mentioned work of the ILC on 'Protection of the Environment in relation to Armed Conflicts' is a testament to this. Several States have agreed with the Commission in 'prohibiti[ng] reprisals against the natural environment, *irrespective of the nature of the armed conflict*'[101] – and this is the position that was ultimately embraced by the ILC.[102] This suggests that States are increasingly accepting the applicability of the notion in NIAC (even if only for the purpose of outlawing such measures in relation to a specific range of targets).[103] But the work of the ILC on this topic has also been

[98] CDDH/II/SR.33, in *CDDH Official Records*, vol. XI, p. 340, para. 6.

[99] CDDH/I/287/Rev.1, in *ibid.*, vol. X, p. 109. In a series of coeval amendments to the reprisals provisions in AP II, Canada suggested the wording 'Acts of retaliation comparable to reprisals' (*ibid.*, vol. IV, pp. 196–201). Later on during the Conference, Canada opposed the introduction of the concept of reprisals in AP II (CDDH/I/SR.73, in *ibid.*, vol. IX, p. 428, para. 9). Even if the delegation submitted that the concept appertained to international law, the decision seems to have been motivated more by practical reasons (risk of escalation in hostilities and fear that States would not become parties to the instrument) than by the legal features of the concept (*ibid.*; see also Canada, CDDH/III/SR.37, 4 April 1975, in *ibid.*, vol. XIV, p. 392, para. 22, stressing the inopportunity of placing 'too many restraints in areas touching upon sovereign rights'). At any rate, this statement (expressed in relation to draft Article 10 *bis*) does not detract either from the previous efforts by Canada to address within the NIAC framework measures that corresponded, in functioning and purpose, to reprisals in IAC, or from its realistic approach to the importance of reciprocity in NIAC.

[100] CDDH/II/SR.49, in *ibid.*, vol. XI, p. 561, para. 73 [emphasis added].

[101] Marja Lehto, 'Third Report on Protection of the Environment in relation to Armed Conflicts', UN Doc. A/CN.4/750, 16 March 2022, p. 65, para. 179 [emphasis added].

[102] See Section 5.1.2.

[103] Lehto, 'Third Report on Protection of the Environment', pp. 65–66, para. 179.

notable for its (embryonic) consideration of the question of accountability of non-State actors, which has prompted the Commission to leave 'without prejudice . . . the rules on the responsibility of non-State armed groups'.[104] Albeit timid, this opening strengthens the equality of rights and obligations in NIAC from the perspective of IHL implementation: by conceptualizing the NSAGs as collective entities to which internationally wrongful acts can be attributed (and against which reprisals can be taken), it brings closer the regimes for holding States and non-State armed groups responsible under international law.[105] Also in the scholarship on the law of NIAC, reprisals and the principle of equality in rights and obligations are treated similarly: the former mechanism is dubbed as 'unfortunate' and undesirable, but 'in fact applicable',[106] whereas the latter principle 'remains intact' notwithstanding suggestions that it is 'unworkable' in NIAC.[107]

5.3 The Purpose and Function of Belligerent Reprisals in NIAC

5.3.1 Equality and Reprisals: The Two Faces of Reciprocity

Section 5.2 has shown that belligerent reprisals must be seen as a particular aspect of the equality in rights and obligations of the parties to a NIAC. Their relationship is one of mutual strengthening: the more equality is embedded in the law of NIAC, the more reprisals are acknowledged as applicable in that context. But what is the rationale behind such a strong correlation? A tempting answer would reason that States have long claimed the right to adopt reprisals, and in light of the principle of equality, NSAGs must be granted the same entitlement. This line of

[104] ILC, 'Draft Principles on Protection of the Environment', draft principle 9(3)(a) and Commentary, p. 125, paras. 11–12. For an earlier approach, see Marja Lehto, 'Second Report on Protection of the Environment in relation to Armed Conflicts', UN Doc. A/CN.4/728, 27 March 2019, p. 28, para. 58 (whereby the 'international responsibility of organized armed groups, while not a legally uncharted area, is a fragmented topic on which few solid conclusions can be drawn', therefore refraining from proposing an article on the issue). In the Sixth Committee, several States welcomed the analysis of the responsibilities of non-State actors in relation to the protection of the environment and invited the ILC to address the issue in more detail ('Topical Summary of the Discussion Held in the Sixth Committee of the General Assembly during its Seventy-Fourth Session', UN Doc. A/CN.4/734, 12 February 2020, p. 21, para. 100). See also Lehto, 'Third Report on Protection of the Environment', p. 37, para. 93.

[105] See Henckaerts and Doswald-Beck, *Customary IHL Study*, vol. I, p. 536.

[106] Sivakumaran, *Law of NIAC*, pp. 452, 457 and 473.

[107] *Ibid.*, p. 243.

reasoning is invalidated by the *travaux préparatoires* of AP II. Various States maintained that they did not have any right to adopt reprisals in NIAC against insurgent forces – a somewhat surprising, but highly self-interested claim. In reality, their argument was more detrimental to NSAGs (which, by virtue of the principle of equality, could not claim a right to adopt reprisals that their State counterpart did not have) than it was for the States themselves (which would in any case rely on the *domaine réservé* to suppress rebellion with considerable leeway).[108]

The connection between reprisals and equality is better explained by the importance of reciprocity for the negotiation, the conclusion and the application of AP II. At the beginning of the CDDH, the ICRC had suggested that the norms enshrined in AP II were unconditional.[109] This claim was immediately challenged by several delegations, which stressed the importance of reciprocity for both the creation and the application of obligations in NIAC. In their view, mutuality of advantages could not exist only as a pre-condition for accepting to be bound (positive reciprocity)[110] – it also subjected continued compliance with the norm to the counterpart's behaviour (negative reciprocity).[111] Equality in rights and obligations and belligerent reprisals are two faces in the coin of reciprocity. The former captures reciprocity in its static form, giving legal vest to the idea that provisions governing NIAC must be 'both practicable and attractive' and present 'an obvious, practical benefit' to each party in the armed conflict.[112] The latter represent the dynamic aspect of such mutuality of interests, ensuring that the equality in rights and obligations is maintained over time and even in the face of attempts by the counterpart at perturbing it through violations.

Suddenly, we notice that the reciprocity paradigm is at the very core of belligerent reprisals in NIAC – perhaps even more than it was for IAC. But if reciprocity justifies the very existence of the mechanism in a context where one (or every) party to the conflict lacks sovereign attributes, would it not necessarily characterize also the purpose and function that reprisals have in NIAC? If one looks at the CDDH, the first

108 Iraq (CDDH/II/SR.32, in *CDDH Official Records*, vol. XI, p. 336, para. 52), Nigeria (CDDH/II/SR.33, in *ibid.*, vol. XI, pp. 342–43, paras. 18–20), India (CDDH/I/SR.32, in *ibid.*, vol. VIII, p. 32, para. 22).

109 ICRC (CDDH/SR.1, in *ibid.*, vol. V, p. 11, para. 22).

110 Canada, amendment concerning Protocol II as a whole in *ibid.*, vol. IV, p. 191, as well as statement in CDDH/SR.56, in *ibid.*, vol. VII, pp. 194–95, para. 6.

111 South Africa (CDDH/SR.19, 11 March 1974, in *ibid.*, vol. V, p. 195, para. 3).

112 Canada, amendment concerning Protocol II as a whole in *ibid.*, vol. IV, p. 191.

impression might well be that on numerous occasions reprisals were being conceived of as a tool of enforcement. Their purpose was sometimes identified as that of 'inducing the adverse party to comply with its obligations',[113] or of 'mak[ing] the adverse Party respect his own obligations'.[114] Furthermore, certain delegations used the idea of 'countermeasure' to indicate reprisals in draft AP II – thereby recalling the assimilation between the two notions that played such a prominent role in entrenching the enforcement dogma for reprisals.[115]

And yet, these references look no more than accidental characteristics of a notion that cannot be separated from its grounding in reciprocity. The real thrust of the proposed provisions on reprisals in AP II resides in their synallagmatic elements. Whether a given article or part of AP II could be breached by way of reprisals, ultimately depended on whether it was seen as commanding '*unconditional* respect' (as per the title of draft Article 10 *bis*) or not.[116] That the retaliatory and reciprocal features of reprisals prevailed over their enforcement purpose is also manifested by the wording of draft Article 10 *bis* that resulted from the work of Committee I of the CDDH: to capture the notion of belligerent reprisals, delegates eventually preferred the idea of breaches '*in response to a violation* of the provisions of the Protocol' than that of breaches '*for the purpose of inducing* the adverse party *to comply* with its obligations'.[117] In sum, the very provisions that were outlawing certain reprisals because of the unconditional quality of the corresponding primary rules

[113] Document CDDH/I/GT/79 submitted by the Sub-group on reprisals in draft Protocol II to Working Group B of Committee I (in CDDH/I/287/Rev.1, in *ibid.*, vol. X, p. 108); for a similar wording, but with 'Party' with capital letter, see Pakistan in *ibid.*, vol. X, p. 109.

[114] ICRC, Proposal II for amendment of draft Article 6(3) (in *ibid.*, vol. IV, p. 19), as well as Proposed amendment to Article 10 *bis* (in *ibid.*, vol. IV, p. 37). See also the proposal of Canada in *ibid.*, vol. X, p. 109, with its emphasis on 'refus[ing] to comply with these provisions [of Protocol II] after being called upon to do so'.

[115] Philippines, in *ibid.*, vol. X, p. 109 ('countermeasures for the purpose of enforcing the provisions'); ICRC, Proposal II for amendment of draft Article 6(3) (in *ibid.*, vol. IV, p. 19), as well as Proposed amendment to Article 10 *bis* (in *ibid.*, vol. IV, p. 37). For the assimilation in relation to IAC, see Section 2.3.

[116] CDDH/SR.51, in *ibid.*, vol. VII, p. 107 [emphasis added] and the comment by Italy (*ibid.*, pp. 120–22). See also, excluding viability of *a contrario* interpretations, the statements by Poland and Mexico in CDDH/I/SR.73, in *ibid.*, vol. IX, pp. 450 and 452.

[117] Compare CDDH/405/Rev.1 (in *ibid.*, vol. X, p. 283) with Report of Sub-group on Reprisals in Draft AP II (Working Group document CDDH/I/GT/95), para. 2 (in *ibid.*, vol. X, pp. 234–35) [emphasis added]. For objections to the formula containing 'in response', see Mexico (*ibid.*, vol. X, p. 234, para. 6) and Indonesia (CDDH/I/SR.64, 7 June 1976, in *ibid.*, vol. IX, p. 310, para. 31).

on protection were at the same time re-affirming reciprocity as the operational logic underlying the working of those reprisals that were not prohibited. The mechanism was better conceptualized in terms of its relationship with a previous breach, than in terms of its purpose of enforcing respect for the law.

If one looks closely, detaching reprisals from enforcement is a further consequence of the delegations' insistence on the difference of status in NIAC. As long as norm-enforcement is conceptualized as the final corollary of a norm-creation process for which sovereignty is required, reprisals would find little (and one-sided) applicability in a context where only one type of actor (i.e., the State) claims the prerogative to contribute to the formation of international (humanitarian) norms. On the contrary, the formalization under the reciprocity paradigm and the link with equality in rights and obligations make reprisals agnostic to the fact that the parties to the conflict might have a different status under international law. If reprisals are conceived of as a self-help tool to maintain a relative equilibrium of rights and obligations, the absolute and exclusive dimension introduced by the issue of sovereignty is removed. The only concern of the mechanism is that of safeguarding such balance and of maintaining the terms of the equation, irrespective of the level (of sovereignty) on which the legal relationship is situated.

5.3.2 *Squaring the Circle: Reprisals, Reciprocity, Equilibrium*

All these considerations confirm, even in the legal framework governing NIAC (and somewhat more urgently here than for IAC), the importance of reciprocity in structuring the idea of belligerent reprisals. Understanding the purpose and function of reprisals between States is important for its implications on the remaining scope of legality of the mechanism and its substantive and procedural requirements – but in the context of NIAC, where the parties to the armed conflict are not necessarily on an equal footing, such an enquiry is key to determining the very applicability of the mechanism. We have established, first, that the defining criterion for the existence of reprisals in NIACs lies not in the difference in status, but in the equality in rights and obligations that characterizes the parties also to this type of armed conflicts. Second, we have concluded that the corresponding formalization of the purpose and function of reprisals in NIAC must be grounded, not in a paradigm of enforcement (with its focus on an abstract ideal-type of sovereignty and a hierarchical demarcation between State- and non-State entities), but in a paradigm of reciprocity (with its focus on a concrete and balanced web of legal relationships). It is now time to consider some wider implications of this re-instatement of reciprocity at the core of belligerent reprisals in NIAC.

First, one may suppose a fundamental inconsistency between, on the one hand, the applicability of the notion of reprisals in NIAC and, on the other, the imputability requirement discussed in relation to the Italian case-law on World War II atrocities. As we saw above, Italian tribunals have long held that German armed forces could take reprisal action only if the breaches of the laws of war committed by Resistance forces could be attributed to the Italian State.[118] This requirement from national case-law could be seen as colliding with the possibility (acknowledged in this chapter) that a State adopt retaliatory action against NSAGs, irrespective of any attribution of the latter's conduct to a sovereign entity. In reality, the fact that imputability is required in relation to the Italian *Resistenza* but not when it comes to modern NIACs is not problematic from a theoretical perspective – on the contrary, it highlights the importance of reciprocity in structuring the purpose and function of reprisals *in both contexts*. The Italian case-law is centred on the attribution of the *Partigiani*'s conducts to the Italian State because the underlying assumption was that of an occupation of the Italian territory on the part of the Reich, and therefore of a state of war (therefore, international armed conflict) between Italy and Germany.[119] Classifying the hostilities between the Resistance forces and the German military as a NIAC was not even taken into consideration by this case-law – so much so that, even if the provision on reprisals in the Italian Royal Decree No. 1415 of 1938 could on its terms apply to NIAC, it has been interpreted by the Italian courts as being limited to the relationship between States.[120] At the time of World War II, when not even Article 3 common to the 1949 GCs (let alone AP II) had been adopted, the international legal system was all the more reticent to recognizing equal rights and

[118] See Section 3.4.2.

[119] See Section 3.4.2, footnote 79.

[120] See Article 8 of Regio Decreto No. 1415 (1938) and Section 3.4.2, *passim*. This is arguably a side effect of the assimilation between belligerent reprisals and countermeasures investigated above. For a similar dynamic in which sovereign elements must characterize both the entity taking, and the one receiving, unilateral measures, see Schmitt (ed.), *Tallinn Manual 2.0*, pp. 112–14, Commentary on Rule 20, paras. 3 and 7–10 (whereby 'countermeasures are not available in response to a cyber operation conducted by a non-State actor unless the operation is attributable to a State').

obligations to insurgent forces.[121] In applying an instrument such as the Royal Decree No. 1415 to criminal cases from that epoch, the requirement that private conducts be attributed to a sovereign State is plausibly the only way to ensure that reprisals maintain a logic of reciprocity and operate as a tool balancing rights and obligations. If we then fast forward to the present regulation of NIAC, a NSAG does not need to rely on imputability and see its conduct attributed to a sovereign in order to claim equal rights and obligations *vis-à-vis* enemy State forces – such equality is already established as a founding element in the legal architecture. Therefore, the requirement of imputability to a State can now be dropped in relation to NIACs without affecting under any respects the reciprocal features that inspire the functioning of reprisals. Either in the form of the imputability requirement in IAC, or as the principle of equality in rights and obligations in NIAC, reciprocity determines the purpose and function of the mechanism.

Second, grounding belligerent reprisals in reciprocity solves a number of objections to the applicability of the mechanism in NIAC that have been raised by the doctrine. One of the arguments used by Bílková to affirm the inapplicability of reprisals in NIAC focuses on their qualification as a circumstance precluding wrongfulness: since reprisals 'remove from the sphere of application of primary norms of IHL an act done in response to a previous violation of IHL', they represent an exception to a rule, as such to be interpreted narrowly and not to be presumed in the absence of explicit provisions.[122] The problem with this line of reasoning (which presupposes once more an assimilation of reprisals with countermeasures) is that it is only valid in an enforcement scenario. Seen under the reciprocity paradigm, reprisals have a much more "physiological" function of safeguarding over time the equality in rights and obligations between the parties to the armed conflict. Their function is, so to say, normalized, and they cease to represent an exception that needs to be specifically provided for. Bílková also argues for the inapplicability of reprisals in NIAC on the basis of the functional international legal personality of armed opposition groups, which would not include 'the freedom to use [reprisals] without any restraints'.[123] Also this point works only with reference to an enforcement-based idea of reprisals,

[121] Outside of the recognition of belligerency: see Moir, 'The Historical Development', pp. 338–50.
[122] Bílková, 'Reprisals in NIACs', pp. 61–62.
[123] *Ibid.*, p. 62.

where the re-establishment of the legal order through unilateral measures is reserved to actors with sovereign prerogatives. Under the reciprocity framework, reprisals flow without any hindrance even from the limited international legal personality of NSAGs, and in a variety of ways. In their simpler form, reprisals would help maintain the balance in rights and obligations disturbed by the counterpart's violations of IHL. But in an even stronger sense, reprisals might represent the very tool to determine the presence and extent of rights and obligations in what would otherwise be a very asymmetric relationship between a State and a non-State actor. The necessity of a reciprocity-construed notion of reprisals in NIAC is as much a question of exercising rights and obligations, as it is one of defining them in the first place.

Third, placing reprisals under the reciprocity paradigm prompts us to re-think the ways in which international law governs internal armed conflict, and to conceive of compliance under a different light. In recent years, the scholarship has struggled to reconcile the theoretical aspiration for a legal framework where all actors are bound by the same rules, with the reality of asymmetric conflicts where the military needs and capacities of NSAGs often differ from those of States. To bridge this compliance gap, authors have re-visited (if not altogether challenged) the application to NIACs of the principle of equality in rights and obligations. Whereas Shany suggests accommodating the principle of equality with the doctrine of common but differentiated responsibilities, standards derived from human rights law, and a selective enforcement of humanitarian norms, Sassòli proposes a capacity-based 'sliding scale' of obligations for NSAGs.[124] Going even further, Provost has argued in favour of 'a shift from formal to substantive equality in humanitarian law applicable to internal conflicts', in which 'the obligations of all participants in a legal regime are interconnected'.[125] These proposals have the merit of re-defining the substance of the principle of equality in the face of critical challenges to its application, but they largely fail to suggest concrete ways of implementing this new understanding in the practice of States and NSAGs.

It is submitted that a reciprocity-based formalization of belligerent reprisals could serve this function, by working as a tool to negotiate a

[124] Marco Sassòli and Yuval Shany, 'Should the Obligations of States and Armed Groups under International Humanitarian Law Really Be Equal?' (2011) 93 IRRC, pp. 430–31. See also Sassòli, 'Taking Armed Groups Seriously', p. 20.

[125] René Provost, 'The Move to Substantive Equality in International Humanitarian Law: A Rejoinder to Marco Sassòli and Yuval Shany' (2011) 93 IRRC, p. 440.

mutually acceptable *equilibrium* for the rights and obligations of parties to a NIAC. The notion of equilibrium, fluid and dynamic, is here preferred to the more rigid and static idea of equality. Only the former conveys the impression of a point of convergence (neither determined in advance nor established once for all) between four factors: the strategic objectives of each fighting side, their willingness to curb their freedom of action in exchange for a comparable (not necessarily identical) limitation by the counterpart, their practical capabilities in enforcing legal requirements, and (last but not least) the safeguard of humanitarian imperatives. These factors are all the more shifting in the context of NIACs, where the rights and obligations of NSAGs could develop as a result of both factual vicissitudes (e.g., exercise of control over territory for the purposes of AP II application) and normative changes (e.g., recognition of belligerency, unilateral commitments, conclusion of agreements). Reprisals would then work as a bargaining tool to devise, maintain or re-calibrate an equilibrium between the rights and obligations of the (State- and non-State-) parties to the NIAC, thereby creating throughout hostilities a 'communit[y] of practices ... linking actors on the basis of shared interests or practices'.[126]

[126] *Ibid.*, p. 441.

6

Belligerent Reprisals in Non-international Armed Conflict

A Quest for Equilibrium

6.1 Informal Avenues to Shared Expectations

The systemic analysis in Chapter 5 has shown that also in the context of NIAC, belligerent reprisals are (i) applicable and (ii) inspired in their functioning by a logic of reciprocity. The place and role of this mechanism in NIAC results from the interaction of several conceptual premises, such as State sovereignty, the international personality of NSAGs, and the principle of equality in rights and obligations; at the same time, reprisals have an active bearing on the relative strength of these principles, because they represent the tool for State- and non-State actors alike to articulate their legal position *vis-à-vis* the enemy in the volatile context of armed conflict. To see how this complex dynamic unfolds, this chapter will take an inductive approach and retrace the process by which belligerents craft an equilibrium of rights and obligations through reprisals.

The idea of an ever-developing legal relationship, whose terms are not necessarily settled in advance but develop as a result of the strategic incentives and operational capabilities of the parties, could prove difficult to accept. It sounds all the more unappealing in a legal framework (that of NIAC) where the already difficult balance between humanitarian considerations and military necessity is further challenged by States jealously protecting their sovereign prerogatives. In such a context, the protection of war victims would appear to be better served by a set of clear and pre-determined rules agreed upon at the multilateral level, than by a seemingly precarious balance of rights and obligations negotiated by deed and guaranteed by the unilateral mechanism of reprisals. However, in their quest for hard rules, international lawyers risk losing sight of the varied ways in which actors can agree on a given course of conduct, even outside of formal undertakings.

6.2 Permissible and Prohibited Reprisals in NIAC

6.2.1 Whence the Prohibition?

A good example of this, with notable implications for the protection of war victims, can be found in the debate on which reprisals are lawful (and which prohibited) in NIAC. Given the lack of specific black-letter rules in the framework of the 1949 Geneva Conventions and their Additional Protocol II,[1] to what criteria should we turn to identify permissible targets of these measures? The answers to this important question have been articulated both within and outside the IHL framework. The ICRC has relied on 'the absolute character of th[e] prohibitions' in Article 3 common to the four GCs and in Article 4(2) of AP II to conclude that 'there is in fact no room left at all for carrying out "reprisals" against protected persons'.[2] Another, even more expansive avenue, inaugurated by General Assembly resolutions[3] and brought to

[1] Geneva Conventions Relative to the Protection of the Victims of International Armed Conflicts, Geneva, 12 August 1949, in force 21 October 1950, 75 UNTS 31; UKTS 39 (1958), Cmd 550; 157 BFSP 229; 6 UST 3114; TIAS 3362; ATS 21 (1958); Protocol Additional to the Geneva Conventions of 12 August 1949, and relating to the Protection of Victims of Non-international Armed Conflicts (Protocol II), Geneva, 8 June 1977, in force 7 December 1978, 1125 UNTS 609.

[2] Sandoz, Swinarski and Zimmermann (eds.), *Commentary on the APs*, p. 1372, para. 4530. More recently, the ICRC has re-affirmed its long-standing view whereby Common Article 3 GCs implicitly prohibits any reprisals involving acts prohibited under items (a) to (d) of paragraph 1 thereof, and in any case any reprisals contrary to the humane treatment of all persons not or no longer taking active part in the hostilities: compare Jean Pictet (ed.), *Commentary to the III Geneva Convention relative to the Treatment of Prisoners of War* (Geneva: ICRC, 1960), p. 40 with ICRC, *Commentary on GC III*, 2nd ed., para. 946. Several delegations at the CDDH also believed that reprisals in NIAC could be ruled out on the basis of common Article 3 GCs, or provisions in AP II mentioning obligations that must be respected 'in all circumstances', 'at any time and at any place whatsoever', or 'as a minimum': see UK (CDDH/I/SR.32, in *CDDH Official Records*, vol. VIII, p. 330, para. 40), Belgium (CDDH/I/SR.40, 14 April 1975, in *ibid.*, vol. VIII, p. 425, paras. 21–23 and CDDH/SR.51, in *ibid.*, vol. VII, p. 109, para. 11), Italy (CDDH/SR.51, in *ibid.*, vol. VII, pp. 120–22).

[3] See UN Doc. A/RES/2444(XXIII), *Respect for Human Rights in Armed Conflict*, 19 December 1968 and especially UN Doc. A/RES/2675(XXV), *Basic Principles for the Protection of Civilian Populations in Armed Conflict*, 9 December 1970 ('*Bearing in mind* the need for measures to ensure the better protection of human rights in armed conflicts of

fruition by the scholarship, would rely on international human rights law to rule out of NIAC reprisals against persons that would otherwise lack similar protection under IHL – notably, civilians and the military.[4] These two lines of reasoning, one based on IHL and another on human rights, can also be combined: this is demonstrated, for instance, by the case-law of the ICTY, where both normative systems contribute to the inference (explicit in *Martić (Rule 61 Decision)*, only implicit in *Kupreškić*) that the prohibition on reprisals against civilians also applies to NIAC.[5]

At the same time, relying on alternative IHL norms or the human rights framework to prohibit (certain) reprisals in NIAC has also met with harsh criticism. Sivakumaran has demonstrated that a ban on reprisals does not follow from either Common Article 3 GCs or AP II (at least beyond the categories of acts proscribed, and of persons protected, by those provisions).[6] While welcoming the process of humanization of IHL under the impulse of human rights law, several scholars have warned against a full ousting of reciprocity from the regulation of armed conflict. For instance, Osiel has highlighted those features of IHL (especially its governing a military confrontation 'between collectivities, not individual persons') that distinguish it from 'newer rules originally devised for times of peace';[7] Provost, on its part, has stressed that '[a]doption of these non-derogable human rights norms . . . does not necessarily create a core of "intransgressible" minimal humanitarian norms applicable even to measures of reprisals taken pursuant to the law of war'.[8] Moreover, as Darcy himself concedes, excluding reprisals from NIAC on the basis of human rights law could work well with regard to States, but not necessarily for NSAGs, given the conceptual hurdles in

all types', as well as '7. Civilian populations, or individual members thereof, should not be the object of reprisals').

4 Darcy, *Collective Responsibility and Accountability*, pp. 175–82.

5 In *Martić* (Rule 61), the ICTY relied, *inter alia*, on General Assembly resolution 2675 and Article 4 of AP II to conclude that 'the prohibition on reprisals against the civilian population or individual civilians . . . is applicable to all armed conflicts' (pp. 6–7, paras. 15–17). In ICTY, *Kupreškić* TC, the prohibition of reprisals against civilians in NIAC on the basis of Common Article 3 works as an *a fortiori* argument for an identical conclusion with respect to IAC (pp. 211–12, para. 534); the Chamber also mentions that 'belligerent reprisals against civilians and fundamental rights of human beings are absolutely inconsistent legal concepts' (*ibid.*, p. 208, para. 529).

6 Sivakumaran, *Law of NIAC*, pp. 450–52. See also Darcy, 'Evolution of Reprisals', p. 219; Frits Kalshoven, 'Belligerent Reprisals Revisited' (1990) 21 NYIL, p. 78.

7 Osiel, *End of Reciprocity*, pp. 121 and 140.

8 Provost, *International Human Rights and Humanitarian Law*, p. 200.

holding them bound by human rights treaties.[9] It is under this light that we should read the strong criticisms that the scholarship has levelled against the ICTY findings on reprisals against civilians in NIAC.[10]

6.2.2 *Consensus at the 1974–1977 Diplomatic Conference*

Existing approaches to the question of which reprisals are lawful in NIAC (and which are not) differ both in the methodology they use and in the conclusion they reach – but in a way they rest on a common assumption. All of them interpret the absence of black-letter prohibitions on reprisals in AP II as evidence that no consensus could be reached on that issue during the 1974–1977 Diplomatic Conference. The idea that no agreement on prohibited reprisals can be gauged from the *travaux préparatoires* is ever-present: in one case, it prompts the interpreter to find the answer in other IHL provisions, if not in an altogether different legal framework; in the other, it induces to consider every instance of State (and only State) practice as if it occurred in a legal vacuum, and not

[9] Darcy, *Collective Responsibility and Accountability*, pp. 180–81. This asymmetry would result problematic from the perspective of equality in rights and obligations: NSAGs would be entitled to adopt reprisals measures forbidden to States, in a paradoxical reversal of the concerns animating States that negotiated AP II.

[10] Kalshoven, 'Two Recent Decisions', p. 15; Darcy, 'Evolution of Reprisals', pp. 233–34 and 240–41; Greenwood, 'Reprisals in the Jurisprudence', p. 556. According to the ICRC, the judgments by the ICTY Trial Chamber and Appeals Chamber in *Martić* would disavow the Tribunal's earlier case-law in *Martić* (Rule 61) and *Kupreškić*: by rejecting the argument on reprisals on the basis of procedural conditions (i.e., the requirements that the reprisal be a measure of last resort and that it be preceded by a formal warning), the ICTY would have implicitly given up the idea that reprisals against civilians are *per se* prohibited in NIAC (ICRC, *Commentary on GC III*, 2nd ed., Commentary on Article 3, footnote 936). This conclusion would signal the Tribunal's attention for the criticism levelled against its previous judgments, but it fails to consider two elements. First, the Tribunal might have learnt from its previous experience and ruled out a defence of reprisals on the basis of the easiest grounds, without venturing into unnecessary considerations. Second, the Tribunal bestows civilian populations a certain level of protection from reprisals ('to the extent possible') by relying on the requirement that reprisals 'respect the "laws of humanity and dictates of public conscience"' (ICTY, *Martić* TC, p. 167, para. 467). This wording echoes the Martens Clause, which in *Kupreškić* had been the keystone to (i) emphasize *opinio iuris sive necessitatis* over *usus* and (ii) conclude that the treaty prohibitions on reprisals against civilians in IAC had crystallized into custom (ICTY, *Kupreškić* TC, pp. 207 and 209, paras. 527 and 531). Contrary to the ICRC's opinion, it seems that by establishing a semblance of prohibition on reprisals against civilians in NIAC on the basis of the Martens Clause, the Trial Chamber in *Martić* seems to re-affirm and expand, rather than disavow, its earlier case-law.

against the background of a standard that determines its lawfulness or unlawfulness. In sum, these approaches fail to acknowledge the potential for a negotiating process to create legal expectations and craft a mutual understanding of future course of conduct, irrespective (and even in the absence) of a black-letter provision that sanctions it.

In reality, the wealth of legally relevant information that can be retrieved from the *travaux préparatoires* of AP II on reprisals prohibited in NIAC belies any impression that international law was silent on the issue in the wake of the CDDH. There exist different ways to formalize this hermeneutical operation. First, recourse to this material could be justified as a 'supplementary means of interpretation' for those provisions of AP II (such as, for instance, Article 4 itself) whose meaning in relation to reprisals in NIAC remains 'ambiguous or obscure'.[11] Second, statements and conduct at international conferences have been recognized as relevant for the purpose of creating and identifying customary international law.[12] Seen under this light, the diplomatic positioning of States at the CDDH can point to widely shared expectations among States concerning reprisals prohibited (or permitted) in NIAC.

Judging from the comments and proposals made during the negotiation of AP II, there was a general consensus that reprisals in NIAC were prohibited against: (i) persons in the power of the enemy who do not take a direct part or who have ceased to take a part in hostilities, whether or not their liberty has been restricted; (ii) the wounded, the sick and the shipwrecked, as well as medical personnel, units and transports; and (iii) the civilian population. Support for protecting from reprisals these categories of persons and medical objects remained strong throughout the Diplomatic Conference. Corresponding prohibitions featured in the

[11] Article 32 of Vienna Convention on the Law of Treaties, Vienna, 23 May 1969, in force 27 January 1980, 1155 UNTS 331.

[12] Henckaerts and Doswald-Beck, *Customary IHL Study*, p. xxxviii ('Verbal acts [of States constituting practice that contributes to the creation of customary international law] include ... comments by governments on draft treaties [and] statements ... at international conferences'); ILC, 'Draft Conclusions on Identification of Customary International Law', p. 141, Commentary on Conclusion 10, para. 6 ('Multilateral drafting and diplomatic processes may afford valuable and accessible evidence as to the legal convictions of States with respect to the content of customary international law'). As these texts demonstrate, the only difference would at worst concern the construction of verbal acts as evidence of practice (as per the ICRC) or *opinio iuris* (according to the ILC) – but see ILC, *ibid.*, p. 133, Commentary on Conclusion 6, para. 2, interpreting verbal conduct as 'also count[ing] as practice'.

original ICRC draft of AP II;[13] in various amendments by States[14] and proposals by the ICRC,[15] the Sub-group on reprisals[16] and Working Group B of Committee I;[17] and in the final version of Article 10 *bis* adopted by Committee I and eventually deleted by the Plenary.[18]

By comparison, the prohibition on reprisals against civilian objects met with much feebler approval. These targets were not protected from reprisals in the original ICRC draft,[19] and were only introduced in the debates through amendments by those States that were willing to have

[13] See respectively draft Articles 8(4) in Part II, 19 in Part III and 26(4) in Part V (*CDDH Official Records*, vol. I, Part III, pp. 35–40). In the original ICRC draft, Article 8(4) only shielded from reprisals 'persons whose liberty has been restricted by capture or arrest for reasons in relation to the armed conflict', thus potentially leaving outside of the protection the wider category of persons who do not take a direct part or who have ceased to take a part in hostilities in draft Article 6 (*ibid.*). This gap was immediately spotted by the Finnish delegation, who tried to extend the prohibition of reprisals to Article 6 (*ibid.*, vol. IV, p. 18 and CDDH/I/SR.32, in *ibid.*, vol. VIII, p. 324, para. 7). By 1976, the ICRC was proposing a corresponding inclusion in Article 6 (*ibid.*, vol. IV, p. 19) and in Article 10 *bis* (*ibid.*, vol. IV, p. 37).

[14] Romania (*ibid.*, vol. IV, pp. 75 and 80), German Democratic Republic (*ibid.*, p. 80), Canada (*ibid.*, p. 191). Early on, Australia submitted an amendment to delete paragraph 4 of Article 26 prohibiting reprisals against the civilian population or civilians (*ibid.*, p. 76). However, States in Committee III either supported the prohibition on reprisals (Finland, Federal Republic of Germany, Norway, USSR, Byelorussia) or reserved their position on the whole article (Mexico, UK, Brazil, Italy) – none was in favour of deleting the paragraph (CDDH/III/SR.8 and CDDH/III/SR.9, in *ibid.*, vol. XIV, pp. 59–75).

[15] *Ibid.*, vol. IV, p. 37. The civilian population is not explicitly mentioned in the ICRC proposed amendment to Article 10 *bis*, but it can be read in the very wide wording 'persons who do not take a direct part or who have ceased to take a part in hostilities'. This interpretation is suggested by the earlier support in the original ICRC draft for a prohibition on reprisals against civilians (see in this chapter, footnote 13), and by the references to Part V in the proposals that followed shortly afterwards (see in this chapter, footnotes 16 and 17).

[16] CDDH/405/Rev.1, in *ibid.*, vol. X, pp. 234–35 ('provisions of Parts II and III and of articles . . .'(sic), with the proposal being 'without prejudice to any relevant decisions that might be taken concerning Part V of the Protocol').

[17] *Ibid.*, pp. 233–34 ('The provisions of /Parts II, III and V/', with some delegations being 'able to agree to a text of the kind proposed only if provisions of Part V are appropriately included').

[18] *Ibid.*, p. 283 ('The provisions of Parts II and III and of Articles 26'). Article 10 *bis* was rejected by a majority that was less than half the number of States participating in the voting (forty-one votes to twenty, with twenty-two abstentions: CDDH/SR.51, in *ibid.*, vol. VII, p. 109). Moreover, as the French delegation explained, by casting a negative vote to support the Pakistani draft, it was not 'expressing any views on the substance of Article 10 *bis*' (*ibid.*, p. 120).

[19] *Ibid.*, vol. I, Part III, pp. 40–41.

similar provisions in the two Additional Protocols.[20] Civilian objects were again left out of the ICRC proposed amendment to Article 10 *bis*,[21] and it was only by way of compromise that Working Group B of Committee I proposed that the general provision on prohibited reprisals contain a reference to Articles 26 *bis* (civilian objects in general), 27 (objects indispensable to the survival of the civilian population) and 28 (works and installations containing dangerous forces).[22] Committee I followed the suggestion, but with a very narrow majority (twenty-nine votes to eleven, with thirty-nine abstentions).[23] Even after the rejection of Article 10 *bis* in the Plenary, there was no attempt to re-introduce a specific prohibition on reprisals in Articles 26 *bis*, 27 and 28.[24] It seems safe to conclude that the diplomatic tussle did not coalesce around a protection of civilian objects from reprisals; as a matter of customary law, this category of items could still be lawfully targeted by way of retaliation.[25]

Finally, even if few delegations warned against *a contrario* interpretations that would allow reprisals against persons and objects not specifically protected therefrom,[26] this does not detract from States' willingness

[20] The German Democratic Republic introduced an amendment to draft Article 26 to protect also civilian objects from attacks by way of reprisals (*ibid.*, vol. IV, p. 80). Other amendments concerned: Article 27 for objects indispensable to the survival of the civilian population (Romania: *ibid.*, pp. 84 and 86; Finland and Sweden: *ibid.*, p. 84; Egypt, Iraq, Syria: *ibid.*, p. 85); Article 28 for works and installations containing dangerous forces (Romania: *ibid.*, pp. 88 and 90; Finland: *ibid.*, p. 89). See also the positive comments on amendments to Articles 27 and 28 by USSR and Yugoslavia (CDDH/III/SR.18, in *ibid.*, vol. XIV, p. 151, para. 3 and p. 159, para. 45), but also the negative ones by Mongolia (CDDH/III/SR.20, in *ibid.*, vol. XIV, p. 176, para. 53). For the need to have identical provisions on this point in the two Protocols, see Finland and Egypt, *ibid.*, p. 176, para. 34.

[21] *Ibid.*, vol. IV, p. 37.

[22] CDDH/405/Rev.1, in *ibid.*, vol. X, p. 231.

[23] CDDH/I/SR.73, in *ibid.*, vol. IX, p. 429.

[24] CDDH/SR.52, in *ibid.*, vol. VII, pp. 135–38. Article 26 *bis* was deleted by consensus, whereas draft Articles 27 and 28 became (with no provision on reprisals) respectively Articles 14 and 15 in the final text of AP II (*ibid.*).

[25] The only potential exception to this conclusion is the case of cultural property, if one were to conclude that the treaty prohibition on reprisals against such category of objects in NIAC (see Section 5.1.1) has crystallized into custom. Rule 148 of the ICRC *Customary IHL Study*, however, does not go this far: its prohibition of 'countermeasures other than belligerent reprisals' in NIAC only covers 'persons who do not or who have ceased to take a direct part in hostilities' (Henckaerts and Doswald-Beck, *Customary IHL Study*, vol. I, p. 526).

[26] Poland and Mexico in CDDH/I/SR.73, in *ibid.*, vol. IX, pp. 450 and 452.

to restrict the prohibition of reprisals in NIAC to 'certain well-defined cases, restrictively enumerated'.[27] In this sense, there were no challenges to the idea that reprisals could be directed against individuals that take a direct part in the hostilities (be they civilians or members of fighting units).[28] The same must be true, if the principle of equality in rights and obligations is to be given actual implementation, for reprisals against the armed forces of a State – notwithstanding States' uneasiness at the idea that 'some non-identified organization' adopt reprisals against their own organs.[29]

In conclusion, the distinction that comes out of the CDDH's work on NIAC is not, as argued by Sivakumaran, between 'belligerent reprisals against persons in the power of the adversary and belligerent reprisals in the context of the conduct of hostilities'.[30] The relevant distinction is rather between persons (who are protected from reprisals unless they take a direct part in the hostilities) and objects (which can be targeted by way of reprisal, except for medical ones). Curiously then, a customary prohibition on belligerent reprisals against the civilian population is easier to argue for NIAC than IAC, even though the legal framework governing the former is far less developed than the latter. This conclusion is less paradoxical than it looks, if only one considers that taking reprisals against its own civilians is significantly different from (and, from a practical point of view, much less convenient than) retaliating against the civilian population of another State.[31] At any rate, the fundamental point here is that the process of negotiating AP II is much more revelatory about reprisals prohibited in NIAC than the treaty itself. Both the ICTY and the scholars commenting on its case-law could have relied on this material to bolster their analysis. The judges could have based their prohibition on reprisals against civilians in NIAC on the more familiar argument of customary law;[32] commentators, on their part, could have

[27] Cameroon (CDDH/I/SR.73, in *ibid.*, vol. IX, p. 455.

[28] According to Article 26(2) in the original ICRC draft, the protection afforded civilians '*by this article*' lasts 'unless and for such time they take a direct part in hostilities' (*ibid.*, vol. I, Part III, p. 40, emphasis added). In the ICRC scheme, the civilian population or individual civilians would enjoy protection from attacks by way of reprisal under draft Article 26 (4) only insofar as they comply with the general condition in paragraph 2 of not participating in hostilities.

[29] ICRC (CDDH/II/SR.28, in *ibid.*, vol. XI, p. 291, para. 63).

[30] Sivakumaran, *Law of NIAC*, p. 450.

[31] *Ibid.*, pp. 452–53.

[32] With regard to *Kupreškić*, however, we have just seen that a prohibition of reprisals against civilians in IAC does not follow necessarily from a corresponding prohibition in

listed these statements and proposals as instances of State practice or *opinio iuris* in support of such prohibition, thereby interpreting cases of unrestricted retaliatory violence against civilians as violations of a customary rule (instead of evidence of the absence thereof).

6.2.3 The Limits of a Formal Outlook

Our analysis of the CDDH highlights the limitations that one encounters (and the failure that they will ultimately meet with) if belligerent reprisals are formalized in formal and static terms. The international legal reflex is to see questions of rights and duties only as a black-or-white issue: when involved in an armed conflict, either States and NSAGs have international legal obligations or they do not, and the full physiognomy of their juridical spheres is fully defined as soon as IHL applies. This view overlooks the fact that the process of determining the legal position of parties involved in a conflict is a much more nuanced and dynamic endeavour. If IHL represents a compromise between military necessity and humanitarian considerations, these traditional poles are not to be understood in abstract terms: they are related to the interests of the various stakeholders, and their relative strength evolves on the basis of what the parties are willing to give in and what they are committed to stick to.

In this sense, the negotiations of AP II and belligerent reprisals in NIAC share a common feature: that of being tools to bargain a workable equilibrium of rights and obligations. Reprisals are not discussed in the relative quiet of a diplomatic setting – they too represent a means of "talking" about the obligations of the parties to a conflict and of evening out their legal position. Just like the *travaux préparatoires* of AP II can complement the deficiencies of the treaty text, belligerent reprisals can be seen as a follow-up tool to clarify, refine and supplement applicable standards of behaviour. Seeing them as an enforcement mechanism founders as soon as one acknowledges the lesser sophistication of the norms governing internal armed conflict; but as an instrument inspired by reciprocity, they could be used to steer and govern the legal relationship between belligerents – even in a situation where one of the fighting

NIAC. If at all necessary for the solution of the case (see Greenwood, 'Reprisals in the Jurisprudence', p. 549), a finding of the customary status of such prohibition in IAC should be based on a different reasoning.

sides would have preferred not to be bound by rigid legal standards (for instance, a government unwilling to bestow rights on rebel forces).

Despite their practical potential, instances of retaliatory non-compliance with IHL norms in NIAC are rarely formalized as belligerent reprisals by legal commentators. These incidents are most often described as isolated examples of breaches of applicable norms, rather than parts of a process of act and response. And yet, contemporary practice upholds also for NIAC the formalization of belligerent reprisals as a reciprocity-inspired mechanism. As we shall see in the remainder of this chapter, this is confirmed both by the language of parties to the various NIACs, and by the work of several UN bodies that have monitored their behaviour throughout hostilities. Such a comprehensive study will show how belligerent reprisals are used for purposes that exceed by far the logic of enforcement: the adoption of non-compliant behaviour follows a pattern of strategic bargaining whereby the warring factions negotiate and sustain an equilibrium in rights and obligations.

Carrying out this form of empiric analysis is all the more important in the present context. When it comes to NIAC, the agreed equilibrium might well have to specify, not only which victims of war will be protected and how hostilities will be conducted, but also which reprisals will be prohibited and which not. Let us not forget that the rules on prohibited reprisals that can be derived from the work of the CDDH stem from proposals and statements of *States*; at the same time, we have considered the web of legal relationships between parties to a NIAC not as a legal given, but as a dynamic endeavour that arises out of the interaction between them.[33] Against this backdrop, State-designed prohibitions on reprisals in NIAC could be subject to approval or contestation just as much as any other substantive rule negotiated through deed by the belligerents. This could lead to a situation where the limits on belligerent reprisals (i.e., to what extent they are prohibited or allowed) are negotiated through recourse to belligerent reprisals themselves! In this sense, the object of contention is also the very tool through which the bargain is carried out. Given these premises, only a reciprocity-based formalization will provide belligerent reprisals with the flexibility that is necessary to forge an equilibrium in rights and obligations between parties to NIAC.

[33] On how IHL instruments become binding on entities (such as NSAGs) that are not High Contracting Parties to them, see ICRC, *Commentary on GC III*, 2nd ed., para. 541.

6.3 Belligerent Reprisals in Action

6.3.1 Monitoring Retaliation

In recent years, a wide range of actors has monitored and reported on IHL compliance in NIAC with increased frequency.[34] These include both human rights fact-finding missions and commissions of inquiry originating from the Human Rights Council, and groups of experts that assist committees in overseeing sanctions regimes. Although their institutional mandates were not primarily (if at all) concerned with IHL, these bodies have not shied away from addressing potential IHL violations whenever they found that a given situation amounted to an armed conflict – for our purposes, a non-international one.[35] They have thus been confronted with a number of instances where the (unlawful) conduct of one party to the conflict was seen as reacting to some behaviour (either lawful or unlawful) of the counterpart – and the way in which this behavioural connection has been construed by the monitoring bodies indicates to what extent belligerent reprisals (and, more widely, reciprocity) are accommodated into the legal framework governing NIAC. This accommodation can be analysed both in static and in dynamic terms. In the former, the notion of belligerent reprisals is distinguished from other examples of reactive behaviour and seen in its specific character of an otherwise unlawful conduct excused by a previous illegality. In the latter, that same notion is understood as taking on several purposes, depending on the evolution of the legal and factual relationship between the parties to the conflict.

Reports of investigative bodies mandated by the Human Rights Council use a panoply of terms to capture the reactive nature of certain violations. These include, beyond reprisals, the notions of revenge, retribution, (collective) punishment, retaliation and response. This is quite surprising in its own merits. Given the fundamental value attached to human rights and the exceptional scope for derogations thereto, one would not expect such bodies to inquire into the factual motivations behind a given breach: the purportedly intransgressible nature of certain IHL norms should be magnified by the strong guarantees in place for the

[34] For an overview and detailed analysis, see Émilie Max, *Implementing International Humanitarian Law through Human Rights Mechanisms: Opportunity or Utopia?*, Geneva Academy Working Paper, October 2019.

[35] For an analysis of the competence of investigative mechanisms created by the Human Rights Council, including some that will be addressed in this chapter, see *ibid.*, pp. 9–13.

protection of human rights. How could we make sense of this tendency to explain the rationale behind behaviours that do not comply *prima facie* with IHL norms?

One could argue that, by highlighting the reactive nature of violations, monitoring bodies wish to stygmatize how arbitrary the trampling on the human rights of the victims, the message being that two wrongs do not make a right. But another explanation would see this tendency as a reflex of the interplay between international human rights law and IHL in the particular context of armed conflict. Under this light, even the simple mention of the reactive nature of a breach (without deriving therefrom further effects in terms of excuse or justification) points to the impact that the fundamentally "horizontal" IHL regime has on the "vertical" relationship governed by human rights law,[36] and to the creeping effect of reciprocity-based elements onto the understanding of legal relationships in a conflict scenario.

6.3.2 *An Exercise in Distinction: Belligerent Reprisals* vis-à-vis *Other Reactive Behaviours*

What is more, acknowledging the fundamentally responsive nature of conducts during hostilities helps formalize the different types of reactive behaviours in a sophisticated manner. At first glance, investigative bodies would seem to use the terms recalled above interchangeably, almost as synonyms. In reality, it is possible to draw rather precise lines of demarcation between the meaning that those notions are given in the different reports; moreover, these meanings appear quite consistent throughout a vast array of commissions of inquiry and fact-finding missions.

For one thing, the notions of 'retribution', 'revenge' and 'collective punishment' are used almost exclusively in relation to harmful, illegal conducts taken against persons perceived as supporting the enemy, irrespective of whether the target's prior behaviour could be characterized as unlawful under IHL.[37] For instance, the Commission of Inquiry on Syria and the Commission on Human Rights in South Sudan resort to these terms to describe such reactive behaviours as: the deprivation of

[36] ICRC, *International Humanitarian Law and the challenges of contemporary armed conflicts*, Report (2011), p. 14.

[37] The question whether such support for the enemy is lawful under national law is irrelevant here.

liberty and of access to food and medicine,[38] enforced disappearance,[39] sexual violence,[40] the use of imprecise weapons in civilian areas,[41] and attacks against civilians ('punitive counter-insurgency').[42] Only on rare occasions, the International Commission of Human Rights Experts on Ethiopia and the Office of the UN High Commissioner for Human Rights (OHCHR) in its investigation on Libya have used the same terms to indicate unlawful behaviours that were characterized by a strong afflictive element *vis-à-vis* previous wrongdoing by the enemy.[43] Overall, the distinguishing features of this category of reactive behaviours appear to be (i) their punitive character, and (ii) in the majority of cases, the fact that the alleged misbehaviour complained of has a political character (i.e., communities and individuals sympathizing for, or simply not opposing, the enemy) rather than a legal one (i.e., a breach of IHL).

A different meaning is the one that can be ascertained for the terms 'retaliation', 'reaction' and 'response'. Compared to the previous batch of terms, this new set of notions has two distinguishing factors: first, the punitive element is much less pronounced;[44] second, the conducts reacted against have a stronger military component, insofar as they stem from the behaviour of the enemy forces (such as attacks on military targets, military operations and offensives, and the gaining of territory)[45]

[38] CoI-S, UN Doc. A/HRC/23/58, 18 July 2013, paras. 65, 69 and 144; CHR-SoSu, UN Doc. A/HRC/45/CRP.3, 5 October 2020, paras. 88, 123 and 144–46.

[39] CoI-S, UN Doc. A/HRC/25/65, 12 February 2014, Annex IV, paras. 2 and 18–21.

[40] CoI-S, UN Doc. A/HRC/37/CRP.3, 8 March 2018, paras. 11, 38, 43 and 52; CHR-SoSu, UN Doc. A/HRC/37/71, 13 March 2018, para. 28.

[41] CoI-S, UN Doc. A/HRC/23/58, para. 104; CoI-S, UN Doc. A/HRC/24/46, 16 August 2013, para. 114.

[42] CHR-SoSu, UN Doc. A/HRC/37/CRP.2, 23 February 2018, paras. 289 and 380; CHR-SoSu, UN Doc. A/HRC/37/71, paras. 24, 38 and 64.

[43] This is the case for acts of rape and sexual violence by Tigrayan forces said by the perpetrators to be in 'revenge for the widespread rape of Tigrayan women and girls' (ICoHRE-E, UN Doc. A/HRC/51/46, 19 September 2022, paras. 64–65) and the beheading by ISIL of Egyptian Copts claimed 'as revenge for "sisters who were tortured and murdered by the Coptic Church of Egypt" five years previously' (OHCHR-Libya, UN Doc. A/HRC/31/CRP.3, 23 February 2016, para. 83).

[44] Although it cannot be ruled out in few pronouncements: OHCHR-Libya, UN Doc. A/HRC/31/CRP.3, paras. 113 and 274; CHR-SoSu, UN Doc. A/HRC/40/CRP.1, 20 February 2019, paras. 759–761; CHR-SoSu, UN Doc. A/HRC/49/78, 15 February 2022, para. 59; CHR-SoSu, UN Doc. A/HRC/49/CRP.4, 21 March 2022, paras. 76 and 82 and p. 20, footnote 120.

[45] CoI-S, UN Doc. A/HRC/24/46, Annex II, para. 15; CoI-S, UN Doc. A/HRC/27/60, 13 August 2014, para. 106; CoI-S, UN Doc. A/HRC/28/69, 5 February 2015, paras. 51 and 266; CoI-S, UN Doc. A/HRC/33/55, 11 August 2016, para. 27.

rather than the feelings of the civilian population. In the majority of cases (and particularly those reported by the Commission of Inquiry on Syria), these terms indicate retaliatory attacks on civilians,[46] objects entitled to specific protection (including hospitals)[47] and objects indispensable to the survival of the civilian population.[48] But even here, it appears largely immaterial whether the conduct motivating the reactive behaviour represents a violation of IHL or a permissible method of warfare: for instance, the notion of 'retaliation' is used by the Commission on Human Rights in South Sudan to qualify attacks against civilians, both when they followed an attack on a religious building, and when they were carried out as a reaction against battlefield losses.[49]

Finally, with a few exceptions[50] the notion of 'reprisals' is used by investigative bodies as a term of art, albeit with two, different meanings. Oftentimes, and in line with the practice of the Human Rights Council, the term covers the harmful conducts (from travel bans and surveillance to arbitrary detention, torture and killing) directed against individuals and groups that seek to cooperate or have cooperated with the United Nations in the field of human rights.[51] However, on several occasions the notion is used as a short-hand for the IHL notion of belligerent reprisals. Although these references take a variety of forms and hint at different understandings of how the mechanism works, they are all based on the assumptions that the notion of belligerent reprisals (i) applies in NIACs, (ii) is subject to some form of legal regulation (i.e., prohibition or limitation of use), and (iii) can take on a variety of purposes.

[46] CoI-S, UN Doc. A/HRC/24/46, Annex II, para. 15; CoI-S, UN Doc. A/HRC/27/60, para. 106; CoI-S, UN Doc. A/HRC/25/65, para. 143.

[47] CoI-S, UN Doc. A/HRC/33/55, para. 27.

[48] CoI-S, UN Doc. A/HRC/28/69, para. 266.

[49] CHR-SoSu, UN Doc. A/HRC/37/CRP.2, paras. 289, 326, 340, 380, 405, 407, 411, 425, 450–451.

[50] For instance, with connotations of revenge and punishment: CoI-S, UN Doc. A/HRC/19/69, 22 February 2012, paras. 47–48, 118 and 133; CoI-S, UN Doc. A/HRC/37/72, 1 February 2018, paras. 21, 25 and 43; CHR-SoSu, UN Doc. A/HRC/45/CRP.4, 5 October 2020, Summary, p. 1.

[51] See HRC resolutions 12/2 (UN Doc. A/HRC/RES/12/2); 24/24 (UN Doc. A/HRC/RES/24/24); 36/21 (UN Doc. A/HRC/RES/36/21); and 42/28 (UN Doc. A/HRC/RES/42/28). See also the OHCHR page dedicated to reprisals at www.ohchr.org/en/reprisals. Examples can be found in: CoI-S, UN Doc. A/HRC/46/55, 11 March 2021, para. 7; Independent Fact-Finding Mission on Libya, UN Doc. A/HRC/48/83, 29 November 2021, para. 13; CHR-SoSu, UN Doc. A/HRC/34/63, 6 March 2017, para. 59; IIFFM-M, UN Doc. A/HRC/51/4, 12 July 2022, para. 42.

It is to the latter meaning that we shall now turn, to see how belligerent reprisals in NIACs have been articulated by warring parties and understood by monitoring bodies. Our analysis will demonstrate two points. First, a passage by the Independent International Fact-Finding Mission on Myanmar will provide further elements supporting the key finding of Chapter 5 – that is, when it comes to the *functioning* of belligerent reprisals, features associated with reciprocity prevail over those flowing from enforcement, even in the context of NIAC. Second, the monitoring of the NIACs affecting Syria and Yemen will highlight how the *purpose* of belligerent reprisals evolves, progressively losing its enforcement aim and embracing the more strategic aspiration of governing the equilibrium of rights and obligations between the parties to the armed conflict.

6.3.3 *The IIFFM-M and the Re-instatement of Reciprocity in the Functioning of Reprisals*

A first foray into how UN investigative bodies treat the notion of belligerent reprisals can be found in the work of the Independent International Fact-Finding Mission on Myanmar (IIFFM-M). The IIFFM-M has so far referred to belligerent reprisals in only one instance, but this single mention branches out with particularly far-reaching ramifications. While analysing what it had classified as a non-international armed conflict between the Government forces of Myanmar (called Tatmadaw) and the Arakan Army,[52] the IIFFM-M has dwelled on an incident involving the ancient town of Mrauk-U. Once the capital of the first Arakanese Kingdom, the city hosts hundreds of 'monuments and structures [with] religious, historical and cultural significance' that 'constitute "cultural heritage" as defined and protected under international law'.[53] As a Tatmadaw convoy was driving through that city in March 2019, it opened fire on monasteries and statues, placed artillery in proximity of historical buildings, and damaged them by digging up trenches and using their stones as bunkers.[54]

In its detailed analysis of the incident, the IIFFM-M strives to co-apply and harmonize several bodies of law, including IHL, the conventions protecting cultural property in the event of armed conflict, international

[52] IIFFM-M, UN Doc. A/HRC/39/CRP.2, 17 September 2018, paras. 52–53; IIFFM-M, UN Doc. A/HRC/42/CRP.5, 16 September 2019, paras. 253 and 273.

[53] IIFFM-M, UN Doc. A/HRC/42/CRP.5, para. 279.

[54] *Ibid.*, paras. 281–83.

human rights law, and even the 1972 World Heritage Convention.[55] The conduct of the Tatmadaw is ultimately assessed in light of (i) the principles of distinction and precaution under IHL and (ii) the obligation to respect cultural property.[56] However, in its overview of applicable norms, the IIFFM-M singles out the absolute prohibition on acts of reprisals against cultural property contained in the 1954 Hague Convention and affirms that it applies also in NIACs.[57] What are the reasons for mentioning this norm in relation to the specific situation under scrutiny?

The reference to belligerent reprisals could be a way to neutralize a defence hinted at by the Tatmadaw and loosely based on a reciprocity argument. On the basis of the information at its disposal, the IIFFM-M had been able to exclude the presence of fighters from the Arakan Army in civilian houses and properties in Mrauk-U where the convoy had passed, thereby ruling out the claim that the cultural sites had become military objectives because of use in support of military action by the enemy.[58] But as the IIFFM-M recalls, the offensive in Mrauk-U had also been justified as a response to an earlier attack that the Arakan Army had launched on a Tatmadaw convoy.[59] Furthermore, the Tatmadaw's suggestion that the attack by the Arakan Army had injured civilians[60] could be seen as adding a supplementary layer of defence, whereby opening fire on cultural property was justified, not by its loss of protection, but by the need to respond to an unlawful conduct by the enemy. In this sense, recalling the explicit prohibition of belligerent reprisals in the 1954 Hague Convention aims to forestall the legality of any hostile act taken against cultural property in reaction to potentially unlawful (and, *a fortiori*, lawful) acts by the enemy.

There is, however, another and deeper way in which the notion of belligerent reprisals permeates the analysis of the attack. At a certain

55 *Ibid.*, paras. 289–96.

56 The Mission concludes that the Tatmadaw had contravened IHL by launching an indiscriminate attack and by failing to take all feasible precautions to avoid or in any event minimize damage to civilian life and property (*ibid.*, paras. 289 and 291); it also found that they had breached the protection afforded cultural property under international law by using it for military purposes, by wilfully damaging, misappropriating and vandalizing it, and by directing acts of hostility against it (*ibid.*, para. 296).

57 *Ibid.*, para. 293. Hague Convention for the Protection of Cultural Property in the Event of Armed Conflict, The Hague, 14 May 1954, in force 7 August 1956, 249 UNTS 215.

58 IIFFM-M, UN Doc. A/HRC/42/CRP.5, para. 284.

59 *Ibid.*, para. 290.

60 *Ibid.*, para. 284, footnote 644.

point, the IIFFM-M seems to suggest that, since the Government of Myanmar had acknowledged the outstanding universal value of Mrauk-U by adding it to its Tentative List,[61] the town 'should be afforded *heightened protection* under the 1954 Hague Convention'.[62] On the basis of textual underpinnings, it is not unreasonable to construe this passage as a reference to the *special* regime of protection provided for under Chapter II of that Convention.[63] According to that regime, certain immovable cultural properties of very great importance only lose immunity from acts of hostility or military use in two situations. The first case is mentioned in Article 11(2) of the 1954 Hague Convention and rests on a purely factual determination: immunity could be withdrawn 'in exceptional cases of unavoidable military necessity, and only for such time as that necessity continues'.[64] The second one, on the other hand, is set forth in Article 11(1) of that treaty and presupposes a breach of the international obligations incumbent on the enemy. If one of the parties to the conflict violates its duty to ensure the immunity of cultural property under special protection (for instance, by using them or their surroundings for military purposes), such property could become a legitimate target 'so long as this violation persists' and

[61] UNESCO defines the Tentative List of each State as 'an inventory of those properties situated on its territory which each State Party considers suitable for nomination to the World Heritage List', containing 'details of those properties which [States Parties] consider to be of potential Outstanding Universal Value and which they intend to nominate during the following years' for inscription on the World Heritage List (World Heritage Centre, *Operational Guidelines for the Implementation of the World Heritage Convention*, WHC.21/01, 31 July 2021, para. 62).

[62] IIFFM-M, UN Doc. A/HRC/42/CRP.5, para. 294 [emphasis added].

[63] *Ibid.*, para. 293, whereby the system established by the 1954 Hague Convention of '*special heightened protections* for cultural property that has been internationally recognized as being culturally significant' is mentioned *in addition to* the other obligations established in that treaty. The problem with this reading is that, in principle, the special regime of protection was crafted to be applied in IAC, and only after a formalized procedure of inscription has been carried out (see respectively Articles 19 and 8(6) of the 1954 Hague Convention). These hurdles could be overcome by reading the passage by the IIFFM-M as a proposal *de lege ferenda* (note the wording 'should be afforded'), or as an extension of (certain) guarantees afforded by the regime of special protection in case of a documented outstanding universal value (for instance, through inscription on Tentative Lists or the World Heritage List).

[64] Article 11(2) of the 1954 Hague Convention. This provision also provides for some procedural guarantees, such as the rank of the decision-maker (an officer commanding a force the equivalent of a division in size or larger) and the duty of advance notification whenever circumstances permit (*ibid.*).

following 'whenever possible' a request to cease the violation within a reasonable time.[65]

Let us focus on the latter way of withdrawing immunity, which Provost has compared to the familiar types of reaction to a breach formalized under international law. He relies on the requirements in Article 11(1) of the 1954 Hague Convention (i.e., the prior breach, the temporal limitation and the request for cessation) to conclude that the measure outlined in that provision is 'closer in nature to reprisals than to the condition of reciprocity', thereby drawing a thick line of demarcation between the two frameworks.[66] However, assuming such a sharp juxtaposition between reprisals and reciprocity leads to paradoxical results: indeed, the targeting of cultural property by way of belligerent reprisal, which is not permitted under the ordinary regime of protection enshrined in Article 4(4) of the 1954 Hague Convention, risks becoming legitimate under the special ("heightened") regime under Article 11(1) thereof!

Whereas Provost proposes to solve this inconsistency by qualifying Article 11(1) as a special rule derogating from the general prohibition of reprisals,[67] it is submitted that a more linear course of action would acknowledge that reciprocity is embedded in this particular type of belligerent reprisals. This conclusion is warranted by several considerations. At the textual level, by setting forth that 'the opposing Party shall ... *be released* from the obligation to ensure the immunity of the property concerned', Article 11(1) of the 1954 Hague Convention adopts a language that is clearly hinting at reciprocity and the suspension of the contractual synallagma.[68] Moreover, reciprocity exerts its influence by circumscribing the scope of permissible retaliatory action, thereby removing the seeming paradox of a reprisal that is first prohibited and then re-introduced against the very property that is particularly worth of protection. Under the ordinary regime set forth in the 1954 Hague Convention, the prohibition of reprisals is meant to shield cultural property from retaliatory action that could potentially follow *any* type

[65] Article 11(1) of the 1954 Hague Convention.

[66] Provost, *International Human Rights and Humanitarian Law*, p. 176.

[67] *Ibid.*

[68] Article 11(1) of the 1954 Hague Convention. The French and the Spanish text of the Convention (which are equally authentic versions according to Article 29(1) thereof), use words that convey similar ideas: 'dégagée de son obligation' and 'desligada ... de su obligación', respectively.

of IHL violation: since belligerent reprisals do not need be in kind, the risk to be averted is that cultural property be targeted in reaction to unlawful war conducts that have no connection with it. By contrast, under the special regime, the reciprocal element ensures that the unlawful military advantage obtained by stripping the specially protected cultural property from immunity is countered through a form of belligerent reprisal that is both strictly linked with the original violation and limited in scope: the release from the obligation to ensure immunity follows and mirrors the counterpart's failure to ensure immunity, and is warranted only to the extent that is necessary and sufficient to re-establish the original equilibrium perturbed by the first violation. In this limited respect, the reciprocal element of the measure is capable of restricting retaliatory action in ways that an enforcement-based understanding of belligerent reprisals would not.

Equipped with this enhanced understanding, let us now go back to the case of Mrauk-U. Also on that occasion, the absence of enemy fighters was instrumental for the IIFFM-M to prove that the cultural site was not being used for military purposes, and therefore to prevent the Tatmadaw from justifying their acts of hostility as a form of *simil*-belligerent reprisals sanctioned under the special protection regime.[69] But the thrust of all the references to belligerent reprisals hides beneath (and goes beyond) the facts of the case. First, by leaning on the text of the 1954 Hague Convention, the IIFFM-M re-affirms the prohibition and, therefore, the abstract applicability of belligerent reprisals even in the context of NIAC. Second, by hinting at a "heightened" protection that reminds of the special regime under the same Convention, it highlights the many points of contact between the withdrawal of immunity under Article 11(1) of that treaty, the features traditionally associated with belligerent reprisals, and the working of reciprocity.

In sum, at the very moment when it makes explicit (albeit very limited) room for a legal tool modelled on belligerent reprisals in NIAC, the IIFFM-M re-instates reciprocity at the core of its functioning. Perhaps inadvertently, the work of the IIFFM-M offers a practical example of how to weave, into the functioning of belligerent reprisals, the logic of reciprocity that the scholarship had strived to keep separated in the theoretical analysis. Let us now turn to the monitoring of the conflicts in Syria and Yemen to see how the grounding of belligerent reprisals in

[69] IIFFM-M, UN Doc. A/HRC/42/CRP.5, para. 284.

reciprocity affects the identification of the purposes associated with these measures.

6.4 Monitoring Bodies and the Purpose of Belligerent Reprisals in NIACs

6.4.1 *The Commission of Inquiry on Syria*

6.4.1.1 Punitive and Deterrent Features Associated with Belligerent Reprisals

Compared to the IIFFM-M, the Commission of Inquiry on Syria (CoI-S) has referred to belligerent reprisals several times in its decade-long mandate. The legal basis for the applicability or the prohibition of belligerent reprisals in NIAC is less clear here,[70] but these mentions advance to a considerable extent our comprehension of the purposes that the investigative body attaches to the notion.

The first notations on belligerent reprisals in the work of the CoI-S are characterized by a strong emphasis on the punitive element of the measure. Already in July 2013, while discussing summary executions and the war crime of murder, the CoI-S stated that revenge killings (most often carried out against detained persons believed to be opposition sympathizers) 'are a direct violation of the prohibition of reprisals'.[71] It also recalled how the public execution in ISIL-controlled Raqqah of three Alawite men had been explicitly motivated in the judgment as a form of 'retaliation' for a massacre of civilians allegedly committed by Government forces and affiliated militias a few days earlier.[72] At first sight, these passages look quite ambiguous. The reference to 'revenge', the accusation of harbouring sympathy for the counterpart and the notion of public show trials and executions could indicate that, in reality, the Commission had the prohibition of collective punishment in mind.

[70] The CoI-S has found that the situation in Syria had met the legal threshold for a non-international armed conflict since the period covered by its third report (mid-February to mid-July 2012): CoI-S, UN Doc. A/HRC/21/50, 16 August 2012, para. 12 and Annex II, para. 3.

[71] CoI-S, UN Doc. A/HRC/23/58, para. 51. Note how this passage subsumes the idea of revenge (mentioned above together with retribution and collective punishment) within the notion (and the prohibition) of belligerent reprisals. This incorporation hints at the capacity of the notion of belligerent reprisals to accommodate within its logical boundaries the many purposes associated with the different types of reactive behaviour, as it was demonstrated with regard to IAC and will be shown with reference to NIAC.

[72] *Ibid.*, paras. 41, 50 and 60.

However, this argument runs against the explicit mention of reprisals and fails to consider that the prohibition of collective punishment is addressed elsewhere in the report, with regard chiefly to arbitrary arrest and detention.[73]

This reference to reprisals would be better understood on its own terms, as a precise consequence of conclusions that the CoI-S had reached concerning the applicable law. Upon finding that the legal threshold for a NIAC had been met,[74] the CoI-S had set out a detailed framework for the 'complementary and mutually reinforcing' application of IHL and international human rights law;[75] the notions of murder as war crime and arbitrary deprivation of life had also been elucidated in light of the interplay between the two bodies of law (as well as international criminal law).[76] The prohibition of reprisals could then be seen, not as an autonomous norm, but rather as a consequence of a particularly elaborate (and stringent) co-application of these regimes.

Alternatively, a parallelism could be drawn between the references to murder and summary executions that are found in the report, on the one hand, and the prohibitions in Article 3 common to the 1949 GCs of 'murder of all kinds' and 'the passing of sentences and the carrying out of executions without previous judgment pronounced by a regularly constituted court, affording all the judicial guarantees which are recognized as indispensable by civilized peoples' for persons taking no active part in the hostilities, on the other.[77] To the extent that the latter acts shall remain prohibited at any time and in any place whatsoever, the prohibition of belligerent reprisals would represent an application, sufficiently inscribed in the IHL domain, of the absolute character of Common Article 3.

In the following work of the CoI-S, the punitive focus of these initial references to belligerent reprisals is replaced by instances where the deterrent element is predominant. A particularly telling example is the use by Jaysh al-Islam of metal cages 'to parade men and women belonging to the Alawite sect through the streets of their stronghold [of

[73] *Ibid.*, paras. 64–69.

[74] CoI-S, UN Doc. A/HRC/21/50, para. 12.

[75] *Ibid.*, Annex II, para. 5.

[76] *Ibid.*, Annex II, paras. 30–35.

[77] Article 3(1)(a) and (d) of the GCs. The latter provision has indeed been interpreted as 'prohibit[ing] "summary" justice or trial by any tribunal that fails to qualify as fair and regular' (ICRC, *Commentary on GC III*, 2nd ed., para. 711). For courts convened by non-State armed groups, see *ibid.*, paras. 725–731.

Duma] in eastern Ghutah'.[78] The CoI-S describes such conduct *vis-à-vis* captured civilians and government soldiers as use of human shields – the prohibition of which in NIAC (even in the inapplicability of AP II due to Syria's not being party to it) can both be found in customary law and derived from the principles of distinction and precaution.[79] At the same time, the CoI-S stresses that the parading occurred '[f]ollowing an air strike on a vegetable market in Duma ... in which at least 50 civilians were killed',[80] and that it aimed to 'deter further aerial attacks and to send a clear message to the Government'.[81]

What does this passage tell us about the CoI-S's thinking? On the one hand, it looks at the conduct by the armed group in isolation from the contextual behaviour of the other parties to the conflict, suggesting a formalization as use of human shields and hinting at its illegality under IHL. On the other hand, it highlights both the reactive nature of the conduct and its forward-looking purpose, nodding to the functioning of belligerent reprisals without naming them explicitly or making a definitive conclusion as to their legality in the case at hand.[82] The CoI-S juggles the reticence of the legal system to formalize belligerent reprisals in NIAC with the acknowledgement of their role in structuring the parties' behaviour. But even so, it enriches our understanding of the purposes of belligerent reprisals with an explicit acknowledgement of their deterrent aim.[83]

6.4.1.2 Belligerent Reprisals to Counter Unlawful Military Advantage

A further piece of analysis by the CoI-S shows that, besides punishment and deterrence, belligerent reprisals can also be used to nullify the

[78] CoI-S, UN Doc. A/HRC/31/68, 11 February 2016, para. 105.

[79] Henckaerts and Doswald-Beck, *Customary IHL Study*, vol. I, p. 338.

[80] CoI-S, UN Doc. A/HRC/31/68, para. 105.

[81] *Ibid.*

[82] The incident is mentioned in a sub-section titled 'Fracturing of communities' in the section on 'Devastation of a nation' (*ibid.*, p. 14).

[83] For a similar understanding, see also CoI-S, UN Doc. A/HRC/23/58, para. 49 (execution of prison inmates 'in response to an attack by anti-government armed groups' and 'in an attempt to stave off attack'); CoI-S, UN Doc. A/HRC/28/69, para. 221 (indiscriminate attacks involving the dropping of barrel bombs on civilian targets in Raqqah explained by interviewees as 'retaliation for ISIS executing captured Government soldiers'); CoI-S, UN Doc. A/HRC/49/77, 8 February 2022, pp. 29–30 (attacks on schools as well as residential and commercial buildings with no military installations or targets, explained by commentators as 'retaliation for an explosion targeting a bus in Damascus').

military advantages that a party to the conflict reaps from its non-compliance with IHL. The relevant passages can be found in the work that the CoI-S has dedicated to the siege and re-capture of eastern Ghouta, during which both pro-Government forces and besieged armed groups were found to have committed 'pervasive war crimes'.[84]

First, the work of the CoI-S reiterates the distinction between different types of reactive behaviour and their separate formalizations under international law. Collective punishment is described as one of the war crimes integrated by the unlawful tactics of pro-Government forces, insofar as they 'aimed at punishing the inhabitants of eastern Ghouta and forcing the population, collectively, to surrender or starve'.[85] The allegiance with the enemy that is chastised through collective punishment is a matter of *subjective appreciation* by one party to the conflict, whose reaction is therefore not exculpated under international law. Conversely, the term 'reprisal' is reserved for those 'attacks' and 'acts' that were directed by besieged armed groups at the Government-controlled areas of Damascus city and Rif Damascus, with the objective of countering unlawful attacks by pro-Government forces.[86] The prior unlawful conduct by the enemy that originates the reprisal is a matter of *legal appreciation*, *objective* to the extent that it can be ascertained on the basis of legal qualification and the application of international law.

Second, the work of the CoI-S can be interpreted as confirming the abstract applicability of the notion of belligerent reprisals in NIACs. In the case at hand, the belligerent reprisal consisted in indiscriminate attacks carried out by employing 'indirect fire artillery systems . . . incapable of accurate targeting' (such as unguided mortars) against densely populated areas.[87] The CoI-S affirms the illegality of these underlying conducts on their own merits – which is necessary for their very qualification as belligerent reprisals.[88] However, it also finds that armed groups 'did not have the right to resort to countermeasures against persons not taking a direct part in hostilities'.[89] This wording is very similar to the second sentence of Rule 148 of the ICRC's *Customary IHL Study* on

[84] CoI-S, UN Doc. A/HRC/38/CRP.3, 20 June 2018, para. 71.
[85] *Ibid.*, para. 27.
[86] *Ibid.*, paras. 28 and 53.
[87] *Ibid.*, paras. 53–57.
[88] The attacks are found to be (i) indiscriminate, (ii) a form of violence intending to spread terror among the civilian population, and (iii) a violation of the most basic human rights, including the right to life, liberty and security of person: *ibid.*, para. 57.
[89] *Ibid.*

reprisals in NIACs;[90] as we have seen above, it also reflects the consensus of most States during the drafting of AP II.[91] What is interesting, however, is that the CoI-S did not quote the first sentence of that Rule, whereby 'Parties to non-international armed conflicts do not have the right to resort to belligerent reprisals'.[92]

In other words, and contrary to the ICRC, the CoI-S does not rule out the possibility that 'the very concept of lawful reprisal in non-international armed conflict has ... materialized in international law'[93] – it simply excludes the lawfulness of the reprisals adopted in the case under review. This choice could not be explained in terms of economy of proof, by saying that the finding of illegality is reached on the basis of the issue that is comparatively less burdensome to prove. Both the question as to the applicability of the notion of reprisals in NIAC and the determination of the permissible target thereof involves a legal (not a factual) determination, and it is not immediately clear which one is easier to answer. But even leaving aside this consideration, inferring from the CoI-S's analysis that belligerent reprisals do not apply in NIACs would run against the numerous textual references to the notion.

Third, one can discern in the CoI-S's reasoning two ways in which belligerent reprisals "meet" the original IHL violation – that is to say, two ways of interpreting the purpose of these measures. For one thing, the reprisal attacks are said to counter the illegality of enemy conduct by 'inducing Government forces to cease their unlawful attacks'.[94] This is the aim of deterrence that is traditionally associated with the measure, also in the previous work of the CoI-S analysed above. At the same time, belligerent reprisals take on a more concrete purpose, by countering the substantive advantages that the counterpart reaps from its misbehaviour. The CoI-S highlights that recourse to belligerent reprisals by besieged armed groups coincided with the three major offensives launched by pro-Government forces to re-capture eastern Ghouta.[95] The retaliatory, concerted launching of unguided mortars from the encircled enclave is seen

[90] 'Other countermeasures against persons who do not or who have ceased to take a direct part in hostilities are prohibited': Henckaerts and Doswald-Beck, *Customary IHL Study*, vol. I, p. 526.

[91] See Section 6.2.2.

[92] Rule 148 of the *Customary IHL Study*.

[93] Henckaerts and Doswald-Beck, *Customary IHL Study*, vol. I, p. 527.

[94] CoI-S, UN Doc. A/HRC/38/CRP.3, para. 57.

[95] *Ibid.*, paras. 5 and 53–57.

as a 'heightened counteroffensive' in late November 2017,[96] or as a 'response to the escalated campaign on eastern Ghouta' on 20 February 2018.[97] The CoI-S specifies that reprisal attacks on Damascus city took a particularly egregious form on the occasion of the third and final offensive and until the re-capture of the area by pro-Government forces.[98]

Can we explain this correlation between military escalation and belligerent reprisals with the argument whereby a party losing ground is more willing to breach IHL? Even the CoI-S seems to embrace this view when it notes that, as besieged armed groups 'gradually ceded territory to pro-Government forces, the frequency and gravity of their attacks correspondingly increased'.[99] The problem with this explanation is that it interprets recourse to belligerent reprisals solely as a function of the counterpart's advances, but fails to consider to what extent such military gains are found to be linked with breaches of the law governing hostilities.

The latter element emerges vividly from a comprehensive reading of the CoI-S's report, where the analysis of belligerent reprisals is encapsulated between two more general findings. On the one hand, the CoI-S states that '[b]etween February and April 2018, tactics employed by pro-Government forces to recapture the enclave were largely unlawful in nature';[100] on the other, it concludes in equally sweeping terms that 'sieges, as they have been conducted in Syria, are unlawful'.[101] It is under this light that the correlation between enemy offensives and belligerent reprisals noted by the CoI-S should be read. Recourse to such measures is seen by the CoI-S as a reaction, not to punctual breaches of IHL, but to a general pattern of behaviour that is found to be illegal.[102]

[96] *Ibid.*, para. 53.

[97] *Ibid.*, para. 54.

[98] *Ibid.*, para. 56.

[99] *Ibid.*, p. 1.

[100] *Ibid.*, para. 27. Besides the above-mentioned war crime of collective punishment, the CoI-S finds that pro-Government forces committed the war crimes of deliberately starving civilians by denying humanitarian aid, launching indiscriminate attacks with both conventional and prohibited weapons in densely populated civilian areas, and denying medical evacuations (*ibid.*).

[101] *Ibid.*, para. 77. This conclusion is all the more relevant given that it was preceded by the acknowledgement that 'under international humanitarian law, sieges as a military tactic are considered lawful when their purpose is to achieve a military objective' (*ibid.*).

[102] A similar reading can be found in a later report by the CoI-S, where military operations to re-take eastern Ghouta are referred to as '[a] series of unlawful attacks, characterized by an escalation in aerial and ground offensives': CoI-S, UN Doc. A/HRC/39/65, 9 August 2018, para. 36.

Correspondingly, their purpose is not (only) that of punishing or deterring, but the more general one of remedying the disadvantageous situation in which a party to the conflict is placed by reason of the counterpart's strategic misbehaviour.

6.4.2 *The Group of Eminent Experts on Yemen and the Panel of Experts on Yemen*

6.4.2.1 Findings on the Applicability of Belligerent Reprisals

Two UN bodies have investigated the purpose and function of retaliatory misbehaviour in the context of the armed conflict(s) in Yemen: the Group of Eminent International and Regional Experts on Yemen (GEE-Y) created by the OHCHR at the request of the Human Rights Council, and the Panel of Experts on Yemen (PoE-Y) established by the UN Security Council. The mandates of these two bodies are of a very different nature, as is the legal basis for their application of IHL.[103] However, these expert bodies have proceeded to a similar classification of the armed conflict(s) in Yemen as non-international in character, and engaged in a thorough review of the parties' compliance with applicable IHL obligations.[104] What is more, both the GEE-Y and the PoE-Y have

[103] The GEE-Y was established by HRC resolution 36/31 'to carry out a comprehensive examination of all alleged violations and abuses of international human rights and other appropriate and applicable fields of international law committed by all parties to the conflict since March 2014' (UN Doc. A/HRC/RES/36/31, para. 12(a)). The PoE-Y, on its part, was established by UN Security Council resolution 2140 (2014) to support the 2140 Sanctions Committee on Yemen in carrying out its mandate, including by feeding the Committee 'with information relevant to the potential designation at a later stage of individuals and entities' as subject to sanctions measures (*ibid.*, para. 21); the same resolution clarifies that '[p]lanning, directing, or committing acts that violate applicable . . . international humanitarian law . . . in Yemen' represent 'acts that threaten the peace, security or stability of Yemen' and, therefore, trigger the designation of individuals and entities (*ibid.*, paras. 17–18).

[104] Throughout its reports, the GEE-Y has maintained the presence of multiple non-international armed conflicts in Yemen – between the armed forces of the Government of Yemen and the Houthis (with the members of the Saudi-led coalition acting as 'cobelligerents on the side of the Yemeni armed forces'), but also 'between the Government of Yemen and other non-State armed groups, including Islamic State in Iraq and the Levant and Al-Qaida in the Arabian Peninsula, and among different armed groups' (GEE-Y, UN Doc. A/HRC/42/17, 9 August 2019, paras. 9–10; see also GEE-Y, UN Doc. A/HRC/39/43, 17 August 2018, para. 15; GEE-Y, UN Doc. A/HRC/42/CRP.1, 3 September 2019, paras. 44–46; GEE-Y, UN Doc. A/HRC/45/6, 28 September 2020, para. 12; GEE-Y, UN Doc. A/HRC/45/CRP.7, 29 September 2020, paras. 31–34; GEE-Y, UN Doc. A/HRC/48/20, 13 September 2021, para. 12). On its part, the PoE-Y concluded

expressed significant views on the meaning of retaliatory misbehaviour in the conduct of hostilities.

Importantly, the remarks that the two monitoring bodies dedicate to the topic do not rest on the same theoretical underpinnings. The PoE-Y has so far advanced an explicit legal basis for the notion of belligerent reprisals in NIAC only once, while discussing an airstrike in mid-February 2020 that resulted in the death of approximately thirty-two people and the injury of twenty-one others (mostly female and children).[105] The attack, which hit the residential area of a village, had followed the downing (claimed by the Houthis) of a Royal Saudi Air Forces fighter jet the night before.[106] Although the PoE-Y's findings are limited to the origin of the explosive devices that hit the area, the Panel also recalled that 'under IHL, reprisals against persons not participating or no longer participating in hostilities, are prohibited';[107] furthermore, it grounded this prohibition in Article 3 common to the 1949 GCs, Article 4 AP II, and Rule 148 of the *Customary IHL Study*, and treated the notion of reprisals separately from that of collective punishment.[108] The PoE-Y could have excluded the very existence of belligerent reprisals in NIAC; however, it interpreted existing IHL as simply prohibiting the adoption of such measures when directed against certain targets. In this passage, the definition of the conceptual and legal boundaries of belligerent reprisals cannot be separated from the implicit affirmation of their applicability in NIAC.

already in its first report that the situation had 'reached the threshold of internal armed conflicts' (PoE-Y, UN Doc. S/2015/125, 20 February 2015, paras. 60–62), and has always dedicated a whole section of its following reports to '[a]cts that violate international humanitarian law'.

105 PoE-Y, UN Doc. S/2021/79, 25 January 2021, Annex 29, Appendix 1, para. 1.

106 The incident has also been analysed by the GEE-Y and the Joint Incidents Assessment Team (JIAT – the investigative mechanism of the Saudi-led 'Coalition to Restore Legitimacy in Yemen'). The former concluded that the Coalition may have failed to comply with relevant IHL obligations (GEE-Y, UN Doc. A/HRC/45/6, paras. 30–31; GEE-Y, UN Doc. A/HRC/45/CRP.7, paras. 72 and 74; GEE-Y, UN Doc. A/HRC/48/CRP.4, 14 September 2021, paras. 15–17). The latter recommended holding the air controller accountable for breaching the rules of engagement, but found that the Coalition's military operations had only affected a civilian building while targeting Houthi armed militia: Saudi Press Agency, 'Joint Incidents Assessment Team Refutes Allegations against Coalition Forces', 25 November 2020 (available at www.spa.gov.sa/2161522).

107 PoE-Y, UN Doc. S/2021/79, Annex 29, Appendix 1, paras. 4 [sic] and 10.

108 *Ibid.*, p. 244, footnote 154.

On its part, the GEE-Y never mentioned the notion of belligerent reprisals explicitly in its reports and detailed findings. This omission might be due to the opinion (expressed in one of the early reports by the GEE-Y) that there exists 'no political basis' for asserting the equality of belligerents in NIACs.[109] However, this notation does not have a bearing on the existence of a *legal* basis for such equality under IHL. What is more, the effects of that remark are circumscribed by the GEE-Y itself to 'the prospect of [the] implementation and enforcement [of the rules governing NIAC] by the non-State actors';[110] therefore, the notation does not affect the prospect of NSAGs *demanding the enforcement* of IHL rules by the enemy (be it a State or not). All of this warns against taking the passage by the GEE-Y as authority ruling out the applicability of belligerent reprisals in NIAC.

Indeed, a comprehensive study of the reports by these two monitoring bodies points to an understanding where (i) misbehaviour by one party to the conflict is often linked to that of the counterpart; (ii) the meaning of retaliatory misbehaviour evolves over time and on the basis of the counterpart's behaviour; and (iii) retaliatory misbehaviour acquires a stronger strategic meaning as the interaction between the parties develops. These dynamics will now be explored in detail.

6.4.2.2 Shifting the Emphasis from Punishment to Reprisal

The early monitoring of both the GEE-Y and the PoE-Y tends to interpret retaliatory non-compliance with IHL norms as a form of (prohibited) collective punishment, irrespective of the State or non-State nature of the party committing it. Two examples can be mentioned in this respect. In its analysis of the 2015 bombing by the Saudi-led 'Coalition to Restore Legitimacy in Yemen' (the Coalition) of the city of Sa'dah (the Houthi stronghold in Northern Yemen alleged to be the origin of the shelling of Saudi villages across the border),[111] the PoE-Y recalls that collective punishment of a civilian population is prohibited 'under all circumstances, including their allegiance or presumed/perceived allegiance to armed opposition groups'.[112] Similarly, when dealing

[109] GEE-Y, UN Doc. A/HRC/42/CRP.1, p. 12, footnote 10.

[110] *Ibid.*

[111] See the leaflet warning dropped over the city prior to the airstrike, especially the reciprocity underlying the parallelism 'We are going to shell the origin of the shelling' (reproduced in PoE-Y, UN Doc. S/2018/192, 26 January 2016, Annex 56, p. 165).

[112] *Ibid.*, Annex 56, p. 163. According to the Panel, 'the targeting of the city of Sa'dah raises extremely serious concerns, including potential violations of the principles of precaution,

with the Battle of Ta'izz in 2015–16, the GEE-Y finds that both parties have failed to comply with their obligations to provide essential supplies and to care for the sick and wounded[113] – but it also indicates that the siege laid over the city by Houthi-Saleh fighters may have represented 'a form of collective punishment on the civilian population residing [therein], for their perceived support of the Popular Resistance and Government-affiliated troops'.[114]

Soon, however, the focus on the punitive features of these conducts is complemented by a stronger emphasis on their retaliatory nature. This is particularly the case for the reflection on the naval and air restrictions enforced by the Coalition in Yemen. According to the GEE-Y, the three-week-long *de facto* total blockade[115] of all the country's borders in November 2017 may have amounted to collective punishment[116] aimed at 'pressurizing the civilian population'.[117] But as both the GEE-Y and the Command of the Coalition have noted, the imposition of access restrictions in November 2017 also represented a 'response' to the launch by the Houthis of a missile towards the Saudi capital Riyadh.[118] When this new element is introduced in the equation, the question becomes what type of link (if any) is established between that strike and the following access restrictions compounded by the blockade.

The answer to this point varies depending on the monitoring body. For its part, the GEE-Y has not assessed the legality of the missile launch, interpreting the retaliatory nature of the blockade only as proof of the 'reactiveness' that distinguishes collective punishment from other unlawful acts.[119] Conversely, the PoE-Y has repeatedly qualified the launch of

proportionality and the principle of distinction' (*ibid.*). See also GEE-Y, UN Doc. A/HRC/39/43, Annex IV, para. 5, whereby the airstrikes occurred 'in response to Houthi attacks on Saudi Arabia launched from the [Sa'dah] governorate'.

113 GEE-Y, UN Doc. A/HRC/42/CRP.1, para. 357.

114 *Ibid.*, para. 358.

115 For the legal qualification of these restrictions, see GEE-Y, UN Doc. A/HRC/39/43, Annex II, p. 29, footnote 1.

116 GEE-Y, UN Doc. A/HRC/42/17, para. 53.

117 GEE-Y, UN Doc. A/HRC/42/CRP.1, paras. 779–780.

118 GEE-Y, UN Doc. A/HRC/39/43, paras. 22, 49 and Annex II, para. 18; GEE-Y, UN Doc. A/HRC/42/CRP.1, para. 115; Emirates News Agency, 'Coalition to Restore Legitimacy in Yemen announces reopening of ports Hudaydah, Sanaa tomorrow', 22 November 2017 (available at https://wam.ae/en/details/1395302648875). Importantly, the restrictions were also justified by the Coalition as a tool to enforce the arms embargo established by UN Security Council resolution 2216 (2015): GEE-Y, UN Doc. A/HRC/39/43, Annex II, para. 18.

119 GEE-Y, UN Doc. A/HRC/42/CRP.1, para. 779.

the ballistic missile on Riyadh as an act violating IHL and attributable to the Houthi leadership.[120] Moreover, it has considered the 'immediate escalation in regional tensions' that culminated in the total blockade by the Coalition[121] as flowing directly from the launch by the Houthis of the ballistic missile in violation of IHL principles (specifically, the prohibition of indiscriminate attacks).[122] As a result, the PoE-Y's understanding of the retaliatory conduct undertaken by the Coalition rests on the explicit qualification of the Houthis' behaviour as unlawful.

Formalizing retaliation as a relationship between IHL violations brings it much closer to the notion of belligerent reprisals than to that of collective punishment. This is not only a hermeneutical operation – it is also reflected in the consequences that the monitoring bodies derive from the application of the idea of belligerent reprisals. The tight interconnectedness between the original and the retaliatory breach becomes particularly evident when the PoE-Y says that '[t]he Houthi forces are also using the population as a pawn when they escalate their strikes against Saudi Arabia, knowing full well the brunt of reprisals will be felt by the civilian population'.[123] This passage is significant, not only because it explicitly qualifies the Coalition's access restrictions as a form of reprisal, but also because it seems to derive from such qualification partial exculpatory effects (at least under the IHL framework). Although the PoE-Y notes regretfully that '[t]he blockade is essentially using the threat of starvation as a bargaining tool and an instrument of war',[124] only the complete and unconditional closure of Sana'a International Airport (i.e., the air component of the blockade) is found to breach Common Article 3 GCs, due to its effects on the sick and wounded prevented from genuinely seeking medical treatment abroad.[125] The

[120] PoE-Y, UN Doc. S/2018/594, 26 January 2018, paras. 90(g) and 179; Annex II, paras. 5 (a), 11(c) and Appendix C.

[121] *Ibid.*, para. 82.

[122] The Panel considered almost certain that the target was the King Khalid International Airport in Riyadh, described as a civilian airport with some military installations and equipment; but even admitting (as claimed by the Houthis) that the attack had aimed at the latter objective, the PoE-Y concluded that 'the commanders who authorized the launch of the missile were reckless and failed to take into consideration, or wilfully disregarded, the fact that a disproportionately number of civilians and civilian objects could be affected by targeting [the airport]' (*ibid.*, Annex 64, Appendix C, paras. 3 and 5).

[123] *Ibid.*, para. 190.

[124] *Ibid.*

[125] *Ibid.*, Annex 70, paras. 10 and 12.

other forms of obstruction of humanitarian assistance (including the restrictions on the import of commercial and humanitarian goods in November 2017) are only found to be 'contrary to the spirit of [UN Security Council] resolution 2216 (2015)'.[126]

Interestingly, this understanding of retaliatory misbehaviour as belligerent reprisal is not reserved by the PoE-Y to State conduct – it also applies to that of non-State actors. As the Panel recalls, shortly after the Coalition enforced the blockade several high-ranking Houthi officials (including the Chairman of the Supreme Revolutionary Committee and the head of the Supreme Political Council) threatened to attack commercial vessels carrying oil, oil installations in Saudi Arabia, as well as the capitals of foreign countries.[127] Arguably, it is the strong link between two conducts highly reproachable under IHL that leads the PoE-Y, also in this case, to interpret these statements as threats of reprisal.[128] The Panel limits itself to stating that attacks on civilians and *prima facie* civilian objects would violate IHL: undoubtedly wary that the situation before it represented the familiar vicious circle of reprisal and counter-reprisal, it does not inquire further whether an actual attack by the Houthis on those targets would be excused.[129] But the absence of any qualms to use the term hints at the theoretical admissibility for a NSAG to invoke and apply belligerent reprisals *vis-à-vis* the counterpart. And although the actual impact of these threats is hard to measure, the gradual lifting of the restrictions in the following weeks might be due to them, at least in conjunction with other factors.[130]

[126] *Ibid.*, para. 189. To the extent that the latter resolution has binding effects in light of its adoption under Chapter VII of the UN Charter, also these other aspects of the *de facto* total blockade would remain unlawful (UN Security Council resolution 2216 (2015), p. 3 and para. 9) – but this would be a consequence only of the higher hierarchical value afforded obligations flowing from the UN Charter under Article 103 thereof. From a purely IHL perspective, the omission by the PoE-Y of a similar finding of illegality seems to be an implicit acknowledgement of the doctrine of belligerent reprisals exerting effects in this case.

[127] PoE-Y, UN Doc. S/2018/594, Annex 64, para. 10(a). A different source reports that the threat of attacking oil installations in Saudi Arabia was linked to a Coalition offensive on the Yemeni port-city of Hudaydah – a condition with no immediate IHL dimension attached to it: see S. Westall, 'Yemen's Houthis threaten to attack warships, oil tankers if ports stay closed', Reuters, 12 November 2017 (available at www.reuters.com/article/uk-yemen-security-idUKKBN1DC0S5).

[128] PoE-Y, UN Doc. S/2018/594, Annex 64, para. 10(a).

[129] *Ibid.*, Annex 64, para. 10(a)-(b).

[130] GEE-Y, UN Doc. A/HRC/42/CRP.1, paras. 771–772. In a statement, the Command of the Coalition announced that the re-opening of the Hudaydah Port (to receive urgent

6.4.2.3 Deterrence and the Strategic Use of Belligerent Reprisals

In their findings on the blockade of Yemen, the monitoring bodies have progressively distanced themselves from an understanding of retaliation in purely punitive terms, in favour of an interpretation that stresses the connection between IHL breaches and their function as belligerent reprisals. But as in the case of the conflict in Syria analysed above, the purposes that can be associated with belligerent reprisals grow more and more sophisticated as the armed conflict unfolds and the interaction between the parties deepens.

The analysis of the Coalition air campaigns in Yemen undertaken by the GEE-Y offers a wealth of material to understand this dynamic. The Group of Experts has noted that Coalition airstrikes peaked in both late 2017 and early 2018 after the launch by the Houthis of ballistic missiles against Saudi cities.[131] These patterns of conduct lead the GEE-Y to remark that a correlation existed between the intensity of the airstrikes and related civilian casualties, on the one hand, and strategic developments in the conduct of hostilities, on the other.[132] Although the GEE-Y does not derive any legal inference from this, this passage is additional evidence of the progressive distancing of retaliatory misbehaviour from the sphere of collective punishment. By linking airstrikes that 'raise serious concerns about the targeting process' and could amount to IHL violations with the wider military context,[133] the Group attributes to them a function that is not only punitive and retrospective, but also forward-looking and interested in shaping the future conduct of the military confrontation.

This understanding of belligerent reprisals is reflected in both parties to the conflict placing a stronger emphasis on the language of deterrence

humanitarian and relief material) and of Sana'a airport (to UN aircraft, designated for humanitarian and relief efforts) followed 'a comprehensive review of the inspection and verification procedures used to implement the United Nations Security Council Resolution 2216' (Emirates News Agency, 'Coalition to Restore Legitimacy in Yemen announces reopening of ports Hudaydah, Sanaa tomorrow', 22 November 2017).

131 GEE-Y, UN Doc. A/HRC/39/43, Annex IV, paras. 11–12; GEE-Y, UN Doc. A/HRC/42/CRP.1, para. 115. The 2017 attack is the one against the King Khalid International Airport of Riyadh mentioned above in this chapter, footnote 122. For details about the Houthi attacks in March 2018, see PoE-Y, UN Doc. S/2019/83, 25 January 2019, p. 32, table 1, as well as UN Doc. S/2018/266, 27 March 2018, p. 1.

132 GEE-Y, UN Doc. A/HRC/39/43, Annex IV, para. 11.

133 *Ibid.*, Annex IV, para. 14.

against attacks on civilians and civilian objects. There exists, however, a significant difference. Over time, the Coalition has circumscribed its understanding of 'deterrent measures' to the destruction of (i) enemy *military* capabilities (ii) in accordance with customary human rights and humanitarian law as well as its rules of engagement – something that, strictly speaking, would not require a justification under the doctrine of belligerent reprisals.[134] The Houthis, on their part, have relied to a bigger extent on the argumentative possibilities opened up by the notion of belligerent reprisals, emphasizing the many purposes that can attach to their use. The language used by Houthi leaders in their statements highlights the strict symmetry (if not the very identity) between the conduct lamented of and the retaliatory behaviour envisaged.[135] The belligerent reprisal almost becomes a faithful mirror of the counterpart's (unlawful) conduct, precisely modelled upon it when possible, or in any case devised so as to create harmful consequences similar to those that have been suffered.

The practice analysed by the GEE-Y highlights how quickly this approach can turn into a vicious circle of reprisals and counter-reprisals.[136] However, stressing the strategic use of belligerent reprisals is not only about acknowledging their deterrent purpose – it also implies that these measures can be harnessed to decrease the overall level of

[134] See several statements by the Spokesman for the Coalition, quoted in: Emirates News Agency, 'Royal Saudi Air Defence intercepts, destroys Houthi UAV: Arab Coalition', 8 April 2019; Emirates News Agency, '"We will take urgent and timely measures against Houthi militia": Coalition to Restore Legitimacy in Yemen', 24 June 2019; Emirates News Agency, 'Coalition downs Saudi-bound Houthi drone', 10 September 2019 and 11 September 2019.

[135] See the speech by the leader of the Houthi movement (quoted in Yemen News Agency, 'Leader of Yemen's Revolution announces new phase of military escalation', 20 December 2017) threatening to bomb Riyadh and Abu Dhabi in retaliation for the bombing of Sana'a, and to target the official seat of the royal court of Saudi Arabia in reaction to an attack on the presidential palace of the Yemeni capital. See also the speech by the Chief of the Houthi political council, quoted in Middle East Eye, 'Houthis promise more missiles if Saudis continue Yemen war', 26 March 2018 ('stop your air strikes and we will stop our missiles[.] If you continue your air strikes we have a right to defend ourselves by all means available'). Finally, see the statement by a spokesperson for the Houthi-aligned military, quoted in Yemen News Agency, 'Riyadh screams of Yemeni missiles', 27 May 2019 (whereby '[t]here will be more salvos [of missiles] until this enemy is deterred, understands the meaning of the Yemeni threat and ceases its crimes').

[136] GEE-Y, UN Doc. A/HRC/42/17, para. 18, whereby drone attacks against oil facilities in Saudi Arabia claimed by the Houthis prompted the Coalition to intensify its air campaign between April and July 2019, which in turn led to an increase in missile attacks originating from the Houthis.

hostilities. Besides leading to a reduction in the number of IHL violations, this would 'level the playing field' by neutralizing the military benefits reaped by the counterpart through its IHL violations, establishing a parity of arms in both legal and practical terms.[137]

Hardly a coincidence, this final aspect of belligerent reprisals can be inferred from the findings of both the GEE-Y and the PoE-Y in relation to the latest years of the armed conflict in Yemen. As the monitoring bodies recall, since August 2019 the Houthis had escalated their military operations, claiming responsibility for the first two attacks on oil facilities in Saudi Arabia in a series of operations significantly dubbed 'Deterrent Balance'.[138] But less than a week after the latter action, the Houthis announced that they would suspend their strikes on Saudi Arabia, 'calling in return for a halt to [Coalition] airstrikes and a lifting of restrictions on access to northern Yemen'.[139] The offer was accepted, which led the PoE-Y to report 'a significant reduction in Coalition air strike on Yemen [and] no reported missile or uncrewed aerial vehicle attacks by the Houthis into Saudi Arabia' throughout October and November 2019.[140]

Although short-lived, this first reciprocal suspension of retaliatory misbehaviour marked on the long run the shared meaning that the parties would attribute to the adoption (or not) of belligerent reprisals. As regards the Houthis, after the resumption of hostilities they launched at least four other operations of economic deterrence,[141] referring in their speeches to 'the equation "Eye for an Eye"' *vis-à-vis* the Coalition's breaches of IHL.[142] But as noted by the PoE-Y, these attacks had the

137 On this aspect, see Yemen News Agency, 'Yemeni ballistic missiles hopes to Level Playing Field in Saudi War: Report', 5 March 2019.

138 PoE-Y, UN Doc. S/2020/326, 28 April 2020, paras. 43 and 56 (attack on 17 August 2019); *ibid.*, Annex 14, para. 11 (attacks on 14 September 2019). Note that the latter report concluded that, notwithstanding their claim of responsibility, the Houthis had not launched the attacks (*ibid.*, para. 19).

139 GEE-Y, UN Doc. A/HRC/45/CRP.7, para. 46. Also the PoE-Y highlighted the conditional offer, stating however that it was subject to the Coalition re-opening Sana'a airport and granting open access for shipping to Hudaydah (PoE-Y, UN Doc. S/2020/326, para. 43).

140 *Ibid.*, para. 46. The Panel also confirmed the successful release of detainees and prisoners by the two parties (*ibid.*).

141 Yemen News Agency, 'Seventh year will be year of victory, decisiveness: Army's spokesman', 22 March 2021; PoE-Y, UN Doc. S/2021/79, para. 69 and UN Doc. S/2022/50, 26 January 2022, paras. 56–59.

142 Interview of a member of the Supreme Political Council al-Houthi with Al Jazeera, quoted in Yemen News Agency, 'Al-Houthi to al-Jazeera: the war is open with Saudi Arabia if it does not stop its aggression against Yemen', 18 August 2020.

primarily political purpose of 'push[ing] Riyadh towards accepting a political settlement beneficial to [the Houthis]'.[143] Similarly on the Coalition's end, the language of retaliation has been relied on to circumscribe the political implications of airstrikes. When a Coalition attack hit Sana'a in March 2020, SaudiArabia's ambassador to Yemen emphasized that it represented a 'response' to the launch of two missiles against Saudi cities by the Houthis, and that it was 'not intended as a re-escalation of the conflict'.[144] Interpreted in light of that prior negotiated understanding, the language of reprisal has limited both the scope of the measure, and the meaning that the counterpart could attribute to it.

The outcome of this long process was the truce of April 2022 between the Houthis and the internationally recognized Government of Yemen, where both parties to the conflict agreed to renounce certain methods of warfare that had resulted in significant IHL violations.[145] It is interesting that the terms of the truce proposed by the Houthis contain two, clearly distinguished elements – a promise and two offers.[146] To start with, the Houthis announced a unilateral suspension for three days of missile and drone attacks on Saudi Arabia, as well as of offensive confrontations on

[143] PoE-Y, UN Doc. S/2022/50, para. 59 – which also stresses the difference from the use of missiles and uncrewed aerial vehicles in Yemen, 'where the aim is maximum lethality'.

[144] W. P. Strobel, 'Saudi Arabia Invites Houthi Rebels to Talks in Riyadh', *The Wall Street Journal*, 30 March 2020. The GEE-Y mentioned a series of airstrikes on Sana'a, but neither it nor the PoE-Y assessed its legality under IHL (GEE-Y, UN Doc. A/HRC/45/CRP.7, para. 48). From available sources, it would seem that the Coalition has maintained that the airstrike had been conducted against legitimate military objectives (Strobel, 'Saudi Arabia Invites'; Crisis24, 'Yemen: Saudi-led coalition strikes targets in Houthi-controlled Sana'a March 30', 30 March 2020), in line with its commitment to 'undertak[e] all preventive measures and necessary precautions to protect civilians and spare them from collateral damage' (Emirates News Agency, 'Coalition forces target ballistic missile capabilities in Sana'a', 23 February 2020). The language of retaliation would then have been used to answer the question concerning the continued validity of the mutually agreed suspension of certain military conducts, rather than the issue of belligerent reprisals. The problem is that that suspension had been premised precisely on the Coalition renouncing airstrikes as a method of warfare; in this sense, the illegality of the airstrike would flow, not from a breach of the principles governing the targeting process, but from the very recourse to the airstrike, in breach of the new understanding for the conduct of hostilities that had been agreed upon by the two parties.

[145] The nation-wide, UN-brokered truce that took effect on 2 April 2022 lasted for six months, but despite failure to extend it, at the time of writing '[t]he overall military situation in Yemen has remained stable' (Hans Grundberg, 'Briefing to the United Nations by the Special Envoy of the Secretary-General for Yemen', 16 January 2023).

[146] Speech by the President of the Supreme Political Council, quoted in Yemen News Agency, 'President announces suspension of missile strikes, drones, military operations for 3 days', 27 March 2022.

all field fronts. Then, the armed group expressed its readiness to turn the suspension of missile and drone attacks into a 'final, firm and lasting commitment' if the Coalition re-opened the Yemeni ports and ceased its airstrikes on Yemen. Finally, it manifested its willingness to transform the suspension of offensive confrontations into a 'final, continuous and permanent commitment' if the Coalition withdrew all external forces from Yemen and ceased supporting local militias therein.[147]

Two notations impose themselves. First, the two offers in the proposal are concerned with different bodies of applicable law. Only the *former* offer of suspension has an immediate IHL dimension, insofar as it relates to those conducts that had been found to cause serious violations of the laws of war (i.e., access restrictions and airstrikes vs. missile and drone attacks). Withdrawal and support to local actors, on their part, concern compliance with other primary norms (such as the rules governing the use of force and the obligation not to intervene in the internal affairs of another State), but their IHL dimension is not apparent. Second, the two prongs are incremental in character. Only the *latter* offer of suspension would have the potential to bring about an effective cessation of hostilities; conversely, renouncing given methods of warfare would not prevent the parties from continuing their fighting through other tactics (such as, precisely, the ground confrontations of the second prong).

If we combine these two elements, we do understand the ultimate purpose attached to belligerent reprisals under this scheme: the playing field is levelled by mutually giving up those forms of retaliatory misbehaviour that had given considerable advantages to the party adopting them. As the interaction between the actors develops, belligerent reprisals are no longer concerned with the short-term objectives of punishment or deterrence for punctual violations – they become focused on the long-term objective of influencing the counterpart by reducing its incentives for IHL violations that affect the military balance. The strategic purpose of these measures would then consist in the opportunity to even out the power relation between the parties to the conflict, by removing the benefits that the wrongdoer reaps from engaging in IHL breaches.

6.5 Belligerent Reprisals as Remedy to Status Inequality

Building on the practice of parties to several NIACs, the reports by the UN monitoring bodies reveal a surprising picture. First, they re-affirm,

[147] *Ibid.*

either implicitly or explicitly, that the notion of belligerent reprisals is applicable in the legal framework governing NIAC. For sure, recourse to these measures has been found to be unlawful in most of the cases analysed; but in reaching their finding of illegality, these bodies have generally (i) recognized the retaliatory nature of the IHL breaches, and (ii) excluded their lawfulness on the basis of a legal prohibition, not of the very absence of the notion from the legal framework governing NIAC. Second, the reports clarify that this notion can be conceptually separated from other types of retaliatory (mis)conduct, such as collective punishment, revenge, reaction or response. Also in the context of NIACs, the defining features of belligerent reprisals consist of (i) their retaliatory character *vis-à-vis* IHL violations by the enemy, (ii) their grounding in reciprocity besides and above their association with enforcement, and (iii) their ultimate concern for the overall equilibrium of the legal relationship between the parties to the armed conflict. Third, the findings by UN monitoring mechanisms bear witness to the wide variety of purposes that belligerent reprisals pursue. As the military confrontation develops and the parties to the conflict refine their understanding of the counterpart's behaviour, belligerent reprisals switch from a punitive and deterrent focus to the more strategic aim of remedying the legal *and* substantive imbalance brought about by the enemy's violations of IHL. Therefore, an interpretation of the concept that excludes the reciprocal elements and is inspired exclusively by the enforcement dimension captures a partial (and arguably not the most relevant) aspect of recourse to belligerent reprisals in this context.

These insights help us re-define the conceptual premises for the discussion concerning belligerent reprisals in NIAC. Parity of status should not be understood as the condition for adopting belligerent reprisals in NIAC, because an even power relationship between State- and non-State actors is precisely the *consequence and objective* of resorting to such measures in that context. As the practice surveyed by the UN monitoring bodies shows, non-State actors are much keener on (and more vocal about) resorting to belligerent reprisals than their State counterparts. It would be reductive to account for this tendency only on the basis of the stronger difficulties that States would face in defending their adoption of such measures.[148] Such an explanation fails to consider

[148] PoE-Y, UN Doc. S/2018/594, para. 190: '[t]he Houthis are relying on public condemnation of Saudi Arabia's reprisals to offset any liability on their part for their actions [i.e., their strikes on Saudi territory]'.

that NIACs are oftentimes marked by a structural difference in status and means between the parties to the armed conflict. In this context, it is the less recognized or the less powerful entity that might have the stronger incentives to adopt belligerent reprisals, in the absence of alternative tools to counter IHL breaches and precisely with a view to remedying the further imbalance created by the counterpart's misconduct. This does not exclude that NSAGs might prefer to maintain a high ground *vis-à-vis* the enemy (and the international community) and continue to comply with IHL norms even when confronted with persistent violations. Nor does it imply that belligerent reprisals would only be permitted when resorted to by the NSAG. But it does call for a more comprehensive formalization of belligerent reprisals in NIACs – one that goes beyond deterrence and enforcement, and underscores the strategic purpose of continuously remedying the legal and practical disparity associated with IHL violations in this type of armed conflict.

Conclusion

The Implications of the New Formalization of Belligerent Reprisals

C.1 Re-uniting Belligerent Reprisals with Reciprocity

In the concluding remarks to his fundamental treatise *Belligerent Reprisals*, Kalshoven noted that, as their role as sanctions of the laws of war was losing legitimacy, belligerent reprisals could take up a different meaning in the relationships between parties to an armed conflict.[1] These measures, he wrote, could be adopted to 'indicate to the adversary that a given step up the ladder of violence is not meant to inaugurate unrestricted warfare, but merely to constitute *a measured reaction to a change in the level of violence applied by the adversary*, and to hint that further steps up the ladder of escalation will only follow if, and to the extent that, his conduct of warfare necessitates these'.[2] While admitting that belligerent reprisals could function 'as a *signal in the military-political power relations between belligerents*',[3] Kalshoven warned that such understanding of the measure was 'totally different'[4] from the one viewing the mechanism as a tool for the enforcement of the laws of war.

As we have seen, a formalization based on reciprocity and interested in the equality of opportunities is not at all extraneous to the notion of belligerent reprisals – it is actually endogenous to it. Chapters 1 and 2 of the book have demonstrated that the paradigms based in enforcement and reciprocity co-existed in the first reflections on belligerent reprisals; it was only the "proceduralization" of the notion that led to a progressive assimilation with non-forcible countermeasures, and resulted in the exclusive and dominant construction of belligerent reprisals as a tool

[1] Kalshoven, *Belligerent Reprisals*, p. 377.
[2] *Ibid.* [emphasis added].
[3] *Ibid.* [emphasis added].
[4] *Ibid.*

entrusted with the enforcement of the laws of war. Chapters 3 and 4 have pointed to several signals in the verbal and physical practice of States that directly challenge an interpretation of the *causa* of belligerent reprisals solely on the basis of the enforcement paradigm; a thorough analysis of retaliatory behaviours in the context of the Iran–Iraq War has further demonstrated that the enforcement paradigm fails to capture the complexity of the interactions of the two frameworks of reference in structuring the adoption of belligerent reprisals in international armed conflict. Finally, Chapters 5 and 6 have delved into the question of belligerent reprisals in non-international armed conflict, disproving conceptual hurdles to the applicability of the notion outside of inter-State confrontations, determining the lawful margins of retaliation, and recognizing the bearing of reciprocity on the adoption of the measure in that context.

As a result of this analysis, the purpose and function of belligerent reprisals (their *causa*) appears under a new light. Resort to belligerent reprisals has consistently served the objective of creating, maintaining or restoring the equality of opportunities between the parties to an armed conflict. To the extent that enforcement of a norm motivated recourse to these measures, it was only instrumental – amid other possible choices – to achieving the over-arching concern for parity of arms between belligerents. As a consequence, the influence of the framework grounded in reciprocity in structuring belligerent reprisals does not represent a deviation (if not an aberration) from the inherent features of the mechanism; quite the contrary, the present research acknowledges and re-instates at the core of the institution the fundamental preoccupation with guaranteeing equality in both a formal and a substantive sense.

In concrete terms, this objective of levelling the playing field takes the form of a re-calibration of the relationship between the parties to an armed conflict, through the re-modulation of one party's conduct in relation to the counterpart's behaviour. Throughout this process, the mutual understanding of belligerent reprisals evolves over time, until it becomes a highly complex succession of action and reaction that governs the escalation (or de-escalation) of *prima facie* unlawful violence. In this sense, belligerent reprisals do represent, as Schelling has authoritatively demonstrated, a form of 'idiom' between belligerents[5] – that is, a form of

[5] Thomas C. Schelling, *Arms and Influence* (New Haven, CT: Yale University Press, 1966), p. 141.

'communication ... by deed rather than by word'[6] that 'maintains a sense of ... diplomatic contact, of a desire to be understood rather than misunderstood'.[7] In these concluding paragraphs, we will analyse a few implications of this new understanding of belligerent reprisals, both for the notion itself and for the wider IHL framework.

C.2 Law-making versus Re-calibrating the Legal Relationship

A first consideration relates to the place and value of this new formalization. At the end of World War II, a few scholars particularly attentive to the dynamics of armed conflict conferred on belligerent reprisals a 'positive legislative function'.[8] Lauterpacht noted that in both World Wars belligerent reprisals had functioned as 'the legal cloak for the departure, *some of which was unavoidable*, from many of the accepted rules of warfare',[9] and that they had 'often fulfilled the function which would normally have been left to agreement between States, namely, that of the adaptation of the law to the changed conditions of modern warfare'.[10] Writing a few years later, Stone recalled the examples of air bombing in World War I and maritime warfare in World War II, and

[6] *Ibid.*, p. 137: 'Communication is by deed rather than by word, and the understandings are not enforceable except by some threat of reciprocity, retaliation, or the breakdown of all restraint'.

[7] *Ibid.*, p. 149. See also *ibid.*, p. 150:

> [w]ords are cheap, not inherently credible when they emanate from an adversary, and sometimes too intimate a mode of expression. The action is more impersonal, cannot be 'rejected' the way a verbal message can, and does not involve the intimacy of verbal contact. Actions also prove something; significant actions usually incur some cost or risk, and carry some evidence of their own credibility. And actions are less ambiguous as to their origin; verbal messages come from different parts of government, with different nuances, supplemented by 'leaks' from various sources and can be contradicted by later verbal messages, while actions tend to be irrevocable, and the fact that action occurred proves that authority is behind it.

[8] Stone, *Legal Controls of International Conflict*, p. 355, footnote 39.

[9] Hersch Lauterpacht, 'The Law of Nations and the Punishment of War Crimes' (1944) 21 BYIL, p. 76 [emphasis added].

[10] *Ibid.* Just a few years later, Lauterpacht would modify his position and understand belligerent reprisals as a tool to 'compel [the enemy belligerent] and his subjects and members of his forces to abandon illegitimate acts of warfare and to comply in future with the rules of legitimate warfare' (Lauterpacht, *Oppenheim's International Law*, vol. II, p. 561, para. 247). Belligerent reprisals would still work as a 'convenient cloak', but simply to 'mask violations of International Law' – no longer to bring about changes in a system of rules perceived as inadequate (*ibid.*, p. 562).

showed how belligerents harnessed the doctrine of belligerent reprisals to depart from outdated and overtly static norms while 'acting "lawfully" ... [and] reserving for the future the attitude to the rules departed from'.[11] Although this view of belligerent reprisals has progressively lost ground and appeal in the field of belligerent reprisals and IHL,[12] the ability of what has been called 'unfriendly unilateralism' 'not only to enforce but also to help generate law' has been investigated in a recent, thorough contribution by Hakimi.[13]

Attributing to belligerent reprisals a legislative function has the considerable merit of focusing the attention on battlefield behaviour and the measure's role in it. However, that theory is at once too ambitious and too limited. Regarding the former aspect, it considers that belligerent reprisals can, almost by themselves, bring about changes in the positive law.[14] This might well have been the case in an epoch where the laws governing warfare were less codified than today, and belligerents' practice played a considerable role in determining standards of conduct and creating shared expectations.[15] However, that theory sits uncomfortably in the contemporary legal framework, characterized by a high degree of codification through treaty-making and robust black-letter law. As for the latter aspect, the theory is too narrow in that it focuses on just one aspect of belligerent reprisals, stressing their legislative function at the expense of other purposes that could be attributed to them both by the parties to the armed conflict and by the legal system.

Compared to the legislative function theory, the model proposed by this book is more comprehensive without entailing the corresponding excesses. By grounding belligerent reprisals in the reciprocity paradigm,

[11] Stone, *Legal Controls of International Conflict*, p. 355, footnote 39.

[12] See Meyrovitz, 'Review of *Belligerent Reprisals*', p. 648, who rejected the view conferring on belligerent reprisals a law-making function.

[13] Monica Hakimi, 'Unfriendly Unilateralism' (2014) 55 *Harvard International Law Journal*, p. 107.

[14] See, for instance, Stone's understanding of belligerent reprisals as 'a powerful instrument for *undermining* or *changing* the law of war': Stone, *Legal Controls of International Conflict*, p. 355 [emphasis in original].

[15] It is hardly a coincidence if the legislative function model was already being talked about as a thing of the past by authors writing between the 1970s and 1980s. For Draper, belligerent reprisals 'in historical terms [have] played a significant role in the development of the law of the war at sea and in some modest curtailment of breaches of the law of land warfare' ('Implementation of International Law', p. 49). For an author who was still considering that belligerent reprisals were used 'to ensure compliance with the law of war, and in some uses perhaps even to promote the lawmaking process itself', see Almond, 'Reprisals: The Global Community', p. 198.

it attributes to the notion a much wider set of legitimate purposes than the one admitted under the enforcement framework and focused on compliance with pre-existing norms. At the same time, it does not go so far as to say that belligerent reprisals can *themselves* bring about changes in the normative system[16] – except, potentially, in liminal and exceptional cases where *any* form of legal regulation is hardly to be found. As we have seen, the core function of belligerent reprisals is that of creating and safeguarding the equilibrium in the relationship between parties to an armed conflict following a perceived breach of the laws of war. Therefore, their focus is not on the coherence or the hold of the legal system as a whole, but, more humbly and more effectively, on the sustenance of a balanced relationship between two sides fighting each other. This feature does not depend at all on the solidity of the legal regime: the legal bond might have to be negotiated, agreed upon and policed even when robust treaties are in place – for instance, because the application or interpretation of certain rules might be unclear. In this sense, belligerent reprisals must be understood as a tool to re-calibrate the legal relationship in a specific context, rather than reforming the whole regime.

C.3 Belligerent Reprisals *vis-à-vis* Compliance Mechanisms

The formalization advanced in this book also helps account for the apparently puzzling resilience of the institution of belligerent reprisals in the face of always new compliance mechanisms. For nearly a century, diplomats, lawyers and policy-makers have devised a considerable number of institutions, measures and regimes geared to monitor violations of, and enhance respect for, the laws of armed conflict. This effort was spearheaded by the formal enquiry procedure, originally established in the 1929 Geneva Convention on the Wounded and Sick[17] but fully developed by the 1949 GCs.[18] The system of Protecting Powers enshrined

[16] Even where a practice different from that expected under positive law were widespread and consistent, it would have to be verified whether the subjective element accompanying recourse to belligerent reprisals meets the threshold of *opinio iuris sive necessitatis* that is necessary for the crystallization of a new customary norm.

[17] Article 30 of the Convention for the Amelioration of the Condition of Wounded and Sick of Armies in the Field, Geneva, 27 July 1929, in force 19 June 1931; no longer in operation following the universal acceptance of the Geneva Conventions of 1949, 47 Stat. 2074; T.S. No. 847; 118 L.N.T.S. 303.

[18] Articles 52, 53, 132 and 149 of the Geneva Conventions Relative to the Protection of the Victims of International Armed Conflicts, Geneva, 12 August 1949, in force 21 October

in the latter instruments[19] as well as in AP I[20] served the similar purpose of 'secur[ing] the supervision and implementation' of IHL.[21] High hopes have also been vested in the International Humanitarian Fact-Finding Commission (IHFFC): established in 1991 pursuant to Article 90 of AP I, this expert body is competent to enquire into any facts alleged to constitute grave breaches and serious violations of IHL, and to facilitate the restoration of an attitude of respect for that body of rules.[22] Finally, in December 2015, the 32nd International Conference of the Red Cross and Red Crescent adopted a resolution on 'Strengthening Compliance with International Humanitarian Law'.[23] Building on a consultation process facilitated by the Government of Switzerland and the ICRC, the Conference '*recommend[ed]* the continuation of an inclusive, State-driven inter-governmental process based on the principle of consensus . . . to find agreement on features and functions of a potential forum of States and to find ways to enhance the implementation of IHL using the potential of the International Conference and IHL regional forums'.[24]

Given this complex monitoring landscape, it is reasonable to wonder why belligerent reprisals (once described as a 'vestigial [and] most primitive' means of reacting to unlawful conduct)[25] still feature at all in the practice and legal parlance of contemporary conflict. How is it even possible that, as the international legal system is crafting more and more refined ways of ensuring the cessation of breaches of *ius in bello* and fostering compliance, voices in the scholarship have revamped the notion of belligerent reprisals in relation to modern-day conflicts, often characterized by asymmetric warfare?[26] How can we explain the fact that even

1950, 75 UNTS 31; UKTS 39 (1958), Cmd 550; 157 BFSP 229; 6 UST 3114; TIAS 3362; ATS 21 (1958).

19 Articles 8, 8, 8 and 9 of the 1949 GCs.

20 Article 5 of the Protocol Additional to the Geneva Conventions of 12 August 1949, and relating to the Protection of Victims of International Armed Conflicts (Protocol I), Geneva, 8 June 1977, in force 7 December 1978, 1125 UNTS 3.

21 *Ibid.*

22 Article 90(2)(c)(i)-(ii) of AP I.

23 32nd International Conference of the Red Cross and Red Crescent, *Strengthening Compliance with International Humanitarian Law*, Resolution 32IC/15/R2, Geneva, 8–10 December 2015.

24 *Ibid.*, operative para. 2.

25 Draper, 'Implementation of International Law', p. 49.

26 See in particular Sutter, 'The Continuing Role', pp. 93–122; Michael A. Newton, 'Reconsidering Reprisals' (2009–2010) 20 *Duke Journal of Comparative and*

the ICRC seems to have admitted (albeit implicitly) the continuing legality and role of certain belligerent reprisals both in its *Customary IHL Study*[27] and in its updated Commentaries to the GCs?[28]

The common answer to this dilemma submits that the residual margin of application of belligerent reprisals is justified (in both practical and moral terms) to the extent that those other compliance mechanisms prove ineffective (or not effective enough).[29] After all – so the argument goes – the compliance mechanisms listed above have failed to gain traction. While formal enquiry procedures have never been launched,[30] Protecting Powers have only been appointed in five conflicts since the adoption of the 1949 GCs.[31] In addition to that, negotiations during the 32nd International Conference of the Red Cross and Red Crescent had already undermined the draft proposal for the Meeting of States on International Humanitarian Law,[32] postponing to an uncertain future

International Studies, pp. 361–388. For a discussion of these debates, see Osiel, *The End of Reciprocity, passim.*

27 Rule 145 adopts a negative formulation: '*[w]here not prohibited by international law*, belligerent reprisals are subject to stringent conditions' (Henckaerts and Doswald-Beck, *Customary IHL Study*, vol. I, p. 513 [emphasis added]). The Commentary on that Rule follows an identical approach when it states that 'the international community is *increasingly opposed* to the use of violations of international humanitarian law as a method of trying to enforce the law' (*ibid.*, p. 514 [emphasis added]).

28 The updated commentary on Article 1 common to the 1949 GCs cautions that 'respect "in all circumstances" does not seem to imply, by itself, an absolute prohibition on [belligerent] reprisals beyond those prohibitions specifically provided for in the Conventions': see ICRC, *Commentary on GC III*, 2nd ed., para. 222.

29 For an early formulation of this answer, see Draper, 'Implementation of International Law', pp. 50 and 58. See also Kalshoven, *Belligerent Reprisals*, p. 375; Greenwood, 'Twilight of Reprisals', p. 56; and (albeit discussing the issue with a more critical eye) Darcy, 'Evolution of Reprisals', pp. 248–51. For a similar idea outside of the scholarship consensus, see ICTY, *Kupreškić* TC, pp. 208–9, para. 530.

30 ICRC, *Commentary on GC III*, 2nd ed., paras. 5331–5336 (which identifies the reasons for the failure in the requirement that 'all interested Parties agree either on the procedure to be followed or on the choice of the umpire', as well as in the lack of institutionalization of the mechanism). See also Jelena Pejic, 'Strengthening Compliance with IHL: The ICRC-Swiss Initiative' (2016) 98 IRRC, p. 319.

31 ICRC, *Commentary on GC III*, 2nd ed., paras. 1297–1302, which attributes to political considerations and to the inapplicability of the mechanism to NIACs the relative failure of the Protecting Powers system. See also Pejic, 'Strengthening Compliance with IHL', p. 320.

32 Compare, in this regard, the language in Resolution 32IC/15/R2 as eventually adopted with that in the official draft resolution submitted to the International Conference (ICRC and Swiss Federal Department of Foreign Affairs, *Strengthening Compliance with International Humanitarian Law – Draft Resolution and Concluding Report*, Doc. 32IC/15/19.2, Geneva, October 2015). For a detailed overview of the process that led to the

the creation of that 'effective, voluntary, and non-politicized institutional forum … for States to meet regularly in order to exchange views on issues related to strengthening respect for IHL'.[33] What is more, in December 2018 the ICRC had to register the impossibility for those participating in the intergovernmental process to reach consensus on the creation of that forum, noting 'the deep sense of mistrust between States in multilateral processes'.[34] On a final note, the first independent forensic investigation carried out by the IHFFC in the Luhansk province of Eastern Ukraine over the summer of 2017, at the request of OSCE,[35] has not dispelled all doubts that the 'sleeping beauty' (as Kalshoven had dubbed the Commission)[36] had finally awakened[37] – not least because of the debatable legal basis of the IHFFC's competence in the presence of a request by an intergovernmental organization.[38] And despite the intense support received by the IHFFC through joint pledges and the

International Conference, as well as the negotiations that took place therein, see Pejic, 'Strengthening Compliance with IHL', *passim*.

33 ICRC and Swiss Federal Department of Foreign Affairs, *Strengthening Compliance with International Humanitarian Law - Draft Resolution and Concluding Report*, operative para. 5. This wording is already characterized by telling departures from an even earlier draft, that had been prepared in September 2015 on the basis of comments from members of the International Conference: see ICRC and Swiss Federal Department of Foreign Affairs, *Draft '0' Resolution on 'Strengthening Compliance with International Humanitarian Law'*, Geneva, September 2015. In the corresponding section, the latter document read 'new, effective and non-politicized institutional space for States to meet regularly in order to *examine* issues related to *compliance* with international humanitarian law, based on dialogue and cooperation' (*ibid.*, operative para. 5 [emphasis added]).

34 Helen Durham, 'Strengthening Compliance with IHL: Disappointment and Hope', *Humanitarian Law and Policy*, 14 December 2018 (available at https://blogs.icrc.org/law-and-policy/2018/12/14/strengthening-compliance-with-ihl-disappointment-and-hope/).

35 IHFFC, *Executive Summary of the Report of the Independent Forensic Investigation in relation to the Incident affecting an OSCE Special Monitoring Mission to Ukraine (SMM) Patrol on 23 April 2017*, 7 September 2017.

36 Frits Kalshoven, 'The International Humanitarian Fact-Finding Commission: A Sleeping Beauty?' (2002) 4 *Humanitäres Völkerrecht - Informationschriften*, pp. 213–16.

37 The question was initially asked (and answered for the most part in the negative) in relation to the 2015 US and Afghan attack on the hospital run by Médecins Sans Frontières in the Kunduz province of Afghanistan: see Catherine Harwood, 'Will the "Sleeping Beauty" Awaken? The Kunduz Hospital Attack and the International Humanitarian Fact-Finding Commission', *EJIL: Talk!*, 15 October 2015 (available at www.ejiltalk.org/will-the-sleeping-beauty-awaken-the-kunduz-hospital-attack-and-the-international-humanitarian-fact-finding-commission/).

38 For an overview of the legal questions raised by the first mandate of the IHFFC, see Cristina Azzarello and Matthieu Niederhauser, 'The International Humanitarian Fact-Finding Commission: Has the "Sleeping Beauty" Awoken?', *Humanitarian Law and*

establishment of groups of friends,[39] the Commission's offers of services in relation to the armed conflicts between Russia and Ukraine, between Armenia and Azerbaijan, and in the Tigray Region of Ethiopia have remained unheeded.[40]

Certainly, this explanation for the continuing role of belligerent reprisals reflects the current track record of existing compliance mechanisms; moreover, it maintains high the hopes that retaliation will eventually be disposed of as soon as those mechanisms gain traction. However, it overlooks the fact that *other* tools, largely external to the IHL regime, are indeed contributing to monitoring respect for IHL. This is the case, for instance, with international criminal tribunals and human rights bodies addressing situations of armed conflict. For sure, this path is not without hurdles, and these new actors face continuous challenges in their endeavours. Still, their mounting practice testifies to the existence (contested, wavering, but nonetheless present) of institutions and mechanisms addressing IHL compliance. Therefore, there must exist a different reason why belligerent reprisals continue to feature in today's armed conflicts – one that does not depend on the difficulties of ensuring respect with IHL, and that flows directly from the character of belligerent reprisals themselves.

This is precisely the point where the formalization of belligerent reprisals under the reciprocity paradigm enters the picture. Their puzzling resilience is motivated by the fact that, far from sharing in the same objective and function as the compliance mechanisms mentioned above, belligerent reprisals serve a purpose (and obey a logic) different from enforcement. Their relevance as a tool to constantly re-calibrate the legal relationship and ensure parity of arms between parties to an armed conflict represents not only their legal *causa*, but also the justification for their continued presence in the IHL framework. Belligerent reprisals still exist *besides and*

Policy, 9 January 2018 (available at https://blogs.icrc.org/law-and-policy/2018/01/09/the-independent-humanitarian-fact-finding-commission-has-the-sleeping-beauty-awoken/).

39 See the IHFFC News Releases of 5 June 2018 ('Organization of American States adopts Resolution referring to IHFFC'), 13 November 2019 ('Launch of the Group of Friends of the IHFFC at the United Nations') and 12 December 2019 ('Support for the IHFFC at the 33rd International Conference') (all available at www.ihffc.org/index.asp?Language=EN&page=news&mode=newsarchive).

40 See the IHFFC News Releases of 29 January 2019 ('IHFFC has proposed its services'), 23 October 2020 ('IHFFC has proposed its services'), 21 January 2021 ('Ethiopia: IHFFC has proposed its services') and 10 March 2022 ('IHFFC has proposed its services') (all available at www.ihffc.org/index.asp?Language=EN&page=news&mode=newsarchive).

notwithstanding compliance mechanisms – or, to put it bluntly, *in spite of* them, and not *in stead of* them. Belligerent reprisals enjoy both a logical and a practical autonomy from institutions designed to ensure abidance by the laws of war. Therefore, the question as to their permanence in the fabric of international law needs to be understood, assessed, and ultimately answered on the basis of their highly peculiar characteristics.

It is easy to appreciate this continued significance of belligerent reprisals if we compare them with two of the most advanced compliance tools mentioned above (devised both outside of, and within, IHL). Let us start with international criminal law. The claim (put forward by the ICTY Trial Chamber II in the *Kupreškić* judgment) that belligerent reprisals have lost their previous 'modicum of justification'[41] because of the 'fairly efficacious'[42] alternative avenue of prosecuting and punishing war crimes and crimes against humanity does not withstand scrutiny. Attributing criminal responsibility for IHL violations pursues the objectives of retribution and special and general deterrence; its focus is on a past to account for and a future to prevent,[43] and its logic is linked to a rather fixed standard, in compliance with the fundamental considerations of justice imposed by the principle of legality. On the contrary, we have seen that belligerent reprisals aim at remedying the consequences of a breach that has created disequilibrium in the relationship between belligerents. As such, their focus is on the present, and their main contribution occurs precisely when a fixed legal standard is contested or unsettled and impossible to reach with lawful means.

A similar conclusion warrants itself with regard to the recently foundered attempt at establishing the Meeting of States on International Humanitarian Law. In the resolution approved during the 32nd International Conference of the Red Cross and Red Crescent in 2015, it was agreed that the consultation process leading to the adoption of such forum of States be guided by the principles of non-politicization, non-selectivity and non-contextuality.[44] These features are in stark contrast

[41] ICTY, *Kupreškić* TC, p. 208, para. 530.

[42] *Ibid.*, p. 209, para. 530.

[43] See *ibid.*: 'the prosecution and punishment of war crimes and crimes against humanity by national or international courts . . . serves the purpose of bringing to justice those who are responsible for any such crime, as well as, albeit to a limited extent, the purpose of deterring at least the most blatant violations of international humanitarian law'.

[44] See 32nd International Conference of the Red Cross and Red Crescent, *Strengthening Compliance with International Humanitarian Law*, Resolution 32IC/15/R2, Geneva, 8–10 December 2015, p. 1, para. 1.

with the main characteristics of belligerent reprisals as unveiled in the present study. Belligerent reprisals are necessarily contextual, in that they are meant to react to specific situations during armed conflict; they are individualized, because they are directed against a well-identifiable addressee; and they are politicized, in the sense that the decision to adopt them will not flow automatically from a breach of *ius in bello* on the part of the enemy, but will be subject to a number of strategic considerations.

C.4 Could We Ever Dispose of Belligerent Reprisals?

If belligerent reprisals remain, it is not despite their irrelevance, but *because of their continued relevance* in the current structure of international law. Their value lies not so much in the tactical reaction to single violations, but in the strategic modulation of the obligations linking the parties to an armed conflict. Strengthening compliance mechanisms remains an important priority of the international regulation of armed conflicts, due to its relevance for victims of breaches and violations. However, improvements in that effort would not automatically result in the elimination of belligerent reprisals. This is because the modicum of justification of belligerent reprisals will not be found outside of them – it is to be looked for within them, in the function that they continue to exert in the current outlook of the laws of armed conflict. Reprisals must be assessed for their capacity to clarify, adjust and strengthen the bundle of rights and obligations linking parties to the armed conflict; for their ability to place belligerents on an equal footing and have them negotiate mutually acceptable standards of conduct; for their unexpected capacity to craft and uphold new forms of legal expectations through reciprocity.

Should we then resign ourselves to the idea that belligerent reprisals are unavoidable? That despite our best efforts, they will continue to enjoy a margin of legality, and in any case challenge through unremitted practice the advances achieved by way of treaty prohibitions? The answer to this question is not necessarily an affirmative one. Belligerent reprisals do not have an autonomous existence that can be separated from the will of those adopting them. This book has focused on the conceptual features of belligerent reprisals, in the belief that mastering the notion is a key passage to approach correctly any subsequent questions concerning both its legal regulation and its policy implications. As an idea, the concept of belligerent reprisals is a tool that policy-makers, militaries, and even the public opinion can freely choose to wilfully use, or wilfully relinquish.

Whatever path is chosen, it will have to be guided by a new theory of belligerent reprisals to prove successful.

If they opt for the former option, it is paramount that the legal formalization that they give to belligerent reprisals corresponds to their actual characteristics. This long-standing feature of armed conflicts must be confronted for what it is, lest we give up all hope to rein in it. It is tempting to construe this institution in a way that suits the direction and policy goals of the laws of armed conflict, highlighting their role in sanctioning norms and contributing to the re-affirmation of fundamental principles. But as we have seen, on the long run this hermeneutical operation could lead to a serious misunderstanding of the dynamics governing the mechanism. Instead, their residual margin of legality, their applicability and their substantive and procedural requirements must be re-assessed in light of the chiefly reciprocal features that characterize the mechanism (most notably the swift and in-kind character of the response).

If they opt for the latter, more ambitious option, it is important to identify correctly what aspects of the international legal architecture governing warfare must be strengthened to replace belligerent reprisals. Buttressing the role of institutions that monitor and enforce IHL would fill an important gap, but it would be a mistake to conclude that this alone would devoid belligerent reprisals of any role. As we have seen, the latter mechanism has much more to it than just the enforcement of norms; their demise would have to be accompanied by initiatives that address the same gaps and issues to which belligerent reprisals were responding. For the law of NIAC, this would entail remedying the structural imbalance between parties that oftentimes characterizes this type of armed conflict; it would also require an availability to thicken the scope of applicable rules, building on minimum standards and devising a more robust range of obligations. With regard to the law of IAC, the priority would be to develop channels facilitating dialogue during conflict, so that belligerents could communicate and argue on protection and conduct of hostilities issues even in the heat of armed confrontation; indeed, the comparatively more sophisticated legal framework of IACs should not blind us to the challenges brought about by new weapons, new enemies and new battlefields, which call for a continuous reflection and negotiation (even among belligerents) on how existing rules should be applied.

If belligerent reprisals are an old mechanism, it is because they answer to ever-present needs. But elusiveness must not be confused with inescapability. Our failures to regulate them, or even to dispense with them, must not be attributed to their inner characteristics. They are rather a consequence of our misconceptions in approaching them, and in construing the purpose that they pursue and the function that they exert in the legal governance of armed conflict. There is hope that a new formalization can adjust these interpretive shortcomings in the short run; and in the long run, that it will help undertake reform paths in a more effective way, allowing for a more robust regulation of, or a definitive departure from, belligerent reprisals.

Appendix

States' and UN Communications Related to the Iran–Iraq War

(Documents are listed by UN Doc. number)

Chemical Warfare

UN Doc. S/15934, 18 August 1983, *Letter Dated 18 August 1983 from the Permanent Representative of the Islamic Republic of Iran to the United Nations Addressed to the Secretary-General*

UN Doc. S/16139, 10 November 1983, *Letter Dated 9 November 1983 from the Permanent Representative of the Islamic Republic of Iran to the United Nations Addressed to the Secretary-General*

UN Doc. S/16154, 16 November 1983, *Letter Dated 16 November 1983 from the Permanent Representative of the Islamic Republic of Iran to the United Nations Addressed to the Secretary-General*

UN Doc. A/38/650-S/16193, 30 November 1983, *Letter Dated 29 November 1983 from the Permanent Representative of Iraq to the United Nations Addressed to the Secretary-General*

UN Doc. S/16220, 16 December 1983, *Letter Dated 15 December 1983 from the Permanent Representative of the Islamic Republic of Iran to the United Nations Addressed to the Secretary-General*

UN Doc. S/16380, 1 March 1984, *Letter Dated 29 February 1984 from the Permanent Representative of the Islamic Republic of Iran to the United Nations Addressed to the Secretary-General*

UN Doc. S/16408, 12 March 1984, *Letter Dated 9 March 1984 from the Permanent Representative of the Islamic Republic of Iran to the United Nations Addressed to the Secretary-General*

UN Doc. S/16433, 26 March 1984, *Report of the Specialists Appointed by the Secretary-General to Investigate Allegations by the Islamic Republic of Iran Concerning the Use of Chemical Weapons*

UN Doc. S/16446, 28 March 1984, *Letter Dated 27 March 1984 from the Permanent Representative of the Islamic Republic of Iran to the United Nations Addressed to the Secretary-General*

UN Doc. S/16454, 30 March 1984, *Note by the President of the Security Council*

UN Doc. S/16498, 19 April 1984, *Letter Dated 18 April 1984 from the Permanent Representative of the Islamic Republic of Iran to the United Nations Addressed to the Secretary-General*

UN Doc. A/39/266-S/16572, 21 May 1984, *Letter Dated 10 May 1984 from the Permanent Representative of the Islamic Republic of Iran to the United Nations Addressed to the Secretary-General*

UN Doc. S/16663, 6 July 1984, *Text of Messages Dated 29 June 1984 from the Secretary-General Addressed to the President of the Islamic Republic of Iran and to the President of the Republic of Iraq*

UN Doc. A/39/374-S/16690, 3 August 1984, *Letter Dated 3 August 1984 from the Permanent Representative of the Islamic Republic of Iran to the United Nations Addressed to the Secretary-General*

UN Doc. A/39/651-S/16827, 13 November 1984, *Letter Dated 13 November 1984 from the Permanent Representative of the Islamic Republic of Iran to the United Nations Addressed to the Secretary-General*

UN Doc. A/40/118-S/16941, 5 February 1985, *Letter Dated 5 February 1985 from the Chargé d'Affaires* ad interim *of the Permanent Mission of the Islamic Republic of Iran to the United Nations Addressed to the Secretary-General*

UN Doc. A/40/154-S/16987, 27 February 1985, *Letter Dated 27 February 1985 from the Chargé d'Affaires* ad interim *of the Permanent Mission of the Islamic Republic of Iran to the United Nations Addressed to the Secretary-General*

UN Doc. A/40/174-S/17027, 13 March 1985, *Letter Dated 12 March 1985 from the Permanent Representative of the Islamic Republic of Iran to the United Nations Addressed to the Secretary-General*

UN Doc. S/17031, 14 March 1985, *Letter Dated 14 March 1985 from the Permanent Representative of the Islamic Republic of Iran to the United Nations Addressed to the Secretary-General*

UN Doc. S/17039, 18 March 1985, *Letter Dated 18 March 1985 from the Permanent Representative of the Islamic Republic of Iran to the United Nations Addressed to the Security Council*

UN Doc. A/40/189-S/17046, 21 March 1985, *Letter Dated 20 March 1985 from the Permanent Representative of the Islamic Republic of Iran to the United Nations Addressed to the Secretary-General*

UN Doc. S/17059, 26 March 1985, *Letter Dated 26 March 1985 from the Permanent Representative of the Islamic Republic of Iran to the United Nations Addressed to the Secretary-General*

UN Doc. S/17088, 9 April 1985, *Letter Dated 8 April 1985 from the Permanent Representative of the Islamic Republic of Iran to the United Nations Addressed to the Secretary-General*

UN Doc. S/17089, 9 April 1985, *Letter Dated 9 April 1985 from the Permanent Representative of the Islamic Republic of Iran to the United Nations Addressed to the Secretary-General*

UN Doc. S/17095, 11 April 1985, *Letter Dated 11 April 1985 from the Permanent Representative of the Islamic Republic of Iran to the United Nations Addressed to the Secretary-General*

UN Doc. S/17096, 11 April 1985, *Letter Dated 11 April 1985 from the Permanent Representative of the Islamic Republic of Iran to the United Nations Addressed to the Secretary-General*

UN Doc. S/17097, 12 April 1985, *Report of the Secretary-General on His Visit to Iran and Iraq*

UN Doc. S/17127, 24 April 1985, *Letter Dated 17 April 1985 from the Secretary-General Addressed to the President of the Security Council*

UN Doc. S/17129, 25 April 1985, *Letter Dated 25 April 1985 from the Permanent Representative of the Islamic Republic of Iran to the United Nations Addressed to the Secretary-General*

UN Doc. S/17130, 25 April 1985, *Note by the President of the Security Council*

UN Doc. S/17143, 2 May 1985, *Letter Dated 2 May 1985 from the Permanent Representative of the Islamic Republic of Iran to the United Nations Addressed to the Secretary-General*

UN Doc. A/39/895-S/17161, 7 May 1985, *Letter Dated 6 May 1985 from the Permanent Representative of Italy to the United Nations Addressed to the Secretary-General*

UN Doc. S/17181, 13 May 1985, *Letter Dated 13 May 1985 from the Permanent Representative of the Islamic Republic of Iran to the United Nations Addressed to the Secretary-General*

UN Doc. A/40/487-S/17342, 16 July 1985, *Letter Dated 16 July 1985 from the Permanent Representative of the Islamic Republic of Iran to the United Nations Addressed to the Secretary-General*

UN Doc. S/17782, 31 January 1986, *Letter Dated 31 January 1986 from the Permanent Representative of the Islamic Republic of Iran to the United Nations Addressed to the Secretary-General*

UN Doc. S/17790, 4 February 1986, *Letter Dated 4 February 1986 from the Permanent Representative of the Islamic Republic of Iran to the United Nations Addressed to the Secretary-General*

UN Doc. S/17822, 12 February 1986, *Letter Dated 12 February 1986 from the Permanent Representative of the Islamic Republic of Iran to the United Nations Addressed to the Secretary-General*

UN Doc. S/17824, 17 February 1986, *Letter Dated 17 February 1986 from the Permanent Representative of Iraq to the United Nations Addressed to the Secretary-General*

UN Doc. S/17829, 14 February 1986, *Letter Dated 13 February 1986 from the Permanent Representative of the Islamic Republic of Iran to the United Nations Addressed to the Secretary-General*

UN Doc. S/17833, 14 February 1986, *Letter Dated 14 February 1986 from the Permanent Representative of the Islamic Republic of Iran to the United Nations Addressed to the Secretary-General*

UN Doc. S/17849, 19 February 1986, *Letter Dated 19 February 1986 from the Permanent Representative of the Islamic Republic of Iran to the United Nations Addressed to the Secretary-General*

UN Doc. S/PV.2666, 24 February 1986, *Provisional Verbatim Record of the Two Thousand Six Hundred and Sixty-Sixth Meeting of the Security Council*

UN Doc. S/17864, 25 February 1986, *Letter Dated 25 February 1986 from the Permanent Representative of the Islamic Republic of Iran to the United Nations Addressed to the Secretary-General*

UN Doc. S/17887, 3 March 1986, *Letter Dated 3 March 1986 from the Chargé d'Affaires* ad interim *of the Permanent Mission of the Islamic Republic of Iran to the United Nations Addressed to the Secretary-General*

UN Doc. S/17888, 3 March 1986, *Letter Dated 3 March 1986 from the Chargé d'Affaires* ad interim *of the Permanent Mission of the Islamic Republic of Iran to the United Nations Addressed to the Secretary-General*

UN Doc. S/17911, 12 March 1986, *Report of the Mission Dispatched by the Secretary-General to Investigate Allegations of the Use of Chemical Weapons in the Conflict between the Islamic Republic of Iran and Iraq*

UN Doc. S/17932, 21 March 1986, *Note by the President of the Security Council*

UN Doc. S/17944, 26 March 1986, *Letter Dated 26 March 1986 from the Permanent Representative of the Islamic Republic of Iran to the United Nations Addressed to the Secretary-General*

UN Doc. S/18028, 22 April 1986, *Letter Dated 22 April 1986 from the Chargé d'Affaires* ad interim *of the Permanent Mission of the Islamic Republic of Iran to the United Nations Addressed to the Secretary-General*

UN Doc. S/18036, 24 April 1986, *Letter Dated 24 April 1986 from the Chargé d'Affaires* ad interim *of the Permanent Mission of the Islamic Republic of Iran to the United Nations Addressed to the Secretary-General*

UN Doc. S/18549, 29 December 1986, *Letter Dated 26 December 1986 from the Chargé d'Affaires* ad interim *of the Permanent Mission of the Islamic Republic of Iran to the United Nations Addressed to the Secretary-General*

UN Doc. S/18553, 2 January 1987, *Letter Dated 2 January 1987 from the Chargé d'Affaires* ad interim *of the Permanent Mission of the Islamic Republic of Iran to the United Nations Addressed to the Secretary-General*

UN Doc. S/18555, 5 January 1987, *Letter Dated 5 January 1987 from the Chargé d'Affaires* ad interim *of the Permanent Mission of the Islamic Republic of Iran to the United Nations Addressed to the Secretary-General*
UN Doc. S/18556, 5 January 1987, *Letter Dated 5 January 1987 from the Chargé d'Affaires* ad interim *of the Permanent Mission of the Islamic Republic of Iran to the United Nations Addressed to the Secretary-General*
UN Doc. S/18574, 9 January 1987, *Letter Dated 9 January 1987 from the Chargé d'Affaires* ad interim *of the Permanent Mission of the Islamic Republic of Iran to the United Nations Addressed to the Secretary-General*
UN Doc. S/18577, 11 January 1987, *Letter Dated 10 January 1987 from the Chargé d'Affaires* ad interim *of the Permanent Mission of the Islamic Republic of Iran to the United Nations Addressed to the Secretary-General*
UN Doc. S/18600, 14 January 1987, *Letter Dated 14 January 1987 from the Permanent Representative of the Islamic Republic of Iran to the United Nations Addressed to the Secretary-General*
UN Doc. S/18605, 15 January 1987, *Letter Dated 15 January 1987 from the Permanent Representative of the Islamic Republic of Iran to the United Nations Addressed to the Secretary-General*
UN Doc. S/18614, 19 January 1987, *Letter Dated 19 January 1987 from the Permanent Representative of the Islamic Republic of Iran to the United Nations Addressed to the Secretary-General*
UN Doc. S/18626, 26 January 1987, *Letter Dated 26 January 1987 from the Permanent Representative of the Islamic Republic of Iran to the United Nations Addressed to the Secretary-General*
UN Doc. S/18628, 23 January 1987, *Letter Dated 23 January 1987 from the Permanent Representative of the Islamic Republic of Iran to the United Nations Addressed to the Secretary-General*
UN Doc. S/18635, 27 January 1987, *Letter Dated 26 January 1987 from the Permanent Representative of the Islamic Republic of Iran to the United Nations Addressed to the Secretary-General*
UN Doc. S/18675, 6 February 1987, *Letter Dated 6 February 1987 from the Permanent Representative of the Islamic Republic of Iran to the United Nations Addressed to the Secretary-General*
UN Doc. S/18676, 6 February 1987, *Letter Dated 6 February 1987 from the Permanent Representative of the Islamic Republic of Iran to the United Nations Addressed to the Secretary-General*
UN Doc. S/18679, 9 February 1987, *Letter Dated 9 February 1987 from the Chargé d'Affaires* ad interim *of the Permanent Mission of the Islamic Republic of Iran to the United Nations Addressed to the Secretary-General*
UN Doc. S/18723, 25 February 1987, *Letter Dated 25 February 1987 from the Permanent Representative of the Islamic Republic of Iran to the United Nations Addressed to the Secretary-General*

UN Doc. S/18728, 27 February 1987, *Letter Dated 27 February 1987 from the Permanent Representative of the Islamic Republic of Iran to the United Nations Addressed to the Secretary-General*

UN Doc. S/18788, 8 April 1987, *Letter Dated 7 April 1987 from the Permanent Representative of the Islamic Republic of Iran to the United Nations Addressed to the Secretary-General*

UN Doc. S/18796, 10 April 1987, *Letter Dated 10 April 1987 from the Permanent Representative of the Islamic Republic of Iran to the United Nations Addressed to the Secretary-General*

UN Doc. A/42/219-S/18799, 13 April 1987, *Letter Dated 13 April 1987 from the Permanent Representative of the Islamic Republic of Iran to the United Nations Addressed to the Secretary-General*

UN Doc. A/42/220-S/18800, 13 April 1987, *Letter Dated 13 April 1987 from the Permanent Representative of the Islamic Republic of Iran to the United Nations Addressed to the Secretary-General*

UN Doc. S/18806, 15 April 1987, *Letter Dated 15 April 1987 from the Permanent Representative of Iraq to the United Nations Addressed to the Secretary-General*

UN Doc. S/18809, 16 April 1987, *Letter Dated 16 April 1987 from the Permanent Representative of the Islamic Republic of Iran to the United Nations Addressed to the Secretary-General*

UN Doc. S/18810, 16 April 1987, *Letter Dated 16 April 1987 from the Chargé d'Affaires of the Permanent Mission of Iraq to the United Nations Addressed to the Secretary-General*

UN Doc. A/42/238-S/18820, 21 April 1987, *Letter Dated 21 April 1987 from the Permanent Representative of the Islamic Republic of Iran to the United Nations Addressed to the Secretary-General*

UN Doc. A/42/253-S/18825, 27 April 1987, *Letter Dated 27 April 1987 from the Permanent Representative of the Islamic Republic of Iran to the United Nations Addressed to the Secretary-General*

UN Doc. A/42/257-S/18829, 28 April 1987, *Letter Dated 28 April 1987 from the Permanent Representative of the Islamic Republic of Iran to the United Nations Addressed to the Secretary-General*

UN Doc. A/42/279-S/18851, 7 May 1987, *Letter Dated 7 May 1987 from the Permanent Representative of the Islamic Republic of Iran to the United Nations Addressed to the Secretary-General*

UN Doc. S/18852, 8 May 1987, *Report of the Mission Dispatched by the Secretary-General to Investigate Allegations of the Use of Chemical Weapons in the Conflict between the Islamic Republic of Iran and Iraq*

UN Doc. A/42/282-S/18855, 8 May 1987, *Letter Dated 8 May 1987 from the Permanent Representative of the Islamic Republic of Iran to the United Nations Addressed to the Secretary-General*

UN Doc. A/42/286-S/18859, 11 May 1987, *Letter Dated 11 May 1987 from the Permanent Representative of the Islamic Republic of Iran to the United Nations Addressed to the Secretary-General*

UN Doc. S/18863, 14 May 1987, *Note by the President of the Security Council*

UN Doc. A/42/294-S/18866, 15 May 1987, *Letter Dated 15 May 1987 from the Permanent Representative of the Islamic Republic of Iran to the United Nations Addressed to the Secretary-General*

UN Doc. S/18870, 18 May 1987, *Letter Dated 18 May 1987 from the Permanent Representative of the Islamic Republic of Iran to the United Nations*

UN Doc. A/42/306-S/18878, 26 May 1987, *Letter Dated 21 May 1987 from the Permanent Representative of the Islamic Republic of Iran to the United Nations Addressed to the Secretary-General*

UN Doc. A/42/315-S/18890, 2 June 1987, *Letter Dated 2 June 1987 from the Chargé d'Affaires* ad interim *of the Permanent Mission of the Islamic Republic of Iran to the United Nations Addressed to the Secretary-General*

UN Doc. A/42/334-S/18910, 10 June 1987, *Letter Dated 10 June 1987 from the Chargé d'Affaires* ad interim *of the Permanent Mission of the Islamic Republic of Iran to the United Nations Addressed to the Secretary-General*

UN Doc. A/42/350-S/18928, 17 June 1987, *Letter Dated 17 June 1987 from the Chargé d'Affaires* ad interim *of the Permanent Mission of the Islamic Republic of Iran to the United Nations Addressed to the Secretary-General*

UN Doc. A/42/360-S/18941, 23 June 1987, *Letter Dated 23 June 1987 from the Chargé d'Affaires* ad interim *of the Permanent Mission of the Islamic Republic of Iran to the United Nations Addressed to the Secretary-General*

UN Doc. A/42/366-S/18947, 25 June 1987, *Letter Dated 25 June 1987 from the Chargé d'Affaires* ad interim *of the Permanent Mission of the Islamic Republic of Iran to the United Nations Addressed to the Secretary-General*

UN Doc. A/42/370-S/18952, 29 June 1987, *Letter Dated 29 June 1987 from the Chargé d'Affaires* ad interim *of the Permanent Mission of the Islamic Republic of Iran to the United Nations Addressed to the Secretary-General*

UN Doc. A/42/371-S/18953, 29 June 1987, *Letter Dated 29 June 1987 from the Chargé d'Affaires* ad interim *of the Permanent Mission of the Islamic Republic of Iran to the United Nations Addressed to the Secretary-General*

UN Doc. A/42/373-S/18955, 30 June 1987, *Letter Dated 29 June 1987 from the Chargé d'Affaires* ad interim *of the Permanent Mission of the Islamic Republic of Iran to the United Nations Addressed to the Secretary-General*

UN Doc. A/42/375-S/18956, 30 June 1987, *Letter Dated 30 June 1987 from the Chargé d'Affaires* ad interim *of the Permanent Mission of the Islamic Republic of Iran to the United Nations Addressed to the Secretary-General*

UN Doc. S/18962, 2 July 1987, *Letter Dated 2 July 1987 from the Chargé d'Affaires* ad interim *of the Permanent Mission of the Islamic Republic of Iran to the United Nations Addressed to the Secretary-General*

UN Doc. A/42/384-S/18967, 7 July 1987, *Letter Dated 7 July 1987 from the Chargé d'Affaires* ad interim *of the Permanent Mission of the Islamic Republic of Iran to the United Nations Addressed to the Secretary-General*

UN Doc. A/42/397-S/18973, 13 July 1987, *Letter Dated 13 July 1987 from the Chargé d'Affaires* ad interim *of the Permanent Mission of the Islamic Republic of Iran to the United Nations Addressed to the Secretary-General*

UN Doc. S/19031, 11 August 1987, *Letter Dated 11 August 1987 from the Permanent Representative of the Islamic Republic of Iran to the United Nations Addressed to the Secretary-General*

UN Doc. S/19621, 15 March 1988, *Letter Dated 15 March 1988 from the Acting Permanent Representative of the Islamic Republic of Iran to the United Nations Addressed to the Secretary-General*

UN Doc. S/19637, 17 March 1988, *Letter Dated 17 March 1988 from the Acting Permanent Representative of the Islamic Republic of Iran to the United Nations Addressed to the Secretary-General*

UN Doc. S/19639, 17 March 1988, *Letter Dated 17 March 1988 from the Acting Permanent Representative of the Islamic Republic of Iran to the United Nations Addressed to the Secretary-General*

UN Doc. S/19647, 18 March 1988, *Letter Dated 18 March 1988 from the Acting Permanent Representative of the Islamic Republic of Iran to the United Nations Addressed to the Secretary-General*

UN Doc. S/19664, 21 March 1988, *Letter Dated 19 March 1988 from the Acting Permanent Representative of the Islamic Republic of Iran to the United Nations Addressed to the Secretary-General*

UN Doc. S/19665, 21 March 1988, *Letter Dated 21 March 1988 from the Acting Permanent Representative of the Islamic Republic of Iran to the United Nations Addressed to the Secretary-General*

UN Doc. A/43/239-S/19682, 25 March 1988, *Letter Dated 24 March 1988 from the Chargé d'Affaires* ad interim *of the Permanent Mission of the Islamic Republic of Iran to the United Nations Addressed to the Secretary-General*

UN Doc. S/19695, 28 March 1988, *Letter Dated 28 March 1988 from the Permanent Representative of Iraq to the United Nations Addressed to the Secretary-General*

UN Doc. A/43/279-S/19726, 4 April 1988, *Letter Dated 4 April 1988 from the Chargé d'Affaires* ad interim *of the Permanent Mission of the Islamic Republic of Iran to the United Nations Addressed to the Secretary-General*

UN Doc. S/19730, 5 April 1988, *Letter Dated 4 April 1988 from the Permanent Representative of Iraq to the United Nations Addressed to the Secretary-General*

UN Doc. A/43/281-S/19733, 4 April 1988, *Letter Dated 4 April 1988 from the Chargé d'Affaires* ad interim *of the Permanent Mission of the Islamic Republic of Iran to the United Nations Addressed to the Secretary-General*

UN Doc. A/43/282-S/19734, 4 April 1988, *Letter Dated 4 April 1988 from the Chargé d'Affaires* ad interim *of the Permanent Mission of the Islamic Republic of Iran to the United Nations Addressed to the Secretary-General*

UN Doc. A/43/288-S/19741, 5 April 1988, *Letter Dated 5 April 1988 from the Chargé d'Affaires* ad interim *of the Permanent Mission of the Islamic Republic of Iran to the United Nations Addressed to the Secretary-General*

UN Doc. S/19759, 12 April 1988, *Letter Dated 11 April 1988 from the Acting Permanent Representative of the Islamic Republic of Iran to the United Nations Addressed to the Secretary-General*

UN Doc. S/19786, 15 April 1988, *Letter Dated 15 April 1988 from the Chargé d'Affaires* ad interim *of the Permanent Mission of the Islamic Republic of Iran to the United Nations Addressed to the Secretary-General*

UN Doc. S/19802, 19 April 1988, *Letter Dated 19 April 1988 from the Acting Permanent Representative of the Islamic Republic of Iran to the United Nations Addressed to the Secretary-General*

UN Doc. S/19816, 21 April 1988, *Letter Dated 20 April 1988 from the Acting Permanent Representative of the Islamic Republic of Iran to the United Nations Addressed to the Secretary-General*

UN Doc. S/19822, 22 April 1988, *Letter Dated 22 April 1988 from the Acting Permanent Representative of the Islamic Republic of Iran to the United Nations Addressed to the Secretary-General*

UN Doc. S/19823, 25 April 1988, *Report of the Mission Dispatched by the Secretary-General to Investigate Allegations of the Use of Chemical Weapons in the Conflict between the Islamic Republic of Iran and Iraq*

UN Doc. S/19886, 16 May 1988, *Letter Dated 16 May 1988 from the Chargé d'Affaires* ad interim *of Permanent Mission of the Islamic Republic of Iran to the United Nations Addressed to the Secretary-General*

UN Doc. S/19892, 19 May 1988, *Letter Dated 19 May 1988 from the Chargé d'Affaires* ad interim *of the Islamic Republic of Iran to the United Nations Addressed to the Secretary-General*

UN Doc. S/19902, 25 May 1988, *Letter Dated 25 May 1988 from the Acting Permanent Representative of the Islamic Republic of Iran to the United Nations Addressed to the Secretary-General*

UN Doc. A/43/410-S/19942, 16 June 1988, *Letter Dated 16 June 1988 from the Chargé d'Affaires* ad interim *of the Permanent Mission of the Islamic Republic of Iran to the United Nations Addressed to the Secretary-General*

UN Doc. S/19948, 20 June 1988, *Letter Dated 19 June 1988 from the Permanent Representative of Iraq to the United Nations Addressed to the President of the Security Council*

UN Doc. S/19954, 22 June 1988, *Letter Dated 22 June 1988 from the Acting Permanent Representative of the Islamic Republic of Iran to the United Nations Addressed to the Secretary-General*

UN Doc. S/19967, 27 June 1988, *Letter Dated 27 June 1988 from the Acting Permanent Representative of the Islamic Republic of Iran to the United Nations Addressed to the Secretary-General*

UN Doc. S/19982, 5 July 1988, *Letter Dated 5 July 1988 from the Permanent Representative of Iraq to the United Nations Addressed to the Secretary-General*

UN Doc. S/20013, 13 July 1988, *Letter Dated 13 July 1988 from the Permanent Representative of Iraq to the United Nations Addressed to the Secretary-General*

UN Doc. S/20049, 22 July 1988, *Letter Dated 22 July 1988 from the Acting Permanent Representative of the Islamic Republic of Iran to the United Nations Addressed to the Secretary-General*

UN Doc. S/20060, 20 July 1988, *Report of the Mission Dispatched by the Secretary-General to Investigate Allegations of the Use of Chemical Weapons in the Conflict between the Islamic Republic of Iran and Iraq*

UN Doc. S/20063, 25 July 1988, *Report of the Mission Dispatched by the Secretary-General to Investigate Allegations of the Use of Chemical Weapons in the Conflict between the Islamic Republic of Iran and Iraq*

UN Doc. S/20074, 29 July 1988, *Letter Dated 29 July 1988 from the Acting Permanent Representative of the Islamic Republic of Iran to the United Nations Addressed to the Secretary-General*

UN Doc. S/20076, 1 August 1988, *Letter Dated 1 August 1988 from the Permanent Representative of Iraq to the United Nations Addressed to the Secretary-General*

UN Doc. S/20077, 1 August 1988, *Letter Dated 1 August 1988 from the Permanent Representative of Iraq to the United Nations Addressed to the Secretary-General*

UN Doc. S/20084, 3 August 1988, *Letter Dated 3 August 1988 from the Minister for Foreign Affairs of the Islamic Republic of Iran Addressed to the Secretary-General*

UN Doc. S/20089, 4 August 1988, *Letter Dated 4 August 1988 from the Permanent Representative of Iraq to the United Nations Addressed to the Secretary-General*

UN Doc. S/20134, 19 August 1988, *Report of the Mission Dispatched by the Secretary-General to Investigate Allegations of the Use of Chemical Weapons in the Conflict between the Islamic Republic of Iran and Iraq*

"War of the Cities"

UN Doc. A/36/842-S/14802, 18 December 1981, *Note Verbale Dated 16 December 1981 from the Chargé d'Affaires* ad interim *of the Permanent Mission of Iran to the United Nations Addressed to the Secretary-General*

UN Doc. S/15270, 2 July 1982, *Letter Dated 1 July 1982 from the Permanent Representative of Iran to the United Nations Addressed to the President of the Security Council*

UN Doc. S/15289, 14 July 1982, *Letter Dated 14 July 1982 from the Permanent Representative of Iraq to the United Nations Addressed to the President of the Security Council*

UN Doc. S/15448, 5 October 1982, *Note Verbale Dated 4 October 1982 from the Permanent Representative of Iran to the United Nations Addressed to the Secretary-General*

UN Doc. A/37/584-S/15471, 1 November 1982, *Letter Dated 28 October 1982 from the Permanent Representative of Iran to the United Nations Addressed to the Secretary-General*

UN Doc. A/37/596-S/15479, 4 November 1982, *Letter Dated 1 November 1982 from the Permanent Representative of Iran to the United Nations Addressed to the Secretary-General*

UN Doc. S/15539, 28 December 1982, *Letter Dated 21 December 1982 from the Permanent Representative of Iran to the United Nations Addressed to the Secretary-General*

UN Doc. S/15579, 8 February 1983, *Letter Dated 2 February 1983 from the Permanent Representative of Iraq to the United Nations Addressed to the Secretary-General*

UN Doc. A/38/165-S/15729, 26 April 1983, *Letter Dated 22 April 1983 from the Permanent Representative of the Islamic Republic of Iran to the United Nations Addressed to the Secretary-General*

UN Doc. A/38/167-S/15735, 27 April 1983, *Letter Dated 26 April 1983 from the Permanent Representative of the Islamic Republic of Iran to the United Nations Addressed to the Secretary-General*

UN Doc. A/38/173-S/15739, 28 April 1983, *Letter Dated 27 April 1983 from the Permanent Representative of the Islamic Republic of Iran to the United Nations Addressed to the Secretary-General*

UN Doc. A/38/177-S/15743, 4 May 1983, *Letter Dated 2 May 1983 from the Permanent Representative of Iraq to the United Nations Addressed to the Secretary-General*

UN Doc. S/15747, 5 May 1983, *Letter Dated 5 May 1983 from the Permanent Representative of the Islamic Republic of Iran to the United Nations Addressed to the Secretary-General*

UN Doc. S/15765, 16 May 1983, *Letter Dated 12 May 1983 from the Permanent Representative of Iraq to the United Nations Addressed to the Secretary-General*

UN Doc. S/15804, 27 May 1983, *Letter Dated 27 May 1983 from the Deputy Permanent Representative of Iraq to the United Nations Addressed to the Secretary-General*

UN Doc. A/38/268-S/15825, 14 June 1983, *Letter Dated 9 June 1983 from the Permanent Representative of Iraq to the United Nations Addressed to the Secretary-General*

UN Doc. S/15834, 20 June 1983, *Mission to Inspect Civilian Areas in Iran and Iraq Which Have Been Subject to Military Attack. Report of the Secretary-General*

UN Doc. S/15874, 19 July 1983, *Letter Dated 14 July 1983 from the Permanent Representative of Iraq to the United Nations Addressed to the Secretary-General*

UN Doc. S/15909, 4 August 1983, *Letter Dated 3 August 1983 from the Permanent Representative of the Islamic Republic of Iran to the United Nations Addressed to the Secretary-General*

UN Doc. S/15926, 15 August 1983, *Letter Dated 12 August 1983 from the Permanent Representative of the Islamic Republic of Iran to the United Nations Addressed to the Secretary-General*

UN Doc. S/15932, 18 August 1983, *Letter Dated 17 August 1983 from the Permanent Representative of the Islamic Republic of Iran to the United Nations Addressed to the Secretary-General*

UN Doc. S/15934, 18 August 1983, *Letter Dated 18 August 1983 from the Permanent Representative of the Islamic Republic of Iran to the United Nations Addressed to the Secretary-General*

UN Doc. S/15962, 9 September 1983, *Letter Dated 7 September 1983 from the Permanent Representative of the Islamic Republic of Iran to the United Nations Addressed to the Secretary-General*

UN Doc. A/38/408-S/15983, 13 September 1983, *Letter Dated 12 September 1983 from the Permanent Representative of Iraq to the United Nations Addressed to the Secretary-General*

UN Doc. S/16000, 22 September 1983, *Letter Dated 22 September 1983 from the Chargé d'Affaires of the Permanent Mission of the Islamic Republic of Iran to the United Nations Addressed to the Secretary-General*

UN Doc. S/16104, 31 October 1983, *Letter Dated 28 October 1983 from the Permanent Representative of the Islamic Republic of Iran to the United Nations Addressed to the Secretary-General*

UN Doc. S/16117, 3 November 1983, *Letter Dated 2 November 1983 from the Permanent Representative of the Islamic Republic of Iran to the United Nations Addressed to the Secretary-General*

UN Doc. A/38/560-S/16120, 3 November 1983, *Letter Dated 1 November 1983 from the Permanent Representative of Iraq to the United Nations Addressed to the Secretary-General*

UN Doc. A/38/591-S/16157, 17 November 1983, *Letter Dated 15 November 1983 from the Permanent Representative of Iraq to the United Nations Addressed to the Secretary-General*

UN Doc. A/38/619-S/16191, 29 November 1983, *Letter Dated 28 November 1983 from the Permanent Representative of Iraq to the United Nations Addressed to the Secretary-General*

UN Doc. S/16204, 7 December 1983, *Letter Dated 6 December 1983 from the Permanent Representative of the Islamic Republic of Iran to the United Nations Addressed to the Secretary-General*

UN Doc. S/16213, 12 December 1983, *Letter Dated 11 December 1983 from the Permanent Representative of the Islamic Republic of Iran to the United Nations Addressed to the Secretary-General*

UN Doc. S/16220, 16 December 1983, *Letter Dated 15 December 1983 from the Permanent Representative of the Islamic Republic of Iran to the United Nations Addressed to the Secretary-General*

UN Doc. A/38/763-S/16225, 19 December 1983, *Letter Dated 14 December 1983 from the Permanent Representative of Iraq to the United Nations Addressed to the Secretary-General*

UN Doc. S/16236, 28 December 1983, *Letter Dated 28 December 1983 from the Permanent Representative of the Islamic Republic of Iran to the United Nations Addressed to the Secretary-General*

UN Doc. S/16260, 9 January 1984, *Letter Dated 6 January 1984 from the Permanent Representative of the Islamic Republic of Iran to the United Nations Addressed to the Secretary-General*

UN Doc. S/16310, 3 February 1984, *Letter Dated 3 February 1984 from the Chargé d'Affaires* ad interim *of the Permanent Mission of the Islamic Republic of Iran to the United Nations Addressed to the Secretary-General*

UN Doc. S/16314, 6 February 1984, *Letter Dated 3 February 1984 from the Chargé d'Affaires* ad interim *of the Permanent Mission of the Islamic Republic of Iran to the United Nations Addressed to the Secretary-General*

UN Doc. S/16331, 9 February 1984, *Letter Dated 9 February 1984 from the Permanent Representative of the Islamic Republic of Iran to the United Nations Addressed to the Secretary-General*

UN Doc. A/38/784-S/16335, 10 February 1984, *Letter Dated 7 February 1984 from the Permanent Representative of Iraq to the United Nations Addressed to the Secretary-General*

UN Doc. S/16337, 10 February 1984, *Letter Dated 10 February 1984 from the Secretary-General Addressed to the Minister of Foreign Affairs of Iraq*

UN Doc. S/16338, 10 February 1984, *Letter Dated 10 February 1984 from the Secretary-General Addressed to the Minister of Foreign Affairs of the Islamic Republic of Iran*

UN Doc. S/16340, 14 February 1984, *Letter Dated 14 February 1984 from the Permanent Representative of the Islamic Republic of Iran to the United Nations Addressed to the Secretary-General*

UN Doc. S/16342, 15 February 1984, *Letter Dated 13 February 1984 from the Permanent Representative of Iraq to the United Nations Addressed to the Secretary-General*

UN Doc. A/38/786-S/16344, 16 February 1984, *Letter Dated 13 February 1984 from the Permanent Representative of Iraq to the United Nations Addressed to the Secretary-General*

UN Doc. A/38/787-S/16345, 16 February 1984, *Letter Dated 14 February 1984 from the Permanent Representative of Iraq to the United Nations Addressed to the Secretary-General*

UN Doc. S/16346, 17 February 1984, *Letter Dated 16 February 1984 from the Permanent Representative of the Islamic Republic of Iran to the United Nations Addressed to the Secretary-General*

UN Doc. A/38/790-S/16350, 17 February 1984, *Letter Dated 16 February 1984 from the Permanent Representative of Iraq to the United Nations Addressed to the Secretary-General*

UN Doc. S/16352, 17 February 1984, *Letter Dated 17 February 1984 from the Permanent Representative of the Islamic Republic of Iran to the United Nations Addressed to the Secretary-General*

UN Doc. S/16354, 19 February 1984, *Letter Dated 18 February 1984 from the Permanent Representative of Iraq to the United Nations Addressed to the Secretary-General*

UN Doc. S/16361, 23 February 1984, *Letter Dated 21 February 1984 from the Permanent Representative of Iraq to the United Nations Addressed to the Secretary-General*

UN Doc. S/16363, 24 February 1984, *Letter Dated 21 February 1984 from the Permanent Representative of Iraq to the United Nations Addressed to the Secretary-General*

UN Doc. S/16370, 24 February 1984, *Letter Dated 23 February 1984 from the Permanent Representative of Iraq to the United Nations Addressed to the Secretary-General*

UN Doc. S/16372, 24 February 1984, *Letter Dated 23 February 1984 from the Permanent Representative of the Islamic Republic of Iran to the United Nations Addressed to the Secretary-General*

UN Doc. S/16374, 27 February 1984, *Letter Dated 27 February 1984 from the Permanent Representative of Iraq to the United Nations Addressed to the Secretary-General*

UN Doc. S/16375, 29 February 1984, *Letter Dated 28 February 1984 from the Permanent Representative of the Islamic Republic of Iran to the United Nations Addressed to the Secretary-General*

UN Doc. A/39/123-S/16389, 6 March 1984, *Letter Dated 2 March 1984 from the Permanent Representative of France to the United Nations Addressed to the Secretary-General*

UN Doc. S/16604, 6 June 1984, *Letter Dated 6 June 1984 from the Permanent Representative of the Islamic Republic of Iran to the United Nations Addressed to the Secretary-General*

UN Doc. S/16606, 7 June 1984, *Letter Dated 6 June 1984 from the Permanent Representative of Iraq to the United Nations Addressed to the Secretary-General*

UN Doc. S/16607, 7 June 1984, *Letter Dated 7 June 1984 from the Permanent Representative of Iraq to the United Nations Addressed to the Secretary-General*

UN Doc. S/16609, 10 June 1984, *Letter Dated 10 June 1984 from the Permanent Representative of the Islamic Republic of Iran to the United Nations Addressed to the Secretary-General*

UN Doc. S/16610, 19 June 1984, *Letter Dated 10 June 1984 from the Permanent Representative of Iraq to the United Nations Addressed to the Secretary-General*

UN Doc. S/16611, 11 June 1984, *Message Dated 9 June 1984 from the Secretary-General Addressed to the Presidents of the Islamic Republic of Iran and the Republic of Iraq*

UN Doc. S/16613, 11 June 1984, *Letter Dated 11 June 1984 from the Permanent Representative of Iraq to the United Nations Addressed to the Secretary-General*

UN Doc. S/16614, 12 June 1984, *Message Dated 11 June 1984 from the Secretary-General Addressed to the President of the Islamic Republic of Iran*

UN Doc. S/16615, 12 June 1984, *Message Dated 11 June 1984 from the Secretary-General Addressed to the President of the Republic of Iraq*

UN Doc. S/16616, 11 June 1984, *Letter Dated 11 June 1984 from the Permanent Representative of the Islamic Republic of Iran to the United Nations Addressed to the Secretary-General*

UN Doc. S/16620, 12 June 1984, *Letter Dated 12 June 1984 from the Permanent Representative of Iraq to the United Nations Addressed to the Secretary-General*

UN Doc. S/16621, 12 June 1984, *Letter Dated 12 June 1984 from the Permanent Representative of the Islamic Republic of Iran to the United Nations Addressed to the Secretary-General*

UN Doc. S/16624, 13 June 1984, *Letter Dated 13 June 1984 from the Permanent Representative of Iraq to the United Nations Addressed to the Secretary-General*

UN Doc. S/16627, 15 June 1984, *Letter Dated 14 June 1984 from the Secretary-General Addressed to the President of the Security-Council*

UN Doc. S/16628, 15 June 1984, *Letter Dated 15 June 1984 from the President of the Security Council Addressed to the Secretary-General*

UN Doc. S/16630, 15 June 1984, *Letter Dated 15 June 1984 from the Permanent Representative of the Islamic Republic of Iran to the United Nations Addressed to the Secretary-General*

UN Doc. S/16631, 17 June 1984, *Letter Dated 15 June 1984 from the Permanent Representative of Iraq to the United Nations Addressed to the Secretary-General*

UN Doc. S/16632, 17 June 1984, *Letter Dated 16 June 1984 from the Permanent Representative of Iraq to the United Nations Addressed to the Secretary-General*

UN Doc. S/16636, 20 June 1984, *Letter Dated 19 June 1984 from the Permanent Representative of the Islamic Republic of Iran to the United Nations Addressed to the Secretary-General*

UN Doc. S/16638, 21 June 1984, *Letter Dated 21 June 1984 from the Permanent Representative of Iraq to the United Nations Addressed to the Secretary-General*

UN Doc. S/16651, 29 June 1984, *Letter Dated 28 June 1984 from the Permanent Representative of the Islamic Republic of Iran to the United Nations Addressed to the Secretary-General*

UN Doc. S/16679, 23 July 1984, *Letter Dated 19 July 1984 from the Chargé d'Affaires of the Permanent Mission of the Islamic Republic of Iran to the United Nations Addressed to the Secretary-General*

UN Doc. S/16750, 19 September 1984, *Note of the Secretary-General on the Report of the United Nations Team in Baghdad Concerning an Inspection Carried Out on 17 September 1984*

UN Doc. S/16793, 23 October 1984, *Letter Dated 22 October 1984 from the Permanent Representative of Iraq to the United Nations Addressed to the Secretary-General*

UN Doc. S/16808, 31 October 1984, *Letter Dated 31 October 1984 from the Permanent Representative of the Islamic Republic of Iran to the United Nations Addressed to the Secretary-General*

UN Doc. S/16878, 2 January 1985, *Letter Dated 31 December 1984 from the Chargé d'Affaires of the Permanent Mission of the Islamic Republic of Iran to the United Nations Addressed to the Secretary-General*

UN Doc. S/16897, 16 January 1985, *Note of the Secretary-General on the Report of the United Nations Team in Teheran Concerning an Inspection Carried Out on 7 and 8 January 1985*

UN Doc. S/16920, 30 January 1985, *Note of the Secretary-General on the Report of the United Nations Team in Baghdad Concerning an Inspection Carried Out on 28 January 1985*

UN Doc. S/16949, 10 February 1985, *Letter Dated 9 February 1985 from the Chargé d'Affaires* ad interim *of the Permanent Mission of the Islamic Republic of Iran to the United Nations Addressed to the Secretary-General*

UN Doc. A/39/870-S/16967, 20 February 1985, *Letter Dated 19 February 1985 from the Permanent Representative of the Islamic Republic of Iran to the United Nations Addressed to the Secretary-General*

UN Doc. S/17002, 5 March 1985, *Letter Dated 5 March 1985 from the Permanent Representative of the Islamic Republic of Iran to the United Nations Addressed to the Secretary-General*

UN Doc. S/17017, 10 March 1985, *Letter Dated 8 March 1985 from the Permanent Representative of the Islamic Republic of Iran to the United Nations Addressed to the Secretary-General*

UN Doc. S/17018, 10 March 1985, *Message Dated 9 March 1985 from the Secretary-General Addressed to the Presidents of the Islamic Republic of Iran and the Republic of Iraq*

UN Doc. S/17019, 10 March 1985, *Letter Dated 10 March 1985 from the Permanent Representative of Iraq to the United Nations Addressed to the Secretary-General*

UN Doc. S/17020, 10 March 1985, *Letter Dated 10 March 1985 from the Permanent Representative of the Islamic Republic of Iran to the United Nations Addressed to the Secretary-General*

UN Doc. S/17025, 12 March 1985, *Letter Dated 12 March 1985 from the Permanent Representative of the Islamic Republic of Iran to the United Nations Addressed to the Secretary-General*

UN Doc. S/17026, 12 March 1985, *Letter Dated 12 March 1985 from the Permanent Representative of the Islamic Republic of Iran to the United Nations Addressed to the Secretary-General*

UN Doc. S/17029, 14 March 1985, *Letter Dated 14 March 1985 from the Permanent Representative of the Islamic Republic of Iran to the United Nations Addressed to the Secretary-General*

UN Doc. S/17036, 15 March 1985, *Note by the President of the Security Council*

UN Doc. S/17037, 18 March 1985, *Letter Dated 16 March 1985 from the Permanent Representative of Iraq to the United Nations Addressed to the Secretary-General*

UN Doc. S/17058, 26 March 1985, *Letter Dated 25 March 1985 from the Permanent Representative of the Islamic Republic of Iran to the United Nations Addressed to the Secretary-General*

UN Doc. S/17073, 1 April 1985, *Letter Dated 1 April 1985 from the Permanent Representative of the Islamic Republic of Iran to the United Nations Addressed to the Secretary-General*

UN Doc. S/17078, 3 April 1985, *Letter Dated 3 April 1985 from the Permanent Representative of the Islamic Republic of Iran to the United Nations Addressed to the Secretary-General*

UN Doc. S/17083, 5 April 1985, *Letter Dated 4 April 1985 from the Permanent Representative of the Islamic Republic of Iran to the United Nations Addressed to the Secretary-General*

UN Doc. S/17097, 12 April 1985, *Report of the Secretary-General on His Visit to Iran and Iraq*

UN Doc. S/17220, 27 May 1985, *Letter Dated 25 May 1985 from the Permanent Representative of the Islamic Republic of Iran to the United Nations Addressed to the Security Council*

UN Doc. S/17221, 27 May 1985, *Letter Dated 26 May 1985 from the Permanent Representative of the Islamic Republic of Iran to the United Nations Addressed to the Secretary-General*

UN Doc. S/17226, 30 May 1985, *Letter Dated 29 May 1985 from the Permanent Representative of the Islamic Republic of Iran to the United Nations Addressed to the Secretary-General*

UN Doc. S/17237, 4 June 1985, *Letter Dated 3 June 1985 from the Permanent Representative of the Islamic Republic of Iran to the United Nations Addressed to the Secretary-General*

UN Doc. A/40/868-S/17617, 8 November 1985, *Letter Dated 8 November 1985 from the Permanent Representative of Iran to the United Nations Addressed to the Secretary-General*

UN Doc. S/17679, 11 December 1985, *Letter Dated 10 December 1985 from the Permanent Representative of the Islamic Republic of Iran to the United Nations Addressed to the Secretary-General*

UN Doc. S/17683, 13 December 1985, *Letter Dated 12 December 1985 from the Permanent Representative of the Islamic Republic of Iran to the United Nations Addressed to the Secretary-General*

UN Doc. S/17687, 19 December 1985, *Letter Dated 19 December 1985 from the Permanent Representative of Iraq to the United Nations Addressed to the Secretary-General*

UN Doc. S/17706, 31 December 1985, *Letter Dated 31 December 1985 from the Permanent Representative of Iraq to the United Nations Addressed to the Secretary-General*

UN Doc. S/17712, 3 January 1986, *Letter Dated 2 January 1986 from the Permanent Representative of the Islamic Republic of Iran to the United Nations Addressed to the Secretary-General*

UN Doc. S/17715, 3 January 1986, *Letter Dated 3 January 1986 from the Permanent Representative of the Islamic Republic of Iran to the United Nations Addressed to the Secretary-General*

UN Doc. S/17720, 7 January 1986, *Letter Dated 6 January 1986 from the Permanent Representative of Iraq to the United Nations Addressed to the Secretary-General*

UN Doc. S/17768, 28 January 1986, *Letter Dated 28 January 1986 from the Permanent Representative of Iraq to the United Nations Addressed to the Secretary-General*

S/PV.2663, 18 February 1986, *Provisional Verbatim Record of the Two Thousand Six Hundred and Sixty-Third Meeting of the Security Council*

UN Doc. S/17872, 28 February 1986, *Letter Dated 28 February 1986 from the Chargé d'Affaires* ad interim *of the Permanent Mission of the Islamic Republic of Iran to the United Nations Addressed to the Secretary-General*

UN Doc. S/17885, 3 March 1986, *Letter Dated 2 March 1986 from the Chargé d'Affaires* ad interim *of the Permanent Mission of the Islamic Republic of Iran to the United Nations Addressed to the Secretary-General*

UN Doc. S/17890, 3 March 1986, *Letter Dated 3 March 1986 from the Permanent Representative of Iraq to the United Nations Addressed to the Secretary-General*

UN Doc. S/17904, 7 March 1986, *Letter Dated 7 March 1986 from the Permanent Representative of Iraq to the United Nations Addressed to the Secretary-General*

UN Doc. S/17909, 11 March 1986, *Letter Dated 11 March 1986 from the Chargé d'Affaires* ad interim *of the Permanent Mission of the Islamic Republic of Iran to the United Nations Addressed to the Secretary-General*

UN Doc. S/17972, 7 April 1986, *Letter Dated 7 April 1986 from the Permanent Representative of the Islamic Republic of Iran to the United Nations Addressed to the Secretary-General*

UN Doc. S/17981, 9 April 1986, *Letter Dated 9 April 1986 from the Permanent Representative of Iraq to the United Nations Addressed to the Secretary-General*

UN Doc. S/18240, 25 July 1986, *Letter Dated 25 July 1986 from the Permanent Representative of the Islamic Republic of Iran to the United Nations Addressed to the Secretary-General*

UN Doc. S/18243, 28 July 1986, *Letter Dated 28 July 1986 from the Permanent Representative of Iraq to the United Nations Addressed to the Secretary-General*

UN Doc. S/18251, 31 July 1986, *Letter Dated 31 July 1986 from the Permanent Representative of Iraq to the United Nations Addressed to the Secretary-General*

UN Doc. S/18258, 4 August 1986, *Letter Dated 2 August 1986 from the Permanent Representative of Iraq to the United Nations Addressed to the Secretary-General*

UN Doc. S/18263, 7 August 1986, *Letter Dated 7 August 1986 from the Permanent Representative of Iraq to the United Nations Addressed to the Secretary-General*

UN Doc. S/18268, 12 August 1986, *Letter Dated 12 August 1986 from the Chargé d'Affaires* ad interim *of the Permanent Mission of Iraq to the United Nations Addressed to the Secretary-General*

UN Doc. S/18284, 18 August 1986, *Letter Dated 18 August 1986 from the Permanent Representative of the Islamic Republic of Iran to the United Nations Addressed to the Secretary-General*

UN Doc. S/18319, 4 September 1986, *Letter Dated 4 September 1986 from the Chargé d'Affaires* ad interim *of the Permanent Mission of the Islamic Republic of Iran to the United Nations Addressed to the Secretary-General*

UN Doc. S/18327, 8 September 1986, *Letter Dated 8 September 1986 from the Chargé d'Affaires* ad interim *of the Permanent Mission of Iraq to the United Nations Addressed to the Secretary-General*

UN Doc. S/18332, 10 September 1986, *Letter Dated 10 September 1986 from the Chargé d'Affaires* ad interim *of the Permanent Mission of Iraq to the United Nations Addressed to the Secretary-General*

UN Doc. S/18335, 10 September 1986, *Letter Dated 10 September 1986 from the Permanent Representative of the Islamic Republic of Iran to the United Nations Addressed to the Secretary-General*

UN Doc. S/18340, 12 September 1986, *Letter Dated 12 September 1986 from the Chargé d'Affaires* ad interim *of the Permanent Mission of Iraq to the United Nations Addressed to the Secretary-General*

UN Doc. S/18345, 16 September 1986, *Letter Dated 16 September 1986 from the Permanent Representative of Iraq to the United Nations Addressed to the Secretary-General*

UN Doc. S/18407, 16 October 1986, *Letter Dated 16 October 1986 from the Permanent Representative of Iraq to the United Nations Addressed to the Secretary-General*

UN Doc. S/18410, 16 October 1986, *Letter Dated 16 October 1986 from the Permanent Representative of the Islamic Republic of Iran to the United Nations Addressed to the Secretary-General*

UN Doc. S/18412, 17 October 1986, *Letter Dated 17 October 1986 from the Permanent Representative of Iraq to the United Nations Addressed to the Secretary-General*

UN Doc. S/18423, 24 October 1986, *Letter Dated 21 October 1986 from the Permanent Representative of the Islamic Republic of Iran to the United Nations Addressed to the Secretary-General*

UN Doc. S/18459, 17 November 1986, *Letter Dated 15 November 1986 from the Permanent Representative of Iraq to the United Nations Addressed to the Secretary-General*

UN Doc. S/18463, 18 November 1986, *Letter Dated 17 November 1986 from the Permanent Representative of the Islamic Republic of Iran to the United Nations Addressed to the Secretary-General*

UN Doc. S/18476, 24 November 1986, *Letter Dated 24 November 1986 from the Permanent Representative of Iraq to the United Nations Addressed to the Secretary-General*

UN Doc. S/18477, 24 November 1986, *Letter Dated 24 November 1986 from the Permanent Representative of Iraq to the United Nations Addressed to the Secretary-General*

UN Doc. S/18482, 25 November 1986, *Letter Dated 25 November 1986 from the Permanent Representative of Iraq to the United Nations Addressed to the Secretary-General*

UN Doc. S/18484, 26 November 1986, *Letter Dated 26 November 1986 from the Permanent Representative of Iraq to the United Nations Addressed to the Secretary-General*

UN Doc. S/18485, 26 November 1986, *Letter Dated 25 November 1986 from the Permanent Representative of the Islamic Republic of Iran to the United Nations Addressed to the Secretary-General*

UN Doc. S/18488, 28 November 1986, *Letter Dated 28 November 1986 from the Permanent Representative of the Islamic Republic of Iran to the United Nations Addressed to the Secretary-General*

UN Doc. S/18507, 7 December 1986, *Letter Dated 7 December 1986 from the Permanent Representative of the Islamic Republic of Iran to the United Nations Addressed to the Secretary-General*

UN Doc. S/18537, 22 December 1986, *Letter Dated 22 December 1986 from the Chargé d'Affaires* ad interim *of the Permanent Mission of the Islamic Republic of Iran to the United Nations Addressed to the Secretary-General*

UN Doc. S/18539, 23 December 1986, *Letter Dated 23 December 1986 from the Chargé d'Affaires* ad interim *of the Permanent Mission of the Islamic Republic of Iran to the United Nations Addressed to the Secretary-General*

UN Doc. S/18540, 23 December 1986, *Letter Dated 23 December 1986 from the Chargé d'Affaires* ad interim *of the Permanent Mission of the Islamic Republic of Iran to the United Nations Addressed to the Secretary-General*

UN Doc. S/18542, 24 December 1986, *Letter Dated 24 December 1986 from the Chargé d'Affaires* ad interim *of the Permanent Mission of the Islamic Republic of Iran to the United Nations Addressed to the Secretary-General*

UN Doc. S/18576, 11 January 1987, *Letter Dated 10 January 1987 from the Chargé d'Affaires* ad interim *of the Permanent Mission of Iraq to the United Nations Addressed to the Secretary-General*

UN Doc. S/18577, 11 January 1987, *Letter Dated 10 January 1987 from the Chargé d'Affaires* ad interim *of the Permanent Mission of the Islamic Republic of Iran to the United Nations Addressed to the Secretary-General*

UN Doc. S/18578, 12 January 1987, *Letter Dated 11 January 1987 from the Chargé d'Affaires of the Permanent Mission of Iraq to the United Nations Addressed to the Secretary-General*

UN Doc. S/18587, 12 January 1987, *Letter Dated 12 January 1987 from the Permanent Representative of the Islamic Republic of Iran to the United Nations Addressed to the Secretary-General*

UN Doc. S/18595, 14 January 1987, *Letter Dated 13 January 1987 from the Permanent Representative of Iraq to the United Nations Addressed to the Secretary-General*

UN Doc. S/18649, 2 February 1987, *Letter Dated 2 February 1987 from the Permanent Representative of the Islamic Republic of Iran to the United Nations Addressed to the Secretary-General*

UN Doc. S/18651, 2 February 1987, *Letter Dated 2 February 1987 from the Permanent Representative of Iraq to the United Nations Addressed to the Secretary-General*

UN Doc. S/18656, 3 February 1987, *Letter Dated 3 February 1987 from the Permanent Representative of the Islamic Republic of Iran to the United Nations Addressed to the Secretary-General*

UN Doc. S/18658, 3 February 1987, *Letter Dated 3 February 1987 from the Permanent Representative of Iraq to the United Nations Addressed to the Secretary-General*

UN Doc. S/18674, 6 February 1987, *Letter Dated 6 February 1987 from the Permanent Representative of Iraq to the United Nations Addressed to the Secretary-General*

UN Doc. S/18678, 9 February 1987, *Letter Dated 9 February 1987 from the Chargé d'Affaires* ad interim *of the Permanent Mission of the Islamic Republic of Iran to the United Nations Addressed to the Secretary-General*

UN Doc. S/18689, 12 February 1987, *Letter Dated 12 February 1987 from the Permanent Representative of Iraq to the United Nations Addressed to the Secretary-General*

UN Doc. S/18702, 18 February 1987, *Letter Dated 18 February 1987 from the Permanent Representative of the Islamic Republic of Iran to the United Nations Addressed to the Secretary-General*

UN Doc. S/18704, 18 February 1987, *Letter Dated 18 February 1987 from the Permanent Representative of Iraq to the United Nations Addressed to the Secretary-General*

UN Doc. S/18717, 23 February 1987, *Letter Dated 23 February 1987 from the Permanent Representative of Iraq to the United Nations Addressed to the Secretary-General*

UN Doc. S/18719, 24 February 1987, *Letter Dated 24 February 1987 from the Permanent Representative of Iraq to the United Nations Addressed to the Secretary-General*

UN Doc. S/18725, 26 February 1987, *Letter Dated 25 February 1987 from the Permanent Representative of the Islamic Republic of Iran to the United Nations Addressed to the Secretary-General*

UN Doc. S/18728, 27 February 1987, *Letter Dated 27 February 1987 from the Permanent Representative of the Islamic Republic of Iran to the United Nations Addressed to the Secretary-General*

UN Doc. S/18730, 2 March 1987, *Letter Dated 2 March 1987 from the Permanent Representative of Iraq to the United Nations Addressed to the Secretary-General*

UN Doc. S/18945, 24 June 1987, *Letter Dated 24 June 1987 from the Chargé d'Affaires* ad interim *of the Permanent Mission of the Islamic Republic of Iran to the United Nations Addressed to the Secretary-General*

UN Doc. S/18954, 29 June 1987, *Letter Dated 29 June 1987 from the Permanent Representative of Iraq to the United Nations Addressed to the Secretary-General*

UN Doc. S/19070, 24 August 1987, *Letter Dated 24 August 1987 from the Permanent Representative of the Islamic Republic of Iran to the United Nations Addressed to the Secretary-General*

UN Doc. S/19071, 24 August 1987, *Letter Dated 24 August 1987 from the Permanent Representative of the Islamic Republic of Iran to the United Nations Addressed to the Secretary-General*

UN Doc. S/19072, 25 August 1987, *Letter Dated 25 August 1987 from the Permanent Representative of the Islamic Republic of Iran to the United Nations Addressed to the Secretary-General*

UN Doc. S/19079, 28 August 1987, *Letter Dated 28 August 1987 from the Chargé d'Affaires* ad interim *of the Permanent Mission of the Islamic Republic of Iran to the United Nations Addressed to the Secretary-General*

UN Doc. S/19096, 2 September 1987, *Letter Dated 2 September 1987 from the Permanent Representative of Iraq to the United Nations Addressed to the Secretary-General*

UN Doc. S/19098, 3 September 1987, *Letter Dated 2 September 1987 from the Chargé d'Affaires* ad interim *of the Permanent Mission of the Islamic Republic of Iran to the United Nations Addressed to the Secretary-General*

UN Doc. S/19105, 3 September 1987, *Letter Dated 1 September 1987 from the Permanent Representative of Iraq to the United Nations Addressed to the Secretary-General*

UN Doc. S/19108, 4 September 1987, *Letter Dated 4 September 1987 from the Permanent Representative of Iraq to the United Nations Addressed to the Secretary-General*

UN Doc. S/19179, 6 October 1987, *Letter Dated 6 October 1987 from the Permanent Representative of Iraq to the United Nations Addressed to the Secretary-General*

UN Doc. S/19198, 12 October 1987, *Letter Dated 12 October 1987 from the Permanent Representative of Iraq to the United Nations Addressed to the Secretary-General*

UN Doc. S/19205, 13 October 1987, *Letter Dated 13 October 1987 from the Permanent Representative of Iraq to the United Nations Addressed to the Secretary-General*

UN Doc. S/19214, 16 October 1987, *Letter Dated 16 October 1987 from the Permanent Representative of the Islamic Republic of Iran to the United Nations Addressed to the Secretary-General*

UN Doc. S/19244, 30 October 1987, *Letter Dated 30 October 1987 from the Permanent Representative of Iraq to the United Nations Addressed to the Secretary-General*

UN Doc. S/19258, 9 November 1987, *Letter Dated 9 November 1987 from the Permanent Representative of Iraq to the United Nations Addressed to the Secretary-General*

UN Doc. S/19282, 19 November 1987, *Letter Dated 19 November 1987 from the Permanent Representative of Iraq to the United Nations Addressed to the Secretary-General*

UN Doc. S/19548, 29 February 1988, *Letter Dated 28 February 1988 from the Chargé d'Affaires* ad interim *of the Permanent Mission of the Islamic Republic of Iran to the United Nations Addressed to the Secretary-General*

UN Doc. S/19550, 29 February 1988, *Letter Dated 29 February 1988 from the Chargé d'Affaires* ad interim *of the Permanent Mission of the Islamic Republic of Iran to the United Nations Addressed to the Secretary-General*

UN Doc. S/19551, 29 February 1988, *Letter Dated 29 February 1988 from the Permanent Representative of Iraq to the United Nations Addressed to the Secretary-General*

UN Doc. S/19554, 29 February 1988, *Letter Dated 29 February 1988 from the Permanent Representative of Iraq to the United Nations Addressed to the Secretary-General*

UN Doc. S/19563, 1 March 1988, *Letter Dated 1 March 1988 from the Acting Permanent Representative of the Islamic Republic of Iran to the United Nations Addressed to the Secretary-General*

UN Doc. S/19583, 5 March 1988, *Letter Dated 5 March 1988 from the Permanent Representative of Iraq to the United Nations Addressed to the Secretary-General*

UN Doc. S/19590, 7 March 1988, *Letter Dated 7 March 1988 from the Permanent Representative of Iraq to the United Nations Addressed to the Secretary-General*

UN Doc. S/19594, 8 March 1988, *Letter Dated 7 March 1988 from the Acting Permanent Representative of the Islamic Republic of Iran to the United Nations Addressed to the Secretary-General*

UN Doc. S/19598, 10 March 1988, *Letter Dated 10 March 1988 from the Permanent Representative of Iraq to the United Nations Addressed to the Secretary-General*

UN Doc. S/19601, 11 March 1988, *Letter Dated 10 March 1988 from the Permanent Representative of Iraq to the United Nations Addressed to the Secretary-General*

UN Doc. S/19603, 11 March 1988, *Letter Dated 11 March 1988 from the Acting Permanent Representative of the Islamic Republic of Iran to the United Nations Addressed to the Secretary-General*

UN Doc. S/19605, 11 March 1988, *Letter Dated 11 March 1988 from the Acting Permanent Representative of the Islamic Republic of Iran to the United Nations Addressed to the Secretary-General*

UN Doc. S/19610, 12 March 1988, *Letter Dated 12 March 1988 from the Permanent Representative of Iraq to the United Nations Addressed to the Secretary-General*

UN Doc. S/19611, 13 March 1988, *Letter Dated 13 March 1988 from the Permanent Representative of Iraq to the United Nations Addressed to the Secretary-General*

UN Doc. S/19612, 13 March 1988, *Letter Dated 13 March 1988 from the Permanent Representative of Iraq to the United Nations Addressed to the Secretary-General*

UN Doc. S/19614, 14 March 1988, *Letter Dated 14 March 1988 from the Chargé d'Affaires* ad interim *of the Permanent Mission of the Islamic Republic of Iran to the United Nations Addressed to the Secretary-General*

UN Doc. S/19615, 14 March 1988, *Letter Dated 14 March 1988 from the Chargé d'Affaires* ad interim *of the Permanent Mission of the Islamic Republic of Iran to the United Nations Addressed to the Secretary-General*

UN Doc. S/19618, 15 March 1988, *Letter Dated 14 March 1988 from the Permanent Representative of Iraq to the United Nations Addressed to the Secretary-General*

UN Doc. S/19619, 15 March 1988, *Letter Dated 14 March 1988 from the Acting Permanent Representative of the Islamic Republic of Iran to the United Nations Addressed to the Secretary-General*

UN Doc. S/19622, 15 March 1988, *Letter Dated 15 March 1988 from the Permanent Representative of Iraq to the United Nations Addressed to the Secretary-General*

UN Doc. S/19626, 16 March 1988, *Note by the President of the Security Council*

UN Doc. S/19630, 16 March 1988, *Letter Dated 16 March 1988 from the Permanent Representative of Iraq to the United Nations Addressed to the Secretary-General*

UN Doc. S/19631, 16 March 1988, *Letter Dated 16 March 1988 from the Permanent Representative of Iraq to the United Nations Addressed to the Security Council*

UN Doc. S/19646, 18 March 1988, *Letter Dated 18 March 1988 from the Acting Permanent Representative of the Islamic Republic of Iran to the United Nations Addressed to the Secretary-General*

UN Doc. S/19652, 21 March 1988, *Letter Dated 19 March 1988 from the Permanent Representative of Iraq to the United Nations Addressed to the Secretary-General*

UN Doc. S/19695, 28 March 1988, *Letter Dated 28 March 1988 from the Permanent Representative of Iraq to the United Nations Addressed to the Secretary-General*

UN Doc. S/19701, 29 March 1988, *Letter Dated 29 March 1988 from the Permanent Representative of Iraq to the United Nations Addressed to the Secretary-General*

UN Doc. S/19707, 30 March 1988, *Letter Dated 30 March 1988 from the Permanent Representative of Iraq to the United Nations Addressed to the Secretary-General*

UN Doc. S/19731, 4 April 1988, *Letter Dated 4 April 1988 from the Permanent Representative of Iraq to the United Nations Addressed to the Secretary-General*

UN Doc. S/19732, 4 April 1988, *Letter Dated 4 April 1988 from the Permanent Representative of Iraq to the United Nations Addressed to the Secretary-General*

UN Doc. S/19743, 6 April 1988, *Letter Dated 6 April 1988 from the Permanent Representative of Iraq to the United Nations Addressed to the Secretary-General*

UN Doc. S/19756, 11 April 1988, *Letter Dated 10 April 1988 from the Permanent Representative of Iraq to the United Nations Addressed to the Secretary-General*

UN Doc. S/19757, 11 April 1988, *Letter Dated 10 April 1988 from the Permanent Representative of Iraq to the United Nations Addressed to the Secretary-General*

UN Doc. S/19760, 12 April 1988, *Letter Dated 12 April 1988 from the Acting Permanent Representative of the Islamic Republic of Iran to the United Nations Addressed to the Secretary-General*

UN Doc. S/19761, 12 April 1988, *Letter Dated 12 April 1988 from the Acting Permanent Representative of the Islamic Republic of Iran to the United Nations Addressed to the Secretary-General*

UN Doc. S/19771, 13 April 1988, *Letter Dated 13 April 1988 from the Permanent Representative of Iraq to the United Nations Addressed to the Secretary-General*

UN Doc. S/19785, 15 April 1988, *Letter Dated 15 April 1988 from the Chargé d'Affaires* ad interim *of the Permanent Mission of the Islamic Republic of Iran to the United Nations Addressed to the Secretary-General*

UN Doc. S/19788, 17 April 1988, *Letter Dated 17 April 1988 from the Permanent Representative of Iraq to the United Nations Addressed to the Secretary-General*

UN Doc. S/19789, 17 April 1988, *Letter Dated 17 April 1988 from the Permanent Representative of Iraq to the United Nations Addressed to the Secretary-General*

UN Doc. S/19792, 18 April 1988, *Letter Dated 18 April 1988 from the Permanent Representative of Iraq to the United Nations Addressed to the Secretary-General*

UN Doc. S/19801, 19 April 1988, *Letter Dated 19 April 1988 from the Acting Permanent Representative of the Islamic Republic of Iran to the United Nations Addressed to the Secretary-General*

UN Doc. S/19805, 20 April 1988, *Letter Dated 20 April 1988 from the Permanent Representative of Iraq to the United Nations Addressed to the Secretary-General*

UN Doc. S/19810, 20 April 1988, *Letter Dated 20 April 1988 from the Permanent Representative of Iraq to the United Nations Addressed to the Secretary-General*

UN Doc. S/19817, 21 April 1988, *Letter Dated 21 April 1988 from the Permanent Representative of Iraq to the United Nations Addressed to the Secretary-General*

UN Doc. S/19818, 21 April 1988, *Letter Dated 21 April 1988 from the Permanent Representative of Iraq to the United Nations Addressed to the Secretary-General*

UN Doc. S/19821, 22 April 1988, *Letter Dated 21 April 1988 from the Chargé d'Affaires* ad interim *of the Permanent Mission of the Islamic Republic of Iran to the United Nations Addressed to the Secretary-General*

UN Doc. S/19825, 25 April 1988, *Letter Dated 22 April 1988 from the Acting Permanent Representative of the Islamic Republic of Iran to the United Nations Addressed to the Secretary-General*

UN Doc. S/19827, 25 April 1988, *Letter Dated 25 April 1988 from the Permanent Representative of Iraq to the United Nations Addressed to the Secretary-General*

UN Doc. S/19837, 26 April 1988, *Letter Dated 26 April 1988 from the Permanent Representative of Iraq to the United Nations Addressed to the Secretary-General*

UN Doc. S/19842, 27 April 1988, *Letter Dated 26 April 1988 from the Acting Permanent Representative of the Islamic Republic of Iran to the United Nations Addressed to the Secretary-General*

UN Doc. S/19847, 28 April 1988, *Letter Dated 28 April 1988 from the Permanent Representative of Iraq to the United Nations Addressed to the Secretary-General*

UN Doc. S/19848, 28 April 1988, *Letter Dated 28 April 1988 from the Acting Permanent Representative of the Islamic Republic of Iran to the United Nations Addressed to the Secretary-General*

UN Doc. S/19852, 1 May 1988, *Letter Dated 30 April 1988 from the Permanent Representative of Iraq to the United Nations Addressed to the Secretary-General*

UN Doc. S/19866, 5 May 1988, *Letter Dated 5 May 1988 from the Permanent Representative of Iraq to the United Nations Addressed to the Secretary-General*

UN Doc. S/19876, 11 May 1988, *Letter Dated 11 May 1988 from the Permanent Representative of Iraq to the United Nations Addressed to the Secretary-General*

UN Doc. S/19884, 16 May 1988, *Letter Dated 16 May 1988 from the Acting Permanent Representative of the Islamic Republic of Iran to the United Nations Addressed to the Secretary-General*

UN Doc. S/19888, 16 May 1988, *Letter Dated 15 May 1988 from the Permanent Representative of Iraq to the United Nations Addressed to the Secretary-General*

UN Doc. S/19893, 19 May 1988, *Letter Dated 19 May 1988 from the Chargé d'Affaires* ad interim *of the Permanent Mission of the Islamic Republic of Iran to the United Nations Addressed to the Secretary-General*

UN Doc. S/19897, 24 May 1988, *Letter Dated 23 May 1988 from the Acting Permanent Representative of the Islamic Republic of Iran to the United Nations Addressed to the Secretary-General*

UN Doc. S/19898, 25 May 1988, *Letter Dated 24 May 1988 from the Permanent Representative of Iraq to the United Nations Addressed to the Secretary-General*

UN Doc. S/19907, 26 May 1988, *Letter Dated 26 May 1988 from the Permanent Representative of Iraq to the United Nations Addressed to the Secretary-General*

UN Doc. S/19914, 31 May 1988, *Letter Dated 31 May 1988 from the Acting Permanent Representative of the Islamic Republic of Iran to the United Nations Addressed to the Secretary-General*

UN Doc. S/19924, 3 June 1988, *Letter Dated 3 June 1988 from the Permanent Representative of Iraq to the United Nations Addressed to the Secretary-General*

UN Doc. S/19929, 6 June 1988, *Letter Dated 6 June 1988 from the Permanent Representative of Iraq to the United Nations Addressed to the Secretary-General*

UN Doc. S/19934, 13 June 1988, *Letter Dated 13 June 1988 from the Permanent Representative of Iraq to the United Nations Addressed to the Secretary-General*

UN Doc. S/19991, 6 July 1988, *Letter Dated 6 July 1988 from the Acting Permanent Representative of the Islamic Republic of Iran to the United Nations Addressed to the Secretary-General*

UN Doc. S/20027, 19 July 1988, *Letter Dated 19 July 1988 from the Acting Permanent Representative of the Islamic Republic of Iran to the United Nations Addressed to the Secretary-General*

UN Doc. S/20035, 19 July 1988, *Letter Dated 19 July 1988 from the Acting Permanent Representative of the Islamic Republic of Iran to the United Nations Addressed to the Secretary-General*

UN Doc. S/20059, 25 July 1988, *Letter Dated 25 July 1988 from the Acting Permanent Representative of the Islamic Republic of Iran to the United Nations Addressed to the Secretary-General*

UN Doc. S/20065, 9 August 1988, *Letter Dated 27 July 1988 from the Acting Permanent Representative of the Islamic Republic of Iran to the United Nations Addressed to the Secretary-General*

BIBLIOGRAPHY

Books

Ambach, Philipp, Bostedt, Frédéric, Dawson, Grant and Kostas, Steve (eds.), *The Protection of Non-combatants during Armed Conflict and Safeguarding the Rights of Victims in Post-Conflict Society* (Leiden: Martinus Nijhof, 2015)

Anzilotti, Dionisio, *Cours de droit international* (Paris: Librairie du Recueil Sirey, 1929, 3rd ed.)

Teoria generale della responsabilità dello Stato nel diritto internazionale (Firenze: Lumachi, 1902)

Arrian, *The Anabasis of Alexander* (tr. Chinnock, Edward J.) (London: Hodder & Stoughton, 1884)

Ben-Naftali, Orna (ed.), *International Humanitarian Law and International Human Rights Law* (Oxford: Oxford University Press, 2011)

Best, Geoffrey, *Humanity in Warfare: The Modern History of the International Law of Armed Conflicts* (London: Weidenfeld & Nicholson, 1980)

Law and War since 1945 (Oxford: Oxford University Press, 1994)

Boothby, William, *Weapons and the Law of Armed Conflict* (Oxford: Oxford University Press, 2016)

Bothe, Michael, *National Implementation of International Humanitarian Law* (Dordrecht: Martinus Nijhoff, 1990)

Bothe, Michael, Partsch, Karl Josef and Solf, Waldemar A. (eds.), *New Rules for Victims of Armed Conflict: Commentary on the Two 1977 Protocols Additional to the Geneva Conventions of 1949* (Leiden: Martinus Nijhoff, 2013)

Bouchet-Saulnier, Françoise, *The Practical Guide to Humanitarian Law* (Lanham, MD: Rowman & Littlefield, 2014)

Brown, Frederic J., *Chemical Warfare: A Study in Restraints* (Princeton, NJ: Princeton University Press, 1968)

Brownlie, Ian, *System of the Law of Nations: State Responsibility* (Oxford: Clarendon Press, 1983), Part I

Cannizzaro, Enzo (ed.), *The Law of Treaties beyond the Vienna Convention* (Oxford: Oxford University Press, 2001)

Cassese, Antonio (ed.), *The New Humanitarian Law of Armed Conflict* (Napoli: Editoriale Scientifica, 1979)

Castrén, Erik, *The Present Law of War and Neutrality* (Helsinki: Annales Academiae Scientiarum Fennicae, 1954)

Clapham, Andrew, *War* (Oxford: Oxford University Press, 2021)

Clapham, Andrew and Gaeta, Paola (eds.), *The Oxford Handbook of International Law and Armed Conflict* (Oxford: Oxford University Press, 2014)

Clapham, Andrew, Gaeta, Paola and Sassòli, Marco (eds.), *The 1949 Geneva Conventions: A Commentary* (Oxford: Oxford University Press, 2015)

Colbert, Evelyn Speyer, *Retaliation in International Law* (New York: King's Crown Press, 1948)

Conforti, Benedetto, *Diritto Internazionale* (Napoli: Editoriale Scientifica, 2006, 7th ed.)

Cordesman, Anthony H. and Wagner, Abraham R., *The Lessons of Modern War. Volume II: The Iran–Iraq War* (Boulder, CO: Westview Press, 1990)

Corney, Jeoffrey S., Hansen, Victor, Jackson, Richard B., Jenks, Chris, Talbot Jense, Eric and Schoettler, James A. Jr., *The Law of Armed Conflict: An Operational Approach* (New York: Wolters Kluwer, 2012)

Corten, Olivier and Klein, Pierre (eds.), *The Vienna Conventions on the Law of Treaties: A Commentary* (Oxford: Oxford University Press, 2011)

Crawford, James, *The International Law Commission's Articles on State Responsibility: Introduction, Text and Commentaries* (Cambridge: Cambridge University Press, 2002)

State Responsibility: The General Part (Cambridge: Cambridge University Press, 2013)

Crawford, James, Pellet, Alain and Olleson, Simon (eds.), *The Law of International Responsibility* (Oxford: Oxford University Press, 2010)

Curtius Rufus, Quintus, *History of Alexander* (tr. Rolfe, John C.), 2 vols. (Cambridge, MA: Harvard University Press, 1946)

Darcy, Shane, *Collective Responsibility and Accountability under International Law* (Leiden: Transnational Publishers, 2007)

Judges, Law and War (Cambridge: Cambridge University Press, 2014)

David, Eric, *Principes de droit des Conflits armés* (Bruxelles: Bruylant, 2012)

De Guttry, Andrea, *Le rappresaglie non comportanti la coercizione militare nel diritto internazionale* (Milano: Giuffrè, 1985)

De Guttry, Andrea and Ronzitti, Natalino (eds.), *The Iran–Iraq War (1980–1988) and the Law of Naval Warfare* (Cambridge: Grotius Publications, 1993)

Decaux, Emmanuel, *La Reciprocité en droit international* (Paris: Librerie Générale de Droit et de Jurisprudence, 1980)

Dekker, Ige F. and Post, Harry H. G. (eds.), *The Gulf War of 1980–1988: The Iran–Iraq War in International Legal Perspective* (Dordrecht: Martinus Nijhoff, 1992)

Delbrück, Jost, *The Future of International Law Enforcement: New Scenarios – New Law?* (Berlin: Duncker & Humblot, 1993)

Des Gouttes, Paul, *Commentaire de la Convention de Genève du 27 Juillet 1929* (Geneva: ICRC, 1930)

Detter, Ingrid, *The Law of War* (Farnham: Ashgate, 2013)

Dinstein, Yoram, *War, Aggression and Self-Defence* (Cambridge: Cambridge University Press, 2005, 4th ed.)

Diodorus Siculus, *Library of History* (tr. Bradford Welles, Charles), 12 vols. (Cambridge, MA: Harvard University Press, 1963)

Distefano, Giovanni, Gaggioli, Gloria and Hêche, Aymeric (eds.), *La Convention de Vienne de 1978 sur la succession d'États en matière de Traités. Commentaire article par article et études thématiques* (Bruxelles: Bruylant, 2016)

Doswald-Beck, Louise, *Human Rights in Times of Conflict and Terrorism* (Oxford: Oxford University Press, 2011)

Fauchille, Paul, *Traité de droit international public. Vol. II: Guerre et neutralité* (Paris: Librairie Arthur Rousseau, 1921)

Fisk, Robert, *Cronache Mediorientali* (Milano: Saggiatore, 2009; it. tr. from *The Great War for Civilization*, Fourth Estate, 2005)

Fleck, Dieter (ed.), *The Handbook of International Humanitarian Law* (Oxford: Oxford University Press, 2013, 3rd ed.)

Fox, Hazel and Meyer, Michael A. (eds.), *Effecting Compliance. Vol. II: Armed Conflict and the New Law* (London: The British Institute of International and Comparative Law, 1993)

Gill, Terry D. and Fleck, Dieter (eds.), *The Handbook of International Law of Military Operations* (Oxford: Oxford University Press, 2015)

Goellner, Aladar, *Pré-caducité, caducité et desuetude en matière de droit international public* (Paris: Rousseau, 1939)

Goldsmith, Jack L. and Posner, Eric A., *The Limits of International Law* (Oxford: Oxford University Press, 2005)

Gomaa, Mohammed, *Suspension or Termination of Treaties for Grounds of Breach* (Leiden: Brill, 1966)

Greenspan, Morris, *The Modern Law of Land Warfare* (Berkeley: University of California Press, 1959)

Greenwood, Christopher, *Essays on War in International Law* (London: Cameron May, 2006)

Greenwood Onuf, Nicholas, *Reprisals: Rituals, Rules, Rationales* (Princeton, NJ: Research Monographs of the Center of International Studies of the Woodrow Wilson School of Public and International Affairs of Princeton University, 1974)

Henckaerts, Jean-Marie and Doswald-Beck, Louise, *Customary International Humanitarian Law*, 2 vols. (Cambridge: Cambridge University Press, 2005)

ICRC, *Commentary on the First Geneva Convention* (Cambridge: Cambridge University Press, 2016, 2nd ed.)

Commentary on the Second Geneva Convention (Cambridge: Cambridge University Press, 2017, 2nd ed.)

Commentary on the Third Geneva Convention (Cambridge: Cambridge University Press, 2021, 2nd ed.)

Jo, Hyeran, *Compliant Rebels: Rebel Groups and International Law in World Politics* (New York: Cambridge University Press, 2015)

Johnson, Rob, *The Iran–Iraq War* (London: Palgrave Macmillan, 2011)

Justinian, *Institutes* (tr. J. B. Moyle) (Oxford: Clarendon Press, 1913)

Kahn, Herman, *On Escalation: Metaphors and Scenarios* (Baltimore: Praeger, 1965)

Kalshoven, Frits, *Belligerent Reprisals* (Leiden: Sijthoff, 1971; re-published Boston: Martinus Nijhoff, 2005)

Kalshoven, Frits and Sandoz, Yves (eds.), *Implementation of International Humanitarian Law: Research Papers by Participants in the 1986 Session of the Centre for Studies and Research in International Law and International Relations of the Hague Academy of International Law* (Dordrecht: Martinus Nijhoff, 1989)

Kalshoven, Frits and Zegveld, Liesbeth, *Constraints on the Waging of War: An Introduction to International Humanitarian Law* (Cambridge: Cambridge University Press, 2020, 4th ed.)

Kelsen, Hans, *Principles of International Law* (New York: Rinehart and Co., 1952)

Kolb, Robert, *Advanced Introduction to International Humanitarian Law* (Cheltenham: Edward Elgar, 2014)

Kolb, Robert, Gaggioli, Gloria and Kilibarda, Pavle (eds.), *Research Handbook on Human Rights and Humanitarian Law: Further Reflections and Perspectives* (Cheltenham: Edward Elgar, 2022, 2nd ed.)

Lauterpacht, Hersch, *Oppenheim's International Law* (London: Longmans, 1952, 7th ed.)

Le Fur, Louis, *Des Représailles en temps de guerre* (Paris: Recueil Sirey, 1919)

Matheson, Michael J. and Momtaz, Djamchid, *Les règles et institutions du droit international humanitaire à l'épreuve des conflits armés récents / Rules and Institutions of International Humanitarian Law Put to the Test of Recent Armed Conflicts* (Leiden: Martinus Nijhoff, 2010)

McDougal, Myres S. and Feliciano, Florentino P., *Law and Minimum World Public Order* (New Haven, CT: Yale University Press, 1961)

Meron, Theodor, *War Crimes Law Comes of Age* (Oxford: Clarendon Press, 1998)

Meyrovitz, Henri, *Le principe de l'égalité des belligérants devant le droit de la guerre* (Paris: Pedone, 1970)

Morrow, James D., *Order within Anarchy: The Laws of War as an International Institution* (Cambridge: Cambridge University Press, 2014)

Osiel, Mark, *The End of Reciprocity: Terror, Torture, and the Law of War* (Cambridge: Cambridge University Press, 2009)

Peeler, Bryan, *The Persistence of Reciprocity in International Humanitarian Law* (Cambridge: Cambridge University Press, 2019)

Pictet, Jean (ed.), *Commentary to the I Geneva Convention for the Amelioration of the Condition of the Wounded and Sick in Armed Forces in the Field* (Geneva: ICRC, 1952)

(ed.), *Commentary to the II Geneva Convention for the Amelioration of the Condition of the Wounded, Sick and Shipwrecked Members of Armed Forces at Sea* (Geneva: ICRC, 1960)

(ed.), *Commentary to the III Geneva Convention Relative to the Treatment of Prisoners of War* (Geneva: ICRC, 1960)

(ed.), *Commentary to the IV Geneva Convention Relative to the Protection of Civilian Persons in Time of War* (Geneva: ICRC, 1958)

Plutarch, *Plutarch's Lives* (tr. Perrin, Bernadotte), 11 vols. (Cambridge, MA: Harvard University Press, 1958), vol. VII, *Life of Alexander*

Provost, René, *International Human Rights and Humanitarian Law* (Cambridge: Cambridge University Press, 2002)

Quintin, Anne, *The Nature of International Humanitarian Law. A Permissive or Restrictive Regime?* (Cheltenham: Edward Elgar, 2020)

Rosenne, Shabtai (ed.), *The International Law Commission's Draft Articles on State Responsibility, Part I, Articles 1–35* (Dordrecht: Martinus Nijhoff, 1991)

The Law of Treaties: A Guide to the Legislative History of the Vienna Convention (Leiden: Sijthoff, 1970)

Salmon, Jean, *Dictionnaire de droit international public* (Bruxelles: Bruylant, 2001)

Samwer, Charles and Hopf, Jules (eds.), *Nouveau Recueil Général de Traités* (Gottingen: Dieterich, 1879)

Sandoz, Yves, Swinarski, Christophe and Zimmermann, Bruno (eds.), *Commentary on the Additional Protocols of 8 June 1977 to the Geneva Conventions of 12 August 1949* (Geneva: ICRC/Martinus Nijhoff, 1987)

Schelling, Thomas C., *Arms and Influence* (New Haven, CT: Yale University Press, 1966)

Schindler, Dietrich and Toman, Jiri, *The Laws of Armed Conflict* (Dordrecht: Martinus Nijhoff, 1988)

Schwarzenberger, Georg, *International Law as Applied by International Courts and Tribunals* (London: Steven and Sons, 1968)

Sereni, Angelo Piero, *Diritto internazionale: relazioni internazionali* (Milano: Giuffrè, 1962), vol. III

Sicilianos, Linos-Alexander, *Les réactions décentralisées à l'illicite: des contre-mesures à la légitime défense* (Librairie générale de droit et de jurisprudence, 1990)

Singh, Nagendra and MacWhinney, Edward, *Nuclear Weapons and Contemporary International Law* (Dordrecht: Martinus Nijhoff, 1989)

Sinha, Bhek Pati, *Unilateral Denunciation of Treaty because of Prior Violations of Obligations by Other Party* (The Hague: Martinus Nijhoff, 1966)

Sivakumaran, Sandesh, *The Law of Non-international Armed Conflict* (Oxford: Oxford University Press, 2012)

Sophocles, *King Oedipus* (tr. Yeats, William B.) (London: Macmillan, 1928)

Spaight, James Molony, *Air Power and War Rights* (London: Longmans, 1947)

Stone, Julius, *Legal Controls of International Conflict: A Treatise on the Dynamics of Disputes- and War-Law* (New York: Rinehart, 1959)

Villiger, Mark E., *Commentary on the 1969 Vienna Convention on the Law of Treaties* (Leiden: Martinus Nijhoff, 2009)

Customary International Law and Treaties: A Manual on the Theory and Practice of the Interrelation of Sources (The Hague: Kluwer, 1997)

Vohrah, Lal Chand, Pocar, Fausto, Featherstone, Yvonne, Fourmy, Olivier, Graham, Christine, Hocking, John and Robson, Nicholas (eds.), *Man's Inhumanity to Man. Essays on International Law in Honour of Antonio Cassese* (The Hague: Kluwer, 2003)

Walzer, Michael, *Just and Unjust Wars: A Moral Argument with Historical Illustrations* (New York: Basic Books, 1977)

Wehberg, Hans (ed.), *Institut de Droit International. Tableau Général des Résolutions (1873–1956)* (Basel: Editions Juridiques et Sociologiques, 1957)

Wilmshurst, Elizabeth and Breau, Susan (eds.), *Perspectives on the ICRC Study on Customary International Humanitarian Law* (Cambridge: Cambridge University Press, 2007)

Zegveld, Liesbeth, *Accountability of Armed Opposition Groups in International Law* (Cambridge: Cambridge University Press, 2002)

Zoller, Elizabeth, *Peacetime Unilateral Remedies: An Analysis of Countermeasures* (New York: Transnational Publishers, 1984)

Articles, Chapters and Contributions

Abi-Saab, Georges, 'The 1977 Additional Protocols and General International Law: Some Preliminary Reflections', in Delissen, Astrid J. M. and Tanja, Gerand J. (eds.), *Humanitarian Law of Armed Conflict: Challenges Ahead* (Dordrecht: Martinus Nijhoff, 1991), pp. 115–26

Ago, Roberto, 'Le délit international' (1939) 68 *Recueil des cours de l'Académie de droit international de La Haye, 1939-II*, pp. 419–554

Albrecht, Arthur R., 'War Reprisals in the War Crimes Trials and in the Geneva Conventions' (1953) 47 AJIL, pp. 590–614

Aldrich, George H., 'Compliance with International Humanitarian Law' (1991) 31 IRRC, pp. 294–306

'Improving Compliance with the Laws Applicable in Armed Conflict: A Work in Progress', in Vohrah, Lal Chand, Pocar, Fausto, Featherstone, Yvonne, Fourmy, Olivier, Graham, Christine, Hocking, John and Robson, Nicholas (eds.), *Man's Inhumanity to Man: Essays on International Law in Honour of Antonio Cassese* (The Hague: Kluwer, 2003), pp. 1–10

'New Life for the Laws of War' (1981) 75 AJIL, pp. 764–83

'Pour le respect du droit international humanitaire' (1991) 282 IRRC, pp. 312–25

'Prospects for United States Ratification of Additional Protocol I to the 1949 Geneva Conventions' (1991) 85 AJIL, pp. 1–20

Ali, Javed, 'Chemical Weapons and the Iran–Iraq War: A Case Study in Noncompliance' (2001) 8 *The Nonproliferation Review*, pp. 43–58

Alland, Denis, 'The Definition of Countermeasures', in Crawford, James, Pellet, Alain and Olleson, Simon (eds.), *The Law of International Responsibility* (Oxford: Oxford University Press, 2010), pp. 1127–36

Almond, Harry H., 'Reprisals: The Global Community Is Not Yet Ready to Abandon Them' (1980) 74 *Proceedings of the American Society of International Law*, pp. 196–201

Barile, Giuseppe, 'The Protection of Human Rights in Article 60, Paragraph 5 of the Vienna Convention on the Law of Treaties', in *International Law at the Time of Its Codification: Essays in Honour of Roberto Ago* (Milan: Giuffrè, 1987), vol. II, pp. 3–14

Barsalou, Olivier, 'The History of Reprisals Up to 1945: Some Lessons Learned and Unlearned for Contemporary International Law' (2010) 49 *Military Law and the Law of War Review*, pp. 335–71

Baxter, Richard R., 'Forces for Compliance with the Law of War' (1964) 58 *Proceedings of the American Society of International Law*, pp. 82–88

Baxter, Richard R. and Buergenthal, Thomas, 'Legal Aspects of the Geneva Protocol of 1925' (1970) 64 AJIL, pp. 853–79

Benvenisti, Eyal and Cohen, Amichai, 'War Is Governance: Explaining the Logic of the Laws of War from a Principal-Agent Perspective' (2014) 112 *Michigan Law Review*, pp. 1363–416

Bierzanek, Remigiusz, 'Reprisals in Armed Conflict' (1987–88) 14 *Syracuse Journal of International and Comparative Law*, pp. 829–46

'Reprisals as a Means of Enforcing the Laws of Warfare: The Old and the New Law', in Cassese, Antonio (ed.), *The New Humanitarian Law of Armed Conflict* (Napoli: Editoriale Scientifica, 1979), vol. I, pp. 232–57

Bílková, Veronika, 'Belligerent Reprisals in Non-international Armed Conflicts', (2014) 63 ICLQ, pp. 31–65

Blum, Yehuda Zvi, 'The Beirut Raid and the International Double Standard: A Reply to Richard A. Falk' (1970) 89 AJIL, pp. 73–105

Boisson de Chazournes, Laurence, La Rosa, Anne-Marie and Mbengue, Makane Moise, 'Commentary to Article 18', in Corten, Olivier and Klein, Pierre (eds.), *The Vienna Conventions on the Law of Treaties: A Commentary* (Oxford: Oxford University Press, 2011), vol. I, pp. 369–403

Bower, Graham, 'The Laws of War: Prisoners of War and Reprisals' (1916) 1 *Transactions of the Grotius Society*, pp. 28 ff.

Bowett, Derek, 'Reprisals Involving Recourse to Armed Force' (1972) 66 AJIL, pp. 1–36

Bristol III, Matt C. C., 'The Laws of War and Belligerent Reprisals against Enemy Civilian Populations' (1979) 21 *Air Force Law Review*, pp. 397–418

Brophy-Baermann, Bryan and Conybeare, John A. C., 'Retaliating against Terrorism' (1994) 38 *American Journal of Political Science*, pp. 196–210

Bunn, George, 'Banning Poison and Germ Warfare: Should the United States Agree?' (1969) 69 *Wisconsin Law Review*, pp. 375–420

Capotorti, Francesco, 'L'extinction et la suspension des traités' (1971) 248 *Collected Courses of the Hague Academy of International Law*, pp. 9–343

Carus, Seth, 'Chemical Weapons in the Middle-East', in Washington Institute for Near Eastern Policy, *Policy Focus – Research Memorandum No. 9* (December 1988)

Casey-Maslen, Stuart, 'The Use of Nuclear Weapons as a Reprisal under International Humanitarian Law', in Casey-Maslen, Stuart, Nystuen, Gro and Golden Bersagel, Annie (eds.), *Nuclear Weapons under International Law* (Cambridge: Cambridge University Press, 2014), pp. 171–90

Cassese, Antonio, 'The Status of Rebels under the 1977 Geneva Protocol on Non-international Armed Conflicts' (1981) 30 ICLQ, pp. 416–39

Clapham, Andrew, 'The Complex Relationship between the Geneva Conventions and International Human Rights Law', in Clapham, Andrew, Gaeta, Paola and Sassòli, Marco (eds.), *The 1949 Geneva Conventions: A Commentary* (Oxford: Oxford University Press, 2015), pp. 701–35

Coulibaly, Hamidou, 'Le rôle des Puissances protectrices au regard du droit diplomatique, du droit de Genève et du droit de La Haye', in Kalshoven, Frits and Sandoz, Yves (eds.), *Implementation of International Humanitarian Law* (Dordrecht: Martinus Nijhoff, 1989), pp. 69–78

Couvreur, Philippe and Berdud, Carlos Espaliú, 'Commentary to Article 72', in Corten, Olivier and Klein, Pierre (eds.), *The Vienna Conventions on the Law of Treaties: A Commentary* (Oxford: Oxford University Press, 2011), vol. II, pp. 1627–40

Crawford, James, 'The Relationship between Sanctions and Countermeasures', in Gowlland-Debbas, Vera (ed.), *United Nations Sanctions and International Law* (The Hague: Kluwer, 2001), pp. 57–68

Darcy, Shane, 'The Evolution of the Law of Belligerent Reprisals' (2003) 175 *Military Law Review*, pp. 184–251

'Prosecuting the War Crime of Collective Punishment: Is It Time to Amend the Rome Statute?' (2010) 8 *Journal of International Criminal Justice*, pp. 29–51

'Reciprocity and Reprisals', in Liivoja, Rain and McCormack, Tim (eds.), *Routledge Handbook on the Law of Armed Conflict* (London: Routledge, 2016), pp. 492–505

'What Future for the Law of Belligerent Reprisals?' (2002) 5 *Yearbook of International Humanitarian Law*, pp. 107–30

David, Eric, 'La Guerre du Golfe et le droit international' (1987) 23 *Revue Belge de Droit International*, pp. 153–83

Davis, George B., 'Doctor Francis Lieber's Instructions' (1907) 1 AJIL, pp. 13–25

De Hemptinne, Jérôme, 'Prohibition of Reprisals', in Clapham, Andrew, Gaeta, Paola, and Sassòli, Marco (eds.), *The 1949 Geneva Conventions: A Commentary* (Oxford: Oxford University Press, 2015), pp. 575–96

De Preux, Jean, 'The Geneva Conventions and Reciprocity' (1985) 244 IRRC, pp. 25–29

Dominicé, Christian, 'Observations sur les droits de l'État victime d'un fait internationalement illicite', in *Droit international* (Paris: Pedone, 1982), vol. II, pp. 1–70

Doswald-Beck, Louise, 'The Right to Life in Armed Conflict: Does International Humanitarian Law Provide All the Answers?' (2006) 88 IRRC, pp. 881–904

Downey Jr., William G., 'The Law of War and Military Necessity' (1953) 47 AJIL, pp. 251–62

Draper, Gerald I. A. D., 'The Enforcement and Implementation of the Geneva Conventions of 1949 and of the Two Additional Protocols of 1978' (1979) 164 *Recueil des cours de l'Académie de droit international de La Haye, 1979-III*, pp. 48–96

'Implementation of International Law in Armed Conflict' (1972) 48 *International Affairs*, pp. 46–59

'Rules Governing the Conduct of Hostilities – The Laws of War and Their Enforcement' (1980) 62 *International Legal Studies Series of the US Naval War College*, pp. 247–62

Dunbar, N. H. C., 'Military Necessity in War Crimes Trials' (1952) 29 BYIL, pp. 442–52

Dupuy, Pierre-Marie, 'Observations sur la pratique récente des "sanctions" de l'illicite' (1983) 87 RGDIP, pp. 505–48

Falk, Richard A., 'The Beirut Raid and the International Law of Retaliation' (1969) 63 AJIL, pp. 415–43

Ferretti, Matthew J., 'The Iran–Iraq War: United Nations Resolution of Armed Conflict' (1990) 35 *Villanova Law Review*, pp. 197–252

Fitzmaurice, Gerald, 'Arbitration between Portugal and Germany Concerning War Damage to Portuguese Property Committed Prior to Portugal's Entry into War' (1932) 13 BYIL, pp. 156–61

Franck, Thomas F., 'On Proportionality of Countermeasures in International Law' (2008) 102 AJIL, pp. 715–67

Gasser, Hans-Peter, 'An Appeal for the Ratification by the US' (1987) 81 AJIL, pp. 912–25

Goldblat, Jozef, 'The Biological Weapons Convention: An Overview' (1997) 37 IRRC, pp. 251–65

Greenwood, Christopher, 'Belligerent Reprisals in the Jurisprudence of the International Criminal Tribunal for the Former Yugoslavia', in Fischer, Horst, Kress, Clauss and Rölf Luder, Sascha (eds.), *International and National Prosecution of Crimes under International Law: Current Developments* (Berlin: Berliner Wissenschaftsverlag, 2001), pp. 539–57

'International Law and the Conduct of Military Operations – Stocktaking at the Start of the Millennium' (2000) 75 *International Legal Studies Series of the US Naval War College*, pp. 179–201

'The Twilight of the Law of Belligerent Reprisals' (1989) 20 NYIL, pp. 35–69

Greig, Donald W., 'Reciprocity, Proportionality, and the Law of Treaties' (1994) 34 *Vanderbilt Journal of International Law*, pp. 295–403

Hakimi, Monica, 'Unfriendly Unilateralism' (2014) 55 *Harvard International Law Journal*, pp. 105–50

Hampson, Françoise J., 'Belligerent Reprisals and the 1977 Protocols to the Geneva Conventions of 1949' (1988) 37 ICLQ, pp. 818–43

'The Enforcement of the International Law of Armed Conflicts' (1993–1994) 4 *King's College Law Journal*, pp. 1–11

Hanke, Heinz Marcus, 'The 1923 Hague Rules of Air Warfare: A Contribution to the Development of International Law Protecting Civilians from Air Attack' (1993) 33 IRRC, pp. 12–44

Hegelsom, Gert-Jan, 'Comments', in Dekker, Ige F. and Post, Harry H. G. (eds.), *The Gulf War of 1980–1988: The Iran–Iraq War in International Legal Perspective* (Dordrecht: Martinus Nijhoff, 1992), pp. 123–28

Heinsch, Robert, 'Judicial "Law-Making" in the Jurisprudence of the ICTY and ICTR in Relation to Protecting Civilians from Mass Violence: How Can Judge-Made Law Be Brought into Coherence with the Doctrine of the Formal Sources of International Law?', in Ambach, Philipp, Bostedt, Frédéric, Dawson, Grant and Kostas, Steve (eds.), *The Protection of Non-combatants during Armed Conflict and Safeguarding the Rights of Victims in Post-Conflict Society* (Leiden: Martinus Nijhof, 2015), pp. 297–331

Henckaerts, Jean-Marie, 'Study on Customary International Humanitarian Law: A Contribution to the Understanding and Respect for the Rule of Law in Armed Conflict' (2006) 82 *International Legal Studies Series of the US Naval War College*, pp. 37–79

Henderson, Christian and Lubell, Noam, 'The Contemporary Legal Nature of UN Security Council Ceasefire Resolutions' (2013) 26 *Leiden Journal of International Law*, pp. 369–97

Hill, David J., 'The Janina – Corfu Affair' (1924) 18 AJIL, pp. 99–103

Hill-Cawthorne, Lawrence, 'Humanitarian Law, Human Rights Law and the Bifurcation of Armed Conflict' (2015) 64 ICLQ, pp. 293–325

Jones, Samuel Vincent, 'Has Conduct in Iraq Confirmed the Moral Inadequacy of International Humanitarian Law? Examining the Confluence between Contract Theory and the Scope of Civilian Immunity during Armed Conflict' (2006) 16 *Duke Journal of Comparative and International Law*, pp. 249–98

Kalshoven, Frits, 'Belligerent Reprisals Revisited' (1990) 21 NYIL, pp. 43–80

'Human Rights, the Law of Armed Conflict, and Reprisals' (1971) 121 IRRC, pp. 183–92

'The International Humanitarian Fact-Finding Commission: A Sleeping Beauty?' (2002) 4 *Humanitäres Völkerrecht – Informationschriften*, pp. 213–16

'Prohibitions or Restrictions on the Use of Methods and Means of Warfare', in Dekker, Ige F. and Post, Harry H. G. (eds.), *The Gulf War of 1980–1988. The Iran–Iraq War in International Legal Perspective* (Dordrecht: Martinus Nijhoff, 1992), pp. 97–114

'Two Recent Decisions of the Yugoslavia Tribunal', in Vohrah, Lal Chand (ed.), *Man's Inhumanity to Man: Essays on International Law in Honour of Antonio Cassese* (The Hague: Kluwer, 2003), pp. 481–509

'The Undertaking to Respect and Ensure Respect in All Circumstances: From Tiny Seed to Ripening Fruit' (1999) 2 *Yearbook of International Humanitarian Law*, pp. 3–61

Kelly, Joseph B., 'Gas Warfare in International Law' (1960) 9 *Military Law Review*, pp. 1–68

Kelly, Michael J., 'Time Warp to 1945: Resurrection of the Reprisal and Anticipatory Self-Defense Doctrines in International Law' (2003) 13 *Journal of Transnational Law and Policy*, pp. 1–38

Kelsen, Hans, 'Unrecht und Unrechtsfolge im Völkerrecht' (1932) 12 *Zeitschrift für öffentliches Recht*, pp. 567–608

Keohane, Robert O., 'Reciprocity in International Relations' (1986) 25 *International Organization*, pp. 1–27

Khaji, Ali, Fallahdoost, Shoaodin, Soroush, Mohammed Reza and Rahimi-Movaghar, Vafa, 'Civilian Casualties of Iraqi Ballistic Missile Attack to Tehran, Capital of Iran' (2012) 15 *Chinese Journal of Traumatology*, pp. 162–65

Klabbers, Jan, 'Off Limits? International Law and the Excessive Use of Force' (2006) 7 *Theoretical Inquiries in Law*, pp. 59–80

Kleffner, Jann K., 'The Unilateralization of International Humanitarian Law' (2022) 104 IRRC, pp. 2153–69

Kolb, Robert, 'The Relationship between International Humanitarian Law and Human Rights Law: A Brief History of the 1948 Universal Declaration of Human Rights and the 1949 Geneva Conventions' (1998) 80 IRRC, pp. 409–19

Krieger, Heike, 'A Conflict of Norm: The Relationship between Humanitarian Law and Human Rights Law in the ICRC Customary Law Study' (2006) 11 *Journal of Conflict and Security Law*, pp. 265–91

Kwakwa, Edward, 'Belligerent Reprisals in the Law of Armed Conflict' (1990–91) 27 *Stanford Journal of International Law*, pp. 49–81

La Brière, Yves de, 'Évolution de la doctrine et de la pratique en matière de représailles' (1929) 22 *Recueil des cours de l'Académie de droit international de La Haye, 1928-II*, pp. 241–94

Lagoni, Rainer, 'Comments: Methods or Means of Warfare, Belligerent Reprisals, and the Principle of Proportionality', in Dekker, Ige F. and Post, Harry H. G. (eds.), *The Gulf War of 1980–1988. The Iran–Iraq War in International Legal Perspective* (Dordrecht: Martinus Nijhoff, 1992), pp. 115–22

Lauterpacht, Hersch, 'The Law of Nations and the Punishment of War Crimes' (1944) 21 BYIL, pp. 58–95

'The Limits of the Operation of the Law of War' (1953) 30 BYIL, pp. 206–43

Lavoyer, Jean-Philippe, 'International Humanitarian Law: Should It Be Reaffirmed, Clarified or Developed?' (2006) 80 *International Legal Studies Series of the US Naval War College*, pp. 287–309

Leiser, Burton M., 'The Morality of Reprisals' (1975) 85 *Ethics*, pp. 159–63

Levie, Howard S., 'Maltreatment of Prisoners of War in Vietnam' (1968) 48 *Boston University Law Review*, pp. 323–59

MacCoby, Simon, 'Reprisals as a Measure of Redress Short of War' (1924) 2 *Cambridge Law Journal*, pp. 60–73

MacCoubrey, Hilaire, 'The Nature of the Modern Doctrine of Military Necessity' (1991) 30 *Military Law and the Law of War Review*, pp. 215–52

Maresca, Louis and Mitchell, Eleanor, 'The Human Costs and Legal Consequences of Nuclear Weapons under International Humanitarian Law' (2015) 97 IRRC, pp. 621–45

Max, Émilie, *Implementing International Humanitarian Law through Human Rights Mechanisms: Opportunity or Utopia?*, Geneva Academy Working Paper, October 2019

McKinnon, Fiona, 'Reprisals as a Method of Enforcing International Law' (1991) 4 *Leiden Journal of International Law*, pp. 221–48

McNair, Arnold D., 'The Legal Meaning of War and the Relation of War to Reprisals' (1925) 11 *Transactions of the Grotius Society*, pp. 29–51

McNaugher, Thomas L., 'Ballistic Missiles and Chemical Weapons: The Legacy of the Iran–Iraq War' (1990) 15 *International Security*, pp. 5–34

Meron, Theodor, 'The Geneva Conventions as Customary International Law' (1987) 81 AJIL, pp. 348–69

'The Humanization of Humanitarian Law' (2000) 94 AJIL, pp. 239–78

Mestre, Achille, Le Fur, Louis and Scelle, Georges, 'Les sanctions internationales: trois opinions de juristes' (1936) 4 *Centre d'études de politique étrangère*, pp. 9–53

Meyrovitz, Henri, 'Review of *Belligerent Reprisals* by Frits Kalshoven' (1972) 66 AJIL, pp. 648–51

Mitchell, Andrew D., 'Does One Illegality Merit Another?' (2001) 170 *Military Law Review*, pp. 155–77

Moir, Lindsay, 'The Historical Development of the Application of Humanitarian Law in Non-international Armed Conflicts to 1949' (1998) 47 ICLQ, pp. 337–61

Moore, John Norton, 'Ratification of the Geneva Protocol on Gas and Bacteriological Warfare: A Legal and Political Analysis' (1972) 58 *Virginia Law Review*, pp. 419–509

Morgenthau, Hans J., 'Théorie des Sanctions Internationales' (1935) 3 *Revue de droit international et de législation comparée*, pp. 3–32 and (1935) 4 *Revue de droit international et de législation comparée*, pp. 809–36

Morriss, David M., 'From War to Peace: A Study of Cease-Fire Agreements and the Evolving Role of the United Nations' (1996) 36 *Virginia Journal of International Law*, pp. 801–932

Morrow, James D., 'Atrocity, Policy and the Laws of War: What Does Political Science Have to Say to Law?', in Kontorovich, Eugene and Parisi, Francesco (eds.), *Economic Analysis of International Law* (Cheltenham: Edward Elgar, 2016), pp. 221–48

'The Institutional Features of the Prisoners of War Treaties' (2001) 55 *International Organization*, pp. 971–91

'When Do States Follow the Laws of War?' (2007) 101 *American Political Science Review*, pp. 559–72

Morrow, James D. and Jo, Hyeran, 'Compliance with the Laws of War: Dataset and Coding Rules' (2006) 23 *Conflict Management and Peace Science*, pp. 93–113

Moschtaghi, Ramin, 'The Relation between International Law, Islamic Law and Constitutional Law of the Islamic Republic of Iran – A Multilayer System of Conflict?' (2009) 13 *Max Planck Yearbook of United Nations Law*, pp. 375–420

Müller, Daniel, 'Commentary to Article 20', in Corten, Olivier and Klein, Pierre (eds.), *The Vienna Conventions on the Law of Treaties: A Commentary* (Oxford: Oxford University Press, 2011), vol. I, pp. 489–534

Murphy, Thomas J., 'Sanctions and Enforcement of the Humanitarian Law of the Four Conventions of 1949 and Geneva Protocol I of 1977' (1984) 103 *Military Law Review*, pp. 3–77

Nahlik, Stanislav E., 'Belligerent Reprisals as Seen in the Light of the Diplomatic Conference on Humanitarian Law, Geneva, 1974–1977' (1978) 42 *Law and Contemporary Problems*, pp. 36–66

Newton, Michael A., 'Reconsidering Reprisals' (2009–10) 20 *Duke Journal of Comparative and International Studies*, pp. 361–88

Noonan, Philip, 'Revolutions and Treaty Termination' (1984) 2 *Dickinson International Law Annual*, pp. 301–30

Obradovic, Konstantin, 'L'interdiction des répresailles dans le Protocole I: un acquis pour une meilleure protection des victimes de la guerre' (1997) 320 IRRC, pp. 562–65

'La protection de la population civile dans les conflits armés internationaux', in Cassese, Antonio (ed.), *The New Humanitarian Law of Armed Conflict* (Napoli: Editoriale Scientifica, 1979), vol. I, pp. 128–60

Palchetti, Paolo, 'Article 18 of the 1969 Vienna Convention: A Vague and Ineffective Obligation or a Useful Means for Strengthening Legal Cooperation?', in Cannizzaro, Enzo (ed.), *The Law of Treaties beyond the Vienna Convention* (Oxford: Oxford University Press, 2001), pp. 25–36

Paulus, Andreas, 'Whether Universal Values Can Prevail over Bilateralism and Reciprocity', in Cassese, Antonio (ed.), *Realising Utopia: The Future of International Law* (Oxford: Oxford University Press, 2012), pp. 89–104

Pejic, Jelena, 'Strengthening Compliance with IHL: The ICRC-Swiss Initiative' (2016) 98 IRRC, pp. 315–30

Pezzino, Paolo, 'Crimini fascisti e crimini tedeschi nell'Italia occupata: la difficile strada della giustizia di transizione (1945–2015)', Presentation at Fondazione per la Formazione Forense dell'Ordine degli Avvocati di Firenze, 10 April 2017 (available at www.fondazioneforensefirenze.it/eventi_view.aspx?cat=7&id=1515)

Pictet, Jean, 'The Principles of International Humanitarian Law' (1966) 6 IRRC, pp. 455–69

Pisillo Mazzeschi, Riccardo, 'Termination and Suspension of Treaties for Grounds of Breach', in Simma, Bruno and Spinedi, Maria (eds.), *United Nations Codification of State Responsibility* (New York: Oceana, 1983), pp. 57–94

Pocar, Fausto, 'Some Remarks on the Continuity of Human Rights and International Humanitarian Law Treaties', in Cannizzaro, Enzo (ed.), *The Law of Treaties Beyond the Vienna Convention* (Oxford: Oxford University Press, 2001), pp. 279–93

Politis, Nikolaos, 'Les représailles entre États membres de la Société des Nations' (1924) 31 RGDIP, pp. 5–16

Provost, René, 'Asymmetrical Reciprocity and Compliance with the Laws of War', in Perrin, Benjamin (ed.), *Modern Warfare: Armed Groups, Private Militaries, Humanitarian Organization, and the Law* (Vancouver: University of British Columbia Press, 2012), pp. 17–41

'The Move to Substantive Equality in International Humanitarian Law: A Rejoinder to Marco Sassòli and Yuval Shany' (2011) 93 IRRC, pp. 437–42

'Reciprocity in Human Rights and Humanitarian Law' (1994) 65 BYIL, pp. 383–454

Reisman, Michael W., 'Assessing Claims to Revise the Laws of War' (2003) 97 AJIL, pp. 82–90

Richemond-Barak, Daphné, 'Non-state Actors in Armed Conflicts: Issues of Distinction and Reciprocity', in Banks, William C. (ed.), *New Battlefields / Old Laws: Critical Debates on Asymmetric Warfare* (New York: Columbia University Press, 2011), pp. 106–29

Roberts, Guy B., 'The New Rules for Waging War: The Case against Ratification of Additional Protocol I' (1985) 26 *Vanderbilt Journal of International Law*, pp. 109–29

Roggof, Martin A., 'International Legal Obligations of Signatories to an Unratified Treaty' (1980) 32 *Maine Law Review*, pp. 266–90

Rousseau, Charles, 'Chronique des faits internationaux' (1980) 84 RGDIP, pp. 351–423

'Chronique des faits internationaux' (1990) 94 RGDIP, pp. 473–518, 1035–1100

Ruffert, Matthias, 'Reprisals', in *Max Planck Encyclopaedia of Public International Law* (available at https://opil.ouplaw.com/display/10.1093/law:epil/9780199231690/law-9780199231690-e1771?prd=EPIL)

Sandoz, Yves, 'L'appel du Comité International de la Croix Rouge dans le cadre du conflit entre l'Irak et l'Iran' (1983) 29 *Annuaire français de droit international*, pp. 161–73

Sassòli, Marco, 'Taking Armed Groups Seriously: Ways to Improve Their Compliance with International Humanitarian Law' (2010) 1 *Journal of International Humanitarian Legal Studies*, pp. 5–51

Sassòli, Marco and Shany, Yuval, 'Should the Obligations of States and Armed Groups under International Humanitarian Law Really Be Equal?' (2011) 93 IRRC, pp. 425–36

Schneeberger, Ernst, 'Reciprocity as a Maxim of International Law' (1948) 37 *Georgetown Law Journal*, pp. 29–41

Schwartz, Jonathan B., 'Dealing with a "Rogue State": The Libya Precedent' (2007) 101 AJIL, pp. 553–73

Schwarzenberger, Georg, 'Review of *Belligerent Reprisals* by Frits Kalshoven' (1972) 48 *International Affairs*, pp. 99–100

Schwelb, Egon, 'The Law of Treaties and Human Rights' (1973–75) 16 *Archiv des Völkerrechts*, pp. 1–27

'Termination or Suspension of a Treaty as a Consequence of Its Breach' (1967) 7 *Indian Journal of International Law*, pp. 309–34

Segal, David, 'The Iran–Iraq War: A Military Analysis' (1988) 66 *Foreign Affairs*, pp. 946–63

Seymour, Philip A., 'The Legitimacy of Peace-Time Reprisals as a Tool against State-Sponsored Terrorism' (1990) 39 *Naval Law Review*, pp. 221–40

Shaw, Malcolm N. and Fournet, Caroline, 'Commentary to Article 62', in Corten, Olivier and Klein, Pierre (eds.), *The Vienna Convention on the Law of Treaties: A Commentary* (Oxford: Oxford University Press, 2011), pp. 1411–33

Sicilianos, Linos-Alexander, 'The Relationship between Reprisals and Denunciation or Suspension of a Treaty' (1993) 4 EJIL, pp. 341–59

Simma, Bruno, 'Reflections on Article 60 of the Vienna Convention on the Law of Treaties and Its Background in General International Law' (1970) 20 *Österreichische Zeitschrift für öffentliches Recht*, pp. 5–83

Simma, Bruno and Tams, Christian J., 'Commentary to Article 60', in Corten, Olivier and Klein, Pierre (eds.), *The Vienna Conventions on the Law of Treaties: A Commentary* (Oxford: Oxford University Press, 2011), vol. II, pp. 1351–81

Sofaer, Abraham D., 'The United States Decision Not to Ratify Protocol I to the Geneva Conventions on the Protection of War Victims: The Rationale for the United States Decision' (1988) 82 AJIL, pp. 784–87

Sutter, Philip, 'The Continuing Role for Belligerent Reprisals' (2008) 13 *Journal of Conflict and Security Law*, pp. 93–122

Taremi, Kamran, 'Ballistic Missiles in Iran's Military Thinking', Conference at Woodrow Wilson International Center, 14 October 2003 (available at www.wilsoncenter.org/event/ballistic-missiles-irans-military-thinking)

Tavernier, Paul, 'La Guerre du Golfe: Quelques aspects de l'application du droit des conflits armés et du droit humanitaire' (1984) 30 *Annuaire français de droit international*, pp. 43–64

Turns, David, 'Implementation and Compliance', in Wilmshurst, Elizabeth and Breau, Susan (eds.), *Perspectives on the ICRC Study on Customary International Humanitarian Law* (Cambridge: Cambridge University Press, 2007), pp. 354–76

Venezia, Jean-Claude, 'La notion de représailles en droit international public' (1960) 64 RGDIP, pp. 465–98

Virally, Michel, 'Le principe de reciprocité dans le droit international contemporaine' (1967) 122 *Recueil des cours de l'Académie de droit international de La Haye, 1967-III*, pp. 5–67

Waldock, Humphrey M., 'The Regulation of the Use of Force by Individual States in International Law' (1952) 81 *Recueil des cours de l'Académie de droit international de La Haye, 1952-II*, pp. 455–514

Watkin, Ken, 'Assessing Proportionality: Moral Complexity and Legal Rules' (2005) 8 *Yearbook of International Humanitarian Law*, pp. 3–53

Watts, Sean, 'Reciprocity and the Law of War' (2009) 50 *Harvard International Law Journal*, pp. 365–434

Westlake, John, 'Reprisals and War' (1909) 25 *Law Quarterly Review*, pp. 127–37

Wolfrum, Rudiger and Fleck, Dieter, 'The Enforcement of International Humanitarian Law', in Gill, Terry and Fleck, Dieter (eds.), *The Handbook of International Humanitarian Law* (Oxford: Oxford University Press, 2008), pp. 675–722

Wright, Lord, 'The Killing of Hostages as a War Crime' (1948) 25 BYIL, pp. 296–310

Yu, Steven Kuan-Tsyh, 'The Development and Implementation of International Humanitarian Law' (1991–92) 11 *Chinese Taiwan Yearbook of International Law and Affairs*, pp. 1–19

Zoli, Corri, 'Humanizing Irregular Warfare: Framing Compliance for Non-state Armed Groups at the Intersection of Security and Legal Analyses', in Banks, William C. (ed.), *New Battlefields / Old Laws: Critical Debates on Asymmetric Warfare* (New York: Columbia University Press, 2011), pp. 190–211

Blogposts

Azzarello, Cristina and Niederhauser, Matthieu, 'The International Humanitarian Fact-Finding Commission: Has the "Sleeping Beauty" Awoken?', *Humanitarian Law and Policy*, 9 January 2018 (available at https://blogs.icrc.org/law-and-policy/2018/01/09/the-independent-humanitarian-fact-finding-commission-has-the-sleeping-beauty-awoken/)

Durham, Helen, 'Strengthening Compliance with IHL: Disappointment and Hope', *Humanitarian Law and Policy*, 14 December 2018 (available at https://blogs.icrc.org/law-and-policy/2018/12/14/strengthening-compliance-with-ihl-disappointment-and-hope/)

Haque, Adil Ahmad, 'Renouncing Reprisals: An Opportunity for the Biden Administration', *Just Security*, 1 April 2021 (available at www.justsecurity.org/75553/renouncing-reprisals-an-opportunity-for-the-biden-administration/)

Harwood, Catherine, 'Will the "Sleeping Beauty" Awaken? The Kunduz Hospital Attack and the International Humanitarian Fact-Finding Commission', *EJIL: Talk!*, 15 October 2015 (available at www.ejiltalk.org/will-the-sleeping-beauty-awaken-the-kunduz-hospital-attack-and-the-international-humanitarian-fact-finding-commission/)

Lythgoe, Gail, 'Nuclear Weapons and International Law: The Impact of the Treaty on the Prohibition of Nuclear Weapons', *EJIL:Talk!*, 2 December 2020 (available at www.ejiltalk.org/nuclear-weapons-and-international-law-the-impact-of-the-treaty-on-the-prohibition-of-nuclear-weapons/)

Milanovic, Marko and Schmitt, Michael N., 'Ukraine Symposium – The Kerch Strait Bridge Attack, Retaliation, and International Law', *Articles of War*,

12 October 2022 (available at https://lieber.westpoint.edu/kerch-strait-bridge-attack-retaliation-international-law/)

Rühle, Michael, 'The Nuclear Weapons Ban Treaty: reasons for scepticism', *NATO Review*, 19 May 2017 (available at www.nato.int/docu/review/articles/2017/05/19/the-nuclear-weapons-ban-treaty-reasons-for-scepticism/index.html)

Schmitt, Michael N., 'Ukraine Symposium – Reprisals in International Humanitarian Law', *Articles of War*, 6 March 2023 (available at https://lieber.westpoint.edu/reprisals-international-humanitarian-law/)

Newspapers, News Agencies and Press Releases

(Documents are listed from the most recent to the most dated)

Euronews, 'Hamas claims responsibility for deadly Jerusalem shooting', 30 November 2023 (available at www.euronews.com/2023/11/30/hamas-claims-responsibility-for-deadly-jerusalem-shooting)

Berman, Lazar, 'Netanyahu: Goal of war is "to defeat the murderous enemy, ensure our existence in our land"', *The Times of Israel*, 28 October 2023 (available at www.timesofisrael.com/liveblog_entry/netanyahu-goal-of-war-is-to-defeat-the-murderous-enemy-ensure-our-existence-in-our-land/)

Omaar, Rageh, 'Israeli president Isaac Herzog says Gazans could have risen up to fight "evil" Hamas', *ITV*, 13 October 2023 (available at www.itv.com/news/2023-10-13/israeli-president-says-gazans-could-have-risen-up-to-fight-hamas)

Slawson, Nicola, 'First Thing: no power, water or fuel for Gaza until hostages are freed, Israel says', *The Guardian*, 12 October 2023 (available at www.theguardian.com/us-news/2023/oct/12/first-thing-no-power-water-fuel-gaza-until-hostages-freed-israel-says)

Fabian, Emanuel, 'Defense minister announces "complete siege" of Gaza: no power, food or fuel', *The Times of Israel*, 9 October 2023 (available at www.timesofisrael.com/liveblog_entry/defense-minister-announces-complete-siege-of-gaza-no-power-food-or-fuel/)

Middle East Monitor, 'Statement by Hamas's Al-Qassam Brigades top military commander', 7 October 2023 (available at www.middleeastmonitor.com/20231007-statement-by-hamass-al-qassam-brigades-top-military-commander/)

Jones, Gareth and Heavens, Andrew, 'Russia vows retaliation for Ukraine's "terrorist attack" on Crimean Bridge', *Reuters*, 12 August 2023 (available at www.reuters.com/world/europe/russia-vows-retaliation-ukraines-terrorist-attack-crimean-bridge-2023-08-12/)

Seddon, Max and Miller, Christopher, 'Vladimir Putin vows retaliation for drone attack on Moscow', *Financial Times*, 30 May 2023 (available at www.ft.com/content/cdde0e44-0e90-41c0-a3be-e5f6849b706b)

Ebel, Francesca, 'Putin admits attacks on civilian infrastructure, asking: "Who started it?"', *The Washington Post*, 8 December 2022 (available at www.washingtonpost.com/world/2022/12/08/russia-attacks-ukraine-infrastructure-putin/)

Beaumont, Peter, Higgins, Charlotte and Mazhulin, Artem, 'Putin warns of further retaliation as Ukraine hit by massive wave of strikes', *The Guardian*, 10 October 2022 (available at www.theguardian.com/world/2022/oct/10/explosions-kyiv-ukraine-war-russia-crimea-putin-bridge)

Hunder, Max and Landay, Jonathan, 'Russia launches biggest air strikes since start of Ukraine war', *Reuters*, 11 October 2020 (available at www.reuters.com/world/europe/russias-ria-state-agency-reports-fuel-tank-fire-kerch-bridge-crimea-2022-10-08/)

Human Rights Watch, 'Armenia/Azerbaijan: don't attack civilians respect absolute ban on targeting civilians, civilian objects', 30 September 2020 (available at www.hrw.org/news/2020/09/30/armenia/azerbaijan-dont-attack-civilians)

Crisis24, 'Yemen: Saudi-led coalition strikes targets in Houthi-controlled Sana'a March 30', 30 March 2020 (available at https://crisis24.garda.com/alerts/2020/03/yemen-saudi-led-coalition-strikes-targets-in-houthi-controlled-sanaa-march-30)

Strobel, Warren P., 'Saudi Arabia invites Houthi rebels to talks in Riyadh', *The Wall Street Journal*, 30 March 2020 (available at www.wsj.com/articles/saudi-arabia-invites-houthi-rebels-to-talks-in-riyadh-11585616096)

Superville, Darlene, 'Trump retreats from threat to attack Iranian cultural sites', *Associated Press*, 8 January 2020 (available at https://apnews.com/article/e456bc97066894a04b23b384fec6cded)

Smith, David and agencies, 'Trump defends "war crime" threat to target cultural sites in Iran', *The Guardian*, 7 January 2020 (available at www.theguardian.com/world/2020/jan/06/suleimani-killing-donald-trump-defends-threat-to-hit-cultural-sites-in-iran)

BBC News, 'Trump under fire for threat to Iranian cultural sites', 6 January 2020 (available at www.bbc.com/news/world-middle-east-51014237)

Woodcock, Andrew, Merrick, Rob and Cowburn, Ashley, 'Iran crisis: Boris Johnson warns Trump not to break international law by bombing cultural sites', *The Independent*, 6 January 2020 (available at www.independent.co.uk/news/uk/politics/iran-war-trump-boris-johnson-cultural-sites-soleimani-iraq-a9272076.html)

Chulov, Martin, Borger, Julian, Abdul-Ahad, Ghaith and agencies, 'Trump vows to hit 52 sites "very hard" if Iran retaliates over Suleimani killing', *The Guardian*, 5 January 2020 (available at www.theguardian.com/world/2020/jan/05/donald-trump-vows-to-hit-52-sites-very-hard-if-iran-retaliates-for-suleimani-killing)

Middle East Eye, 'Houthis promise more missiles if Saudis continue Yemen war', 26 March 2018 (available at www.middleeasteye.net/fr/news/Houthis-vow-stop-missiles-if-Saudi-Arabia-ends-bombardment-Yemen-1027249923)

Westall, Sylvia, 'Yemen's Houthis threaten to attack warships, oil tankers if ports stay closed', *Reuters*, 12 November 2017 (available at www.reuters.com/article/uk-yemen-security-idUKKBN1DC0S5)

Chiacu, Doina and Maler, Sandra, 'After Obama apology, MSF still wants independent investigation of Kunduz: statement', *Reuters*, 7 October 2015 (available at www.reuters.com/article/uk-afghanistan-attack-msf-liu-idUKKCN0S12FR20151007/)

Tyler, Patrick E., 'Both Iraq and Iran gassed Kurds in war, U.S. analysis finds', *The Washington Post*, 3 March 1990, quoted in UN Doc. S/21329, 23 May 1990, p. 4

The New York Times, 'Iran–Iraq war: eight brutal years', 22 July 1988

Anderson, Jack and Van Atta, Dale, 'Iran may turn chemical tables on Iraq', *The Washington Post*, 2 October 1985, p. F-11

Churchill, Winston, BBC broadcast, 1 October 1939

Databases

ICAN (International Campaign to Abolish Nuclear Weapons), 'Which countries have nuclear weapons?' (available at www.icanw.org/nuclear_arsenals)

ICRC (in partnership with the British Red Cross), *Customary IHL Database* (available at https://ihl-databases.icrc.org/customary-ihl/eng/docs/home)

Treaties, States Parties and Commentaries Database (available at https://ihl-databases.icrc.org/ihl)

INDEX

www.ingramcontent.com/pod-product-compliance
Lightning Source LLC
LaVergne TN
LVHW011703200926
848484LV00004B/1054
* 9 7 8 1 1 0 8 8 3 1 8 4 0 *